THE GRANDEST LARCENY

THE GRANDEST LARCENY
THE FOUNDATION OF ISRAEL

J. E. THOMAS

Fonthill Media Language Policy

Fonthill Media publishes in the international English language market. One language edition is published worldwide. As there are minor differences in spelling and presentation, especially with regard to American English and British English, a policy is necessary to define which form of English to use. The Fonthill Policy is to use the form of English native to the author. J. E. Thomas was born and educated in the UK and now lives in the UK, therefore British English has been adopted in this publication.

www.fonthill.media
office@fonthillmedia.com

First published in the United Kingdom
and the United States of America 2023

British Library Cataloguing in Publication Data:
A catalogue record for this book is available from the British Library

Copyright © J. E. Thomas 2023

ISBN 978-1-78155-884-3

The right of J. E. Thomas to be identified as the author of this work has been asserted by him in accordance with the Copyright, Designs and Patents Act 1988.

All rights reserved. No part of this publication may be reproduced, stored in a retrieval system or transmitted in any form or by any means, electronic, mechanical, photocopying, recording or otherwise, without prior permission in writing from Fonthill Media Limited

Typeset in 10pt on13pt Sabon
Printed and bound in England

To the memory of our friend Adnan Abdul Rahim, one of many Palestinians who never did go home.

To Carol Thomas, fulfilling a promise.

Contents

Acknowledgements		9
Note on Spelling and Quotations		10
Introduction		11
1	Myths and the Makers of Myths	15
2	The Political Art of Lies and Ambiguity: The McMahon Letters and the Sykes–Picot Agreement	36
3	After Balfour: 'The document is undoubtedly the starting point of the whole trouble'	71
4	Escalation: 'The Mandate ... itself had lighted the fire'	124
5	The British Government Disregards the Law: 'No one can give what they don't have: *nemo dat quod non habet*'	156
6	The Israeli Prime Minister Sets the Goal: 'And if dozens of Arabs get killed—that's exactly what we want'	198
7	Terrorism, Violence, and the Expansion of the State	240
8	New Lamps For Old? The Treatment of Palestinians and the 'New Antisemitism'	282
Glossary		330
Endnotes		332
Bibliography		363
Index		371

Acknowledgements

We all know that behind every book there are many people who made it happen. In this case, *inter alia*, this includes the staff of the Hallward Library at the University of Nottingham, especially those in the inter library loan department, and the staff of the Nottinghamshire County Library in West Bridgford, who carried on despite the pandemic. My thanks go to both. My thanks also go to Elaine Watts, cartographic unit manager at the School of Geography, University of Nottingham, for the illustrative maps, which were so carefully drawn and so promptly delivered.

I am indebted to Simon Thomas and Carol Thomas who introduced me to the quintessential legal rule *nemo dat quod non habet,* discussed in chapter five.

Photographs tell so much. Philip Thomas brought his research skill to bear in helping me identify photographs and their various sources. My debt to his skill and industry is enormous: especially for his critical help with the final version of the index. Also thanks to Colleen McDonnell for much help with the index.

I want to thank Joseph McDonnell Thomas for drawing my attention to several sources and Emily McDonnell Thomas for obtaining some of these. Thanks to Nick Brown for help in improving the quality of photographs.

I thank Tilda Yolland and Olwen Thomas for reading my drafts, surely the least interesting of occupations, and eliminating those howlers which can adorn a book. Any errors that remain are mine. I want to thank Jasper Hadman, my editor, for his prompt attention and his considerable skill in the shaping of this book's final form.

Finally, and as ever, I can never thank Hazel Mills enough. She has always taken control of the technical problems of setting out the script of my books, and making them presentable to a publisher. Writing a book seems easy by comparison.

Note on Spelling and Quotations

Arabic and Hebrew words are spelt in a variety of ways in English. I have used what appear to me to be the standard forms in literature. When quoting I have copied the form used in the quotation.

Unless otherwise stated in square brackets, the use of italics for emphasis in quotes should be attributed to the author of the quote.

Introduction

This book is about one of the most astonishing events of the twentieth century: the handing over of an entire country, by a country that did not own it, to people who simply laid claim to it. Put so boldly, it would appear to be a fantasy, but it happened, and in the process caused hundreds of thousands of deaths, millions of injuries, and one of the biggest evictions of people from their homes in recorded history. It has resulted in the destabilisation of a whole geographical region. This was the price for granting Palestine to the Jews.

There had been, for some time, a wish on the part of some sections of the Jewish population to establish a state in Palestine. At the end of the nineteenth and beginning of the twentieth century this began to be articulated by what came to be known as the Zionist movement. Dominated mainly by Jews from Eastern Europe, and stimulated in part by persecution, the movement became formalised and organised; it set out to achieve the aim of generating support for the idea of a 'return' to Palestine. This book analyses the course of this movement and the ultimate achievement of its goal: the state of Israel.

We begin with the alleged basis of the right to return: the biblical Old Testament. I attempt to explain the prophecies, their force and their fallacies. I then examine how these beliefs came to be supported by key political figures, notably in Britain, and how this support was translated into political action.

The fall of the Turkish Ottoman empire, of which Palestine was a part, at the end of the First World War, gave the Zionists the chance they needed. They had critical support among key members of the British government, one of whom was the foreign secretary, Arthur Balfour. It was he that penned, and gave his name to, the short statement known as 'The Balfour Declaration'. It is not only short; it is ambiguous to the point of being incomprehensible, and it was to set the Middle East aflame.

In the peace settlement of the post-war period, Britain was given a 'mandate' to govern a number of countries, including Palestine. The 1920s witnessed considerable Jewish immigration to Palestine and resistance from the native Arab Palestinians, who made up the majority of the population. Fighting ensued, and a bevy of reports and investigations were commissioned to find a solution to an insoluble problem.

The situation rapidly descended into chaos, but Britain was, in a sense, given a breathing space with the onset of the Second World War. By the end of the war, several Jewish terrorist organisations had established themselves in Palestine; their attacks contributed to the British decision to hand back the mandate to the newly formed United Nations. The Holocaust was an important factor in the debates about the future of Palestine; the war had left thousands of refugees homeless, and many of them were Jews. Eventually, it was decided to partition the country between Jews and Arabs.

Partition led to an escalation in violence, and sucked other countries into the conflict. These wars enabled the fledgling Israeli state to gain territory: territory they have resolutely refused to return to its rightful owners. International condemnation of Israeli governments has proven ineffective because Israel has been able to rely on the consistent support of Western governments, particularly those of the United States.

It has become clear that the basic tenet of the founding Zionist movement, that Israel is only for Jews, is being realised. More and more, land belonging to Arabs is being stolen from them, and there is no sign of a cessation of this practice. Israeli policies have led to outspoken disapproval around the world, but the global Zionist movement has developed a simple tactic of deflection: condemnations are met with accusations of a modern incarnation of antisemitism described as 'new antisemitism'.

This book finishes with an examination of the prospects for the Palestinian people, who are systematically being deprived and ill-treated.

Introduction

Palestine/Israel today.

1
Myths and the Makers of Myths

Myths and myth-making are a cornerstone of social structure. The solidarity of nations, and of religions, depend upon them. There are broadly two kinds of myths: those which cannot have any basis in fact, and those which are based upon a grain of truth. And there is also a continuum between the two, along which may be ranged those which, while important, are difficult to categorise.

An example of a myth which is incredible, but of great historical significance, is the legend of Romulus and Remus. These brothers were, so the myth goes, the founders of Rome. Their lives were saved by a she-wolf, which suckled them. The mythology which has developed around them is a study in itself: their story has been discussed by Roman authors and modern scholars at extraordinary length; they have been depicted in countless forms of art; and in the ancient world, people believed their story in a literal sense.

The 'Solutrean hypothesis' is a modern example of a myth that lacks any credibility, but has been adopted and believed by some nonetheless. It seeks to prove that Europeans lived in America before the arrival of Asian immigrants, today's Native Americans. The hypothesis is based upon similarities found between stone tools dug up in Spain belonging to the Solutrean culture, which existed there some 20,000 years ago, and those discovered among artefacts belonging to the prehistoric Clovis culture in New Mexico. This is the sum total of the evidence linking the two cultures, but from this has stemmed the suggestion—and in some cases the assertion—that Europeans were the original inhabitants of America, and were probably wiped out by invaders from Asia. This has been used as a basis for arguing that, in spreading across America, European settlers did not dispossess Native Americans of their lands but merely took back what had belonged originally to their ancestors. Science journalist Angela Saini sums up the power of this myth, even on intelligent, educated people, by referring to the 'small number of American archaeologists who have staked their careers on it'.[1]

An example of a myth which may include a speck of truth is the legend of King Arthur. It is claimed that such a leader did truly exist in pre-Saxon Britain. From this bare fact—if it can be called a fact—there has developed a vast literature in several languages about his court, his knights, and his code of chivalry. His legend has been appropriated on several historical occasions for the benefit of the appropriator. For example, in the fifteenth century, having usurped the English throne, King Henry VII claimed that he was, in some mystical fashion, the heir to the Arthur. To help substantiate this claim, he named his son and heir after the legendary king.

There are some myths that are difficult to classify because scientists, and pseudo-scientists, produce alleged 'evidence' in support of them. Evidence, no matter how dubious, can be used to thrust myths, whether ancient or newly conceived, into the modern political toolbox. Theories of racial and genetic differences fall into this category. The establishment of apartheid in South Africa sprang from the theory that black and brown people are inherently inferior to white. It is obviously the case that *physically* they are different, but every kind of serious empirical study has proven that in all other respects race has no bearing whatsoever on intelligence. Yet, during apartheid, for a significant proportion of white South Africans, the belief that mental capacity was dependent on race was unshakeable. Similarly, across the globe, the erroneous scientific theory of eugenics was widely accepted by apparently well-balanced people in the nineteenth and twentieth centuries, with terrible consequences that shaped the history of those centuries.

Much of what is commonly accepted as Jewish history falls within the general definition of myth. These myths are often amplified by politicians advancing the case that the land of Palestine belongs to the Jews. David Ben-Gurion, the first prime minister of Israel, told the Peel Commission in 1937 'that the Bible was the Jewish people's "Mandate"'.[2] He read the Bible 'as history', and set out to establish a parallel between the victories of the biblical warrior Joshua and the Israeli victories in the war of independence.[3] To that end he convened a Bible study group to prove it. 'So interpreted,' writes historian Rachel Havrelock, 'the Bible operates to sanction and justify the actions of the state as legitimate and, to a certain degree, blessed.'[4] Not only could modern Israelis relate to the processes of conquest and settlement, but through the prism of Joshua they could also understand these processes as re-enactments of the biblical past.[5]

This parallel was reinforced at every opportunity. For example, in February 1955 Israel mounted an attack on Gaza, codenamed Operation Black Arrow. Thirty-eight Egyptians were killed and many more injured. There is a memorial to the event, upon which are inscribed five quotations from the Hebrew Bible. One of these is as follows:

And stay ye not, but pursue after your enemies, and smite the hindmost of them; suffer them not to enter into their cities: for the Lord your God hath delivered them into your hand.[6]

As well as using the Bible to justify his political aims, Ben-Gurion engaged in historical fantasy. He would have people believe that the Canaanites whom Joshua encountered, according to the book of Joshua, were Jews who had never left for exile in Egypt. According to Ben-Gurion's interpretation, they had lost their faith and their culture, but were brought back to their original state by Joshua. Thus Ben-Gurion claimed that Palestinians were actually Jews who had remained in the land following the Roman expulsion and eventually converted to Islam. 'The Arabs,' he wrote, 'who are flesh of our flesh, can adapt once again, assimilate and return to our midst.'[7]

It follows that, rather like the legend of Europeans living in America before the arrival of Asians, Jews were the first settlers in Palestine, and therefore no one else has a claim to the land.

Putting aside such fantasies, the cornerstone of Jewish and Zionist claims to the land of Palestine is the Old (Hebrew) Testament of the Bible, reinforced by the Torah. It is often supposed that the Jewish Holocaust of the Second World War was the driving force behind the establishment of the state of Israel, but well before the Holocaust, Zionists were using the Bible as a divine writ to establish a Jewish state in Palestine via the killing and eviction of the non-Jewish inhabitants.

The Balfour Declaration of 1917 opened the gateway to statehood. Dr Joseph Herman Hertz, chief rabbi of Britain and the empire, turned to the Bible to attempt to express what this moment meant for Jews:

For the interpretation of their true feelings today ... [the Jewish people] must turn to Scripture. Twenty-five hundred years ago Cyrus issued his edict of liberation to the Jewish exiles in Babylon ... Theirs was a similar feeling of joy and wonder ... that caused them to explain: 'We shall see it done and done consummately, the thing so many have thought could never be done!'[8]

Menachem Begin, one-time terrorist and later prime minister of Israel, is typical of those who believe that 'Eretz Israel', the 'Land of Israel', 'has always comprised what came subsequently to be called Palestine on both sides of the river Jordan, that is to say not only Western Palestine, but also the territory formerly occupied by three of the twelve Hebrew tribes, Manasseh, Gad, and Reuben.'[9] It may be noted that these tribes, if they existed at all, lived on the east bank of the River Jordan, and so Begin is reminding us that, for some branches of Zionism at least, the claim includes what is today the kingdom of Jordan. So far, Zionists have been denied possession of this East Bank.

To Begin, there could be no argument about the Zionist claim: 'To whom did Palestine belong? The Jews of course. It said so in the Bible.'[10] The British, as he saw it, were using the Jewish cause as a means to help them get hold of Palestine.

British policy, therefore, was ready to back a great ideal which would enable Britain to take over control of Palestine without seeming to. The ideal was at hand: the Jews to whom the Bible had promised Palestine, were persecuted and needed a home. The ideal was very appealing. Britain would promise the Jews a Home in Palestine. Not Palestine as a Home, but a Home *in* Palestine. Britain would have Palestine, and the Jews would have a Home in it. Such a policy would also help British interests in America, for the Jews there had influence.[11]

Put another way, Britain was not being altruistic in contributing to the creation of a 'homeland' for the Jews, but was exploiting what Begin considered as the Jewish inheritance. He was vocal in his criticism of British governance in Palestine:

> The dispute over the Wailing Wall and the Old City is a reflection of the whole struggle for Eretz Israel. British policy ... directed its shafts at the heart of Jewish tradition. As elsewhere it used Arabs or Moslems. As usual an Inquiry Commission was set up and published its 'verdict'—this time in the form of the 'Order-in-Council, 1929'. There they wrote with superb impertinence that the Moslems had the sole right of ownership and possession of the Wailing Wall, as well as the right of ownership to the adjacent courtyard and the area overlooking the Wall. And there they decreed 'Jews are forbidden to blow the Shofar at the Wailing Wall' ... This was the house, and this the country which, with its seers and kings and fighters, was ours before the British were a nation.[12]

Sometimes Begin could be restrained in his criticism: 'I do not make this analysis in a critical spirit towards British policy. I do not deny that British policy often benefited humanity. But also at times the contrary happened.'[13] Usually, however, his views reflected a pathological hatred of the British.

The central question underlying the Zionist claim is whether or not the Bible is a true record of what God said. If it is not a true record, then the whole Zionist case is baseless. But the claim itself, that God talks to individuals and gives them guidance and instruction, is amazing when put into the context of modern political decision-making.

Below I outline some of the most common examples of Old Testament scripture used by Zionists to substantiate their claim on Palestinian land. The Bible from which I quote is the King James Version.

> Now the Lord had said to Abram, get thee out of thy country, and from thy kindred, and from thy father's house, unto a land that I will shew thee.
> And I will make of thee a great nation, and I will bless thee, and make thy name great, and thou shalt be a blessing.[14]

The same vague promise is made again in the book of Deuteronomy:

> And the Lord thy God will bring thee unto the land which thy fathers possessed, and thou shall possess it; and he will do thee good, and multiply thee above thy fathers.[15]

The Lord is more specific in a later chapter:

> In the same day the Lord made a covenant with Abram, saying, Unto thy seed have I given this land, from the river of Egypt unto the great river, the river Euphrates.[16]

The covenant is very specific, mentioning 'the river of Egypt' and the Euphrates. The same promise of territory is made again in Genesis:

> The land was granted by God to the people of Israel as an everlasting possession. God spoke to Abraham: 'I will give unto thee and thy seed after thee the land wherein thou art a stranger, all the land of Canaan'.[17]

On another occasion, also reported in Genesis, God appears to Jacob in a dream. Of 'a certain place', he says,

> And, behold, the Lord stood above it, and said I am the Lord God of Abraham thy father and the God of Isaac: the land whereon thou liest, to thee I will give it, and to thy seed.[18]

The book of Deuteronomy is an especially important source for the Jewish claim to Palestine:

> Turn you and take your journey, and go to the mount of the Amorites and unto all the places nigh thereunto, in the plains, in the hills, and in the vale, and in the south, and by the seaside, to the land of the Canaanites, and unto Lebanon, unto the great river, the river Euphrates.
>
> Behold, I have set the land before you: go in and possess the land which the Lord sware unto your fathers, Abraham, Isaac, and Jacob, to give unto them and to their seed after them.[19]

A very detailed description of the borders of this 'promised land' is given in the book of Numbers:

> Command the children of Israel, and say unto them, when ye come into the land of Canaan; (this is the land that shall fall unto you for an inheritance, even the land of Canaan with the coasts thereof).

> Then your south quarter shall be from the wilderness of Zin along by the coast of Edom, and your south border shall be the outmost coast of the salt sea eastward.
> And your border shall turn from the south to the crescent of Akrabim, and pass on to Zin: and the going on thereof shall be from the south to Kadeshbarnea, and shall go on to Hazaraddar, and pass on to Azimon.
> And the border shall fetch a compass from Azimon unto the river of Egypt, and the goings out of it shall be at the sea.
> And as for the western border, ye shall have even the great sea for a border: this shall be your west border.
> And this shall be your north border: from the great sea ye shall point out for you mount Hor.
> From mount Hor ye shall point out your border unto the entrance of Hamath; and the going forth of the border shall be to Zedad.
> And the border shall go on to Ziphron, and the goings out of it shall be at Hazarenan: this shall be your north border.
> And ye shall point out your east border from Hazarenan to Shepham.
> And the coast shall go down from Shepham to Riblah on the east side of Ain; and the border shall descend and shall reach unto the side of the sea of Chinnereth eastward.
> And the border shall go down to Jordan, and the goings out of it shall be at the salt sea; this shall be your land with the coast thereof roundabout.
> And Moses commanded the children of Israel, saying, this is the land which ye shall inherit by lot, which the Lord commanded to give unto the nine tribes, and to the half tribe.[20]

Some borders are not so precise:

> And if the Lord enlarge thy coast, as he has sworn unto thy fathers, and give thee all the land which he has promised to give unto thy fathers.
> If thou shalt keep all these commandments to do them, which I command thee this day, to love the Lord thy God, and to walk ever in his ways: then shalt thou add three cities more for thee, beside these three.[21]

The eighth chapter of Deuteronomy goes into detail about the richness of the land and the easy life there:

> For the Lord thy God bringeth thee into a good land, a land of brooks of water, of fountains and depths that spring out of valleys and hills.
> A land of wheat, and barley, and vines, and fig trees, and pomegranates; a land of oil olive and honey;
> A land where thou shalt eat bread without scarceness, thou shalt not lack anything in it; a land whose stones are iron, and out of whose hills thou mayest dig brass.[22]

In Exodus there is a promise to solve the problem of the existing inhabitants:

> I will not drive them out from before thee in one year, lest the land become desolate and the beast of the field multiply against thee. By little and little I will drive them out from before thee until thou be increased and inherit the land.
>
> And I will set thy bounds from the Red sea even unto the sea of the Philistines, and from the desert unto the river; for I will deliver the inhabitants of the land into your hand: and thou shalt drive them out before thee.[23]

Ben-Gurion was apparently so convinced of the inevitability of this promise that he kept a copy of the passage on his desk.[24]

It is perhaps not surprising, considering the number of contradictions in the Bible, that challenges to the claim that God promised the land to the Jews can be brought on biblical grounds. Drawing on biblical evidence, Dr Alfred Guillaume, a professor of Old Testament studies, pointed out that the words 'thy seed' in Genesis 23, 'inevitably include Arabs, both Muslims and Christians, who claim descent from Abraham through his son Ishmael'. So, God said, 'I will make a nation, because he [Ishmael] is thy seed.'[25]

Zionist propaganda of the nineteenth and early twentieth centuries made little reference to the violent, seizing aspects of the Bible's prophecies and injunctions. Speaking to the prophet Moses, the Lord said:

> And ye shall dispossess the inhabitants of the land, and dwell therein for I have given you the land to possess it.
>
> But if ye will not drive out the inhabitants of the land before you; then it shall come to pass, that those which ye let remain of them shall be pricks in your eyes, and thorns in your sides and shall vex you in the land wherein you dwell.[26]

In Deuteronomy, God authorises his people, the Jews, to take for themselves the property belonging to the inhabitants of the land.

> And when the Lord your God brings you into the land which he sware unto your fathers, to Abraham, to Isaac, and to Jacob, to give thee great and goodly cities, which thou buildedst not.
>
> And houses full of good things which thou filledst not, and wells digged which thou diggedst not, vineyards and olive trees, which thou plantedst not.[27]

The exhortation to kill occurs many times. For instance, in Deuteronomy:

> When the Lord thy God shall bring thee into the land whither thou goest to possess it, and hath cast out many nations before thee, the Hittites, and the Girgashites, and the Amorites, and the Canaanites, and the Perizzites, and

the Hivites, and the Jebusites, seven nations greater and mightier than thou.

And when the Lord thy God shall deliver them before thee; thou shalt smite them and utterly destroy them; thou shalt make no covenant with them, nor shew mercy unto them.[28]

Joshua, who may be described as the biblical Genghis Khan for his imperial ambitions and mass slaughter of his enemies, is acknowledged as a founding father of an everlasting state. He entered into the policy of slaughter with gusto. At the battle of Jericho, the book of Joshua relates that 'they utterly destroyed all that was in the city, both man and woman, young and old, and ox, and sheep, and ass with the edge of the sword.'[29] Before Jericho, 'according unto the word of the Lord which he commanded Joshua', Joshua dealt with the city of Ai:

> And so it was, that all fell that day, both of men and women, were twelve thousand, even all the men of Ai. For Joshua drew not his hand back, wherewith he stretched out his spear, until he had utterly destroyed all the inhabitants of Ai.[30]

On another occasion Joshua was more merciful, albeit at considerable advantage to himself and his people. The people of Gibeon had heard what he had done in Ai and Jericho, and so they surrendered, along with neighbouring tribes:

> And Joshua made them that day hewers of wood and drawers of water for the congregation, and for the altar of the Lord, even unto this day, in the place which he should chose.[31]

In more recent enlightened times, such brutal accounts have posed a problem for people who believe in the veracity of the Bible as a historical text. And so there has grown up a considerable literature which seeks to modify or excuse what is alleged to have happened. Thus, apologia have been made variously that these killings were an attempt to destroy paganism, that the Lord did not order them, that the Jews misunderstood God's commandment, that this Lord is not the same as that of the New Testament, and so on.

In modern times, to remind people of this violent tradition is to invite accusations of antisemitism. In *The New Antisemitism* (1974), Forster and Epstein criticised Russian writer Y. Yevseyev's 1972 article 'Fascism under the Blue Star':

> 'Frequently in the Old Testament' he [Yevseyev] said 'extermination is advocated'. He then quoted ... Holbach ... to remind us that the Hebrew God, as represented by Moses, always advised 'violence and murder' as part of Jewish foreign policy. Such interpretations of the Old Testament are widely condemned. Instead there is insistence that Judaism advocates peace.[32]

The Old Testament is undoubtedly an invaluable text for scholars of ancient history, but almost all serious scholars agree that it does not amount to a reliable historical source. It is not known, with any precision at least, when its various books were written (although the authors were certainly not eye-witnesses to the events they wrote about) or by whom, but it is acknowledged that historical accuracy was never the purpose for which the Old Testament was written. It follows that if the Old Testament is a hotch-potch of myths based only on scattered grains of truth, then the prime justification for a 'return' of the Jews evaporates. The mere fact that millions of people may believe in the literal truth of the Old Testament cannot justify the cruelty and dispossession carried out in the name of securing a Zionist state.

Yet faith has conquered truth and logic. In his *History of Palestine*, Gudrun Kramer wrote that when 'the rabbis proclaimed a duty for all Jews to remain in Eretz Israel or to acquire land there ... they encouraged the immigration of Jews and threatened to punish any sale or rent of land to non-Jews'.[33] Jewish biblical scholars have always insisted that the Bible banned all non-Jews from the 'land' and banned all social contact, including, for example, intermarriage: 'Neither shalt thou make marriages with them.'[34]

Despite the manifest absurdity of biblical exhortations, many of which were purportedly given by God, people continue to believe them and this has made them dangerous:

> Many religious Jews believe that the conquest of biblical Judea and Samaria [in 1967] was an act of divine intervention, restoring the nation to its historical homeland and hastening the coming of the Messiah.[35]

There is much else in the Hebrew Bible which bolsters the Zionist claim that Palestine 'belongs' to the Jews, and this raises a fundamental question: wherein does the authority of the Bible exist?

It is generally accepted that the Old Testament was written by multiple authors many years after the events it describes. Many of those events, such as Moses's parting of the Red Sea, are miraculous. Throughout, prophets and leaders engage in conversations with God and receive instructions directly from him. To accept what is written in the Old Testament as fact demands a suspension of logic and reason which can only be embraced by those possessed of what is called 'faith'. It is, in essence, religious fundamentalism. As long as this faith does not result in the persecution of those who do not share it, little harm is done. However, the political mobilising of faith in the Hebrew Bible by Zionists has caused an almost inconceivable amount of suffering for the Palestinian Arabs.

Questions have been raised: What authority do these prophesies have over the rights of human beings? Are they relevant? Do they make any sense? Considering their impact on world events, the matter is of the utmost significance; not only have biblical prophesies been used as a linchpin in the argument for the return of Jews to Palestine, but they continue to be brought into play as eternal and indubitable facts.

Serious scientific enquiry has been put into assessing the veracity of the Bible, and sober enquiry examines evidence. It is possible to challenge the Bible's historical accuracy and end up accepting or rejecting alternative interpretations and meanings. Much more difficult to reject is the physical evidence of archaeology. It is this evidence which undermines the historicity of the Bible.

Palestine has always been a popular theatre for archaeological fieldwork, and naturally, there has always been special interest in attempting to marry up biblical accounts with hard physical evidence. On the whole the results have been difficult for the fundamentalists to accept.

The attempt to trace the path of the major event of the Exodus from Egypt—'the very foundation upon which the biblical edifice was erected'—so far has ended with the summary that, 'in fact, no one has found any archaeological evidence for the Exodus from Egypt'.[36] Rabbi David Wolfe of Los Angeles sums up the evidence:

> The truth is that virtually every archaeologist who has investigated the story of the Exodus, with very few exceptions, agrees that the way the Bible describes the Exodus is not the way it happened, if it happened at all.[37]

In the case of the heroic battles fought by Joshua, these are positively disproved by archaeological findings. The account of the destruction of the city of Ai cannot be true, as by the time Joshua is supposed to have conquered it, it was already a ruin. These excavations were, according to archaeologist and Old Testament scholar William G. Dever, 'a major blow to the "conquest theory"'.[38]

Even more devastating was the revelation that Jericho could not have been destroyed by Joshua. The archaeologist Kathleen Kenyon investigated Jericho in the 1950s and reported that at the time of Joshua's alleged attack the site was deserted.[39] In summary, Nadav Na'aman, described by Dever as a 'relatively moderate critical scholar', concludes:

> The comprehensive conquest saga in the Book of Joshua is a fictive literary composition aimed at presenting the entire Land of Israel, initiated and guided by the Lord and carried out by the twelve tribes under Joshua.[40]

Some archaeologists, troubled by the evidence that salient 'historical' aspects of the Hebrew Bible are based on fabrication, have tried to modify the facts. And so theories of 'peaceful infiltration' and an 'immigration model' have been promulgated, claiming that the Israelites did indeed move into Canaan, but that it was a gradual process and not the result of invasion and slaughter. But this is pure supposition, devoid of evidence, and as Dever points out, 'there was never any archaeological evidence to support it'.[41] Still, Dever is reluctant to dismiss Old Testament stories as complete fabrication: 'Even propaganda and myth, like caricature, must necessarily contain some objective truth, lest they be completely unbelievable and thus ineffective.'[42] This may offer some consolation to believers, but it stretches the meaning of myth to a point at which the word itself can be alleged to mean anything. As we have seen, there are myths that cannot possibly contain any objective truth.

When it comes down to it, the use of the Bible to justify the eviction of Palestinians and the return of the Jews may be described as logical reasoning based on a false premise. It is sophistry. Yet it is what has brought the state of Israel into being.

The Jewish state was abolished in the years following the Roman invasion of 63 BC. Then, in AD 70, in response to a rebellion, the Roman general and later emperor, Titus, destroyed Jerusalem. The Jews were dispersed and so the Jewish diaspora was set in train. For the next two millennia, the region which came to be known as Palestine was part of a succession of empires, including the Byzantine, Arab, Crusader and Ottoman. Thus for over eighteen centuries, although some Jews remained there, Palestine was never a Jewish state, and for most of that long period the majority of the population was mixed.

Zionists of the late nineteenth and early twentieth centuries were faced with three principal issues that weakened their case for the formation of a Jewish state in Palestine: 1.) the unreliability of the Bible as a historical source; 2.) the vast stretch of time since the Jewish people had ruled parts of Palestine; and 3.) the relatively small number of Jews living in Palestine at the time. The Zionists not only had to convince governments (especially the British) that they had every right to Palestine, they also had to persuade Jews all over the world that they had a common cause.

In 1920 in the Israeli newspaper *Haaretz*, Jewish historian Joseph Klausner warned Arabs against challenging Jewish ambitions in Palestine with a declaration of Jewish unity:

> Our campaign will include all 13 million Jews in all the countries of the world. And everyone knows how many statesmen, and how many opinion makers, how many people of great wisdom and great wealth and influence we have in Europe and America.[43]

In their dealings with the British government, Zionist spokesmen always insisted that the Jews were a coherent and cohesive group, and that they were solidly behind the demand for what they called the 'return'. This is aptly illustrated by a conversation that took place between Zionist leader Chaim Weizmann and the British foreign secretary, Arthur Balfour, in 1906—their first meeting:

Balfour asked Weizmann whether there were many Jews who thought like him and was told there were millions. 'It is curious,' Balfour said. 'The Jews I meet are different.' Weizmann's response: 'Mr. Balfour, you meet the wrong kind of Jews.'[44]

But such evasive tactics were not always good enough. To properly convince people that the Jews were a cohesive group, Zionists had to 'take a diverse collection of humanity, encompassing in the Jewish case Rothschild barons in Mayfair and barefoot goatherds in Yemen, linked by little more than devotion to an ancient text ... and to translate them into a "people" who, in terms of modern European nationalism, had a claim on a territorial nation-state.'[45] It was a sizeable challenge, but there were many high-ranking British politicians and officials who were ready and waiting to be swayed to the Zionist viewpoint.

Sir Mark Sykes, diplomat and co-author of the controversial Sykes–Picot Agreement, was an enthusiastic supporter of Zionism. He had a deeply colonial attitude, reflected in his secret treaty of 1916 with French diplomat François Georges-Picot, which divided the Middle East into French and British spheres of influence. Sykes saw a Zionist movement that reflected his own preconceptions, that is of a united world Jewry rather than the divided reality of world Jewry: a collection of disparate communities.[46]

Another myth, diligently promoted by Jewish Zionists, was that Britain had always been sympathetic to the idea of the 'return'. After the signing of the Balfour Declaration in 1917, Albert Hyamson, a civil servant and fanatical Zionist, founded The Jewish Bureau in the Department of Information. The bureau published a stream of material that attempted to justify the signing of the declaration and also to prove that Britain had always been sympathetic to the plight of the Jews.

> To those to whom the History of the Jews in England is familiar the adoption by the British Government of the Zionist cause ... will not have come altogether as a surprise, for both as regards the restoration of the Jews to Palestine and the position of the Jews in the Diaspora, without as well as within the British Empire, successive governments ever since the time of Oliver Cromwell have been consistently sympathetic.[47]

We shall see that this was far from the case.

Theodor Herzl (1860-1904), an Austro-Hungarian Jew and founding father of the organised Zionist movement, was one of the first to recognise the importance of myth in the formation of a national identity. According to Robert S. Wistrich, professor at Hebrew University in Jerusalem, 'he reinvented the Jewish past and instrumentalised Judaism for secular, nationalistic ends.'

> The heroic, chivalrous Jew that he had sketched could not be expected to identify with the Diaspora, when Jews had become universally stigmatised pariahs and

their culture had stagnated in the ghetto. The new Jew, according to Zionism, must overcome this aberration of 2000 years of isolationism and self-contempt and hark back to the glory of the Maccabees.[48]

The history of the Zionist movement is brimming with references to folklore, myths, legends and national heroes. Ze'ev Jabotinsky, a militant Zionist, was 'wrapped by his disciples in layer upon layer of myth and legend'.[49] Avraham Stern, leader of the notorious Stern gang in the 1940s, took on the underground name of 'Yair' in tribute to the commander of the zealots at Masada. Bar-Giora was an early militant Zionist group named after Simon Bar-Giora, leader of one of the major Judean rebel factions in the first century AD. 'Operation Nachshon' was the codename of the first major assault by Jewish forces in the 1948 War, named after Nachshon Ben-Aminadav, a biblical tribal leader who was the first to enter the Red Sea as it split apart at Moses's command. 'The methods of organisation, agitation and propaganda employed by political Zion might be modern,' wrote Robert Wistrich, 'but its emotional appeal resided in much more ancient, even archaic symbols like the "Promised Land", the Covenant or the "faith of the fathers".'[50]

But mythmaking, in some cases, can be counter-productive. Masada is the site of a hilltop fortress to which Jewish rebels fled in AD 73 during the First Jewish–Roman War. The account of what happened was written by a Jewish writer called Josephus, who later joined the Roman court and devoted his life to historical writing under the emperor's patronage.[51] He described the mass suicide of 960 men, women and children, although this is not supported by archaeological evidence, which can only account for the remains of twenty-eight people.[52] Jewish religious authorities have questioned whether suicide should be accepted, and much less applauded, especially as a 'mass suicide' that includes children must include the murder of children. But questioning of this sort has been set aside in the development of Masada as a beacon of Jewish strength and resistance. '"Never again shall Masada fall"… became a national slogan and a patriotic vow that was used in ceremonies conducted at the site,' wrote Yael Zerubavel.[53] But there is also a view that the propagation of the legend has caused a 'Masada complex' among the global Jewish community. Yael Zerubavel explains:

> The outbreak of the 1973 Yom Kippur War, the 1982 Lebanon War and the *intifada* were taken as evidence of the endless cycle of wars to which a Masada psychology can lead … By identifying the situation of contemporary Israel with that of Masada and Holocaust it has been argued the Likud government was reinforcing its view of Israel as 'a people dwelling alone' in a hostile world and shaping its policies accordingly.[54]

The Israeli government denies this, saying it is not a 'complex' but 'a realistic assessment, based on Jewish historical experience'.[55]

David Ben-Gurion, the first prime minister of the state of Israel, was a prolific myth-maker. He began with his own name. Born David Grün, he changed to Ben-Gurion, after Joseph Ben-Gurion, a prominent Jewish leader in the First Jewish–Roman War of AD 66-73. He did this in 1906 after migrating from Poland to Palestine; according to historian Tom Segev, 'changing one's name was an accepted practice at the time. It was meant to disconnect the person from life in exile, and create a new Hebrew identity in Palestine.'[56]

David Ben-Gurion devoted himself to reinforcing and adding to biblical myth. In the Bible he recognised 'the revelation of the genius of our people'. The Bible, he said, 'forged the image of the Jewish nation to a greater extent than did any book shape any other nation'.[57] And he understood how it could be used to galvanise nationalistic fervour:

> The tales of the forefathers 4,000 years ago, the story of Abraham's life and travels, the wanderings of the Children of Israel in the desert after the exodus from Egypt, the wars waged by Joshua and the Judges who succeeded him, the lives and deeds of Saul, David and Solomon, the tales of Uziah King of Judah and Jeroboam 11 King of Israel, all these are more relevant, more current, more fascinating and more vital for the new generation which was born and raised in Israel, than all the speeches and disputes of the Basel congresses put together.[58]

Of course, in Ben-Gurion's mind there was no doubt about Jewish claims to the land of Palestine. In *Israel Among the Nations* (1953) he set out a curious mystical link between the Jews and the 'land':

> The tremendous, unparalleled role that the Jewish people played in the history of the human spirit and culture, is a result of the mutual interaction between the people and the land.

At times Ben-Gurion went so far as to state that until the arrival of the new Hebrew, the 'tiller from the People of Israel', the expanses of the land were 'barren'.[59]

Like all mythmakers he tumbled into mythological absurdity. In 1906 he wrote of 'the foul miasma which rises from the fallow earth when it is ploughed for the first time in 2,000 years'. This allegation of pollution is explained by Rachel Havrelock in *The Joshua Generation: Israel Occupation and the Bible*:

> Behind the conquest [of Joshua] stands the idea that the practices of the Canaanites contaminate the very soil of Canaan to the point that God cannot reside therein, so if Israel wants to establish a sanctified country, then the offending residents must be annihilated. In the place of local covenants of peace Israel is to abide by *the* covenant with God.[60]

Like so many sophisticated Jews, when Ben-Gurion came into contact with Jews from the diaspora, or those who survived the concentration camps, he found many of them uninterested in his national project, and unlikeable. He wished away the periods of exile, turning, in the words of his former secretary Ze'ev Tzachor, 'a blind eye to a period which he felt deserved to fall into oblivion—the period of Israel's exile. Among Ben-Gurion's hundreds of articles and the thousands of historical references in them, there is hardly a single positive remark to be found concerning the course of Jewish history outside of the Land of Israel.'[61]

In England, the idea of a Jewish 'return' to Palestine had found support in some quarters long before the formation of an organised Zionist movement. It was an idea that had risen out of a long history of persecution.

In 1290, in a culmination of anti-Jewish feeling, Edward I expelled the Jews from England. The ostensible reason was that they had continued to practise usury after its prohibition in 1275 with the statute of the Jewry. Hatred of Jews, however, was based more on the common belief of antisemitic myths. It was widely believed, for example, that Jews murdered Christian children and used their blood to make Passover bread. An estimated 16,500 Jews were expelled from England, although a small number were converted to Christianity and remained.[62]

After the Reformation, there developed a new obsession with Hebrew studies, which led to an idealisation of the Jews. Early in the seventeenth century, Leonard Busher, a pioneering writer on religious toleration, declared that the Jews 'shall inhabit and dwell under his Majesty's dominion, to the great profit of his realms and their furtherance in the faith'.[63] New-found interest in the Old Testament was accompanied by an expectation that the Jews, for all their wickedness, could be converted, and that their conversion would pave the way to the *Parousia*, the second coming of Christ. There also emerged at this time the idea that Christians were the true inheritors of God's destiny, and moreover, that 'the English were the new Israel'.[64]

These debates culminated in around 1656, when Oliver Cromwell was lord protector of England, Scotland and Ireland. Most historians agree that this was the year in which Jews were officially welcomed back to England. The change was due largely to a European Jew named Menasseh Ben-Israel, who wrote an 'address' to Cromwell in about 1651, pleading 'free exercise of our Religion' in the English Commonwealth and the repeal of 'those rigorous Lawes made under the Kings against so innocent a people'.

In a precursor to the persuasive strategy employed by later Zionists, Ben-Israel called on the Scriptures to support his case. Quoting the book of Daniel, he pointed out that 'the restoring time of our nation into their native Country is very near at hand'; to achieve this, he continued, 'people of God must be first dispersed into all places and Countries of the World'. There were no Jews in England, but according to Ben-Israel's somewhat questionable interpretation of the words of

Daniel 12:7, if there were, the fulfilment of this prophesy would be brought a step closer.⁶⁵

Ben-Israel then moved on to more earthly incentives. 'Profit is a most powerful motive,' he wrote, 'and which all the world prefers before all other things.' He went into detail about the 'Importation and Exportation of Goods' and 'the profit that I conceive this Commonwealth is to reap' from the readmission of Jews into English society.

Some sections of the Anglican Church had other, more elevated reasons for supporting readmission. Prime among these was the ambition to convert Jews to Christianity, a desire inherited by later Christian Zionists. In addition, the idea that Jews should be settled in their own land—some suggested Palestine—started to emerge in the early seventeenth century. The belief was that it would lead to a second coming of the Messiah.

The clergyman Thomas Brightman was an early advocate for the idea of a Jewish 'return'. In about 1615 he published a treatise entitled 'Shall they return to Jerusalem again?' In it he insisted that the Jews be returned to the Holy Land: 'There is nothing more certain: the prophets do everywhere confirm it and beat upon it.' Around the same time, as the Puritans 'sailed across the Atlantic to seek religious freedom,' wrote historian Simon Sebag Montefiore, 'they read of Jerusalem and the Israelites in their Bibles and saw themselves as the Chosen People blessed by God to build a new Zion in the wilderness of Canaan. "Come let us declare in Zion the word of God" prayed William Bradford as he disembarked from the *Mayflower*.'⁶⁶

After the readmission of the Jews in England, there was much debate about the extent to which they should be integrated into the wider community. In 1753, when there were about 8,000 Jews in the country, mostly 'foreign born', a Naturalisation Bill was proposed, popularly called the 'Jew Bill'.⁶⁷ Heated debates took place about whether the bill would speed up conversion or whether it would lead to the swamping of Christianity and the undermining of societal values. It was also questioned whether naturalisation would be against God's will, considering that the Bible insisted that the Jews must suffer.⁶⁸ On the other hand, it was argued that 'the wealth of the Jew and the increase in trade that they would stimulate would benefit the whole economy'.⁶⁹

Amid the debate, speculation that the Jews might be sent to Palestine began to re-emerge. This was not, however, suggested for their benefit, but as means of getting rid of them. (The same reasoning recurred continually in British political debate, right through to the twentieth century.) The act 'may in some measure strengthen [the Jews] in England to depart both earlier and easier to their own land'.⁷⁰ The act was passed, but in December of the same year, it was repealed.

In the eighteenth century, the status of Jews in Britain came under the spotlight. There was a persistent faith, even among highly intelligent men such as Isaac Newton, that Jews could be converted to Christianity. Linked to this was an expectation that they would return to the 'favour' of God through their acceptance of Jesus. Joseph Priestley, one of the most distinguished scientists and liberal philosophers of his time, wanted Jews to become Unitarians: 'When you shall be obedient to God,' he wrote, 'in consequence of it He shall restore to you the possession of your own country.'[71]

Across the Channel in France, the state's attitude towards Jews changed dramatically with the social and political upheaval of the French Revolution. In 1791, the revolutionary government accorded Jews the full rights of ordinary citizens. At the same time, other European societies indulged in a growing fascination with the mystical. This resulted in a greater interest in and attention to biblical prophesies. This, in turn, spawned an outpouring of pseudo evidence of a return to the Holy Land.

It was the popular belief in England that France would attack the Ottoman empire, settle the Jews in Jerusalem, and that converted Jews from England would go there and establish the second kingdom of Christ.[72] This was not entirely fanciful. During the siege of Acre in 1799, the French newspaper *Gazette National* reported that Napoleon had 'published a proclamation in which he invites all the Jews of Asia and Africa to gather under his flag in order to re-establish the ancient Jerusalem'. Eight years later, in 1807, Napoleon convened a Sanhedrin (an assembly) in Paris. There is no doubt that his adventures in the Middle East contributed to the belief in a 'return'.

At the beginning of the nineteenth century there were about 20,000 Jews in England. There was plenty of antisemitic feeling and expression, but less so than in most other European countries, and so England was perceived a relatively safe place for Jews.

But like other non-Church of England people, Jews still suffered legal discrimination. They were, for example, barred from membership of the Inns of Court, from public office, from attendance at universities, and from commercial business in the City of London. In spite of these hindrances, many Jews achieved great success. They formed the British Board of Deputies in 1760 to promote and safeguard the interests of British Jews, and in the early nineteenth century, members of the board such as Moses Montefiore, Isaac Goldsmid, and Nathan Rothschild rose to extraordinary heights of wealth and influence.

In 1826 the Philo-Judaean Society was established. It was an association of predominantly evangelical Anglicans whose wealth and social standing helped accelerate the drive for Jewish emancipation. In 1830, two bills were introduced into the House of Lords and House of Commons respectively to remove Jewish disqualification: one was introduced by Lord Bexley and the other by Robert Grant. Both men were Christians and both were enamoured by Jewish biblical heritage.

The rich and powerful earl of Shaftesbury objected to the bills. He wanted to keep Jews apart in society in the hope that they would sooner go to Palestine, and there convert to Christianity. Thus they would 'become once more the husbandmen of Judea and Galilee'. He asserted that if the 'five powers of the West [could] guarantee the security of life and possessions to the Hebrew race, they would flock back [to Palestine] in rapidly augmenting numbers'.[73]

In 1809 this theme of conversion had been organised in the form of The London Society for the Promotion of Christianity Amongst the Jews. One of its proponents, an Anglican priest named Leigh Richmond, attracted large audiences. The society served to better inform people about the Jewish community, but the number of successful conversions was negligible. Some rabbis banned Jews who read conversion tracts from attending synagogues, 'and in one case the Jews threw the tracts back at the missionaries'.[74] There may have been some converts in mainland Europe, but broadly speaking, these efforts 'throughout modern history have been one great exercise in futility'.[75]

As has been mentioned, the Jews were not the only people to take up the Zionist cause. Since its beginnings, there has been a powerful faction of Christian Zionists motivated by a belief in biblical prophesy and/or a desire to exclude Jews from Christian society. In the early twentieth century, the influence of the Bible on the critical debates about the future of Palestine was considerable. Like many brought up in the tradition of biblical education, key figures like Jan Smuts, Winston Churchill, and Arthur Balfour often quoted the Bible as justification for Zionist demands. For example, in November 1931, Churchill wrote an article in the *Sunday Chronicle* about Moses, 'the supreme law-giver', extolling him for his role in developing ethical codes:

> We believe that the most scientific view, the most up-to-date and rationalistic conception, will find its fullest satisfaction in taking the Bible story literally, and in identifying one of the greatest of human beings with the most decisive leap-forward ever discernible in the human story.[76]

Yet the Bible's relevance to the modern age remains highly questionable. As A. J. P. Taylor wryly observed, 'Maybe Lloyd George and Balfour merely took their knowledge of Palestine from the Bible, which in this respect happens to be out of date.'[77]

Focus on Jerusalem, a Christian Zionist publication founded in 1995, published an article in 2006 entitled 'The Bible and Palestine'.[78] It claimed that Jews have an exclusive right to the land of Palestine. This is one of two fundamental arguments of Zionism. The other is that the Bible is unquestionably true. The article, written by Darrell Young, exemplifies the views of a fanatical strain of Christian Zionism.

Among the usual plethora of biblical quotations, which are of no relevance, Young argued that there was never a political entity which could be accurately described as Palestine, and that there was never, until the rise of Zionism, a people called Palestinians. This is controversial. The word Palestinian existed, but included all who lived in that region. Arab Palestinians usually called themselves Muslims or identified by clan or tribe. The area later known as Palestine, Young asserted, following the standard Jewish narrative, is the 'Land of Canaan', which afterwards was named 'Eretz Yisrael' or 'Land of Israel'.[79] Young conceded that the name Palestine has been used since Roman times, but that it was 'the Roman Emperor's method of eradicating the memory of Israel from anything to do with the Biblically Promised Land ... to show the world that Rome had forever annulled the covenant of Abraham'.[80]

> From the beginning of history to this day, Israel–Judah–Judea has had the only united, independent, sovereign nation-state that ever existed in "Palestine" west of the Jordan river.[81]

The author called the name Palestine 'anti- Israel, anti-Christian', and said 'those Christians who promote a Palestinian state have placed themselves in alliance against God's providential designs for Israel. (Psalm 83.5).'[82]

Like all arguments based upon the presumed truth of the Bible, this article is inherently flawed, but a final point made by the author illustrates the way in which these views can shape contemporary politics to the detriment of Arab Palestinians. Speaking of present-day Palestinians, Darrell Young asserted that they 'do not qualify for the protections to be given to those under Israel's God ordained ordinance'.[83]

Evangelical Christian support for Zionism and Israel is a major force in modern US politics. In the 1980 presidential race, Jimmy Carter's use of the term 'Palestinian homeland' in a speech sparked outrage. Full-page advertisements appeared in national newspapers calling for an affirmation of 'belief in biblical prophecy'. In consequence, Carter lost the evangelical 'right' and went on to lose the election.[84]

A few decades later, President Obama believed that 'there was an essential bond between the Black and the Jewish experiences', but 'those shared values also made it impossible for me to ignore the conditions under which the Palestinians in the occupied territories were forced to live'.[85] He was, however, left with little choice:

> A strong group of white evangelicals—the GOP's most reliable voting bloc—believed that the creation and the gradual expansion of Israel fulfilled God's promise to Abraham and heralded Christ's eventual return. On the Democratic side, even stalwart progressives were loath to look less pro-Israel than Republicans, especially since many of them were Jewish themselves or represented sizeable Jewish constituencies.[86]

He did, however, express disapproval of settlements in Arab sectors of East Jerusalem. But it has made no difference. Even a president as courageous and liberal as Obama had to cave in.

As expected, Netanyahu's initial response to our proposed settlement freeze was sharply negative, and his allies in Washington were soon publicly accusing us of weakening the US–Israel alliance. The White House phones started ringing off the hook, as members of my national security team fielded calls from reporters, leaders of American Jewish organisations, prominent supporters and members of Congress, all wondering why we were picking on Israel and focusing on settlements when everyone knew that Palestinian violence was the main impediment to peace.[87]

In *Zionism and the State of Israel: A Moral Enquiry*, author Michael Prior identified ten organisations of the evangelical 'right' which campaign for Zionist causes. In his interview with a leader of one of these, he observed that his 'perspective excluded all consideration of human rights issues, against the background of the overriding allegedly divine authorisation of the affairs of the state of Israel'. The organisation in question proclaimed that God had given the Jews 'absolute rights over the whole of it [Israel]' and that 'God will bless, or curse nations in accordance with their treatment of the Chosen People of Israel'.[88]

This type of unequivocal Christian support for Zionism is nothing new. 'The Balfour Declaration ... was born out of the Christian Zionist movement of the late 1800s, and appropriated with the political Zionism movement of the Jews,' wrote Darrell Young in his 2006 article 'The Bible and Palestine'.[89] Historian N. A. Rose called Balfour 'the most eminent Gentile Zionist of his day'. He named David Lloyd George, Jan Smuts, and Winston Churchill as among the principal Gentile Zionists of their times, but also shone a light on lesser-known figures who had a significant impact, like Colonel J. C. Wedgwood.

Colonel Wedgwood, 1st Baron Wedgwood, was a Liberal and Labour politician who published a book in 1928 called *The Seventh Dominion*. It advocated for the creation of a Jewish state with dominion status within the British Commonwealth. In 1929 Wedgwood formed the 'Seventh (Palestine) Dominion League' and held a series of meetings to realise his vision. The league attracted enthusiastic membership, but it faded away amid the deterioration in relations between Zionists and the British government.[90] Wedgwood's book, however, still provides a valuable insight into the mentality of the 'Gentile Zionist':

> The Anglo-Saxon, more than any other race, wants to sympathise with the Jews, and would like to settle up for these last two thousand years ... we are both moneylenders, and unpopular ... we too, find in the Old Testament, or Torah, convenient justification for all that needs justification in our relations with mankind ... no doubt we can understand the Jew better than can those to whom the Old Testament is not familiar from infancy. To the foreigner the word Jew is a hissing in the street; to us the word suggests Solomon and Moses, and a thousand cradle stories. So often have we used their names for our own children

that they seem now to be our fathers, specially our Puritan forefathers ... When my ancestors hewed down the aristocrats at Wigan Lane and Naseby they were armed with the names of Aaron and Abner ... Moses led out of Egypt the first non-conformists, the first free thinkers to break away from idolatry and priestly rule ... Towards such a people one has a feeling almost of awe, they are so well known, and yet so old and eternal.[91]

Such sentiments were commonly expressed at the time, most notably by Winston Churchill.

Of equal significance was the support of British officials who subscribed to Christian Zionist claims. Brigadier Wyndham Deedes, chief secretary in the Mandatory Palestine Government between 1920 and 1922, was a devout Christian and Zionist. According to historian Tom Segev, he once said to one of his colleagues that 'the more he could assist in the return of the Jews to the Holy Land, the quicker he would hasten the second coming of the Lord'. Norman Bentwich, a life-long Zionist who became attorney-general in Deedes's administration, described Deedes as 'a modern saint'.[92]

From the Palestinian Arab point of view, none of the theology about 'promises' and 'returns' has ever made any sense. This was pointed out in the Palin Commission Report on the Jerusalem riots of 1920:

[This] profound religious sentiment which appeals so strongly to those European and American peoples who have absorbed the Old Testament narrative and prophesies with their earliest essays in their native tongue, means less than nothing to a people who see themselves menaced with deprivation by a race they have hitherto held in dislike and contempt. So far as the claim is historic, they can only see in the Jews a people, who, after an independent history of less than three hundred years, were twice expelled from their territory.[93]

It is not surprising that anyone who was not brought up to believe in the extraordinary myths expounded in the Bible would be capable of understanding the degree of emotion encapsulated in the Balfour Declaration. Unfortunately the Arabs had few voices to speak up for them, while behind Zionist ambitions was an impressive array of powerful forces. It is that Arab weakness and Zionist strength which we will now discuss.

2
THE POLITICAL ART OF LIES AND AMBIGUITY

The McMahon Letters and the Sykes–Picot Agreement

The notion of a 'return' to Palestine had been mooted in Jewish religion and culture since the settling of the diaspora, and supported latterly, as we have seen, by Christian sects and individuals. Zionists have always stressed, some would say stretched, the mystical attachment felt by Jews for the Promised Land, especially for Jerusalem.

Advocacy campaigns for a Jewish homeland in Palestine culminated in the first World Zionist Conference held in Basle in 1897. This led to the establishment of the World Zionist Organisation, an English branch of which, the English Zionist Federation, was set up in 1899. At the centre of the conference programme was the intention to establish a home for the Jewish people in Palestine, secured under public law.

Nothing has dogged the debate about Palestine more than the interpretation of the meaning of words. The meaning of 'home' is a good example. Its slide into 'state' or 'commonwealth', both of which are manifestly different, has fuelled interminable argument, and even at this first conference in 1897 there was heated discussion about what word to use.

The architect of the conference was Theodor Herzl (1860-1904), a native of Hungary in the then Austro-Hungarian empire. He became a symbol of Zionist success. In a panegyric to Herzl in 1951, David Ben-Gurion, the first prime minister of Israel, attributed to him 'the might of a Macabee, the cunning of David, the bravery of Rabbi Akiva ... the humility of Hillel, the beauty of Judah Hanassi and the burning love of Judah Ha-levi.'[1] Ben-Gurion later altered his view, saying in 1975 that Herzl was 'neither Joshua nor David, neither Judah Maccabee nor Rabbi Akiva and Bar-Kochba'.[2] He lacked what Ben-Gurion had come to recognise as a mystical connection with the land of Palestine, which could only be experienced through birth and upbringing in that land.

Herzl was chiefly a journalist by profession. In 1896 he published *Der Judenstaat* (The Jewish State), a highly influential book which advocated for a Jewish settlement in Palestine. In 1901, after several attempts, he met the Turkish sultan Abdul Hamid II and offered him Jewish money to pay Ottoman debts. He met him again the following year and this time offered the sultan money for land in Acre and its surrounding areas. The sultan declined. From then until his early death at the age of forty-four, Herzl was the pivot of the Zionist movement.

In France and across Europe, the idea of a homeland for Jews gained traction in the popular uproar that followed the wrongful conviction for treason of a French officer named Captain Alfred Dreyfus in 1894. Dreyfus was sent to Devil's Island, part of the penal colony in French Guiana, where he was kept in solitary confinement and subjected to especially cruel treatment. He had been there for four years when, in a famous newspaper article entitled 'J'Accuse', the French writer Emile Zola drew attention to the injustice he had suffered. The 'Dreyfus Affair', as it became known, exposed the endemic nature of antisemitism in French culture and across Europe. Theodor Herzl and the Zionist movement seized upon the case as proof that the Jews would never be accepted in their 'home' societies.[3]

So how was this grand aim of a 'homeland' to be achieved? Already, at this early stage, the policies of the Zionists had begun to crystallise. The core tactic was to be always rigid and unyielding. There was only one target, and this was to occupy the whole of what was supposedly biblical Palestine. This included land on the west bank of the River Jordan and on the east bank—in present-day Jordan—encompassing an area far beyond the boundaries of present-day Israel.

The land, of course, was occupied, and to overcome this obstacle the Zionists adopted a policy of deceit. The settled Arab population was told that their rights would be respected and that they would share in the administration of the land, when in fact the desired aim was to expel them. The inevitability of this would seem to be inescapable. Palestine was a small country, and if tens of thousands of immigrants were to arrive, some, or ideally all of the existing inhabitants would have to be removed.

The Zionists have always been open about their ambitions. Very early in the debates about the future of Palestine they submitted a map to the 1919 Paris Peace Conference, which showed the outline of the proposed Jewish state. This included not only the whole of what was to become the mandated territory, but the south of Lebanon, parts of Syria, including the Golan Heights, and part of the east bank of the River Jordan, including the town of Aqaba. Handing over the latter would have left Jordan with no access to the sea. A piece of Egypt was also included on the map, north of a line from El-Arish to the Gulf of Aqaba. Existing populations were to be expelled. This policy has been reiterated on many occasions by many prominent Zionists including Ben-Gurion, Chaim Weizmann, Moshe Dayan and Menachem Begin. The policy was also recognised by a US general, Patrick J. Hurley, who reported it to President Roosevelt in 1943:

The Zionist organisation in Palestine has indicated its commitment to an enlarged programme for:
1. A sovereign Jewish state that would embrace Palestine and probably eventually Transjordan.
2. An eventual transfer of the Arab population from Palestine to Iraq.[4]

Some of these goals were achieved when Arabs were dispossessed of land later in the twentieth century, and the Golan Heights and the West Bank were purloined in 1967.

There were two other essential aspects of Zionist policy. The first was to disregard the truth. There could be no deviation from the cause of return, and if the truth hindered the cause, there was, it was agreed, no point in being truthful or objective. The second was to disregard criticism, either of aim or method. This policy became manifest years later when dozens of United Nations resolutions criticising the behaviour of Israel were ignored, denied, or attributed to antisemitism. Above all, only Palestine was acceptable as a destination for the Jews. This last was one of the few factors which initially divided the Zionists. It is only by acknowledging these policies that the process which culminated in the foundation of the state of Israel and Israel's treatment of the Arabs can be understood.

Zionist ambitions were viewed with mixed feelings in Britain at the beginning of the twentieth century. Antisemitism was rife in society and parliament, but when it came to action, MPs were either indifferent, as shown by wild swings in voting patterns, or immensely supportive of the Zionist cause. Without this political support, the Balfour Declaration of 1917 could not have been signed. Moreover, the attitude of the British ruling class towards Arabs was decidedly negative; as a group they desperately lacked political clout in parliament. This was outlined in May 1939 by Conservative MP Anthony Crossley during a debate on the much hated (by the Jews) White Paper, which restricted Jewish immigration into Palestine:

> There are no Arab members in Parliament. There are no Arab constituents to bring influence upon their members in Parliament. There is no Arab control of newspapers in this country. It is difficult to get a pro-Arab letter in *The Times*. There are in the City no Arab financial houses which can control amounts of finance. There is no Arab control of newspaper advertising in the country. There are no ex-colonial Secretaries.[5]

The same point was made by Arab historian George Antonius in 1938:

> The fact that a number of members of both Houses are Jews is in itself a guarantee that the Zionist case does never go by default; and as no such

representation is open to the Arab side, the one-sidedness of the debates is further accentuated.[6]

Even arch-Zionist Jan Smuts conceded to this point: in November 1929 he reported that Lord Passfield, whose controversial report I will discuss later, had said 'the Arabs are not represented, they are nowhere'.[7] This was in contrast to the situation of the Jewish lobbies, whose power, if it could be marshalled, was enormous.

Power and influence were determining factors in the events which led to the Balfour Declaration and its aftermath. A convincing proof of this can be seen in the contrasting fates of Jews and Romani after the Second World War.

The Romani or Roma seem to have arrived in Europe towards the end of the thirteenth century. It was thought for many years that they came from Egypt—hence the name 'Gypsy'—but philological studies have indicated that they are most likely of Indian origin. The Roma have suffered from persecution ever since their arrival in Europe, and never more so than under Nazi policy, when they were as much of a target for extermination as the Jews. As noted by the Holocaust survivor Miriam Novitch, 'It was the wish of the all-powerful Reichsführer Adolf Hitler to have the Gypsies disappear from the face of the earth.'[8]

The Roma were subjected to all the same 'laws' as the Jews: they could not marry 'Aryans' and they were categorised as second-class citizens. Just as Kristallnacht signified a dramatic increase in anti-Jewish violence and persecution in Germany and Austria in November 1938, so 'Gypsy Clean-Up Week' in June of the same year marked the mass arrest and deportation by the Nazis of thousands of Roma to concentration camps. The Nazis categorised Roma people as racially impure, criminal and anti-social. The infamous 'Final Solution' applied to them as much as the Jews, and in Auschwitz, both groups were the victims of the grotesque experiments of Dr Josef Mengele, the SS 'Angel of Death'.[9]

The genocidal policy of the Nazis resulted in the deaths of around half of the Roma population of Europe: certainly in excess of 500,000, and possibly more than 1.5 million.[10] The accuracy of these numbers is complicated by a lack of census records for Roma populations, the paucity of records kept in concentration camps, and the fact that many Roma were murdered outside the camps.

The fate of the Roma in the Holocaust is often neglected by historians. 'More energy is expended on making their case by those seeking to distance Romanies from the Holocaust than on examining the relevance of the Holocaust to the Romanies' present day condition,' wrote Roma scholar Ian Hancock.[11] He described this deliberate attempt to exclude the Roma as a 'meanly motivated and defensive attitude', which is 'unscholarly and unprofessional in the context of the Holocaust'.[12] Hancock attributes much of what he calls the 'minimising rhetoric' to Jewish authors, but acknowledges at the same that other Jewish scholars support the recognition of Roma suffering.[13] This recognition has increased in recent times with the hosting of memorial ceremonies and the commissioning of physical memorials, such as the one in Berlin erected in October 2012.

There are many reasons why the fate of the Roma under the Nazis has not been recognised as prominently as that of the Jews. The Roma have always been among the poorest and most deprived groups in Europe, with low rates of literacy and zero political influence. Throughout European history, they have been arguably more unpopular than the Jews, and in countries like Hungary and Romania, an official policy of persecution persists today. Above all, however, the lack of recognition is due to an insistence by Jewish lobbies on 'owning' the Holocaust. As British Labour party leader Jeremy Corbyn found in January 2011, when he sponsored a bill to that effect, any attempt to include others in its story is firmly resisted. The fate of the Roma was not of any interest to Zionists, who had but one goal: Palestine.

Many Jews in Britain and elsewhere did not support the Zionist notion of settlement in Palestine. Most notably, there was the considerable initial opposition of Orthodox Jewry. As noted by historian Tom Segev, by 1918, when the Zionist Commission was founded, 'the conflict between the ultra-Orthodox and the Zionists had already emerged as a central issue'.[14]

Orthodox Jews believed that the return to Jerusalem should not be attempted or achieved by mankind, but that the intervention of God—i.e. the coming of the Messiah—should be awaited. There was also an admonition in the Talmud, the primary source of Jewish religious law, which ordered that Jews should not 'rebel against the nations'.[15] The 'chief concern' of Orthodox Jews, however, according to Islamic scholar Gudrun Kramer, 'was not the physical oppression and persecution of the Jews, but rather their estrangement from their Jewish faith and identity through assimilation'.[16]

This condemnation of assimilation was not shared by the majority of Jews, many of whom regarded assimilation as the best way of improving their lot in the country in which they lived. In Russia, for example, where Jews lived outside of mainstream society, they were badly treated and severely disadvantaged, while in Britain, where most Jews were integrated into society, they lived in relative harmony with their host community, despite the existence of antisemitism.

Most British Jews who occupied high-ranking places in society supported assimilation, but the argument in its favour also led to confusion. In the words of American Zionist Louis D. Brandeis, associate justice of the US Supreme Court and founder of the Jewish American Provisional Executive Committee, 'loyalty to America demands ... that each American Jew become a Zionist'. On the other hand, Brandeis asserted that Jews in America must 'preserve their distinct identity', and that 'assimilation is national suicide'.[17]

In Britain, the principal supporters of assimilation were a group of wealthy Jewish families known as 'the Cousinhood'. These families moved in aristocratic circles and were closely associated with the British political elite. Their names were well known. The most famous, and arguably the wealthiest, were the Rothschilds. Edwin Montagu, secretary of state for India between 1917 and 1922 and a significant opponent of Zionism, and his cousin Herbert Samuel, first high commissioner of Palestine under the British Mandate, were also members of the Cousinhood.

The principal organisational opposition to Zionism came from the Conjoint Foreign Committee, 'the recognised spokesman of the British Jews in matters affecting Jewish communities abroad'.[18] The term 'conjoint' referred to the fact that committee was comprised of two organisations: the Board of Deputies of British Jews (established in 1760) and the Anglo-Jewish Association (established in 1871). These organisations were made up of highly successful Jewish members of society; together they sought to improve the position of all Jews in British society. They disagreed with the Zionist proposition to establish a Jewish homeland because it encouraged the sense in the wider British society that Jews did not really belong.

This base of Jewish opposition was eventually worn down, and on 24 May 1917, when David Alexander, president of the Board of Deputies, put a statement in *The Times* claiming that British Jews opposed Zionism, he was immediately faced with a motion of no confidence. A few days later, the Foreign Office asked Lord Walter Rothschild and Chaim Weizmann to hold the aristocratic title, and for Chaim Weizmann to submit proposals for a Jewish homeland.

This division among Jews was exacerbated by another chronic, and to some, still unsolved question. Is Judaism a religious or a racial category? Claude Goldsmid Montefiore, member of the Cousinhood, president of the Anglo-Jewish Association (1892-1921), long-standing joint president of the Conjoint Committee and co-signatory of Alexander's letter, argued the former. He believed that even in Russia, where half the global population of Jews resided in the late nineteenth century, integration was possible, but only if the word 'Jew' denoted a religion and not a nationality.[19] 'We have come forth from the Ghetto to be worldwide and free,' he wrote, 'we cannot again be cribbed and confined by geographical limitations.'[20]

The author and journalist Arthur Koestler expressed the alternative opinion in 1949:

> The Jewish religion is not merely a system of faith and worship, but implies membership of a definite race and potential nation ... to be a good Jew one must profess to belong to a chosen race, which was promised Canaan, suffered various exiles and will return one day to its true home. The 'Englishman of Jewish faith' is a contradiction in terms.[21]

Koestler regarded the position of the Jew to be metaphysical: '"the human condition carried to its extreme"'.[22] The existence of the state of Israel, to his mind, presented Jews with a problem of understanding where they belonged:

The conclusion is that since the foundation of the Hebrew State the attitude of Jews who are unwilling to go there, yet insist on remaining in some way apart from their fellow-citizens, has become an untenable anachronism.[23]

Likewise, the famous editor and owner of *The Manchester Guardian*, C. P. Scott, spoke of 'the Jew as a whole Jew, with a country and a patriotism to which any other country and any other patriotism will be secondary or adoptive'.[24]

During the First World War it became obvious that a compromise between the Zionists and the Conjoint Committee was impossible. What seems to have given a boost to the former was the warming support of two of the Rothschilds—Lord Walter and his younger brother Charles. They were part of an international network of Rothschilds, one of whom, Baron Edmond, head of the French branch of the family, had already helped financially in the development of Jewish settlements in Palestine.

Early in the history of the Zionist movement, the possibility of a settlement somewhere other than in Palestine had existed, and several alternatives were suggested. Among them were East Africa, Eritrea, Cyprus, Tripoli, the Sinai peninsula, and even Brazil. Little regard was given to the native populations of these places and it took King Victor Emmanuel III of Italy to remind Herzl that these people might raise objections to a sudden influx of thousands of Jewish immigrants.[25]

Joseph Chamberlain, the British colonial secretary, raised the question of East Africa—modern Uganda—in 1903 after a visit there the previous year. This proposal seems to have aroused the most interest and the most controversy among Zionists. At that time there was an attack on Jews in the Russian city of Kishinev, and the matter of asylum seemed paramount. Some were distressed at the challenge to the sole idea of Palestine. Segev tells us that Ben-Gurion, then a boy, 'broke into tears'.[26] Others were happy to settle for a home anywhere.

Despite the split among Zionists, Herzl reluctantly agreed to prepare a report for Chamberlain on the feasibility of East Africa as a homeland for the Jews. Interestingly, the report was compiled by Lloyd George, Roberts and Company, a well-known firm of solicitors at the time.

Chamberlain passed the report to the foreign secretary, with a guarded letter enclosed which was read out to the Sixth Zionist Conference, held in August 1903. In the letter, Chamberlain gave his agreement with the proposal to take over land in East Africa.[27] The debate that followed caused turmoil among the Zionists. 'It is a historical curiosity that at that time the Jews in Palestine itself, with very few exceptions, were fanatical "Ugandists",' wrote Koestler.

> The passion for Uganda soon became associated with a deadly hatred for Palestine... their only name for Palestine was 'a land of corpses and graves', a land of malaria and eye-diseases, a land which destroys its inhabitants... the

whole of Palestine was in a state of ferment ... all opposition to Uganda came from outside of Palestine.[28]

This somewhat bizarre idea soon fell apart. The land was already occupied, and the proposed disposal of the inhabitants of East Africa was not discussed—certainly, the inhabitants themselves were not consulted. This subject was raised briefly by Chamberlain when he spoke at a public meeting in December 1904, expressing the hope that 'these poor exiles [the Jews]... could live in safety [in a place] where they could find subsistence without in any way interfering with the subsistence of others'.[29] There was also the matter of the European settlers, especially in Kenya, led by the formidable Lord Delamere, a pioneering settler in Kenya and a large landowner, who protested against 'the introduction of alien Jews'.[30] The local British commissioner also did not recommend the scheme.

Despite a debate in the Commons in June 1904 in which there was the usual sympathy expressed for the Jews, there was increasing opposition from those Zionists who would accept nothing other than Palestine. They had their way when the Seventh Zionist Congress in July 1905 determined that only settlement in Palestine was acceptable. This showed the power of the Zionists. They relied, as always, on the weakness of British resolve and their opponents' lack of influence.

Before East Africa came under consideration, Herzl and Chamberlain had met in 1902 ostensibly to discuss a settlement in Cyprus or in El Arish in Egypt. Herzl believed that either could be used as a base for infiltration into Palestine. Cyprus was ruled out, but there was discussion in the Colonial Office and the Foreign Office about El Arish. In the case of Brazil, a Jewish physician named Dr David Eder, later chairman of the 'Zionist Commission', was sent by his cousin, the writer Israel Zangwill, to investigate the possibility of a Jewish settlement. In the end, neither El Arish nor Brazil came to anything.

Zangwill established the Jewish Territorial Organisation whose guiding principle was that any reasonable land would be acceptable for a settlement. In 1939, because of Nazi persecution, it was suggested in a conversation between Churchill and an Albanian diplomat that perhaps Albania could take in refugees. This idea died when Mussolini invaded that country.[31]

As late as April 1942, Churchill suggested turning two former Italian colonies—Eritrea on the Red Sea and Cyrenaica and Tripolitania (part of today's Libya) on the Mediterranean—'into Jewish colonies, affiliated, if desired, to the National Home in Palestine'. At the Potsdam Conference in 1945, Churchill, one supposes as a joke, said 'it appeared the Jews were not very smitten with this suggestion'.[32]

From time to time the Negev, a desert region south of Jerusalem, sparsely inhabited by nomadic Bedouin tribes, came up as another viable option. Weizmann had written to Churchill twenty years earlier about the possibility of the Jews developing the region and Churchill had liked the idea, although nothing was done about it at the time.

Years later, the Zionists were to obtain the Negev. The fate of the nomads living there was presumably of little concern, and this provides an example, in accordance with nineteenth-century colonial thinking, of the astonishing disregard for the rights of people who had lived in the land for hundreds or even thousands of years. What is remarkable is that although such attitudes have been discredited and discarded in modern times, they have persisted in Palestine and are still guiding the twenty-first-century policies of Israeli governments.

The presence of two peoples in the same country and their relationship is a matter that has concerned liberal Jews since the beginning of modern Zionism. Erik Cohen is one who addresses the question, pointing out that, although the Israeli Declaration of Independence offers assurances on several issues—religion for example—there is no mention of nationality:

> This omission points to the ambivalence of Israel's Founding Fathers as to the problem of the national status of Arabs in a Jewish state. This problem was to become one of the basic points of structural strain in Israeli society at a later stage.[33]

This historical colonialist hangover was surprising to many, including the liberal Count Folke Bernadotte, the United Nations representative appointed to try to sort out the mess that was Palestine after the Second World War:

> The reply was in the negative: the Jewish Government could under no present circumstances permit the return of Arabs who had fled or been driven from their homes during the war. I observed that I was surprised that the representatives of the Jewish people in particular should look at this problem from such a narrow viewpoint, that they should regard it purely as a political problem without taking into account the humanitarian side of the matter.[34]

When Count Bernadotte said 'in particular', he clearly meant that after their recent history in the Holocaust, it was almost incomprehensible that the Jews should have no sympathy for the dispossessed.

Part of the explanation for this disregard of human rights is to be found in the source of the Jewish immigration to Palestine. The bulk of the early migrants came from Eastern Europe, in particular Russia. These countries were ruled by dictators who ruthlessly kept their populations under control. Events such as the Enlightenment had passed over them, leaving them untouched by its questioning about human rights. Many of the leaders of the immigrants were from Eastern Europe, including three who were to become prime ministers: Ben-Gurion, Begin and Shamir, who judging by their treatment of Arabs, had no notion of the humanitarian traditions which had developed in the West.

Those Jews who emigrated from the West often found the standards of behaviour of fellow Eastern Jews deplorable. Nor was the position improved by the post-First World War immigration, since most of the immigrants were Eastern Europeans with none of the traditions of humanitarian thought of Western Europe. And it is notable that the members of murderous gangs, such as the Stern, were not of Western European origin. Churchill recognised the differences in the cultures of West and East:

> It would be a measureless disaster if Russian barbarism overlaid the culture and independence of the ancient States of Europe.[35]

Palestinian Arabs noticed the harsh traditions which Eastern European Jews brought with them, as was commented upon in the Palin Commission Report of 1920:

> The Orthodox Jew born in the country has never inspired the Arab or Christian with any particular feelings of distrust for, as has been observed before, he has been recognised as an inoffensive creature practically dependent for existence on foreign charity. But they already notice that the latest immigrants from Eastern Europe are men of a very different type imbued with all shades of the political opinions which have plunged Russia into a welter of anarchy, terrorism and misery during the past few years.[36]

Jewish immigration to Palestine exposed the fact that the Jews were by no means a homogenous group. This is such a cardinal matter that it is necessary to analyse it. At the foundation of the state, Ben-Gurion had to accept the fact that he had to allow non-European Jews into Israel if he wanted to outnumber the Arabs. But he did not like them. For him, almost all the newcomers, Holocaust survivors and Jews from the Islamic world, were foreign and alien. They were Jews, he said, 'only in the sense that they are not non-Jews'. As he saw it, the Jews of the Arab countries were a poor substitute for the murdered Jews of Europe.[37]

In recent years the situation has become exacerbated:

> During the past five years [1990-1995] the mass Aliya [immigration] of over 500,000 Jews into Israel from the ex-USSR has changed the face of the nation in unexpected ways. These Russian-speaking immigrants, unlike the more Zionist orientated wave of the 1970s, show little inclination to identify with Israeli culture. Instead they have created their own sub-culture in its midst— an unprecedented phenomenon which, given the size of this migration (10 per cent of the total Jewish population of Israel) is likely to continue in this generation. The xenophobic hostility of the native population, the media and even some politicians to this influx and their stereotypical responses, suggest that Israel may have reached a saturation point in its current ability to absorb new immigrants.[38]

It may be noted here that the 'native population' refers presumably to Jews. Many years later there was an attempt by President Sadat of Egypt to initiate peace talks with Israel. At that time the Likud party was in power, led by the extremist hardliner, Menachem Begin, who was Russian born. These talks were dominated by his intransigence, which led Ezer Weizman, the Israeli defence minister, to conclude after a fractious meeting in January 1978, 'it was a meeting between the Middle East (the Egyptian mentality) and Eastern Europe (the Israeli mentality)'.[39] It is the case therefore that during the mandate the British administration made a grievous mistake in assuming that the standards of Western society would be manifest in Jewish thought and behaviour.

Such vestiges of Western enlightened thought that found their way into Zionist thought and action were under early attack. In the early twentieth century the balance was disturbed by the need to bring in Jews, *any* Jews, to replace the 'mass exodus of European Jewish immigrants who had arrived in the Second Aliyah'.[40] The Zionists, in the shape of the Palestine Office, 'discovered the Jews of Yemen',[41] and it suited Arthur Ruppin, chief of the Palestine Office, to import them as part of Zionist policy to displace Arab labour. They had the advantage that although they were paid more than Arabs, they were paid less than European Jews, and as Ben-Gurion said, 'they did not have many needs'. There was a problem about their dark skin colour, but Ruppin insisted: 'There was no such thing as a dark-skinned Jew, but hoped that he could also find fairer Jews in Yemen.' The consequence of their differences was that 'many of them encountered prejudice and humiliation'.[42]

In the period after independence the 'cultural' balance became even more distorted. There had been mass immigration of Jews from North Africa and the Yemen. In the 1950s the Israeli Defence Forces (IDF) produced the Lavi Plan. In its review of Israeli's situation it stated that:

> Among the dangers facing the country, other than the hatred of the Arabs, the Report cited the composition of its Jewish population. During the coming several decades, about a third of Israelis would belong to the 'backward ethnic groups whose natural increase will be greater than the rest of the inhabitants.' As a result, Israel was in danger of 'Levanti-Sation', which could weaken social solidarity and strength. To achieve what the study called 'qualitative enhancement', Israel would need the immigration of high-quality Jews from overseas, meaning mostly the United States and the Soviet Union.[43]

Ben-Gurion himself was concerned about the heartless, not to say murderous, behaviour of 'oriental' Jews in the IDF. The situation in the terrorist Irgun was even more worrying, but at least explicable since

> Its recruits were mostly from among the Yemenite and Sephardic Jews who were taught Polish underground tactics.[44]

The problem of the 'kind' of Jews who arrived in Palestine was always being faced by the planners. Choices had to be made, and Ben-Gurion 'would choose young people, not old'. There was established 'a special fund to pay the cost of sending back to Europe immigrants "who had become a burden on the public and its social institutions"'.[45]

Returning to the early years of Zionism, the World Zionist Executive Headquarters were moved to Berlin in 1911, a fact which is not much dwelt upon in official or academic histories, but was of the greatest relevance in 1914, when public hatred of all things German exploded into violence against Germans, or people of German ancestry resident in Britain. The Zionist movement was dominated either by Germans or East Europeans who had strong ties with Germany. Herzl, in the last years of the nineteenth century, met the German Kaiser on several occasions and hoped that the establishment of a friendship, or even a protectorate under the Turks, would lead to permission to settle in Palestine. Nothing came of this. Nor, as we have seen, did attempts to deal directly with the sultan.

Before the First World War, Palestine was Turkish territory, the Turks were allied to the Germans, and it was not clear who would win. It followed that the Turks should be courted, even to supporting the idea of raising a force to join them. David Ben-Gurion, believing that the Turks would win, proposed recruiting a battalion to join the Turks in their fight against the Allies. In the fast moving style of the times, Ben-Gurion eventually joined the British Army in the ranks of the Jewish Legion.

For many years the Ottoman empire had been in crisis, and in 1908 to 1909 there was a revolution in Turkey. The idea gained ground that the Jews were allying themselves with the Germans and the Turks and were therefore undermining Britain's interests. This is illustrated by a Foreign Office handbook published later in 1920, which read:

> Only after the Revolution of 1908 could the German–Jew institutions, which had come into existence to take control of the Hebrew movement in Palestine, begin to make headway, and the German era of Jew colonisation increased materially the number and holdings of alien settlers.[46]

It is generally agreed by Jewish historians that Constantinople was an active source of Jewish propaganda, with an important branch of the Zionist Agency, and its publication *Le Jeune Turc* which 'lent itself to German propaganda and more than once published articles unfriendly to Great Britain', while the director of the Zionist Agency, Victor Jacobson, Russian-born but educated in Germany, 'gave a free hand to German or pro-German writers'.[47] There were, naturally, attempts by Jews to deny such allegations and to emphasise that Zionism did not favour one nation or another but was concerned only with the position of the Jews. Meanwhile British Jews were to face a home-grown crisis.

By the end of the nineteenth century there was much debate about the numbers of Jews arriving in Britain from Russia. Despite Joseph Chamberlain's expressions of sympathy, evidenced by his taking seriously the Cyprus and El Arish proposals, this immigration was of concern to him, especially since it was causing resentment in the East End of London. At Limehouse in December 1904, he expressed his sympathy for the locals:

> You are suffering from the unrestricted import of cheaper goods. You are also suffering from the unrestricted immigration of the people who make these goods.[48]

This influx had at its source the assassination of Tsar Alexander II in March 1881. The new Tsar, Alexander III, decided that Jews had been responsible and set in train 'pogroms'—attacks on Jewish communities. In 1881 pogroms were recorded in 166 Russian towns.

Largely as a result of this persecution in Russia, especially at the end of the nineteenth century, large numbers of Jews sought refuge in Britain. This led to a widespread feeling that there were too many Jews, and the numbers had to be controlled. Their numbers were especially noticeable in the East End of London, and gradually and especially in that part of the city, there developed resentment at their presence.

This resentment was widespread. Those who advocated restricting immigration appealed to working class people with the allegation that the new arrivals were undercutting wages and forcing British people out of their houses. Even the Trades Union Congress supported controls. Jewish trade unionists countered by saying that the numbers were exaggerated, and that the presence of immigrants was not the cause of the misery of the poor. This was due, in fact, to 'the consequences of class rule and class exploitation'.[49] The press drew a very negative picture of the immigrants:

> These were the penniless refugees and when the relief committee passed by they hid their gold, and fawned and whined, and in broken English asked for money for their train fare.[50]

An organisation called the British Brotherhood League was set up in 1901 and attracted wide support, including that of a very distinguished MP who had been born in India, and was himself an immigrant: Mancherjee Bhownaggree. The best known member was the MP for Stepney, Major William Evans-Gordon, who wrote that it was bad to have 'settlement of large aggregations of Hebrews in a Christian land'.[51] Like the Blackshirts in the 1930s, the league held marches and meetings, notably in the East End of London. At one of these an MP, Henry Norman, 'was applauded when he advised other nations to "disinfect their own sewage" adding that Englishmen "would not have this country made the dumping ground for the scum of Europe"'.[52]

The league, of course, demanded that immigration should be controlled. This pressure resulted in the setting up of a Royal Commission on Alien Immigration in 1902, which reported in August 1903. It relied heavily on the evidence presented by Evans-Gordon, who had travelled extensively in Europe on a fact-finding journey.

The commission duly set out suggestions for restricting immigration. These included a provision that if, within two years, anyone was 'reasonably supposed to be a criminal, a prostitute, living off prostitution, or of notoriously bad character', such a person could be deported, as could anyone who was 'a charge upon public health', except for ill health. Those arriving who were suffering from 'infectious or loathsome disease' or mental incapacity should be refused entry. With regard to the alleviation of overcrowding, certain areas should be designated as unsuitable for the acceptance of immigrants.

The government now felt it had to act and an Aliens Bill was presented to the House of Commons in 1905. Arthur Balfour, the prime minister, the same Balfour who was to utter the devastating 'Declaration' of 1917, made his views clear. Speaking to the House on 2 May 1905, he denied 'absolutely' the claim that the bill would restrict the right to asylum. 'Why,' he asked, 'should we admit into this country people likely to become a public charge? Are we bound to support every man, woman, and child incapable of supporting themselves who choose to come to our shores? That argument seems to me to be preposterous.' He argued that there had to be control because 'these foreign immigrants go into a small area of the East End of London, and they produce the evil of overcrowding'. Although some spoke out against the bill, it was clear that it was a popular measure, and the act received the royal assent in August 1905. An interesting curiosity is that all four Jewish Conservative MPs voted for the bill, while of the four Jewish Liberals, one abstained and three voted against.

The act had some effect:

> In 1906 more than 500 Jewish refugees were granted political asylum. In 1908 the number had fallen to twenty and by 1910, just five. During the same period, 1378 Jews, who had been permitted to enter as immigrants but were found to be living on the streets without any visible means of support, had been rounded up and deported back to their country of origin.[53]

But the act was too late, as were subsequent acts designed to restrict immigration. Already by the end of the nineteenth century about 15,000 Jews had arrived, and they were to affect significantly the social picture in London. It was over this agonising about immigration that Winston Churchill first made his name as a champion and defender of Jews and Zionism. It was a position from which he never wavered.

At the time of this agitation, Winston Churchill was active in politics. He was to prove a relentless advocate of Zionism: indeed, so consistent was he in his support that it may be said that it was sometimes mindless. His first major intervention occurred early in his career. It was linked to his move from the Conservative to the Liberal party. Not only was Churchill going to lose his Oldham seat because he had left the Conservative party, he needed a Liberal seat. His chance to ingratiate himself with the powerful Jewish group in Manchester came when there was a previous attempt, in 1904, to pass an Aliens Act. Nathan Laski was a very influential Jewish figure in Manchester and he sent Churchill briefing papers designed to prevent, if possible, the passing of the bill. Laski, Churchill recognised, would be able to arrange his candidacy for the Liberal party.

On the day he crossed the floor, Churchill sent a letter to *The Times*, *The Manchester Guardian* and the *Jewish Chronicle* 'denouncing the Unionists' Government Bill, which was intended to restrict the immigration into Britain of Jews escaping from pogroms in Tsarist Russia'.[54] He wrote that the bill 'is expected to appeal to insular prejudices against foreigners, to racial prejudice against Jews, and to labour prejudice against competition', and that the bill was in conflict with British traditions of hospitality. A 'common informer' could abuse the bill for personal reasons. 'The letter itself was intended as an electoral gambit—one third of his new constituency's voters were Jewish.'[55] In June Churchill spoke in the House as a Liberal, and tried to insist on a debate, when the government did not want one. Instead the bill was sent to a grand committee, upon which Churchill managed to secure a place. There the Liberal representatives insisted on going into such detail that the government decided to abandon the measure.

There is much in the letter which informs us about Churchill. There is first his hypocrisy, for there are few national political figures who have so abused 'foreigners' as him. Leaving aside the 'Hun' which was a wartime necessity, he profoundly disliked Indians, and, significantly, Arabs. When there was a prospect of Gandhi holding discussions with the viceroy of India, Churchill deplored this, describing him as 'striding up the steps of the Viceregal palace ... such a spectacle can only increase the unrest in India and the danger to which white people there are exposed'.[56] Again:

> I do not admit, for instance, that a great wrong has been done to the Red Indians of America, or the black people of Australia. I do not admit that a wrong has been done to these people by the fact that a stronger race, a higher grade race, or, at any rate, a more worldly-wise race, to put it that way, has come in and taken their place. I do not admit it. I do not think the Red Indians had any right to say, 'The American Continent belongs to us and we are not going to have any of the European settlers coming here'. They had not the right, nor had they the power.[57]

This statement goes a long way in explaining Churchill's lack of concern for the rights of the Palestinian Arabs. Linked with this were his emotional feelings for the Jews:

Churchill's philo-Semitism, so rare on the Tory benches was invaluable in allowing him to see sooner than anyone else the true nature of the Nazi regime. 'I remember the tears pouring down his cheeks one day before the war in the House of Commons,' Attlee recalled many years later, 'when he was telling me what was being done to the Jews in Germany'.[58]

Churchill deplored the second bill which was enacted in 1905, but this time he failed to stop it. He did, though, suggest that a Liberal government could repeal it. In February 1907 he wrote to the home secretary, Herbert Gladstone, setting out his objections: because people were poor, it did not mean they were undesirable. Similarly there was no correlation between being wealthy and being a suitable immigrant. The officials responsible for applying the act acted cruelly, for example: 'children were parted from their parents ... the Act was both useless and vexatious ... I am sure the Liberal party would support the repeal of such a foolish piece of legislation.'[59] Despite Churchill's pleading, the party failed to repeal the act when it ousted the Conservatives in the election of 1906. Although some of the Tory candidates tried to capitalise on the immigrant issue, they lost heavily. Even Arthur Balfour lost his seat. But the Aliens Act stood.

Churchill became home secretary in 1910, and his actions in that position have always been attended by controversy. This centred on his use of troops to deal with social protest. There was what came to be known as the 'Siege of Sidney Street' in 1911, when a group of anarchists was discovered in that street and a gun battle took place. The fact that they were foreigners was widely discussed and must have had an adverse effect on the perception of immigrants. Then Churchill sent in troops to quell striking miners in South Wales, an action that tarnished his reputation there for the rest of his life.

What is less well known is that in 1911, in South Wales, there were attacks on Jewish shops and homes. It was alleged that Jewish landlords had evicted miners who could not pay the rent. On the third day of the violence, Churchill sent a hundred soldiers to Tredegar. After a few days the rioting subsided. No Jews had been killed, but the rioters were punished, and some sent to prison. Despite a petition, Churchill refused to interfere with the sentences. He received the thanks of the Board of Deputies of British Jews. The Jewish historian Martin Gilbert writes of his approval of Churchill's behaviour: 'From his position of authority, Churchill had acted without hesitation to stamp on violence in Britain.' Churchill's legacy would have been much less poisonous to some if he had shown some mercy to the rioters. This would, of course, have been impossible given the mood of the time and the mental makeup of Churchill. It can be certain that the issuing of severe punishments could not have done much to improve relationships between the Jews and the wider community.[60]

It would only be a relatively short time before Britain was in turmoil. There was a war such as had never been seen, the outcome of which, while requiring every resource, was far from certain. In the Middle East the war was being waged against the Turks, still in possession of a vast empire. The future of Palestine and the question of a 'return' by the Jews was hardly a national priority, which ostensibly made the advancement of the cause difficult, and yet paradoxically easier because the cause could not properly be addressed by key decision makers. This environment was one that the Zionists were able to exploit.

At the start of the First World War, it was fairly clear that the Ottoman empire would not survive; other nations began to consider their individual stakes in the wreckage. France, for example, had considerable interests in Syria, and it wanted these to remain.

The start of the war, although it offered opportunity to the Zionists, also posed a number of problems for them. Their headquarters were in Germany and there were many Jews living there. Thousands of these, of course, volunteered for the German Army, not only because they were patriotic, but because they hoped it might improve their status in German society. They also hoped that a German victory over the Russians would lead to a lessening of the persecution of Jews in that country. As always, the Zionist interest in the war focused on what would happen to Palestine, and the main Zionist player in this regard was to be Chaim Weizmann. His manipulation of a constantly changing situation must rank as one of the political phenomena of the period.

Weizmann was born in 1874 in Russia. As a young man he studied chemistry in Germany and Switzerland, and in 1904 he went to live in Manchester, where he took up a post in the university. He lived in Manchester for most of the rest of his life. In 1910 he became a British citizen. Although his views on the future of Jewry were very contentious amongst the Jews, over the next twenty years, by skilful manipulation of political events, he became recognised as their spokesman, especially and most importantly by the British government. He combined his rise to power with practical measures: for example when in Jerusalem in 1907 he helped organise the Palestine Land Development Company, which was to continue the acquisition of Arab land which had begun in the previous century.

Weizmann had been of some use to the war effort through his development of acetone, a central component of explosives. This vital work had led him to make contact with key players in the government, notably David Lloyd George, minister of munitions, and Arthur Balfour, the first lord of the Admiralty. Both were to become even more important during the war: Lloyd George as prime minister and Balfour as foreign secretary. Weizmann was helped in his government contacts because he had a crucial sympathiser in the person of C. P. Scott, the editor of *The Manchester Guardian*. 'It is doubtful whether Weizmann would have got to Lloyd George and Balfour without Scott's help ... During the course of the war Weizmann spoke with Lloyd George at least seven times, once they dined together at the home of Lady Astor.'[61]

The Political Art of Lies and Ambiguity

A meeting between Balfour and Weizmann, which was to have profound consequences, took place in January 1905 after a political meeting in Manchester. Balfour invited Weizmann to visit him in London. There were several failed attempts to meet, and when they did meet Balfour said to Weizmann: 'Mind you come again to see me. I am deeply moved and interested. It is not a dream. It is a great cause, and I understand it.'[62] Weizmann also wrote that 'he listened for a long time and was, I assure you, most deeply moved—to the point of tears'.[63] Palestine seems to have been a subject which often provoked tears in cabinet ministers. On one occasion Weizmann found Lloyd George 'weeping in 10 Downing Street reading the psalms'.[64]

These meetings between Balfour and Weizmann continued until March 1917, when Weizmann reported that

> We had a serious talk on practical suggestions connected with Palestine. He gave me a good opening to put before him the importance of Palestine from a British point of view, an aspect which was apparently new to him.[65]

We shall go on to see that Balfour had changed his attitude to Jews a good deal since his attack on them during the debates on the immigration bills. By 1917 he had become as lyrical and excessive as Churchill:

> The Jews are the most gifted race that mankind has seen since the Greeks of the fifth century. They have been exiled, scattered and oppressed ... if we can find them an asylum, a safe home in their native land, then the full flowering of their genius will burst forth and propagate.[66]

Herbert Samuel was a critical political figure both before and after the Balfour Declaration. He was a member of that well-established, well-connected British Jewish constellation, which was a source of opposition to Zionism, although he did not share in that opposition. He was a Liberal, and served as chancellor of the duchy of Lancaster in 1909, as postmaster-general, as president of the Local Government Board, and as home secretary. He was also the leader of a much-fractured Liberal party from 1931 to 1935.

Samuel claimed to have abandoned religious beliefs, but this did not weaken his resolve to support Zionism, despite the fact that he seemingly cultivated a cool and detached demeanour: it was famously said that he 'conveys no impression of enthusiasm and is as free from passion as an oyster'.[67] Despite some evidence of his caution in the timing of a Jewish bid for power in Palestine, his manipulation of the Palestine debate shows that he was passionate about the cause. His freedom from 'passion' was to prove invaluable in restraining the excesses of some Zionists at critical phases of the struggle. At first his support for Zionism seemed doubtful, but he soon became a champion of the cause, and unlike other Jews pressing the case, he was a government minister.

Very soon after war broke out in November 1914, Herbert Samuel went to see Sir Edward Grey, the foreign secretary, and suggested 'perhaps the opportunity might arise for the fulfilment of the ancient aspiration of the Jewish people and the restoration [in Palestine] of a Jewish state'.[68] On the same day Samuel went to see Lloyd George, at that time chancellor of the exchequer. Only months before the latter had described Samuel as a 'greedy, ambitious and grasping Jew with all the worst characteristics of his race'. On this occasion, however, he said that he was 'very keen to see a Jewish state established there'.[69] Even though the two remarks would appear to be somewhat contradictory, this was no surprise. Lloyd George would typically say what seemed to be politic, regardless of truth.

During 1915, Samuel continued his canvassing of Lloyd George and Sir Edward Grey, and in March of that year he submitted a document to the prime minister, Herbert Asquith, setting out a possible future for Palestine, including large-scale Jewish immigration. Samuel also pointed out the advantage to Britain of Palestine as a buffer to protect Egypt and the Suez Canal. This argument gained mounting force as the Zionist campaign developed. In the final version of the document, Samuel marshalled what were to become familiar arguments in support of a Jewish takeover, the principal argument being that no European power, especially France, should be trusted near the Suez Canal. There should be a British protectorate, and then, having said that a Jewish state was not possible, he immediately contradicted himself:

> Under British rule facilities would be given to Jewish organisations to purchase land, to found colonies, to establish educational and religious institutions, and to try to co-operate in the economic development of the country, and that Jewish immigration, carefully regulated, would be given preference, so that in the course of time the Jewish inhabitants, grown into a majority and settled in the land, may be conceded such degree of self-government as the conditions of that day might justify.[70]

Such a proposal would provide a bulwark against French ambitions, and the French would be unlikely to oppose such a humane proposal. Asquith, the prime minister, was not especially keen, and stated, with a passing reference to the 'race' question,

> I am not attracted by this proposed addition to our responsibilities, but it is a curious illustration of Dizzy's [Disraeli's] favourite maxim that 'race is everything' to find this almost lyrical outburst proceeding from the well-ordered and methodical brain of H.S.[71]

Stein's summary is that 'Samuel's memorandum does not seem to have made any marked impression on his colleagues'.[72] This is hardly surprising when thousands were being killed in seemingly endless slaughter: what was happening in a remote country could hardly have been of interest.

It was time for Samuel and Weizmann to meet. When C. P. Scott suggested it to Weizmann, he was reluctant since he believed Samuel was hostile to the Zionists. But although Samuel may have had earlier reservations, by this time he was a convert, to the unutterable delight of Weizmann and the other Zionists.

The debates about Zionism and its purpose were not confined to Europe. At the end of the nineteenth century, some two million Jews had arrived in the United States so that by the outbreak of the First World War there was a Jewish population there of approximately three million. But as in Britain, among the wealthier there was little interest in Zionism, and the poorer new arrivals had more urgent concerns like surviving. There were, of course, factional struggles amongst American Jews. There were Zionists and anti-Zionists, supporters of Germany, pacifists, and those worried, like their British counterparts, about being accused of conflict between their loyalty to a new Palestine and the country of their birth or adoption. A British ambassador to the US, Spring-Rice, expressed this in a letter in November 1917, in which he pointed out that there were only a few American Zionists: 'the great masses of Jews appear to be bitterly opposed to the Zionist leaders, and the rich Jews are divided among themselves'.[73]

There was, though, plenty of publicly expressed opinion that the notion of a Palestinian homeland was widely supported. Every view could be alleged as representative because there was no single body deputed to speak for all Jews. Weizmann spent a good deal of time trying to bring American Jews into line. He sent emissaries to liaise with key American organisations and officials. As a result of a conference called by Zionists in August 1914, an American organisation was established called 'The Provisional Executive for General Zionist Affairs'.[74]

Naturally some Americans did not support the Jews. One, a Colonel House, was a key adviser to President Wilson. It was because he was such an important influence that he was nicknamed 'Colonel'. He later served on the League of Nations Commission on Mandates. He is reported as having said that 'the Jews from every tribe descended in force, and they seemed determined to break in with a jimmy if they are not let in'.[75] But there is also evidence that some Americans were in favour of the Zionists. There was also discussion about the possibility of the US taking over in Palestine:

> At the end of the War the idea of an American protectorate was revived. Unreal though it was, for there was never any likelihood of commending itself to the Americans, it was seriously discussed, and on the eve of the Peace Conference there was in some British circles a decided feeling that the United States should be invited, and indeed, pressed, to become responsible for Palestine.[76]

Since the attitude and behaviour of the American people and government to Zionism has always, and continues to be, of paramount importance, it is vital to note the patterns in the early days of Jewish immigration to the United States.

Large numbers of the Jewish population were German in origin. Some of the Germans naturally supported their homeland—it must be remembered that the US was not yet in the war—and some still had connections there. When it is remembered how Jews had suffered under the Tsars, it is to be expected that, when war broke out, Russian emigrants hoped for a German victory. But as Stein points out, this did not mean they were anti-Allies or pro-German: rather that they were anti-Russian.[77] What this amounted to was quite considerable support for Germany, which of course angered the British. The British ambassador painted a very treasonous picture where 'the Germans and the German Jew bankers are toiling in a solid phalanx to compass our destruction'.[78] It was another reference to the widespread belief in the influence of Jewish money.

Britain realised that it was essential to get active American involvement in the war. This wish was cultivated by a group of Jews who saw it as a useful tool with which to persuade the British government (and other governments) to express sympathy for Zionism. These Jewish 'activists' were 'from the USA, England, Russia and Egypt, Horace Kallen, Lucien Wolf, Vladimir Jabotinsky, and Edgar Suares ... together they endorsed the increasingly accepted belief in pro-German intrigues and influence among the masses of American Jewry, and the existence of a powerful German-Jewish financial clique.'[79]

An effective solution was the issue of a statement that the British desired a protectorate in Palestine, which would be sympathetic to the Zionist cause.[80] The American Provisional Executive Committee did what it could to advance the cause of Zionism, especially in helping Palestinian Jews survive the vagaries of Turkish rule:

> From the day when war broke out Palestine had appealed to America for help. America was at that time the one country which, through its political and financial position, was able to save Palestine from permanently going under.[81]

The attitude of President Wilson of the United States was at first not supportive. Stein points out that having been asked by the British for his views, 'he sent a discouraging reply'. Such was the power of the US, even then, that his reply 'had come near to killing the Balfour Declaration'. But when Britain asked again, he expressed approval of it. Had this 'reply been equally chilling, it is quite possible that the Declaration would never have seen the light'.[82]

By 1916 it was already becoming obvious that the Jewish vote in US politics was going to be an important influence, as it has been ever since. Because it was becoming clear that Jewish voters would vote for those candidates who supported Jewish and Zionist interests, regardless of broader considerations, 'there is some reason to believe that in 1916 Woodrow Wilson gave a prominent New York Zionist an assurance of his benevolent interest in Zionism in return for a promise of support in the presidential campaign of that year.' Stein quotes I. S. Meyer who wrote, 'President Wilson ... was the first occupant of the White House to feel the full force of Zionist pressure.'[83]

While the activities of the Zionists were being debated in Europe and the United States, there was intense diplomatic and political activity in the Middle East. The Turkish Ottoman empire had been slowly crumbling during the later nineteenth century, and early in the twentieth it was clear that it could not last. The 'Young Turk' Revolution in Turkey of 1908-09 restored a constitutional monarchy, which in turn enabled the emergence of a plethora of parties and organisations in Palestine, including two generally known as the Jewish Social Democratic Labour party and the Arab al-Fatat. The former was set up by German Jews who were settlers, and the latter, at first, was committed to the idea of equal rights with the Turks within the empire. Such an idea was totally unacceptable to the Turkish government, and so the movement developed a policy of Arab independence. Together with another Arab organisation called al-'Ahd, they set out their ambitions in the 'Damascus Protocol' in 1915.

These potential rebels were organised, and could probably command considerable support. But to succeed they needed the critical help of arguably the most powerful Arab in the empire, Grand Sharif Hussein of Mecca. The sharif had four sons who feature in the history of the time: Ali, Abdullah, Feisal and Zeid. Of these, Ali took very little part in the momentous events which were to follow. The most prominent, and the most memorable, was Feisal, whose name is always associated with the exploits of T. E. Lawrence (Lawrence of Arabia), although it was Feisal's brother Abdullah, who was to be the greater influence in the events which surrounded the establishment of the Zionist state. It was Feisal who managed the difficult task of negotiating the Byzantine tangle of Ottoman politics, convincing the Turks that he and his family were to be trusted, and at the same time in early 1915 listening to revolutionary Arab leaders and eventually persuading his father to support their cause.

The sharif was faced with a big problem when it came to the question of whether to support the Turks or the British. After all, as the Jews had found, it was not clear at the beginning of the war who would win. British policy was to persuade the Arabs to side with them and to rise against the Turks. In early 1915, out of the clandestine Arab meetings, came the Damascus Protocol.

The Damascus Protocol put Great Britain firmly in place as a nation that would support the Arabs with economic benefits and a mutual defence arrangement. The privileges granted to foreigners would be abolished. But the central aim was to establish an Arab state which would run from the borders of Anatolia, following the Red Sea, embracing the whole of Arabia and Mesopotamia, to the border with Persia and the Persian Gulf, but excepting—here a concession to

British interests—Aden. The proposed state, of course, included Palestine, which in any case was often regarded as being part of Syria.

The man on the ground in charge in Cairo was Sir Arthur Henry McMahon, newly arrived from India, and with no experience of the Middle East. His colleagues did not leave a very flattering picture of the man who was to negotiate some of the most difficult diplomacy of the day. 'He is a nice man,' said one, 'and I like him very much, but his ability is of a very ordinary type while his slowness of mind and ignorance of French must be serious drawbacks to him.'[84] Another complained that 'his slowness and absolute determination never to give a decision if he can possibly help it are at times quite disconcerting ... he is quite the laziest man I have met.'[85]

In the background of the McMahon Letters was something called 'an official Proclamation from the Government of Great Britain to the natives of Arabia and the Arab provinces'. This was issued by the British authorities in Cairo. It announced that

[Britain] has decided not to attack you nor initiate war against any of you nor [Kedourie describes this as 'its most startling passage'] does she intend to possess any part of your country neither in the form of conquest and possession nor in the form of protection or occupation.

It went on to assure the Arabs that if the Turks were driven out 'we will give up those places to them at once' and the Arabs would 'take the reins of the Government of their country' and 'your perfect independence' would be recognised.[86]

With the full authority of all the important officials, locally and in London—including, most notably, that of the foreign secretary, Sir Edward Grey—McMahon began negotiations with the sharif. Grey sent a message which read, 'His Majesty's Government will make it an essential condition in any terms of peace that the Arabian peninsula and its Moslem Holy Places should remain in the hands of an independent Sovereign Moslem state'.[87] By July 1915 Sharif Hussein had made up his mind. The assurance was given because it was believed there was a real danger that the Germans, or the Turks, might persuade the Arabs to join with them. In the event the outcome was that the Arabs did join the British, to very good effect, and there arose the Hussein–McMahon Correspondence, consisting of only eight letters, which were to have unbelievable ramifications.

The argument surrounding these letters is so important to historical events that it must be reviewed at some length. For the purpose of this analysis it is only necessary to examine the controversial question as to the place of Palestine in this maelstrom, but it should be noted that there has been argument about intent, honesty, misunderstanding, the meaning of words, and the quality of translation in respect to all of the correspondence. The latter was, and is, a matter of considerable dispute.[88] To these complexities should be added the historic rivalry between the India Office, the Indian government, and the Foreign Office, and the anger of the British government at the assurances that McMahon was giving to the Arabs. And these are only a few of the issues. The Zionists were conscious of these rivalries, and were skilled at understanding and exploiting them.

With regard to Palestine, the central question was whether or not it was to be included in the new Arab state. There is no doubt that it is included in the Damascus Protocol. It would be essential for the Zionist cause that doubt was thrown on the intention to include Palestine. Prior draws attention to the clarity of that intent to include Palestine:

> Sir Henry McMahon, the British High Commissioner in Egypt, with certain important reservations, agreed ... 'to recognise and support the independence of the Arabs within the territories included in the limits and boundaries proposed by the Sharif of Mecca', i.e. from Cilicia in the north to the Indian Ocean in the south, and from the Mediterranean to Iran.[89]

It may be emphasised that this absolutely, and clearly, includes Palestine. Hussein replied on 14 July 1915 to McMahon making a number of proposals. These included agreement to the setting up of a caliphate, mutual defence, and setting out precise boundaries of the new Arab state. McMahon replied on 30 August agreeing that the Arab countries would be independent, but that the 'question of frontiers and boundaries, negotiations would appear to be premature and a waste of time on details at this stage'.[90] It looked as though the project would collapse when McMahon issued this, the first of his caveats, which were to confuse the issue for ever afterwards.

Hussein replied that the whole promise turned on acceptance of the borders as set out in the protocol. He wrote that he was disappointed at the 'the obscurity and the signs of lukewarmth and hesitancy' about the matter of frontiers and boundaries.[91] This prompted the most important and controversial letter of all.

On 24 October McMahon wrote that he had not intended to be hesitant or 'lukewarm', and then came the sentence which was to change the course of history:

> The districts of Mersin and Alexandretta, and portions of Syria lying to the west of the districts of Damascus, Homs, Hama and Aleppo cannot be said to be purely Arab, and must on that account be excepted from the proposed delimitation.[92]

He then went on to say:

> Subject to the modifications above, Great Britain is prepared to recognise and uphold the independence of the Arabs in all the regions lying within the frontiers proposed by the Sharif of Mecca.[93]

Hussein's reply was mostly a history lesson, in which he points out that Aleppo and Beirut and the western maritime coasts are 'purely Arab provinces'. McMahon's reply on 13 December was to say that the

> Government of Great Britain have fully understood your statement in that respect and noted it with the greatest care. But as the interests of their ally France are involved in those two provinces, the question calls for careful consideration.[94]

The Arab position was that the matter was a simple one of geography: Palestine was well south of the areas marked for exclusion. They must have been baffled too by the statement that some districts were not 'purely Arab'. The matter did not rest. For the next twenty years and beyond there were attempts to address the question as to whether McMahon said what he meant, or did not mean what he said.

Lord Curzon's Eastern Committee of the war cabinet was quite clear. At their meeting on 5 December 1918, Lord Curzon, at that time leader of the House of Lords, concluded the following:

> The Palestine position is this. If we deal with our commitments, there is first the general pledge to Hussein in October 1915, under which Palestine was included in the areas as to which Great Britain pledged itself that they should be Arab and independent in the future.[95]

Curzon went on to observe that 'a new feature was brought into the case' by the Balfour Declaration, but then expressed concern about Jewish immigration, and 'the fact that the Zionists have taken full advantage—and are disposed to take even fuller advantage of the opportunity which was then offered to them'. They even 'claim to spread across the Jordan into the rich countries lying to the east, and, indeed there seems to be small limit to the aspirations which they now form'.[96] Curzon was right: the Zionist claim was that what is now Jordan should be included in their 'homeland'.

Arnold Toynbee was at the time working for the government and he was asked to comment on some of the documentation. He wrote in a memorandum in October 1918, 'we are pledged to King Hussein that this territory shall be "Arab" and "independent"'.[97] His note reflected the view of many. However, this was unlikely to carry much weight since he was only a junior civil servant—a temporary Foreign Office clerk.

> Surely our foundation should be a *Palestinian* State with *Palestinian citizenship* for all inhabitants, whether Jewish or non-Jewish. This alone seems consistent with Mr. Balfour's letter. Hebrew might be made an official language, but the

Jewish element should not be allowed to form a state within the state, enjoying greater privileges than the rest of the population.[98]

Kedourie examines the possibility that Toynbee did not have access to all the documentation, having been called upon to produce a report six weeks before the armistice. He had only been in the department since March 1918. This led him to some 'peculiar and erroneous conclusions'.[99]

Even though Toynbee worked on the papers at the time, his interpretation has been challenged notably by Isaiah Friedman.[100] In a memorandum for the Paris Peace Conference, H. Erie Richards, referring again to the October letter, states that Britain was prepared to support Arab independence within certain limits, and 'Palestine was within those territories'.[101] But in November 1920 a Hubert Young of the Foreign Office prepared a memorandum for a visit by Feisal to London. This exploited longstanding arguments about the meaning of words used by the Turks to demarcate districts, and in consequence what those districts comprised. Young proposed that the 'western boundary', mentioned in McMahon's letter, was marked by a line from Lake Tiberias to Aqaba via the Dead Sea.[102] It follows that Palestine was excluded from the promise to Hussein. This highly speculative and devastating conclusion, which is based upon fiction, laid the basis for subsequent challenges to what everyone, not least the Arabs, had assumed.

In the next year, Eric Forbes Adams wrote a letter to Sir John Shuckburgh in which he noted that 'Toynbee, who went into the papers, was quite sure his interpretation was right and I think his view was more or less accepted until Young wrote his memorandum'.[103] An Arab delegation in London in December 1922 gave copies of the correspondence to several newspapers and *The Daily Mail* correspondent, J. M. N. Jeffries, published articles entitled 'The Palestine Deception' which demanded the cancelling of the Balfour Declaration and a British withdrawal from Palestine.[104] But the damage was done, and despite further insistence that Palestine should be included in the promises to the Arabs, the pressure was to prove irresistible. Then, McMahon himself began to intervene. He persistently denied that Palestine was included in his promise to the Arabs, and his denial was wheeled out on many occasions to justify the *volte face*.

His method was that of all politicians who want to rewrite history. They start by saying that they did not write (or say) something. Then, if the evidence is clear that they did, to claim that the interpretation is wrong. And finally they say that whatever is written is not what they meant to say. McMahon's defence—for it must be judged as such—must be dismissed in the form in which it was made in a letter to *The Times* on 22 July 1937:

> I feel it my duty to state, and I do so definitely and emphatically, that it was not intended by me in giving this pledge to King Hussein to include Palestine in the area in which Arab independence was promised.

In the same month the head of the Eastern Department of the Foreign Office wrote a minute about that letter, in which he said the only thing that made sense: 'the short answer is that if we did not want to include Palestine, we might have said so in terms, instead of referring vaguely to areas west of Damascus'. He goes on: 'It would be far better to recognise and admit that H.M.G. made a mistake and gave flatly contradictory promises—which of course it did.'[105] Until Hubert Young's rewriting of geography there can be no doubt that there is no reason to suppose that Palestine would be excluded from the proposed Arab country.

The most amazing letter of all from McMahon was sent to Sir John Shuckburgh in March 1922. McMahon had been asked why Palestine and Jerusalem had not been mentioned in his original letters. He replied:

> There was no place I could think of at the time of sufficient importance for purposes of definition further south of the above [i.e. Damascus, Hama, Homs and Aleppo] ... it was fully my intention to exclude Palestine as it was to exclude the more northern tracts of Syria.

Even more jaw-dropping was his statement that he had not set the Jordan as a western boundary of Arab control as 'he thought it might be "desirable" at some later stage of the negotiations to find some "suitable frontier line" between the Jordan and the Hedjaz railway'.[106] This latter area, in present-day Jordan (east of the river), the Zionists hoped to purloin as it was the home of Jewish tribes in prehistory in biblical fable. The Jordan and its relationship to the borders of Israel remain a source of speculation for some:

> Who were the people who made up Israel? Each time the question was asked, the response created new borders, as well as new relationships to Israel's most significant border, the River Jordan.[107]

In 1922 Churchill wrote a 'White Paper', a policy document setting out proposals for future legislation, which will be discussed later. It is sufficient to say at this point that Churchill, predictably, claimed that Palestine was excluded. His statement was bold:

> It is not the case, as has been represented by the Arab delegation that during the war His Majesty's Government gave an undertaking that an independent national government should be established in Palestine.

He went on to make the familiar allegation that Syria west of Damascus, and that includes Palestine, was not included in McMahon's offer. In March 1923 Lord Islington, in a Lords' debate, rejected Young's and Churchill's arguments, concluding that 'Mr. Churchill, with considerable ingenuousness, of which, when in a difficult situation, he is an undoubted master, produced an entirely new description of that line'. The duke of Devonshire agreed. The meaning of the words 'west of the district of Damascus ... has to be somewhat strained in order to cover an area lying considerably to the south, as well as the west, of the City of Damascus'.[108]

Sir Gilbert Clayton (1875-1929) held several major posts in the war in the Middle East, including head of the Arab Bureau in Cairo and military governor of Jerusalem. It was claimed that he wrote an informal note in April 1923, which was described by Herbert Samuel in 1937 in a debate in the House of Lords. He explained that Clayton gave him, quite unofficially, a note dated 12 April, 1923.[109] This note said: 'I can bear out the statement that it was never the intention that Palestine should be included in the general pledge given to the Sharif, the introductory words of Sir Henry's letter were thought at that time—perhaps erroneously—clearly to cover that point'. By the time Samuel produced the letter, Clayton was dead. An unofficial note, not before in the public domain, dated some eight years earlier and now promulgated by a Zionist ex-minister, is hardly strong evidence upon which to support policies affecting millions. The situation was summed up by Lord Edward Grey, the former foreign secretary, who was McMahon's senior when the correspondence took place. In a debate in March 1923, he concluded:

> A Zionist home, my Lords, undoubtedly means or implies a Zionist government over the district in which the home is placed, and if 93% of the population of Palestine are Arabs, I do not see how you can establish other than an Arab Government, without prejudice to their civil rights. That one sentence alone of the Balfour Declaration seems to me to involve, without over-stating the case, very great difficulty of fulfilment.[110]

In 1939 a committee was set up 'to Consider Certain Correspondence ...' in preparation for a White Paper in 1939. Faced with a welter of documentation the conclusion was that it was

> ... evident from these statements that His Majesty's Government were not free to dispose of Palestine without regard for the wishes and interests of the inhabitants of Palestine, and that these statements must all be taken into account in any attempt to estimate the responsibilities which—upon any interpretation of the Correspondence—His Majesty's Government incurred towards those inhabitants as a result of the Correspondence.

In fact, all of this furore was compounded by incompetence. McMahon was temperamentally unsuitable for the task, and he had no experience of the Middle East. He was asked to assure the Arabs of eventualities which the government had no intention of bringing about, and was then reprimanded when he tried. His defence demonstrates that the wording of his letters was studiously vague:

> I found myself at the moment in the difficult position of having to give in great haste such assurances in respect to a nebulous state of affairs, both present and future, as would satisfy a somewhat nebulous community and prompt them into taking sides with us instead of the enemy. I had necessarily to be vague as on the one hand HMG disliked being committed to definite future action, and the other any detailed definition of our demands would have frightened off the Arab.[111]

There are many other examples which show that Britain was merely using the Arabs. A British official, Sir Arthur Nicolson, said that the idea of an Arab state was 'an absurdity' since the Arabs were 'a heap of scattered tribes with no cohesion and no organisation'.[112]

It was not until 1939 that the correspondence was published in a White Paper.[113] This episode was the first of many to sully any reputation the British government might have had in the Middle East. However, despite the manifest evidence, some Jewish historians advance conclusions based upon very questionable premises, but they are conclusions which set in train the eventual concession to the Zionists. Segev's view is representative:

> The affair proved embarrassing for the government, but at most the Arabs won on a technicality; the letters did not decisively confirm that Palestine would be included in the independent state the British had promised the Arabs.[114]

The conclusion by Stein is even more removed from the evidence. He writes:

> The question is not merely whether the choice of language was such as to close any possible loophole for the contention that the British undertaking, literally construed, could be made to extend to Palestine.[115]

At this point it is apposite to ask why. He goes on: 'It is material to enquire whether it was so intended by the British government and so understood in good faith by the Sharif'.[116] The answer is that despite McMahon's later attempt to redefine what he thought he said and meant, the British government surely meant to include Palestine, and it is inconceivable that the sharif did not assume so. Yet, Stein's somewhat tortuous conclusion is that

> the truth seems to be that while, on a minute examination of the language used by McMahon in describing the areas outside of his assurances, a case can be made out for the view that Palestine was not ambiguously excluded, it is a purely verbal case, unrelated to the substance of the matter and devoid of

merits. This is not to say that the position in Palestine was unaffected by British encouragement of Arab national aspirations; but if the question is whether the British government had committed itself in 1915 to leaving Palestine under Arab control, the answer seems clearly to be that there was no such commitment.[117]

Karsh abruptly rejects the Arab case: 'Actually, McMahon excluded Palestine from such an empire'.[118]

Whatever is claimed T. E. Lawrence may have said or done on the subject of the Middle East, on the McMahon dispute Lawrence is unambiguous: 'The dismissal of Sir Henry McMahon confirmed my belief in our essential insincerity.'[119] In fact it was Lawrence who disclosed the existence of the correspondence immediately after the war, albeit under the signature of a journalist in *The Daily Telegraph*.[120]

For the Arabs, much worse was to come. At the same time as these exchanges were going on towards the end of the war, the European powers were carrying on other secret negotiations. The Allies—Britain, France, Russia and Italy—all wanted pieces of the decaying Ottoman empire, and from the moment Turkey entered the war, there was diplomatic discussion about the division. These debates were coloured by the antique enmity between Britain and France, both of which were determined to outdo the other in grabbing as much as possible. These were to culminate in a pure expression of colonialist ambition and treachery: the Sykes–Picot Agreement.

Although Sykes–Picot was an Anglo-French discussion, Russia, at that time still an ally, and Italy had interests in the matter of the division of the Ottoman empire when the war was won. An important spur to the negotiations was that in early 1915, Russia announced to its allies that it intended to take and keep Constantinople, thus procuring a much-needed warm water port. There was also a fear that the Germans and/or the Turks might start negotiations with the Arabs, which would interfere with British and French machinations.

The two men deputed to debate the issue were Sir Mark Sykes and François Georges-Picot. Sykes was an English country gentleman, a Conservative MP, very widely travelled and seen by many as typical of his time and class. T. E. Lawrence expressed his opinion of him in an unflattering summary:

> [He is the] imaginative advocate of unconvincing world-movements … also a bundle of prejudices, intuitions, half-sciences. His ideas were of the outside; and he lacked patience to test his materials before choosing his style of building. He would take an aspect of the truth, detach it from its circumstances, inflate it, twist and model it, until its own likeness and its new unlikeliness together drew a laugh; and laughs were his triumphs.[121]

Sykes was a key player in the events in the Middle East at the time. Naturally, he brought all the historical baggage of colonial Britain:

He dismissed the idea of Arab nationalism as 'absurd'. These views were in no way mitigated by his belief that urban Arabs were 'cowardly', 'insolent yet despicable', 'vicious as far as their feeble bodies will admit', and that Bedouin Arabs were 'rapacious, greedy ... animals'.[122]

He also gave the impression that 'he was fluent in both Arabic and Turkish. In fact he could speak neither.'[123] He was hardly a likely ally for Arab aspirations, especially since 'during the war he was converted to Zionism'.[124] Georges-Picot was a professional diplomat with a deep understanding of the Middle East. He had been, for example, consul-general in Beirut. He was also a committed nationalist and imperialist with ambitions for French expansion, especially for the retention of French interests in Syria.

For our discussion, the relevant terms of the agreement, to which Russia and Italy assented, were that Britain would control the coastal strip between the Mediterranean and the River Jordan, Jordan, the south of Iraq, and the ports of Haifa and Acre. France would control south-eastern Turkey, northern Iraq, and Syria. Palestine would be split between France and Britain, with Jerusalem being internationalised.

This followed the recommendations of a committee chaired by Sir Maurice Bunsen, set up in 1915 to review British interests in the Ottoman empire after the war. This committee reported that 'they see no reason why the sacred places of Palestine should not be dealt with as a separate question' and where 'both belligerents and neutrals are alike interested'.[125] This seems to have been in part because France was very reluctant to hand over Palestine to the British. Russia and Italy would get portions of the Ottoman empire which are not relevant to this discussion. The Arabs would be allowed to keep the Arabian Peninsula. Roughly, the fate of Palestine would be decided after further consultation. This was Britain's first step in the practice of giving away territory which they did not own, and in which people lived, but who were to have no say in their future.

The Sykes–Picot Agreement was signed by Sir Edward Grey for the British government, and Paul Gambon for the French. It was dated 16 May 1916. It was a manifest contradiction to the promises to the Arabs made in the McMahon Correspondence, and has been regarded ever since, rightly, as a most treacherous move on the part of the 'Entente' powers. The Arabs were not told about the negotiations. As to the McMahon Correspondence, this had to be obliterated somehow. Although Sykes was told about McMahon, he could not, and did not, take any account of it in his deliberations. The agreement became public knowledge when the Russian revolutionary government published the details, and this was followed up by publication in *The Manchester Guardian* on 26 November 1917.

As for Arthur Balfour, his statements on every aspect of the Palestine controversy are charged with ambiguity, inaccuracy, and denial of indisputable fact. I give many examples in this account, but one of the worst examples is contained in a memorandum he issued on 11 August 1919:

The Political Art of Lies and Ambiguity 67

> The fundamental conception underlying the Sykes–Picot Agreement should be maintained—namely a French sphere of influence centring around Syria, a British sphere centring around the Euphrates and the Tigris, *and a home for the Jews in the valley of the Jordan* [my emphasis].[126]

There is no mention in the Sykes–Picot Agreement of such a 'home', indeed there is no mention of Jews at all. Such bizarre statements are so persistent that it must be concluded that Balfour was careless, or had a bad memory, or was a liar, or all three. Perhaps his behaviour makes sense if his famous aphorism is taken seriously. In this much-quoted remark he was probably honestly expressing his approach: 'Nothing matters very much and few things matter at all'.

As for Weizmann and the Zionists, they were naturally concerned about the proposed division of Palestine between Britain and France. Weizmann heard about this 'secret' treaty from C. P. Scott, and immediately saw how it could pose a threat to the proposed Jewish state.[127] Weizmann may well have noticed that while the Arabs would have every reason to feel betrayed by this new imperialism, the status of Palestine was still not, in the remotest sense, allocated to any putative Hebrew state in the Sykes–Picot Agreement.

The Sykes–Picot Agreement was one of the most unrealistic political manoeuvres of the time. It was an attempt by the British and the French both to gain territory for themselves and to prevent one another gaining any advantage. It reflected, again, the many years of European bickering over colonial expansion, but it was also an attempt by both countries to try to collaborate after so many years of war and rivalry. So obsessed were the participants in their 'diplomacy' that it is difficult to believe that they thought anyone could agree with them. The Arabs were not consulted, nor for that matter, though for less reason, were the Jews. President Wilson of the United States, whose central demand was that subject peoples, after the war, should be involved in decisions about their own future, could not countenance it, and this was a view supported by the Bolsheviks.

As in the case of the McMahon Correspondence, Jewish historians naturally take a view not in sympathy with the Arab position. Schneer, for example, asks an amazing question: Did the agreement shortchange the Arabs?[128] There is no point in this question since it is manifestly the case that it did. Schneer also dismisses Arab objections: 'When they [the Arabs] learned what the British and French had done, the sharif and his followers may or may not have had legitimate cause for complaint.'[129] The most controversial action of the British government was yet to come, and would prove to be the cornerstone of calamitous breakdown in the Middle East: the Balfour Declaration.

What then were the forces which were behind the Zionist campaign, and which resulted in such a remarkable political act as the Balfour Declaration? It is impossible to be sure of all the reasons why the declaration was made, or how and in what order any of the people behind it should be rated. There was, though, one dominant, key factor which drove the Zionist movement to success. It was the power mobilised by powerful Jews.

This power is defined by some opponents of the Jews as 'conspiracy'. This, it is claimed by people who subscribe to it, is a malevolent force, responsible for any number of ills in society. The behaviour of Jews in the matter of the declaration is better described as coordination, organised above all by Weizmann, who was well aware of the importance of organised pressure. For example, when he was speaking at a meeting of Jews and Arabs in Jaffa in May 1918 after denying that it was 'our aim to get hold of the supreme power and administration in Palestine', he used the threat of 'world Jewry' and added, 'though the Jews here number but a few, yet the 14 million extant in all parts of the world agree with us and confirm our sayings'.[130]

These allegations, that the Jews were universally supportive of the Zionist cause, and that they wielded huge power, are under constant challenge. Renton is one writer who questions such assumptions:

> The picture of Jewry as a powerful, anti-allied and predominantly Zionist community that was presented to the British Government by the Zionists was far removed from the reality of the Jewish Diaspora.[131]

This version of the universality of Jewish community and its views was accepted by British decision makers because 'it matched the pre-existing assumptions of British officials and politicians, who projected their own sense of culture and desires onto a mythical Jewry'.[132]

Central in this debated influence is the role of Jewish finance, which is also a matter of dispute. Ever since the seventeenth century when reasons were put forward for allowing Jews to return to Britain, the fact that they brought money with them was advanced both by Jews and Gentiles as attractive. In this case Lloyd George had no doubt:

> It was also believed that such a Declaration would have a potent influence upon world Jewry outside Russia and secure for the Entente the aid of Jewish financial interests. In America their aid would have a special value when the Allies had almost exhausted the gold and marketable securities available for American purchases.[133]

The Arabs certainly saw the Jews as highly organised, and backed by financial power. They believed them to be

> past masters in all the arts of ousting competitors whether on the market, in the farm or the bureaucratic offices, backed by apparently inexhaustible funds given by their compatriots in all lands and possessed of powerful influence in the councils of the nations, prepared to enter the lists against him in every one of his

normal occupations, backed by the one thing wanted to make them irresistible, the physical force of a great Imperial power, and he [the Arab] feels himself overmastered and defeated before the contest is begun.[134]

Kaiser Wilhelm II agreed. He spoke of 'the tremendous power represented by international Jewish capital in all its dangerousness', and how Germany should therefore be pro-Zionist.[135]

Later Jewish historians were anxious to play down or deny that this was a motive for the creation of the Balfour Declaration, arguing that the mobilising of massive Jewish finance was a myth. Stein writes that there 'may have been a vague idea that there were financial as well as political advantages to be gained from an appeal to the Jewish feeling for Palestine'. But 'what is hard to believe is that at the time of the Balfour declaration the British Government was angling for the support of American Jewish bankers'. In fact, 'everywhere the Jewish financial magnates had, almost to a man, fought shy of Zionism'.[136]

Despite such protests, it is difficult to deny that Jewish finance was an influence on decision-making. In the early days of Zionist activity, Herzl tried to bribe the Ottomans, saying, 'supposing His Majesty the Sultan were to give us Palestine, we could in turn undertake to regulate the entire finances of Turkey'.[137] It is also impossible to ignore the financial help given by the Rothschild family to early settlements in Palestine. Balfour, in his position as foreign secretary, went to America, where he certainly believed in Jewish influence.

> A Foreign Office note observes that 'during this visit the policy of the declaration as a war measure seems to have taken more definite shape'. It was supposed that American opinion might be favourably influenced if His Majesty's Government gave an assurance that the return of the Jews to Palestine had become a purpose of British policy.[138]

It was hoped that the sympathy of Jews for the Allied cause might be aroused and would counter anti-Russian feeling. Many American Jews came from Russia and because of violent antisemitism there, they could not support a Russian government. There were also many Jews of German extraction who had mixed loyalties. It has been suggested that this fear of an alliance between American Jewry and Germany was a very important engine in the march towards the declaration:

> The image of a potentially pro-German Jewry that could be swept up by a German initiative at any moment had added an even greater sense of urgency, and pushed Balfour to request a draft declaration from the Zionists.[139]

Smuts was one of many who knew that American support was a crucial element in the decision. Reflecting on these events in 1949 to a body of Zionists, he said that an important motivation for the declaration had been that 'it would rally Jewry on a world-wide scale to the allied cause'.[140]

By April 1917, when the Russian Revolution had begun, the situation became even more confused. The British government was anxious to keep Russia in the war. The British ambassador was asked what the effect would be in Russia if the British government expressed sympathy for 'Jewish national aspirations'. Such 'sympathy', it was hoped, 'might counteract Jewish pacifist propaganda in America'.[141]

This wish to plant a fear of American Jewry in respect of its attitude to the war had been assiduously cultivated by four Jews. The ground had been well prepared, notably Renton claims, by the quartet mentioned earlier: Kallen, Wolf, Jabotinsky and Suares. Another was Nahum Sokolow. The latter was especially influential in gaining support for Zionism. He even convinced Pope Benedict XV of the justice of the cause. These individuals played upon British fears about the loyalty of American Jews, and managed to engender a belief that these Jews were very sympathetic to the German cause, especially because they wanted to punish the Russian government for their antisemitic activities. They also persuaded the government that rich Jewish American financiers might support Germany: a belief which Renton describes as 'this imagined problem'.[142] This question of American support was important, but there were other pressures to establish a Jewish state, some of which were in existence before the First World War. It is some of these pressures, personal and political, which will be explored next.

3
After Balfour

'The document is undoubtedly the starting point of the whole trouble'[1]

In September 1917, Mark Sykes, a key figure in the events leading to the Balfour Declaration, drafted a memorandum which he discussed with Weizmann at a time when the future of the declaration was uncertain. In one part, which according to Stein he did not discuss with Weizmann, Sykes set out 'what the Zionists desire and what they do not desire'. Amongst the things they did not want were:

II   To set up a Jewish Republic or other form of State in Palestine or any part of Palestine.
III To enjoy any special rights not enjoyed by other inhabitants of Palestine.[2]

Nobody would have been more aware than Sykes that these non-wishes were fictional. He may have been setting out a position which was more acceptable to the doubters. In any case, with his experience, he must have known better.

The agitation for years by the Zionists for the establishment of a permanent all-powerful Jewish presence in Palestine took a critical turn when Balfour was canvassed by Weizmann and Lord Rothschild to issue some sort of a statement about British intentions (presumably support) for Palestine. This was probably in June 1917. Balfour agreed, and according to Weizmann, '[Balfour] asked me to submit to him a declaration which would be satisfactory to us, and which he would try and put before the war cabinet'.[3] Naturally, the drafting was attended by much argument on the part of the group of Zionists who took it upon themselves, but in July 1917 Lord Walter Rothschild sent a draft. Considering the magnitude of the decisions to be made, it is brief, but the demands were huge:

1   His Majesty's Government accepts the principle that Palestine should be reconstituted as the National Home of the Jewish People.

2 His Majesty's Government will use its best endeavours to secure the achievement of this object and will discuss the necessary methods and means with the Zionist Organisation.[4]

Stein carries out a magisterial analysis of the progress of this document, and the reservations expressed by individual members of the government. The government tried three drafts of its own before the final version appeared. Perhaps the most noticeable feature of these drafts was that the third mentioned 'existing non-Jewish communities in Palestine'.[5] Another important proviso was that there should be no upsetting of 'rights and political status' of Jews in their existing communities: this was clearly intended to offset the persistent claim of anti-Zionist Jews that they would no longer be regarded as 'true' citizens.

The final version was dated 2 November 1917, addressed to Walter, the second Lord Rothschild, although the identity of the author(s) is debatable. Stein points out that the choice of Rothschild as the addressee 'had the decisive advantage of associating the Declaration with the most potent name in Jewry'.[6] The Balfour Declaration reads:

Foreign Office,

November 2nd, 1917

Dear Lord Rothschild,

I have much pleasure in conveying to you, on behalf of His Majesty's Government, the following Declaration of sympathy with Jewish Zionist aspirations which has been submitted to, and approved by, the Cabinet.

'His Majesty's Government view with favour the establishment in Palestine of a national home for the Jewish people, and will use their best endeavours to facilitate the achievement of this object, it being clearly understood that nothing shall be done which may prejudice the civil and religious rights of existing non-Jewish communities in Palestine, or the rights and political status enjoyed by Jews in any other country.'

I would be grateful if you would bring this Declaration to the knowledge of the Zionist Federation.

Yours,

Arthur James Balfour.

The declaration is not only notorious for its dubious moral base, but its wording is deeply ambiguous. Thus 'the' national home of the Zionist draft has become 'a' national home. The ubiquitous Weizmann requested some amendments, of which one was accepted: that Jewish 'race' be replaced with Jewish 'people'.[7] And there was extensive consultation with Zionists, especially Nahum Sokolow about the drafts. Sokolow was a pioneer Zionist, colleague of Weizmann, who gained the support of several eminent figures for the cause, including, as we have seen, Pope Benedict XV.

Morris claims that the Zionists were quite clear about the meaning of 'national home':

> All the declaration's architects believed that a state would emerge once the Jews had attained a majority in Palestine. In internal correspondence Zionist officials spoke at the time of their hope for 'a Jewish state in Palestine'. Representatives of the Yishuv, at their first formal post-Balfour gathering in December 1918, the so-called Eretz-Yisrael Conference, resolved by a vote of 55 to1 that the Zionist movement intended to establish not a 'national home' but a *'medina ivrit'* (a Jewish state).[8]

The Zionists were far from satisfied. As was clear from earlier drafts of the declaration, it was not intended that the Arab 90 per cent of the Palestinian population should be mentioned. When concern was expressed that the first three drafts did not mention the indigenous population, they were included in the fourth: not as Arabs, but as 'non Jewish communities'. All sorts of objections to their inclusion, especially being labelled as in need of protection, were put forward. There was indignation from Rothschild who regarded the implication that the 'other' people would be put in danger as offensive. 'Personally I think the proviso is a slur on Zionism, as it presupposes the possibility of a danger to non-Zionists, which I deny.'[9]

No Zionist case would be complete without due reference to the Bible. The chief rabbi drew upon Leviticus 19:34 as the guarantee of the well-being of the local people. For there it is written:

> The stranger that dwelleth with you shall be unto you as one born among you and thou shalt love him as thyself.[10]

It can be seen that the words 'non-Jewish communities' is a nice way of side-lining the fact that the word Arab is not used. The implication is that the Jews are the dominant force and the Arabs are a minority. In their evidence to the Peel Commission the Arab Higher Committee complained that:

> The terms of the Mandate are drafted in such a manner that the student might understand that there existed in Palestine a Jewish majority and a non-Jewish

minority, the other sections of the population. On the contrary the Arab inhabitants of Palestine form the overwhelming majority and are owners of the territory of which the Mandate system was created; yet throughout the Mandate they are referred to as the 'non-Jewish' population—a misleading and humiliating term.[11]

The fact that the committee had to remind the world of such an obvious fact is testimony to the skill of the Zionists in their choice of seemingly simple words. An example of the subtlety in the use of language when discussing Palestine is in Efraim Karsh's long denunciation of Palestinian intransigence: 'recent declassification of millions of documents ... reveal that there was nothing inevitable about the Palestinian–Jewish confrontation, let alone the Arab–Israeli conflict'. He advances the case that had the Arabs been reasonable:

> There would have been no war and no dislocation in the first place, for the simple reason that the Zionist movement was amenable both to the existence of a substantial *non-Jewish minority in the prospective Jewish state* [my emphasis] on an equal footing, and to the two state solution.[12]

It was not long after the declaration that the British government seems to have realised the enormity of what they had done. British apprehension was in evidence very soon. This was realised when the widely predicted violence broke out. A new chief administrator, Major-General H. D. Watson, reported in August 1919 that:

> The antagonism to Zionism of the majority of the population is deeply rooted—it is fast leading to hatred of the British—and will result, if the Zionist programme is forced upon them, in an outbreak of a very serious character necessitating the employment of a much larger number of troops than at present located in the territory.[13]

The future of Palestine and the question of a 'return' by the Jews was hardly a national priority, which made the advancement of the cause difficult, and yet easier, because the cause could not properly be addressed by key decision makers. This environment was one which the Zionists were able to exploit. As far as Palestine was concerned, the furore created by the Sykes–Picot Agreement was quickly dissipated, as the Jews sought new ways of influencing the British government. The presence of other mammoth distractions, such as the war, may be listed as amongst those turns of good fortune which seem to have always attended the efforts of the Zionists.

The Zionists' most serious challenge would come from the Arabs. In March 1921 a Palestinian committee had submitted a lengthy protest against the turn of events. It warned that the global population of Muslims were angry and that the Balfour Declaration was a 'gross injustice'. Jews were nationals of many nations, it read, and 'the Jew ... is clannish and unneighbourly ... he amasses the wealth of a country and then leads its people, whom he has impoverished, where he chooses ... he encourages wars when self-interest dictates'. The Palestinian committee asked, *inter alia*, for the idea of a national home for the Jews to be 'abolished', and that there should be instead a national government, elected by the Palestinian people who had lived in Palestine before the war.

Churchill rejected all allegations and demands, reciting the same arguments he always did: that the Jews deserve a homeland, and that this would be of benefit to all the people of Palestine and so on. The Jewish historian Gilbert concludes: 'The Arab deputation withdrew, its appeal rejected, its arguments rebutted'.[14] 'Rebutted', it may be countered, is a word which implies that the 'rejection' was manifestly logical, which it was not.

A Jewish deputation followed, again rehearsing familiar arguments, especially that they would not be a threat to the Palestinian Arabs:

> Our kinship in language, race, character and history give the assurance that we shall in due course come to a complete understanding with them.[15]

Ben-Gurion, the master of assurances, made even more extravagant promises. In 1915 he stated, with patronising words, that:

> The Jewish settlement is not designed to undermine the position of the Arab community; on the contrary, it will salvage it from its economic misery, lift it from its social decline, and rescue it from physical and moral degeneration.[16]

Apart from the persistent canvassing, the Zionists had now to try to ensure the legality of their actions. The first step was to gain official, international approval in a very confused post-war world.

The Peace Conference began at Versailles on 1 January 1919. Out of this came the Covenant of the League of Nations which embraced, amongst other things, a system of mandates. The idea of mandates seems to owe a lot to the initiative of the South African Jan Smuts who suggested the establishment of 'International Mandates' at the Peace Conference. The territories which were to be subjected to mandates were the former 'dependent' colonial possessions of the vanquished Germans and Turks.

The theory of mandates, embodied in the Covenant of the League of Nations, contained a somewhat precious phrase: 'sacred trust of civilisation'. Their operation, in theory, would be scrutinised by the League through the Permanent Mandates Commission. There would be three classes of mandated territory: Class A would comprise ex-Ottoman lands which could have independence when they were judged mature enough to take on the responsibility of self-government. Some of these were already at that stage, but the mandate for Palestine was exceptional, as explained by Norman Bentwich, a Jew, who became legal adviser to the mandatory government:

> The principle of self-determination had to be modified because of the two national selves existing in Palestine, and the majority Arab population could not be allowed to prevent the fulfilment of the Mandate in relation to the minority Jewish population.[17]

As always the Zionists were prepared. In November 1918 they sent a number of proposals regarding a 'Jewish national home' in Palestine, drafted by a committee chaired by Herbert Samuel. The fact that he was the chairman ought to have removed any lingering doubts about where Samuel's interest and loyalties lay. These proposals appeared to be well in excess of what many British government ministers had assumed. For example, definite territorial boundaries were set out. A critical statement in the 1918 document was that:

> The most important work to be undertaken by the Council [a putative Jewish Council for Palestine] will be the promotion of Jewish land settlement and the acquisition of land for the purpose.

There is much else which proves, if proof were needed, of the colonising ambitions of the Zionists, including that the Jewish Sabbath should be set as an official day of rest, and that Hebrew should be the 'official language of the Jewish population'.[18] All of this was within the context of 'the increase of the Jewish population, so that in accordance with the principles of democracy it may develop into a Jewish Commonwealth'.[19]

The next significant post-war event was the convening of an Inter Allied Conference in London in February 1920. France had never given up its wish to be involved somehow in the future of Palestine, and in many of the discussions which sought to resurrect the Sykes–Picot Agreement, French delegates claimed that France had a long association with the Holy Places which it could not forego. To deflect these claims and to bolster their own claims over Palestine, Britain had to agree that France should be given a mandate in Syria. There was no discussion of the Balfour Declaration.

The role of the US and its president was important in these debates. From early times there was opposition by American Reform Jews to the idea of settling in Palestine: 'Isaac Mayer Wise (1819-1900), the most prominent leader of the American Reform Movement' led the attack on the idea:

> He wrote extensively in rejection of Jewish nationalism and in opposition to Zionism which he regarded as an anathema. He detested both its premise, that

Zionist proposal to the Paris Peace Conference of 1919 for the delineation of the Jewish state.

anti-Semitism was an absolute condition in every place wherein Jews were a minority, and its proposed solution, the establishment of a Jews-only nation state.[20]

Already in 1879 he had written:

> The colonisation of Palestine appears to us a romantic idea inspired by religious visions without foundation in reality... the idea of Jews returning to Palestine is not part of our creed. We rather believe it is well that the habitable become one holy land and the human family one chosen people.[21]

A petition signed by 300 Reform Jews was presented to President Wilson in March 1919 for submission to the Peace Conference. This denied the Jews had any claim to be a nation, since the nation was abolished some 2000 years ago. Like others, they reiterated the belief that Jews should work for the bettering of their condition in those countries where conditions were unsatisfactory. They listed five objections including the following:

> Palestine was peopled by non-Jews. Violence was inevitable.

> The bulk of western Jews would not wish to give up their nationality to become part of a Jewish homeland.

> To recreate a theocracy would be a retrograde step. Modern nations should be tolerant and multiracial.

Such arguments would not appeal to Balfour. As he said in the earlier debates about Jewish immigration, Palestine provided an opportunity to solve the western Jewish 'problem'.

Brandeis, the head of the American Zionist movement, disagreed with the petitioners, and also signalled the direction of future American sympathy. In an interview with Balfour, he stated:

> First, that Palestine should be the Jewish homeland and not merely that there be a Jewish homeland in Palestine. That, he assumed, is the commitment of the Balfour Declaration, and will, of course be confirmed by the Peace Conference. Secondly, there must be economic elbow room for a Jewish Palestine; self-sufficiency for a healthy social life. That means adequate boundaries not merely a small garden within Palestine. Thirdly the Justice urged that the future Jewish Palestine must have control of the land and the natural resources which are at the heart of a sound economic life.

The minute records that 'Mr Balfour expressed entire agreement with the three conditions which the Justice laid down', although 'he then proceeded to point out the difficulties which confronted England'.[22] It may be noted that the expulsion of Jews to Palestine was not an especial British or American solution. It was advocated in Hungary in June 1878 by Gyozo Istoczy in the Hungarian Diet, and for what seemed to be a universal reason: that the Jews would not integrate with society. He 'claimed that the Jews were an aggressive, socially exclusive cosmopolitan caste which had tenaciously resisted assimilation for nearly 4,500 years.'[23]

The US president, Woodrow Wilson, always an advocate of democracy, believed that an inquiry should be set up to ask the local people what they wanted. Because of obstruction by European governments (for political reasons, especially on the part of the French, who declined to take part), the resultant commission in reality was American: both authors, Henry C. King and Charles R. Crane, were American. Balfour was alarmed by the prospect, and wrote to Samuel that he had 'great hopes that Palestine will be eliminated from the scope of any Commission'.[24] It was a muddled, but understandable hope, since Palestine, it could be clearly seen, presented the greatest problem. For the British that problem was that if the Arabs were asked, they would want self government. What else?

In June 1919 the King–Crane Commission arrived in Palestine. It took evidence from many organisations and notably received a submission from the Syrian Congress, whose membership included Muslim, Christian and local Jewish people. They encountered spoiling tactics from the British. One of their advisers, William Yale, was warned by a British official 'not to provoke the growing tensions in the country: "If you show any partiality or commit any indiscretion, Yale, there will be bloodshed."'[25]

There was hostility too from the French. The perennial battle between the French and the British flared up again, with the French declaring that the British had tried to prejudice the commissioners against them. The situation was complicated by the fact that as the commission arrived in Damascus, the 'General Syrian Congress' issued a 'total rejection of the French'.[26]

The commission made several inflammatory recommendations. These included that there should be no French presence in Syria, that Feisal should be king of Syria, and that the USA should hold the mandate for Syria. The report paid a good deal of attention to the matter of a Jewish 'homeland', and pronounced that it was a bad idea. This view was based on extensive interviews in Palestine, where almost 90 per cent of the people were against the Zionist proposals. In any case, only 10 per cent of the population was Jewish.

The commission considered the position of the Balfour Declaration, especially its concern for the provision for the rights of non-Jews. King–Crane did not believe that in a Jewish state this would happen. Indeed, it noted the fact, ultimately to be realised, that 'Zionists looked forward to a practically complete dispossession of the present non-Jewish inhabitants of Palestine, by various means of purchase'.

What the commission, prescient though it was, could not foresee, was the forcible eviction, and theft of Arab lands.

The religious complications also featured strongly. Palestine was of course the home of much that was sacred to the three religions, and they did not believe the Jews would be seen by the other two as 'proper guardians of the holy places, or custodians of the Holy Land as a whole'. To a country, and a president, disapproving of 'imperial' activity, this warning would have had a powerful appeal:

> Not only you as President but the American people as a whole should realize that if the American government decided to support the establishment of a Jewish state in Palestine, they are committing the American people to the uses of force in that area, since only by force can a Jewish state in Palestine be established or maintained.

The context of this warning was the suggestion that the US should take over the superintendence of affairs in the country. The commission's report was quickly overtaken by events, including the serious illness of the president and the hostility of the European governments. It was not, in any case, published until December 1922, and then only in the *Editor and Publisher* (New York). It was described as a 'Suppressed Official Document of the United States Government'. By this time the US Congress had approved the setting up of a Jewish national home, as Balfour had recommended. And so the report joined the many thousands of reports on the reality of the situation in Palestine, and the potential for disaster consequent upon disregard of that truth. It was ignored.

The British Middle East Committee met in January 1918 and decided to send a 'Zionist Commission' to Palestine. The reasons were 'the need for putting the assurances given [in the Balfour Declaration] into practice: the inadequacy of existing Zionist representation in Egypt and Palestine: the necessity of bringing the British authorities in Egypt and Palestine into contact with the responsible leaders of the organisation in *Entente* countries'. The government hoped for the establishment of a Jewish university and a medical school, and 'the establishment of good relations with the Arabs and other non-Jewish communities in Palestine'.[27]

This highly provocative decision to establish a Zionist Commission was the most astonishing coup by Weizmann, who of course was the *provocateur*. Its prematurity is shown by the fact that no decision had yet been taken internationally about the future of Palestine and that the British were yet to be awarded the mandate. The only serious opposition came from experienced people in Palestine, especially in the British Army, who could see what should have been obvious: that the Arabs would never accept this intervention placidly.

> The arrival of the Zionist Commission took the military administration by surprise, and its subsequent activities were regarded by the military authorities

as completely contrary to the principle of maintaining the status quo in the occupied territories.[28]

This disapproval is just one example of the continuing opposition of the army to the excesses of Zionist pressure, before and after the Balfour Declaration. Weizmann must have been surprised since, despite Sykes' report that the commission was 'much struck by [the] cordiality of their reception' by local worthies, for his part, after only six days, Weizmann wrote, 'we find among the Arabs and Syrians, or certain sections of them, a state of mind which seems to us to make useful negotiations impossible at the present moment'.[29]

Weizmann 'took a pretty odd crew with him'.[30] There were Jews from Britain, France and Italy. Not at first, but later, there were representatives from the US and Russia. Included was Dr Montague David Eder, British, of Lithuanian descent, who was to become very powerful. He was much criticised in official reports for his false allegations and lies, and he became ever more extreme in his demands for influence in Palestine. He eventually became head of the commission. Eder's demands included his views expressed to the Haycraft Commission that there can only be one national home in Palestine, and that a Jewish one, with no equality in the partnership between Jews and Arabs. This demand was, at the time, so outlandish that a senior official in the Colonial Office, Sir Gerard Clauson, suggested that the only way to convince people of the sincerity of the government 'would be the removal of Dr Eder from his present position, a step which I think we are fully entitled to invite the Z.O., in its official position as the Jewish Agency, to take.'[31] No action was taken.

The commission quickly moved from merely giving advice to active interference in the administration of Palestine. They found the Jews there, collectively called the *Yishuv*, in a fairly parlous position, with large numbers being reliant on charity: the *chalukkah* (distribution system). The commission provided food, and gave money to poor families. It supported religious schools, all with money donated by Jews worldwide. It dealt with petitions of every kind: Weizmann wrote that the petitions ranged 'from long-term loans to granting a divorce, and from building a synagogue to getting a thief released from prison'. He did not much like the people whom he was helping: 'tiresome people', he called them. Another commentator wrote that 'there is no other city in the world, where almost eighty per cent of the inhabitants receive support of various kinds and in this support they see no dishonour, baseness and diminishment of the soul'.[32]

The commission seems to have done more. It helped Jewish immigrants, founded settlements, and helped to set up businesses. All designed to deal with what Weizmann saw as 'complete moral corruption' of which he was 'ashamed and frightened'.[33] Yet Weizmann saw that this dependency had its uses, since the generic 'conflict between the ultra-Orthodox and the Zionists had already emerged as a central political issue'.[34] This conflict was lessened by 'the willingness of its ultra-Orthodox residents to accept money from the Zionist Commission [which] was tantamount to recognising its authority.'[35]

Even so, Weizmann tried to gain favour with the ultra-Orthodox by attempting to buy the Western Wall, but this proved to be one of his more outrageous ambitions. More successful was the establishment of a Hebrew University, a long-standing Jewish ambition. The foundations were laid as early as July 1918 while the war was still on. Then there was the campaign to give equality (or priority) to the Hebrew language. There had been protests about Hebrew not appearing on licence plates and on post offices. Eventually, the military government allowed Hebrew to appear on government publications.

Control of the public use of a language is a critical element in cultural attack. The subordination of indigenous languages has been a feature of imperialistic tactics throughout history, from nineteenth-century Wales to German aggression towards the Danes in Schleswig-Holstein in the same century. This is true of modern Israel. Arabic is the subject of controversy because the rulers of Israel are well aware of the centrality of language in identity. Since 2008, three bills have been proposed in the Knesset to abolish Arabic as an official language. In 2018 a basic law was passed—'Israel as the Nation-State of the Jewish People', which went some way along the path to abolition. Arabic was reduced from being a 'co-official' to an 'auxiliary' language, although it has still to be used in official documents. In the early days, the commission's take-over of Jewish secular schools, where German was replaced by Hebrew as the medium of instruction, was of great importance.

Official reports were dominated by the poor relationships between the commission and the British military. This, Segev claims, was because 'the Zionist Commission turned almost every event and decision into a political issue'.[36] The commission also pioneered the practice of alleging that any criticism of Zionism (or later the state of Israel) was actually antisemitism, an important conflation highly developed in the twenty-first century, as we shall see.

Criticism of the operation of the commission was not confined to casual reports by unsympathetic soldiers. They occur in sober documents, such as the Palin Report. This report was the result of a court of inquiry convened by the order of the high commissioner and commander-in-chief in April 1920 to explain the Nebi Musa disturbances, which will be discussed later.[37] As well as examining the events, the report is very critical of much of the way in which Palestine was being run, especially the behaviour of the Zionist Commission.

The report deplores the 'interference with the measures of the Administration manipulated by pressure brought to bear on superior authority in London ...'

> [and] the gradual development of the Zionist Advisory Commission into a body bearing a distinct resemblance to an independent administration apparently able to control the actual Administration ... All these things are done when the Mandate has not yet been given.[38]

The report gives examples of this happening when 'they had failed to persuade the administration to accept their views directly'.

The three examples were concerning the land ordinance, the establishment of the Egyptian bonded warehouses, and agricultural loans.[39] These are technical matters, but deserve some explanation. At one point the British proposed that there should be 'limited transactions' in land. It was very important to do this, as illegal transactions in which Jews were buying land were still being reported. The Zionist Commission 'was at that time in financial straits', and was frightened that if sales were allowed and formalised, the price of land would rise 'previous to the settlement of the country'. The chief administrator tried to point out that the proposed measure was in the interests of everyone. But 'the Commission succeeded in interposing their veto', and a letter from Lord Curzon stopped any change.

The case of the Egyptian bonded warehouses involved 'a body of Jaffa Jews' who wanted to share in the services provided by the warehouses. The administration refused this because the Jews had no experience, but also because there would be a massive conflict of interest. In the end, the Egyptian Bonded Warehouse Company was restricted to a short-term lease which 'would not be binding on the future government'.

With regard to agricultural loans, it was proposed that the government should help cultivators with loans. This money the government borrowed from the Anglo–Egyptian Bank. The Zionists objected, demanding that the Anglo–Palestine Bank—a Jewish bank—should have been given the chance to advance money. The British Foreign Office stopped all further loans. The effect, the report states, was that 'the [Arab] people at once came to the conclusion that the Zionists had interfered in order that they should be left in great straits and should ultimately have to sell their lands to the Zionists at any price'.[40]

There are other serious examples where the Zionist Commission effectively eroded the legal authority. It set up 'peace courts', a fully-fledged legal system independent of the constituted legal system.[41] It demanded that it should appoint all Jewish candidates for the police service, 'and it is still more remarkable that the administration should have admitted the claim'.[42] They also set up a private army which 'drilled in public places'. This 'private' arming by Jews was not new. At a convention in Jaffa in 1907, the Bar Giora, an armed force, was established both to protect settlers and to get rid of Arab and Circassian guards who at the time performed that function. Bar Giora was the name of one of the leaders of the revolt against the Romans in AD 66-70. In April 1909 this was replaced by Hashomer ('The Watchman').

The Palin Report described how the Zionist Commission had an intelligence department which 'has access to all postal and telegraph matter and no documents of the administration are secret from it. [It obtains] through its private Intelligence department of the most secret official documents in the possession of that administration.' I will discuss the Zionist spy ring later.

The commission's public health was run by the American Zionist Medical Unit which showed 'a marked tendency to try and work independently of the public health department of the administration and to annex all the credit for sanitary work done in the country'.

Besides all of this, Weizmann interfered with the staffing of the British authorities. A Colonel Gabriel was in charge of the budget of the military administration. In Weizmann's opinion he favoured the Catholic Church and the Arabs, and therefore 'should not be allowed to return to Palestine'—so Weizmann 'ruled' at a Zionist Commission meeting. Herbert Samuel spoke to Churchill, and Weizmann to Balfour, with the result that Gabriel did not return to Palestine. The foreign secretary, Lord Curzon, who was trying to be impartial, drew the line at this:

> This is allowing the Jews to have things too much their own way ... It is intolerable that Dr Weizmann should be allowed to criticise the 'type of men' employed by H.M. Govt.[43]

When there was rioting in 1929, 'Passfield also concurred in Weizmann's strongly worded complaints about the behaviour of the Palestine administration, and agreed to suspend two senior officials, Mr Luke and Mr Cust, on the grounds of incompetence.'[44]

The report summed up by stating how baffling it all was:

> It is curious to note that the Commission seem to be in a position to define their own mission, nor does it seem to have occurred to the Government to establish any similar body entrusted with the duty of advising as to native interests. The whole of the arrangements appear to have been made in England by the Zionist organisation there ... The situation is, in truth, intolerable.[45]

The increasingly visible Eder was so powerful that he 'would eventually run the delegation single-handedly ... not many remember his name, but he ought to go down in history as the Zionist's first prime minister'.[46] This judgement would seem to prove the case that Eder exercised too much power based upon questionable authority.

I have discussed the most inflammatory issue: that of immigration. The *numbers* of Jews was the principal source of contention, but for the putative state there were two other major problems. These were the difficulty in retaining immigrants, and their diversity in terms of language, culture and general social behaviour.

> Between 1882 and 1914, around 2.6 Million Jews left Russia and its neighbouring territories, most of them to begin a new life in America. For the most part they did so without reflecting deeply on identity and political change. Of all the Jews who after the pogroms of 1881-1882 [in Russia] ... less than 5 per cent went to Palestine.[47]

Not all of the immigrants were from Russia:

> The immigrants of the so-called First Aliya (from 1882 to 1903-1904) ... a considerable number came from Middle Eastern countries, especially from Yemen, Kurdistan and the Maghreb.[48]

There was a Second Aliya from 1904 to 1914:

> [This was] triggered by the Kishinev pogrom (in present-day Moldavia, then Bessarabia) of April 1903 and the Russian Revolution of 1905, which were followed by a fresh wave of anti-Semitism, [which] brought 35,000–40,000 to Palestine, among them many of the future leaders.[49]

One of these was David Ben-Gurion. The Second Aliya also had the highest percentage of emigrants leaving Palestine after a brief stay ... 'a percentage that in some years reached a full third of the immigrants'.[50] Both the Second and the Third Aliya (from 1918 to 1923) 'made every effort to distinguish themselves from the immigrants of the First Aliya. The two later ones brought people who believed in "Jewish labour" or rather "Hebrew labour"... and the difference between the two is significant'.[51] Their 'basic values' were:

> A pioneering spirit, modest lifestyle, high esteem for manual labour (especially agricultural labour), self-defense, self-reliance, and a future-oriented outlook. The idea was to revive *Hebrew* culture as opposed to the *Jewish* culture of the diaspora—the very epitome of everything they despised.[52]

For the most part, as fervent Zionists complained, the immigrants did not share a vision of the return as a mystical matter to which everything should be subordinated. Many did not settle in Palestine/Israel. As late as 1953, 'for the first time, the number of Jews who left Israel to live elsewhere—most of them of European origin—exceeded the number of immigrants who arrive'.[53] Quite often life was hard in Palestine, but in a tradition which would last indefinitely, rich Jews supported them, notably the extensive Rothschild family. They were also helped financially, and of course morally, by the Zionist movement

Concomitant with this immigration was the loss of Arab land. The Turks had tried to restrict buying and selling of land by Jews, but because of corruption and incompetence, this had proved impossible. And so began the acquisition of Arab land, at this time legally: 130,000 acres, had been acquired by 1914 with the help of wealthy patrons. By now there were 'about' 85,000 Jews in Palestine, comprising 'perhaps one-ninth of the Palestinian population'.[54]

At one point, as Ingrams shows:

Matters came to a head when the Sursok family, Lebanese absentee landlords, sold 50,000 acres of land in Palestine to the Zionist Commission, and some 8,000 Arab tenants were evicted. A Land Commission was appointed, and in October 1920 a Land Transfer Ordinance was published designed to protect agricultural tenants from eviction when land was sold by landlords.[55]

It is not surprising that the native Arabs soon began to resent this intrusion. Not only was land falling into the possession of newcomers, but this land often comprised large estates, upon which Arabs were employed as labourers. It became a common tenet of Zionist dogma that only Jews should work in Palestine.[56] This impossible restriction had to be ignored because Arabs were better workers, and willing to work for lower wages.[57] But this did not diminish the racist attitudes of the settlers who defined the Arabs by their 'backwardness'.[58] The situation was a premonition of what was happening in countries where minorities ruled majorities, hence the twentieth century insistence of comparing Israel with apartheid South Africa.

Especially after Balfour, the question of Jewish immigration into Palestine became a focus of heated argument, but also a focus of lies. The new high commissioner, Herbert Samuel, prevented Arab attempts to restrict Jewish immigration. In this Samuel was naturally supported by Churchill, who informed his Colonial Office officials in June 1921 that there could be no representation by Arabs since 'that would give them the power to halt Jewish immigration'.[59] There was a meeting in July 1921, held because it was judged that there had to be an answer to Weizmann's complaint that Balfour was being undermined, even by Samuel, and that the Balfour Declaration 'meant an ultimate Jewish majority' which Samuel's policy would spoil. Lloyd George and Balfour stated 'that by the Declaration they had always meant an eventual Jewish State'.[60]

But many in the British parliament remained uneasy and hostile to the Zionist cause. Despite the fact that there was tumult in the country, and the declaration seemed to be a short and certainly ambiguous statement, there were those who spotted that it was of the greatest significance. Lord Curzon, one of the war cabinet, composed a document entitled 'The Future of Palestine', in which he expressed grave doubts about it. He wanted to avoid Jewish control of the country, but paradoxically he went on to say that this did not preclude Jewish immigration, or Jewish purchase of land. 'If this is Zionism, there is no reason why we should not all be Zionists'.[61] But Curzon was not sufficiently foolish to believe that this was the limit of Jewish ambition. Nor that it was simple. He wondered 'how was it proposed to get rid of the existing majority of Mussulman inhabitants and to introduce the Jews in their place?... [Jewish] repatriation on a large scale he regarded as sentimental idealism, which would never be realised, and that His Majesty's Government should have nothing to do with it.'[62]

The Zionists had had an extraordinary piece of good luck when Churchill was appointed to the War Office. Further amazing good fortune appeared again when he was appointed secretary of state for the colonies in January 1921, since Palestine was now part of his remit.

In the years immediately after the end of the First World War, the Arabs, increasingly aware of the real aims of Zionists and the strength of the support they were getting from the British cabinet, came to realise that they would have to become involved in sophisticated political pressure if they were to deflect events away from the disastrous course ahead. This can be illustrated by a secret report by Wyndham Deedes, in which he noted:

> a considerable growth in political consciousness among the Arabs, even in hitherto 'inarticulate' districts such as Gaza and Beersheba, adding that this growth was one of many symptoms of a general tendency which was noticeable in all fields of activity, religious, educational and economic as well as political, 'towards the attainment of an increased measure of cohesion and solidarity' among the Muslims.[63]

This should not have been a surprise. To those who banked on the amazing hope of Arab indifference, ignorance and inaction, the years would disillusion, but not discourage them:

> Arabic calls the Balfour Declaration *Wa'd Balfur,* literally the 'Balfour Promise' (although *wa'd* has a hint of threat as well). Whether the land was promised by God or by Balfour didn't matter: a promise, an Arabic saying goes, 'is the sound of thunder; its fulfilment is the fall of rain'. And in this case, the thunder was ominous, telling of the flood to come. The omens were correct: the deluge came.[64]

This threat did not lessen Jewish delight over the declaration. Weizmann, like all Zionists, was overjoyed at the news. 'He spoke ... in biblical terms':

> Since Cyrus the Great, there was never, in all the records of the past, a manifestation inspired by a higher sense of political wisdom, far-sighted statesmanship, and national justice towards the Jewish people than this memorable declaration.[65]

There was remarkable indifference generally in Britain to the news of the declaration, considering that it was a British government that had effected it. This is not surprising when it is remembered that, however important the declaration was to Zionists and anti-Zionists, the war was still on and the Russian Revolution was in full swing. Competing with such events it may well have been the case, as observed by Sir Ronald Storrs that 'with ninety-five of my friends in Egypt and Palestine (as in England) the Balfour Declaration ... passed without notice'.[66] A colonial secretary, at the time of Arab riots in the 1930s, made a similar point to Weizmann. An Anglo–Arab conflict would anger the 'man in the street'.

> [He] had no interest in implementing the Balfour declaration, or the mandate, or the MacDonald letter. It would be bound to result in an outcry to clear out of Palestine.[67]

Britain at the time of the declaration was, of course, in turmoil. There was a war such as had never been seen, the outcome of which, while requiring every resource, was far from certain. In the Middle East, where the war was still being waged against the Turks, the news of the declaration had to be carefully handled. Such was the apprehension that the new British military government was too frightened to make a statement in Palestine. It was not until May 1920 that there was a public announcement by Sir Louis Bols, the chief administrator of Palestine. The need for suppression amazed some observers. A *Daily Mail* correspondent wrote:

> Now what does that mean, put in plain English? It means that the British Government has issued a Declaration so high-handed, unwarranted and dangerous that it was an impediment to the progress of the British Army; it had to be suppressed ... has any British Government before been censored by its own forces in the field, as if its pronouncements had been written by the enemy.[68]

Even Balfour began to worry. He wrote to Samuel from the Peace Conference which began in January 1919, expressing concern about the behaviour of the Zionists in Palestine, news of which had reached the conference. He wrote on 1 January 1919: 'May I take this opportunity of stating frankly that the position in Palestine is giving me considerable anxiety'.[69] In fact the position was much the same as it had been before the declaration, in that the dynamics of support and opposition were unchanged.

On the one side there was the unswerving determination of Weizmann and the Zionists. For them the declaration was only the beginning of their plan and they retained the support of influential Jews such as Lord Walter Rothschild. There was also constant propaganda about the degeneracy of the Arabs and their unsuitability to rule themselves. This expressed itself, precisely and forcibly, in the classification of Palestine in the mandate, which successfully invalidated Arab claims to rule the supposedly newly liberated land.

Yet the opposition to Zionism remained firm. There continued to be active criticism in parliament to the principle of Zionism and to the financial costs to the British government. This opposition from many public figures was persistent, notably in the House of Lords, and most especially by Lord Curzon. In November 1919 Curzon wrote to Field Marshal Allenby:

There was no intention of allowing 'spoliation or eviction of the present landowners in Palestine or the grant of profitable concessions to individuals or the Government of a majority by a minority. Those who profess to apprehend this consequence overlook the fact that the Administration of Palestine will be controlled by a great Power or combination of Powers under the Mandate'.[70]

Such assurances, which no doubt Curzon at the time believed, and I will mention others, had no effect. The British government developed two contradictory and parallel policies. The one expressed above by Curzon, and the other persistently pursued by Churchill and other sympathisers which supported handing over Palestine to the Jews. The developing evidence of utter incompatibility can be seen by the ambitions of the Zionists, which is a constant theme in this account, as is the immoveable position often set out by the Arabs:

> The country is ours and has been so of old. We have lived in it longer than they did. Our historical and religious relations with it, we Moslems and Christians, far exceed those of the Jews. Therefore, their claim to their ancient historical rights in the country do not give them the right of appropriating it, in as much as in our historical rights we Arabs cannot justify our claims in Spain, our old home ...[71]

The analogy used of an Arab return to Spain which they ruled for over 400 years is often used. Huneidi was one of many who drew attention to the absurdity of a case for returning power to a people, who had long lost authority in a territory where, in any case, the bulk of them no longer lived.[72]

The British military were worried both at the incipient injustice, and the conflict which assuredly lay ahead. Sir Louis Bols was an experienced and distinguished soldier, and wrote after the Jerusalem riots of 1920: 'I think the Zionist Commission should be broken ... [It] has grown into an Administration [which] cannot continue within OETA [Occupied Enemy Territory Administration South]'. He also complained that:

> My own authority and that of every department of my Administration is claimed or impinged upon by the Zionist Commission, and I am definitely of opinion that this state of affairs cannot continue without grave danger to the public peace and to the prejudice of my Administration.[73]

Nor was he likely to regard as helpful a visit from the US judge, Louis Brandeis, with his view that 'ordinances of the military authorities should be submitted first to the Zionist Commission'.[74] Bols' views were not welcome in London. An official called O. A. Scott wrote that 'to accede to either of General Bols' proposals would be immediately interpreted by all Moslems as a sign of weakness'. Another went further advocating a favoured solution to opposition: 'It looks as if General Bols ought to be moved'.[75] In any case, in 1920 he was replaced by Herbert Samuel.

The attitude of the Zionists towards the senior army officers was hostile. This was because as far as the Zionists were concerned, anyone who was less than totally supportive of their cause was an enemy. Sir Mark Sykes summed up the Zionists 'complaints' about the military in 1918 as being:

(I) That the military authorities do not give sufficient prominence to the Zionist position.
(II) That the military authorities are allowing the Arabs to propagandise and agitate against the Zionists.
(III) That the military authorities are biased in favour of the Arabs especially of the Moslems.
(IV) That the Arabs are growing aggressive and are taking advantage of the weakness of the authorities.[76]

Another senior officer, General Congreve, commander of the British Army in Egypt and Palestine, sent a report to Samuel in May 1921 raising the question of a change of policy. He concluded:

What we have got to face is the fact that as long as we persist in our Zionist policy we have got to maintain all our present forces in Palestine to enforce a policy hateful to the great majority—a majority which means to fight and continue to fight and has right on its side.[77]

His concerns were easily dismissed, since the report went to Samuel, and Churchill, and was commented upon by the senior civil servant John Shuckburgh, who wrote that it 'restates the case from the local point of view against our policy in Palestine'. Churchill agreed, as did Meinertzhagen, who 'dismissed Congreve as a "partisan provocateur"'.[78] We shall go on to see that both Shuckburgh and Meinertzhagen were ardent supporters of Zionism. This explains why, despite the authority and experience behind such concerns, they were dismissed. This contempt for the opinions of people on the ground can therefore be included amongst the reasons why the Zionist tank rumbled on.

The experience expressed by the British military authorities was very worrying for the Zionists. Samuel visited Palestine in January 1920 and his reports make this clear. He noted that the distaste of the military was a barrier to the objective of a national home. The military had to accept the policy because it was official policy but 'not with any conviction of the wisdom of that policy'. Samuel stressed the necessity of bringing into the administration 'a number of new officers'.[79] The antagonism between the military and the Zionists infuriated the latter, and every effort was made to discredit the British Army: Ben-Gurion said of the 1920

Jerusalem riots that: 'direct guilt lay not with the "inciters", but with Bols and Allenby.'[80]

T. E. Lawrence was one of the soldiers who had fought with the Arabs, and felt that they had been badly treated. He summed up a general disgust when he wrote in *The Seven Pillars of Wisdom*: 'The Arab Revolt had begun on false pretences'. He goes on to discuss the McMahon promises and the Sykes–Picot Agreement. Of the Sykes–Picot plan he writes:

> Neither Sykes nor Picot had believed the thing really possible, but I knew that it was, and believed that after it the vigour of the Arab Movement would prevent the creation—by us or others—in Western Asia of unduly 'colonial' schemes of exploitation.[81]

He writes that the Arabs asked him to 'endorse the promises of the British Government':

> Having tested my friendliness and sincerity under fire, [they] asked me, as a free agent, to endorse the promises of the British Government. I had had no previous or inner knowledge of the McMahon pledges and the Sykes–Picot treaty ... But, not being a fool, I could see that if we won the war the promises to the Arabs were dead paper ... Had I been an honourable adviser I would have sent my men home, and not let them risk their lives for such stuff. Yet the Arab inspiration was our main tool in winning the Eastern war. So I assured them that England kept her word in letter and spirit. In this comfort they performed their fine things: but, of course, instead of being proud of what we did together, I was continually and bitterly ashamed.[82]

Jewish historical writers cope with the Arab performance in Lawrence's recital of 'fine things' by minimising the significance of the Arab Rising. Morris is an example:

> Hussein at last rose in revolt. But it never developed into the grand national movement that he had promised; no large Arab contingents of the Ottoman army defected to join his forces; no grand rebellion engulfed the Levant. The action was limited to a few thousand Hejazi tribesmen who were aided by British gunboats along the Red Sea coast, advisers, and large amounts of gold bullion.[83]

T. E. Lawrence knew the reality facing the Arabs, and he knew too that although some politicians had a low opinion of them, they were not going to take whatever Europeans thought would be best for them. He wrote a paper as early as 1915 in which he described the 'German Zionist Jews' in Palestine as 'the most foreign, most uncharitable part of the whole population'. The attitude and role of Lawrence in these developments is one of the very intriguing questions in this conflict. On the one hand there is the seemingly unequivocal view of support for the Arab cause:

> I vowed to make the Arab Revolt the engine of its own success, as well as handmaid to our Egyptian campaign: and vowed to lead it so madly in the final victory that expediency should counsel to the Powers a fair settlement of the Arabs' moral claims.[84]

On the other there are hints of slight support for the opposition. There are examples where Lawrence is reported to have expressed such support verbally. Some of these are questionable, but there are instances where there is documented evidence that he did so. For example, after the Jaffa riots of 1921, when General Congreve expressed concern about British policy and its adverse effects upon the Arabs, Lawrence wrote that 'there was a personal bias behind [Congreve's] opinions'.[85] He also wrote—it is impossible to know why—that in the conference in Cairo in 1921, Churchill 'made straight all the tangle ... so we were quit of the war-time Eastern adventure, with clean hands, but three years too late to earn the gratitude which peoples, if not states, can pay'.[86] Perhaps it was because so much of his effort had been put into the advancement of the Hashemites, and their elevation at that conference which led him to approve of Churchill's policy. One baffled Arab historian decided that such a conclusion was 'so palpably untenable as to cast doubts on Lawrence's understanding of the issues involved'.[87] This is just one of the questions about Lawrence. Antonius raises others in an evaluation which concedes his critical contribution to the Arab Revolt, but wonders about how much that contribution relies too much on Lawrence's own account.

Lawrence was involved in the peace talks, notably as interpreter to Feisal, and they naturally resisted colonial ambitions and advocated the Arab case. He later was an adviser to Churchill in the Colonial Office. He told Churchill in January 1921 that Feisal had agreed to give up all claims to Palestine if the Arabs could have Baghdad, Amman and Damascus.[88] This could be interpreted as some kind of support for Zionist ambitions, but as can be seen, since the Arabs did not get all of those cities, that conversation is irrelevant in any search for truth about the 'return'. Feisal's statement had the potential to negate Arab, or at least eminent Arab, opposition to Jewish takeover. Whatever interpretation is put on this, he simply could not have believed that the outcome was satisfactory for the Arabs. His final verdict, perhaps of the whole war, but certainly of that of the Middle East, was that:

> We lived many lives in those whirling campaigns, never sparing ourselves; yet when we achieved and the new world dawned, the old men came out again and

took our victory to re-make in the likeness of the former world they knew ... we stammered that we had worked for a new heaven and a new earth, and they thanked us kindly and made their peace.[89]

Despite opposition, there was a new dimension of increased support for the Zionists. First, there was a detectable shift in the attitudes of some British Jews to the declaration. Their earlier hostility eventually made no impact upon the outcomes. But it is also possible to detect among those British Jews who had not been happy about the campaign, the beginning of an acceptance of a *fait accompli*. A diplomat, George Kidston, wrote in a minute of 1919:

> Mr Balfour ignores completely the recent manoeuvres of Orthodox and anti-Zionist Jewry. There is ample evidence that this party, even in this country, is yielding to circumstances and is now prepared to come to a compromise with the Zionists—or at least to give to the Allies the impression that it accepts the Zionist ideal.[90]

This shift in attitudes was not universal. Objections were still expressed by Jews who voiced their opposition, even after the declaration had been made. Key figures such as the president of the council of the Anglo-Jewish Association, Claude Montefiore, still regarded the declaration 'with grave and serious misgivings'.[91] This opposition by prominent Jews was surprising, but it existed. Most of it still centred upon the belief that the Jews would be better off improving their circumstances in the countries where they lived.

The second element in the unfolding events which favoured the Zionists was the establishment of a Middle East Department in the Colonial Office. The Middle East Department was to oversee the affairs of the newly freed Arab mandated territories. From the end of the war, such responsibility had been split between the War Office, the Colonial Office and the India Office, which predictably led to confusion. Because of this confusion in the administration of the territories freed from the Turks, it was decided to establish, in February 1921, this Middle East Department. The people chosen to be at the head of the department were John Shuckburgh as assistant under-secretary of state, Robert Vernon and Hubert Young as joint assistant secretaries, T. E. Lawrence as political adviser, and Richard Meinertzhagen as a military expert.

We have encountered Meinertzhagen previously. He was a very odd choice. He was a fantasist, a liar and a fraud. He was of German descent, but wove an unbelievable story that he was Danish. He was an accomplished ornithologist, but one who stole birds from museums and fabricated specimens, which he then passed off as newly discovered varieties. It is a fact that he served as an officer in the British Army, and did serve with Allenby. He is 'routinely discussed as the chief intelligence officer of General Allenby's army in 1917, but he was nothing of the kind'.⁹² He was appointed to the Middle East Department 'by Churchill's special request'.⁹³ This is not surprising since, although he was not Jewish, he was a convinced and vocal Zionist supporter: 'Weizmann and David Ben-Gurion praised him for his earnest efforts in behalf of the Zionist cause'.⁹⁴

He liked to describe himself as a murderer, and for once there seems to have been some truth in this claim According to Lawrence, as well as being 'logical, an idealist of the deepest', he 'took as blithe a pleasure in deceiving his enemy (or his friend) by some unscrupulous jest, as in spattering the brains of a cornered mob of Germans one by one with his African knob-kerri.'⁹⁵ The Palin Report singled him out:

> The Administration was considerably hampered in its policy by the direct interference of the Home Authority and particularly by the fact that the late Chief Political Officer, Colonel Meinertzhagen, acted as a direct channel of communication with the Foreign Office ... not only independent of the High Commission, but at times contrary to the latter's considered opinion.⁹⁶

Garfield sums up one of the many damaging results of his bizarre behaviour:

> Unfortunately Meinertzhagen's fun wasn't harmless. Too many books and articles about Israel, about various wars, about science, and about the European presence in the Middle East, Africa, and India during the first half of the twentieth century, have used his diaries as primary source materials. They are not.⁹⁷

Weizmann was ready for the change of control of Palestine. He wrote to Samuel:

> The handing over of the responsibility of Palestine to a new Committee under the aegis of the Colonial Office terminates our direct connection with the Foreign Office and marks the beginning of a new period in which it will be our aim to be in contact with the new authorities, as circumstances shall require.⁹⁸

The establishment of the Middle East Department was not only an unmitigated disaster for the Arabs, but in the judgement of one experienced official, worse. E. T. Richmond, political secretary to two chief secretaries resigned in 1924. He wrote that he was convinced that:

> The Zionist Commission, the Middle East Department of the Colonial Office and the [Palestine] Administration are dominated by a spirit which I can only regard as evil, and that this spirit is, through the agencies I have mentioned, acting in a manner that is not merely unwise and impolitic but evil.⁹⁹

Meinertzhagen's activities raise another important matter which deserves more attention than it has received in the literature on Palestine: the network of spies used by the Zionists. At least from the date of the declaration, the Zionists had access to secret and confidential information, either overtly through sympathetic politicians, or through spies. Meinertzhagen was, by any definition, a Zionist agent and he now told Leonard Stein, secretary of the Zionist organisation, all about any discussions taking place. On the basis of what he was told on one occasion, Stein, supposing a potential disaster, persuaded Weizmann to return from Europe 'immediately'.[100]

From the beginning of Zionist agitation the connections Weizmann had made and cultivated over the years continued to open almost every door in London to Zionist leaders. One Foreign Office official claimed that the Jewish Agency virtually had the status of a foreign embassy.[101] Balfour's niece, Blanche (Baffy) Dugdale was a devout Christian and a Zionist like her uncle. She volunteered to be a spy. She was well placed to be so, since she worked in British Naval Intelligence, and was a British delegate to the League of Nations. She spoke openly at meetings, and wrote about her support for Zionism.

> [She] had an intimate relationship with a government minister, whom David Ben-Gurion and Moshe Shertok identified in their diaries only as 'a friend'. This was Walter Elliott; he served in the government in various posts during most of the 1930s. The information he leaked to his 'Baffy' was of no small assistance to the Zionist's movement's endeavours; she spoke to him at least once a day ... Ben-Gurion compared her to the prophet Deborah [notice once again resort to biblical parallels]. Dugdale was an intelligent person, and Weizmann and Ben-Gurion did more than just exploit her personal connections. They made her a true partner in their diplomatic labours.[102]

Had she not been so well connected, in the normal operation of security she would surely have been dismissed, or imprisoned, or even executed. Later, there was a police officer in Palestine called Raymond Cafferata. He was a target for murder by the extremists. They never succeeded. He had a secretary who 'as it turned out ... was a secret agent for the Zionists: she copied every letter he dictated to her and sent it to the Haganah'.[103]

Arab fears about the future were kept at bay, because the British government kept assuring the Arabs that they would be given independence. In this lie they were supported by France. George Antonius draws attention to an attempt to seek clarity by a group of seven Arabs from Cairo: 'men of standing and influence ... with their own confidence in the good faith of the Allies profoundly shaken'. They 'formed themselves into a group to concert action'.[104] They prepared a memorial which found its way to London, and on 16 June 1918 the Foreign Office replied.

The detailed reply is set out by Antonius, and he informs us, 'in Arab circles this Declaration is usually known as the Declaration to the Seven'.[105] The Arab countries were classified into four groups of territories: those which were free and independent before the war; those liberated from the Turks by the Arabs; those liberated by the Allies; and those still under Turkish rule. For the purposes of our discussion, 'those liberated by the Allies' included 'most of Iraq 'and the southern half of Palestine inclusive of Jerusalem and Jaffa'. The statement drew attention to the proclamations already made about the latter.

> [These] define the policy of His majesty's Government towards the inhabitants of those regions, which is that the future government of those territories should be based upon the principle of the consent of the governed. This policy will always be that of His Majesty's Government.

There was talk of 'freedom and independence', and assurances that the British government would 'give every support'.[106] 'Despondency ... gave place to a fresh outburst of enthusiasm'. The statement seemed clearer than the Hussein–McMahon agreement, since 'it was more comprehensive, free from any territorial reservations, and it had the added merit of being a public utterance'.[107] It even seemed to trump Sykes–Picot and the Balfour Declaration. Despite the strength of the promises, 'strangely enough, it has remained one of the least known outside the Arab world'.[108] Not so strange when it is remembered the grip the Zionists had on how information was to be shaped and disseminated.

The French now added to the deception. A crisis arose when, just before the entry of Allied troops into Beirut, the Arabs raised their flag. The French objected, and Allenby removed it. This led to violent protests, compounded by the news that the French were going to 'occupy' and that Zionist ambitions in Palestine were becoming very clear. To deflect the anger, the Allies issued an 'Anglo–French Declaration' of 7 November 1918, addressed to the people of Syria and Iraq. Also reprinted in Antonius it once again assured them of:

> The complete and definite emancipation of the peoples so long oppressed by the Turks, and the establishment of national Governments and administrations deriving their authority from the initiative and free choice of the indigenous populations ... [The Allies] far from wishing this or that system upon the populations of those regions, their only concern is to offer such support and efficacious help as will ensure the smooth workings of the governments and administrations which those populations will have elected of their own free will to have.[109]

The Turks, meanwhile, upon learning of Sykes–Picot, made an offer which ostensibly looked promising. It was contained in a letter of November 1917 addressed to Feisal. It pointed out that now the real intentions of the Allies had been revealed. There is an appeal to their brotherhood as Muslims. Hussein had 'fallen into the trap laid for him by the British, allowed himself to be ensnared by their cajoleries, and committed his offence against the unity and majesty of Islam'.[110] The Turks, with the agreement of the Germans, would grant autonomy to all the Arab provinces. Feisal sent the message to his father, who told him to reject it. Hussein asked London what was the 'secret Agreement' mentioned in the letter. Balfour replied that this was a piece of skulduggery by the Turks and complimented the king for rejecting it. It finished with the usual blatant lie:

> An emphatic assurance that Great Britain, in accordance with her former pledge, would stand by the Arabs in their struggle for liberation and assist them in obtaining their freedom.[111]

The news of the Balfour Declaration naturally disturbed Hussein, and once again he asked London for clarification. This time Dr D. G. Hogarth of the Arab Bureau in Cairo was sent to Jeddah. He gave the king

> an explicit assurance that 'Jewish settlement in Palestine would only be allowed in so far as it was consistent with the *political and economic freedom of the Arab population*.' The message was delivered orally, but Hussain took it down, and the quotation I have just given is my own rendering of the note made by him in Arabic at the time.[112]

Antonius goes on to point out that the italicised words were crucially different from the words in the Balfour Declaration which guarantees only 'the *civil and religious rights* of the Arab population'.[113] The king believed Hogarth. The Arabs persisted in their belief that the Allies meant what they said, but the Arab situation was hopeless. As far as Syria was concerned the French took over. In Palestine the Balfour Declaration became British government policy. But it was far from universally welcomed, and not only by Arabs. The Zionists had a hard battle ahead. Especially inevitable was the move to physical resistance by the Arabs.

The next milestone was an Allied Supreme Council of the Paris Peace Conference held in San Remo in Italy in April 1920. This was set up to try to finalise a peace treaty with the Turks, to settle their future, and in particular to plan for the future of Palestine, Syria and Iraq. Britain had already been warned by Meinertzhagen that the Arabs would not agree to any decisions unless Feisal was present.[114] There was some alarm in Britain and it was recommended by several officials that Feisal should be reassured: 'our only chance is to emphasise Palestine for the Palestinians (with the necessary reservations to protect Zionist interests)'.[115] Weizmann, perhaps because of information from his spies, wrote to Curzon's office in March, before the conference opened, to offset any change in what he believed to be British policy. The letter is a combination of inaccuracies, half-truths and wishful thinking:

> Unless there is clear pronouncement from the Peace Conference respecting the establishment of Palestine as the Jewish National Home there is bound to be a certain amount of uneasiness and unrest in Palestine ... All the Allied and Associated Powers are definitely committed to the principle of the Jewish National Home ... The case of Palestine is different from all other mandated areas belonging to the Turkish Empire ... The other mandated areas are to be administered in the national interests of the present inhabitants but the mandate of Palestine is to have as its guiding object the establishment of the Jewish National Home, the rights of the present inhabitants, of course, being adequately guarded.[116]

It may be noted that any 'unease' or 'unrest' would not only be on the part of the Arabs; that the 'Powers' were not *all* committed; that the 'case' of Palestine was only 'different' because of Zionist ambition; and that it was that ambition which would define the 'guiding object': the Jewish national home.

The conference was again dominated by French intransigence over its presumed rights in Palestine and the Balfour Declaration. The French were reluctant to include the latter in the discussion, mainly because, as always, and correctly, it was extremely questionable whether the Allies had ever agreed to it. However, in the end it was accepted as part of the treaty. In terms of the future, it was agreed that Britain would get the mandate over Palestine and Mesopotamia, and France would get that over Syria. Thus failed the ambition of T. E. Lawrence in the quaint language of the day, 'to biff the French out of all hope of Syria'.[117] Apart from the interminable demands of the French to be involved in Palestine, and the equally persistent insistence by the British to include the Balfour Declaration, there was a third mantra, again repeated by the French; it was that the rights of 'non-Jewish' people in Palestine should be protected. In the debates which followed, this was dealt with variously by lies, assurances, and a denial that the Arabs were entitled to, or even understood those rights.

The next stage in the elimination of Arab ambitions was the signing of the Treaty of Sèvres on 10 August 1920 by the Allies. Article 95 of this treaty is relevant to this discussion. It concerned 'the administration of Palestine':

> Within such boundaries as may be determined by the Principal Allied Powers to a Mandatory to be selected by the said Powers. The Mandatory will be responsible for putting into effect the declaration originally made on 2 November 1917 by the British Government, and adopted by the other Allied Powers, in favour of the establishment in Palestine of a National Home for the Jewish people, it being clearly understood that nothing shall be done which may prejudice the civil and religious rights of existing non-Jewish communities in Palestine, or the rights and political status enjoyed by Jews in any other country.

After Balfour

The newly formed League of Nations formally approved the handing over of the mandate on 24 July 1922. Britain was to hold it until 1948. In its preamble, the document issuing the authority reiterated the essence of the Balfour Declaration: that there would be a 'national home' and that the rights of non-Jews would be protected, as would the rights of Jews living in other countries. Implementation of the mandate did not actually begin until September 1923 because of arguments and disputes between the several countries involved.

Meanwhile the Arabs had been busy. A potential bombshell emerged when on 8 March 1920, while Weizmann was writing his letter, and a month before San Remo, a General Syrian Congress declared Palestine, Syria, Transjordan and Lebanon together as a state, with Feisal as king. Allenby wrote that if this reality were ignored, the Arabs would be alienated and 'I feel certain war must ensue'.[118] He was asked how the situation could be accepted, and specifically: 'How would this procedure be applied to Palestine and how would recognition of Feisal as King be reconcilable with Zionist aims?' Allenby repeated his prediction of trouble. Samuel seems to have been alarmed, and wrote to Curzon: 'I can see no sufficient reason for recognising Feisal King of Palestine. I doubt whether he or his supporters expect it ... [It] would tend to take life out of Zionist movement.'[119]

The French too were having none of Arab ambitions. They sent Feisal an ultimatum in July 1920. It contained demands which showed that the French were going to take over: for example that anti-French hostility should be stopped. They attacked Feisal's forces in the battle of Maysalun, outside Damascus, on 24 July 1920, advanced on Damascus, occupied Syria, and turned Syria into a French mandate. For the French, it was a supreme colonial moment and a textbook example of colonial arrogance. Feisal was 'invited' to leave Syria, and at the end of July he did so. In December he was invited to London:

> Shortly after his elder brother Abdullah was charged with taking care of Transjordan, which until July 1920 had been administered as part of the Arab kingdom of the Hijaz, and was now subject to the authority of the British High Commissioner in Jerusalem.[120]

To placate Feisal, Churchill 'gave' him the throne of Iraq, an act which Churchill would often quote as an example of his generosity towards the Arabs. It was not until 1946 that Abdullah was proclaimed king. The Zionists disapproved of this, since the land east of the Jordan was considered by them to be part of biblical Israel, and that it should be part of the 'homeland'. One result was that a group of violent 'revisionists' broke away from the main body. It was led by Ze'ev Jabotinsky. He was to become a very dangerous man.

On 26 April 1920 the conference ended 'after scenes that President Wilson once described as "the whole disgusting scramble" for the Middle East'.[121] These scenes were a continuation of the interminable battle for colonial supremacy in the region, and of course no account of the wishes of the people of the region was taken. The outcome of the conference was joy for the Zionists, since Britain was given the mandate for Palestine. The Zionist lobby knew that their influence in Britain was set, and any threat from France, regarded by them as hostile, was removed. Those Jews who cared were ecstatic. The Zionist Organisation of America, for example, stated:

> The San Remo decision of the Supreme Council of the peace Conference crowns the British declaration by enacting it as part of the law of the nations of the world.[122]

The Arab reaction was less publicised, but it embraced the warnings evinced by Allenby:

> The national demonstrations which the people all over the country had made and the strong continual protests which were submitted to you as well as to all the European Powers have altogether proved that the nation refuses the Zionist Emigration and hates that Palestine should become the prey of greediness, and we say that the nation is prepared to protect this sacred charge, the charge of our fathers and forefathers with all its power.[123]

The wording of the mandate had now to be drafted. There had been discussion about this before the San Remo Conference ever took place. What was the habitation of the Jews in Palestine to be called? A state? A home? A commonwealth? Curzon was always alert to the manipulation of the use of the word commonwealth. He constantly objected to it. At the San Remo Conference he also objected to the inclusion of terms such as 'the historic connection of the Jewish people with Palestine' in the draft mandate:

> I object to the phrase *in toto*, as certain to be the basis upon which the Zionists for all time found their most extreme pretensions and I told Dr Weizmann in an interview that I could not accept it.[124]

In a telegram sent by Weizmann, reference was made to 'a Jewish Commonwealth', and Curzon asked his staff what the word meant. One of his officials replied that the 'idea of a Jewish commonwealth' was 'looming in the background'. Curzon had asked in January 1919:

> What then is the good of shutting our eyes to the fact that this is what the Zionists are after, and that the British Trusteeship is a mere screen behind which to work for this end?[125]

Curzon also tackled Balfour about the speed and direction of Zionist activity. He reported the anxieties expressed to him both by Sir Arthur Money, the administrator under Allenby, and Allenby himself. They felt that:

A Jewish *Government* in any form would mean an Arab rising, and the nine-tenths of the population who are not Jews would make short shrift with the Hebrews. As you may know, I share these views, and have for long felt that the pretensions of Weizmann and Company are extravagant and ought to be checked.

Balfour's reply was, as often, weak and a lie:

As far as I know Weizmann has never put forward a claim for the Jewish *Government* of Palestine. Such a claim is in my opinion certainly inadmissible and personally I do not think we should go further than the original declaration which I made to Lord Rothschild.

The latter phrase ignores the fact that the declaration was incomprehensible. Curzon was far from convinced. He wrote again on 26 January 1919: 'As for Weizmann and Palestine, I entertain no doubt that he is out for a Jewish Government, if not at the moment then in the near future'.[126] Alive to the significance of the wording, especially the use of 'Commonwealth', Curzon, once again, would not accept the latter which was in a Foreign Office draft promulgated in March 1920. He protested:

'Development of a self-government Commonwealth'. Surely most dangerous. It is a euphemism for a Jewish state, the very thing they accepted and we disallow.[127]

A senior civil servant, Eric Forbes Adam, tried to placate him by saying that it is 'a particularly popular word in America!' He further resorted to some imagined problem in translation, writing that 'the use of the word 'commonwealth' can hardly alarm the Arabs because there is no precise Arabic equivalent for this word or for 'democracy' or 'republic' and probably the word would have to be translated 'state' in the Arabic version of the mandate.'

Once again, it was hoped that the Arabs, being simple people, would not understand the meaning of words. Curzon was a rare politician, in that he could not easily be consoled by the blandishments of civil servants:

Is Mr. Forbes Adam serious when he points out that we do not use the words *Jewish* Commonwealth? Of course not—As however we do not mean *Arab* or *Syrian* Commonwealth—why not be honest and say Jewish Commonwealth at once? That would be intelligible—But as it is contrary to every principle upon which we have hitherto stood, I at any rate cannot accept it.[128]

In respect of the mandate, when the term 'self-governing Commonwealth' was replaced with 'self-governing institutions', Curzon wrote in March 1920, 'it all turns on what we mean. The Zionists are after a Jewish state with the Arab as hewers of wood and drawers of water ... that is not my view. I want the Arabs to have a chance and I don't want a Hebrew state.'[129] For once, amusingly, Curzon had here used the Bible, a principal weapon in the Zionist armoury, against them: 'Let them live; but let them be hewers of wood and drawers of water unto all the congregation.'[130]

In the same note Curzon made observations on another minute written by a civil servant. He is at his most frank. He is frustrated and angry, and feels as though vague forces are in charge The most astonishing of these observations, considering he was foreign secretary, was as follows:

> I have never been consulted as to this mandate at an earlier stage, nor do I know from what negotiations it springs or on what undertakings it is based ... I think the entire conception wrong. Here is a country with 580,000 Arabs and 30,000 or is it 60,000 Jews (by no means all Zionists). Acting upon the noble principles of self-determination and ending with a splendid appeal to the League of Nations, we then proceed to draw up a document which reeks of Judaism in every paragraph and is an avowed constitution for a Jewish State. Even the poor Arabs are only allowed to look through the keyhole as a non-Jewish community. It is quite clear that the mandate has been drawn up by someone reeling under the fumes of Zionism. If we are all to submit to that intoxicant, this draft is all right.[131]

Britain's allies were supportive of those who shared Curzon's fears. The Vatican was very critical of Zionist ambitions. The secretary of state said that it was well to give the Jews equal civil rights, but the draft mandate aimed at 'the absolute preponderance of Jews over all other peoples in Palestine'. This was 'seriously damaging' to the rights of other nationalities, and contradicted the Treaty of Versailles.[132] This was not the first time the Catholic Church had expressed concerns about Zionist activity. A Cardinal Bourne wrote a letter dated 25 January 1919:

> Christians of various kinds and Moslems have approached me on the subject [of a Jewish takeover]. They feel they are being handed over unjustly to those whom they dislike more than their late Turkish oppressors ... the Zionists too claimed that they had obtained the approval of the Holy City and thereby gained the support of some Catholic Bishops in the United States and in England. There is no foundation for this claim. The whole movement appears to be quite contrary to Christian sentiment and tradition.[133]

Balfour's response in a letter to the prime minister was, by his standards, straightforward. It was also predictable:

I think the opposition offered by so many Roman Catholics to the Zionist policy is very little to their credit, and cannot be easily reconciled with the tenets of their religion!¹³⁴

In June 1920 Robert Vansittart of the Foreign Office wrote to Curzon of the French reaction:

As to the Palestinian mandate, Berthelot said that Millerand had nearly jumped out of his skin when he had shown it to him. Berthelot added that, frankly, he himself was both surprised and alarmed by it. They both think it much too judaised and judaising—full of red flags indeed ... You will remember that you toned down the first draft, and I toned it down still further. If it should be watered down a bit more (there are some in the Cabinet like Mr. Montague [*sic*] who may press for this), it will ease our position, vis à vis of the Zionists in having the French urge us however mildly.¹³⁵

Curzon noted 'I am quite willing to water the Palestine mandate which I cordially distrust'.

Vansittart tried again, only to incur Curzon's displeasure. It was about 'the historical connection, etc. in the Preamble'. Curzon ordered it removed but 'now I find that Mr. Vansittart has gone and put it back again ... I do not myself recognise that the connection of the Jews with Palestine, which terminated 1200 years ago, gives them any claim whatsoever'. His exasperation shows when he concludes: 'On this principle we have a stronger claim to parts of France'.¹³⁶ Thus he drew a parallel with the Arab view of the absurdity of any claim by them to Spain which they had ruled in more recent than biblical times.

Vansittart also raised the question as to whether the Zionists should see the draft *before* the cabinet. Curzon's view was predictable: 'I greatly dislike giving the draft to the Zionists'.¹³⁷ Sir John Tilley pointed out, again an amazing admission from such a powerful person: '*I believe* [was he not sure?] every draft of the mandate has been shown to the Zionists ... My feeling is that if at the last moment we make important alterations without telling them we shall be regarded as having played them false.'¹³⁸ Further exchanges revealed that the 'historical connection' phrases 'were drafted last year in Paris by Mr. Balfour himself and I believe Mr. Balfour attached the importance to their appearance in the mandate as an explanation of the essence of Zionism'. As to Weizmann, he 'attaches more importance to it [the phrase] than he does to the detailed provisions on the mandate itself'.¹³⁹

Weizmann also turned his attention to the matter of borders. He went straight to Balfour with a letter stating that unless the matter of frontiers were settled 'there was serious danger of the National Home being crippled economically'.¹⁴⁰ Since Balfour was by now lord president of the council, he sent the letter on to Charles

Hardinge, the permanent under-secretary of state for foreign affairs, with a note containing typical Balfour contradictions. On the one hand: 'Our Jewish friends, who are not always easy to deal with, sometimes get dreadfully perturbed over matters of comparatively small moment.' But, on the other hand: 'The question of frontiers is *really* vital, because it affects the economic possibilities of developing Palestine, and on these economic possibilities depend the success or failure of Zionism.' They should be given land which is 'now useless to everybody'.[141]

To return to the immediate reaction to the declaration, the continuing opposition of probably the majority of important Jews who were sufficiently aware of what was being done did not deter the Zionists. It was such opposition which led to the establishment of the League of British Jews, designed to undo Zionist plans. They would find that a difficult task. After all, the Zionists had the official support of the British government (and soon the US) as exemplified by the action of the Foreign Office in setting up 'a special branch for Jewish propaganda'.

> Propaganda material was distributed to virtually every known Jewish community in the world ... leaflets containing the text of the Balfour Declaration were dropped over German and Austrian territory; pamphlets in Yiddish were distributed to Jewish troops in Central European armies ... which read: 'Jerusalem has fallen! The hour of redemption has arrived ... Palestine must be the national home of the Jewish people once more ... Remember! An Allied victory means the Jewish people's return to Zion'.[142]

There was set up in the Department of Information a 'Jewish Section'. That this was suggested by Jabotinsky is another example of the bizarre way in which the future of Palestine was being handled. The head of it was a former civil servant in the Post Office called Albert Hyamson. He was Jewish, and he explained that the aims of the Jewish Section were:

> To conduct British propaganda among Jews in all parts of the world "giving it special tone required by Jewish temperament" [*sic*], and the Jewish branch was to promote the Zionist movement.[143]

The London Zionist Bureau moved swiftly. It set up a propaganda committee to work with the Department of Information. Hyamson was elected chairman of that too. This meant that huge government resources were devoted to the nurturing of Zionist propaganda, all done openly. The result was the distribution of vast amounts of material throughout the world, especially in America, most of it originating in the Zionist Propaganda Committee. This 'paid special attention to visual media such as film, picture post cards, posters, illustrated lectures and Yiddish plays'.[144] Hyamson did not stop there. His career received a boost when, in 1921, Samuel appointed him to be in charge of the Palestinian administration's Immigration Department. Zionists realised that certain categories of people had to be rejected: communists, the seriously ill, prostitutes and so on, and Hyamson's careful scrutiny of applicants, paradoxically, led to him being labelled 'a Jewish anti-semite and as first-class scum'.[145]

There were two main questions which tormented everyone who had influence: exactly *who* was to exercise authority in Palestine, and where were its borders. On this first question, Lloyd George and the Zionists were in agreement. Zionism would flower under the tight control of Britain. Any question of the resurrection of French influence was simply brushed aside, as is illustrated by this anecdote by T. E. Lawrence, recalling the day that the victorious forces entered Jerusalem:

> [Picot] said in his fluting voice: 'and tomorrow, my dear general, I will take the necessary steps to set up civil government in this town.' It was the bravest word on record: a silence followed, as when they opened the seventh seal in heaven. Salad, chicken mayonnaise and foie gras sandwiches hung in our wet mouths unmunched, while we turned to Allenby and gaped. Even he seemed for the moment at a loss. We began to fear that the idol might betray a frailty. But his face grew red: he swallowed, his chin coming forward (in the way we loved), whilst he said, grimly, 'in the military zone the only authority is that of the Commander-in-Chief-myself'.[146]

There was also some support for the idea that the US should take charge. Once again Balfour displayed his chronic erraticism. He wanted the US to be considered for the management of Palestine. As always his utterances were charged with ambiguity, but he certainly did say to the war cabinet in October 1917 that he would like to see 'some form of British, American or other protectorate'.[147] It may be noted that this statement does not further the discussion very much. Yet, even though Lloyd George seems to have been in little doubt about Britain seizing power, he managed to discuss the possibility of US involvement on several occasions with Americans, including with Colonel Edward House, already mentioned as a key adviser to the president.

There was the question of what actually constituted Palestine. A Greek version of the name was used by Herodotus in the fifth century BC. Palestine was never in historical times regarded as a 'country'. It was part of a greater entity, notably Syria. The problem was compounded by the fact that it had no indisputable natural boundaries, except for the Mediterranean. Zionists had already, in November 1918, proposed boundaries to the Foreign Office: 'In the East, a line close to and west of the Hedjaz railway.' Their proposal, as might have been expected, included the land to the east of the Jordan. Lloyd George, then prime minister, called a meeting in September 1919 to discuss where the borders were. The questions discussed were basic but vital. Should Lake Tiberias be included?

Should Mount Hermon? Lord Allenby said that 'the Zionists stretched Palestine far to the north and would like to include Hama. Their idea was to fix the boundaries similarly to those of Solomon's empire.'[148] Havrelock sums up the quagmire which the border question became, especially its epicentre, the River Jordan.

> With ever-changing constituent parts, the chronicle as well as the nation of Israel is a work in process. The continual morphing of ancient Israel through alliance, absorption, and the defection or defeat of its component groups involves recurrent acts of boundary drawing. Groups of people move in and out of insider and outsider positions. And as the group undergoes shifts, so does the nation and the territory change. Who were the people who made up Israel? Each time the question was asked, the response created new borders, as well as new relationships to Israel's most significant border, the River Jordan.[149]

The problem remains in the twenty-first century, especially because of the wars which resulted from Israeli expansion. A major campaigner in this regard was Moshe Dayan who believed that the 1967 war had led to biblical fulfilment about the destiny of Israel, which was to occupy all of what was, allegedly, biblical Palestine. As the architect of victory, Dayan 'assumed the Joshua avatar':

> We are the biblical generation of the settlement, following the Joshua conquest, and the helmet and the sword are essential requirements ... [Dayan] saw the question of state borders as his personal purview with his authority leaving its stamp on the 'historic land', 'Israel of our times', and 'future borders'. His merger of past, present, and future carried an implicit argument for territorial maximalism—that the land conforms to the very borders achieved in the 1967 war.[150]

When the reference to biblical myth is set aside, what this means is that the territories under occupation, especially the West Bank, should never be returned to the Arabs.

The background to all of this, and the very root of the problem, was the irreducible fact that Palestine was an Arab country. Throughout every discussion there were implications that this was a 'problem' which could be overcome. Many in the British government, and many of the educated public, were conscious of the devastating effects of a Jewish takeover would have on the Arabs. Antisemitism was widespread in British society, but there was also resentment about that large numbers of immigrant Jews had avoided military service in the war because they were not British citizens. But the principal concern, however, was that Britain had made definite promises to the Arabs upon the condition that they would fight the Turks, and these promises included control over their countries. The Balfour Declaration manifestly broke those promises, a situation which was compounded by the emerging ambitions of France, which were to see Arab leaders ousted from the most symbolic area of all: Syria.

The Zionists were well aware that there would be considerable concern about the future of the overwhelmingly Arab population. Their main tactic in deflecting this was to deny that there would be a Jewish takeover. Rather, there would be some sort of sharing of power. After all, the two peoples had the same heritage. Norman Bentwich, a Jew who held an important post in Palestine, wrote:

> There is ample room for the children of Esau and of Jacob to live in harmony on the land. [It ought to be possible] to secure a good understanding ... between the two elements that are in origin akin and stand in material need of each other.[151]

The 'problem' had always occupied Zionists. After the declaration, Herzl's deputy 'identified the Arab question as the foremost obstacle to the Zionist enterprise [since] "when we return to our ancestral homeland we will find there some 600,000 Arabs"'.[152]

A Harry Sachet wrote a letter in 1917 which shows how Zionist thinking was becoming positively warped. In it, having described the Arabs as 'our most tremendous problem', he goes on: 'I don't want us in Palestine to deal with the Arabs as the Poles deal with the Jews, and with the lesser excuse that belongs to a numerical minority'.[153] There was much propaganda along the same lines. The parallel with other 'colonial' societies is striking. How to deal with the racial majority was a favourite topic of conversation in British colonial Africa. White people there seemed to forget that they were vastly outnumbered by Africans, and discussed the 'problem' as if the Africans were not the majority.

At an international level there were broadly two dimensions to the attempts to placate the Arab authorities. The first was to constantly express the belief that in some way the Zionists would handle any difficulties. The second was to assure the Arabs that their interests were paramount. We have seen examples of this and it was again deployed by Ronald Storrs in November 1918, when he told an Arab audience, sickened by the flaunting of Zionist flags at a celebration of the anniversary of the declaration, 'that the Allies did not intend to force a government on the people of the land against their wishes ... Palestine, he added, was free to choose its own government'.[154]

Accompanying these assurances there was a policy of keeping the facts away from the Arabs: the Sykes–Picot Agreement was only the most blatant demonstration of this. To this mixture were added the deliberate lies told by Weizmann to the Arabs, as in an address in April 1918 to local leaders in Palestine:

> All the fears expressed openly or secretly by the Arabs that they are to be ousted from their present position were due either to a fundamental misconception of Zionist aims and intentions or to the malicious activities of their common enemies.[155]

There *were* attempts to address the future by Jewish and Arab leaders. Weizmann and Feisal held discussions several times but they proved to be futile, as they had to be. In June 1918 they had a meeting in which it seemed Feisal agreed to the most unlikely accords, including the acceptance of the declaration and Jewish immigration. It was to be claimed that he accepted the Zionist ambition. Weizmann, in a letter to Balfour on 19 April 1919, made one more of his extravagant claims, which was that 'between the Arab leaders, as represented by Faisal, and ourselves there is complete understanding, and therefore, no doubt complete accord'.[156] But to add to the confusion as to what had been agreed or not agreed, Feisal wrote a postscript. This stipulated that the agreement turned on the acceptance of Arab independence. This, like so much of the documentation drawn up, is questioned by Jewish writers.

Like Lawrence, the British authorities on the ground had first-hand experience of the danger in a situation which was built on massive contradictions. The head of the military administration in Palestine, General Money, pointed out that Britain could not be acceptable as a mandatory power if it was evident that at the centre was to be the implementation of the Balfour Declaration.[157] The British government, faced with such news, which of course implied a reversal of British policy, were confused.

Balfour, from then until he left office, became increasingly erratic and rather desperate in his attempts to keep his policy in place. Instructions were sent in August 1919 in a spirit of optimism which had no basis in reality; they were intended to stabilise the situation by being firm. These instructions stated that the British position was unchanged: the Balfour Declaration would be implemented and the Arabs must accept the fact.

On the question of the mandate, Balfour wanted to absolve Britain of responsibility: instead he proposed, as I have said, that the US should take it on. It would appear that, at last, he realised that he had created an impossible situation, summed up in his massive understatement that 'Palestine presented a unique situation'.[158] He was puzzled by the US president's support for both Zionism *and* for self-determination. As we have seen, Balfour's 'solution' was that 'self-determination ... could not be indiscriminately applied to the whole world, and Palestine was a case in point'. After all, he did not think 'that Zionism will hurt the Arabs'.[159]

In October 1919 Balfour was able to free himself of the colossal problems ahead by being appointed lord president of the council. He was replaced by Lord Curzon. Although Curzon had been a critic of much of the policy towards Palestine, he now behaved responsibly and professionally by trying to promote his government's policy while maintaining his concerns about the direction events were taking. On 30 November Curzon protested again in a cabinet memorandum about the wording of the mandate. He pointed out that at first the French objected because 'of its almost exclusively Zionist complexion and of the manner in which the interests and rights of the Arab majority ... were ignored. The Italian Government expressed similar apprehensions. The mandate, therefore, was largely rewritten, and finally received their assent.'[160]

It was also clear that Weizmann had seen the draft—'it has been shown to him by several people outside the F.O.'.[161] But, as always, Weizmann wanted more. He wanted it to be formally communicated to him. People, including Curzon, objected to this, since the draft had not even been approved by the League of Nations.[162]

Even before the mandate was formalised, a new British civil administration was established, headed by a high commissioner for Palestine, and Sir Herbert Samuel was given the post in 1920. This appointment was another astonishing benefit for the Zionist cause, even though there were many who thought the appointment of a Jew would be quite unacceptable. This was the view of Field Marshal Allenby, who believed that the appointment of a Zionist to this post was 'highly dangerous'. The Arabs, he said, 'would regard appointment of a Jew as first Governor, even if he is a British Jew, as handing [the] country over at once to a permanent Zionist Administration ... we must be prepared for outrages against Jews, murders, raids on Jewish villages.'[163]

His colleague, Major General Bols, stated that the appointment was noted with 'consternation, despondency and exasperation by Muslims and Christians, the Christians being, if possible even more bitter than the Moslems ...'

> It is impossible to induce either party in their present spirit to accept Mr. Herbert Samuel as a British statesman of Jewish religion, they look upon him first and foremost as a Jew and a Zionist. They are convinced that he will be a partisan Zionist and that he represents a Jewish and not a British Government.[164]

Samuel was consulted and 'considered these Reports unduly alarmist, but said he would consult a delegation representing the Palestine Jewish community which was in London at the time'.[165] Not surprisingly considering the membership, the delegation expressed the view that such reports were indeed alarmist. Most unusually, Curzon officially may have supported the appointment, telling Allenby that the 'appointment of Mr. Herbert Samuel as High Commissioner for Palestine has been decided upon because they are convinced that his high reputation and administrative experience render him particularly qualified for the task and because his authority with the Zionists, coupled with his well known sympathy for the Arabs, will enable him to hold scales even, and to exercise a pacifying and moderating influence at the outset of new system of civil administration'.[166]

In a House of Lords debate in July 1922, there were objections to the appointment of a Jew as administrator. As usual, Churchill constantly tried to deflect the objections from the many who thought the appointment of a Jew would be quite unacceptable. Churchill had an answer. Turning a seeming disadvantage on its head, he wrote to senior colleagues, pointing out that Samuel was evenly 'holding the balance between Arabs and Jews and how effectively he was restraining his own people, *as perhaps only a Jewish administrator could* [my emphasis]'.[167]

Predictably, Samuel, during his reign, helped consolidate the putative Jewish hold on Palestine. He at once, upon his appointment, began clearing the way for a Jewish takeover by passing ordinances which ranged from enabling immigration, to easing land purchase, to the recognition of Hebrew as an official language. He granted a Jew, Pinhas Rutenberg, an *éminence grise* of whom we will learn more, exclusive permission to produce electricity in both Palestine and Transjordan.

Samuel, as a Jew and Zionist governing an Arab country, was in the most difficult of situations. As he was to find out, whatever he did would upset everybody. But he did try. He arranged for the arming of Jewish colonies for their defence, incidentally condoning the establishment of illegal 'armies'. He announced temporary restrictions on immigration: these were removed a few months later. There was also established a Supreme Muslim Council, although with no real power to do anything, and he proposed a truly radical step, which was the abolition of the Zionist Commission and its replacement by a representative body.

Such actions did not please the Zionists, since they believed that the Balfour Declaration gave exclusive possession to the Jews, and any concessions to Arabs were a betrayal. There was talk of trying to have Samuel dismissed, but it was realised that such a step would seem very odd considering what he was, and it was difficult to see how any replacement could be more sympathetic than a Zionist Jew. The extent of Samuel's support for Zionism is evident, but his skill at hiding that support was so refined that even the Zionists themselves doubted his commitment. A measure of that support can be gauged from the lies contained in his valedictory report when he gave up the post in 1925:

> In the first place, the people discovered that the disasters, which they were told were about to fall upon them, did not in fact occur ... the attacks upon their villages by well-armed Jewish colonists, which some of the agitators had announced, did not take place ... the day when a hundred thousand Jews were to disembark in Palestine in order to occupy their lands came and went, and there was no such invasion ... it is difficult, under such conditions, to maintain indefinitely an attitude of alarm; people cannot be induced to remain constantly mobilised against a danger which never eventuates.[168]

And, as always, the Zionists had to cope with the Arabs. In 1921 when Churchill became colonial secretary, he convened a two-week conference in Cairo in March.[169] There had been a revolt in Mesopotamia in 1920, during which hundreds of British troops had been killed, and the conference was intended, in part to address that problem, but more generally to try to move forward in the settling of the chaos which the Middle East had become. This had recently been complicated by Abdullah's forming a force to fight the French in Syria.

Local people were not invited to Cairo, apart from two Arabs who were members of the mandate administration. On 22 March a Palestinian Arab delegation met Churchill, but he refused to discuss politics, and said he would see them in Jerusalem, after the conference.[170]

The major results of the conference were substantially propelled by T. E. Lawrence, who was there as adviser to Churchill. These were that Feisal was to be given authority over Iraq, Abdullah over Transjordan, and Hussein over the Hejaz. Herbert Samuel tried a last ditch attempt to persuade Churchill to include Transjordan in Palestine, but Churchill's priority and hope was that the considerable support given to the Hashemites would quell Arab nationalism. Zionist ambitions for land to the east of Jordan were seemingly squashed.

On 24 March Churchill went to Jerusalem. On 28 March he met Abdullah. Abdullah asked what was going to happen. Was there to be a Jewish state west of the Jordan? Churchill lied. Churchill said that there would be no mass Jewish immigration. But if Abdullah did not interfere in eastern Palestine, Zionism would not apply to Transjordan. Abdullah wanted Palestine to be included in the proposed territory, but 'it was explained to him that His Majesty's Government were already far too committed to a different system in Palestine for them to be able to accept this proposal'.[171]

This ambition of Abdullah's to include Palestine in his country was the guiding light of his political ambition. He had to wait until April 1950 until at least a part of the land west of the Jordan came to him: the West Bank was included in his regime.

Churchill then met with a delegation of Palestinians. A memorandum given to him was a catalogue of grievances. They questioned the legality of the Balfour Declaration, found the appointment of a Jew as high commissioner abhorrent, deplored the economic advantages being given to the Jews, said the Jews were becoming the rulers, and wanted an end to immigration.[172] Churchill's response was familiar. The paper was biased and made untrue statements. The national home for the Jews would be good for the world, good for the Jew, good for the Arabs who dwell in Palestine. He leapt to the defence of Samuel, the essence of which was that since he was a Jew 'he was believed by them when he said that he was only doing what was just and fair'.[173]

Churchill was then presented with a document by the Jewish National Council of Palestine. They thanked Britain for 'the rebuilding of the Jewish National Home', and hoped it would include 'its historical frontiers'. After all it is little alongside 'all the Arab lands'. And they described the progress over the last forty years. Churchill's response was rather different from that meted out to the Arab delegation: 'The cause of Zionism is one which carries with it much that is good for the whole world... you were animated by the very highest spirit of justice and idealism.' But they were warned that the majority population would cause trouble. He had read the memorandum 'with great interest and sympathy'. Churchill compounded this hyperbole in a speech he made at the Hebrew University in Jerusalem on 29 March: 'he spoke words of encouragement that thrilled his listeners'—as well they might.[174] 'Palestine would transform into a paradise as foretold in the scriptures, "a land flowing with milk and honey, in which sufferers of all races and religions will find a rest from their sufferings"'.[175]

Emir Hussein, once absolutely central to events in the region and to British support in the Middle East, refused to accept a treaty of friendship with Britain because it would mean accepting the declaration and with it Zionist policy. T. E. Lawrence was dispatched to try to persuade him to change his mind, but the obstinate refusal of Hussein to forego his principles meant that Lawrence was wasting his time. In 1924 Abdulaziz Ibn Saud of the sultanate of Nejd attacked Hussein. On 22 December 1925, after a series of battles, Saud was pronounced king of Hejaz, and so ruler of Arabia. Hussein asked Britain for help, which was refused on the grounds that Britain did not interfere in religious disputes. In fact, Hussein was of no further use to Britain, and was becoming an obstacle to the achievement of Palestinian policy. He was exiled to Cyprus, and died in Amman in 1932.

The Zionists were displeased at the 'loss' of the land east of Jordan. Their displeasure that was hinted at by James de Rothschild many years later when thanking Churchill:

> You laid the foundation of the Jewish State by separating Abdullah's kingdom from the rest of Palestine. Without this *much-opposed* prophetic foresight there would not have been an Israel today [my emphasis].[176]

Weizmann never gave up. Now he wanted the whole of Transjordan to be included in the area arrogated to the Jews, and he wrote to Churchill, once again drawing on semi-historical, but ancient beliefs that three tribes of Israel had lived there: those of Reuben, Gad and Manasseh, who had on that land 'first pitched their tents and pastured their flocks'.[177] Mercifully Churchill was not persuaded, thus avoiding making an intolerable situation even worse.

When Transjordan was set up as an independent state, the Zionists were displeased. Transjordan consisted of four fifths of the original mandate. But the Zionists did not give up hope, as Morris explains:

> They reasoned—and were to continue to reason until the end of the 1930s—the arrangement was only temporary: Transjordan might still be opened up for Jewish settlement and conquest. The right wing periphery of the movement, the Revisionists, continued to dream of conquering Transjordan down to the 1950s and 1960s, and some, even later; their slogan continued to be "two banks to the Jordan: one is ours and the other too".[178]

After Balfour

However, there remained a glimmer of hope for the Zionists. The conference delineated boundaries for Palestine, but 'on the east, the boundary is undefined'.[179] And so it was that Zionist hopes of taking over Transjordan were thwarted. Many Zionists realised that they had to come to terms with the reality that the presence of a pro-British Arab regime was, for Britain, a tactical advantage.

The creation of the kingdom of Transjordan caused a significant split in the Zionist ranks. The breakaway group was led by Vladimir (Ze'ev) Jabotinsky. The 'loss' of the territory on the east bank of the Jordan was for him clear evidence that the Zionist leadership was too moderate. Mention has been made of Jabotinsky forming a breakaway 'Revisionist' group called, variously, the World Union of Zionist Revisionists or the Alliance of Revisionist–Zionists, with its military arm *Irgun Zvai Leomi* (National Military Organisation in the Land of Israel). This was to be an especially vicious terrorist body that carried out murderous attacks on the Arabs and the British, which dominated events in Palestine during the 1930s and 1940s. In 1936 Jabotinsky was the author of an 'evacuation plan' to move 1.5 million Jews from Europe to Palestine, which was supported by the Polish government but forbidden by the British, and which was, in any event, stopped by the onset of the war.

There are those who claimed that Jabotinsky was 'liberal'. This is based on statements that he made to a British parliamentary group in July 1937, but here he was anxious to deny the Peel Report's description of him as an extremist:

> But at least I never dreamt of demanding the Arab inhabitants of the Jewish state to emigrate ... the notion of 'uprooting' masses of people is nothing but idle talk.[180]

What he should have said was that he 'dreamt' of little else: his actions towards the Arabs were to be murderous.

Jabotinsky was, it seems, very persuasive. He wrote to Churchill pleading for his support for the development of Jewish Palestine, arguing for massive immigration, insisting that a Jewish state would be no threat to the Arabs, and that such a state should include territory on both banks of the Jordan:

> Churchill was impressed by these arguments, and saw Jabotinsky again a few days later, for an hour in the House of Commons. Jabotinsky's points had made their mark. When the Commons debated the Peel Report on 21 July [1937], Churchill opposed any final commitment to partition.[181]

The mandate was eventually confirmed by the League of Nations on 24 July 1922. The second paragraph of the preamble made clear that the mandate was designed above all to implement the Balfour Declaration:

> The Mandatory should be responsible for putting into effect the declaration originally made on 2 November 1917 by the Government of His Britannic Majesty, and adopted by the said Powers, in favour of the establishment in Palestine of a national home for the Jewish people.

There has been recognition 'to the historical connection of the Jewish people with Palestine and to the grounds for reconstituting their national home in that country'. And so it can be seen that the effort by Curzon to obliterate the historical connection had been swept aside, and, further the use of 'reconstituting' fulfils another Zionist tactic, which was to allege that the 'home' was not new, but was a return. The detailed articles are replete with admonitions to ensure Jewish domination. Article 4 notes that: 'An appropriate Jewish agency shall be recognised as a public body for the purpose of advising and co-operating with the Administration of Palestine ... The Zionist Organisation, so long as its organisation and constitution are in the opinion of the Mandatory appropriate, shall be recognised as such agency.'

Article 6, after the usual consolation that the position 'of other sections of the population are not prejudiced', states that the administration shall facilitate Jewish immigration under suitable conditions and shall encourage, in cooperation with the Jewish agency referred to in Article 4, close settlement by Jews on the land, including state lands and waste lands not required for public purposes. Article 7 dealt with nationality. There should be a law which would 'facilitate the acquisition of Palestinian citizenship by Jews who take their permanent residence in Palestine'. Article 11 deals with 'development':

> The Administration may arrange with the Jewish agency mentioned in Article 4 to construct or operate, upon fair and equitable terms, any public works, services and utilities, and to develop any of the natural resources of the country, in so far as these matters are not directly undertaken by the Administration.

There should be 'a reasonable rate of interest' on any capital used for these purposes. Hebrew takes its place as one of the official languages and 'the holy days of the respective communities' are instituted as 'legal days of rest' (Articles 22 and 23). One somewhat mysterious article announces that the provisions set out do not include 'the territories lying between the Jordan and the eastern boundary of Palestine as ultimately determined'.

This can only refer to the Zionist ambition to include land east of the Jordan in the new Zionist state. The word Arab does not occur in the mandate. The Arabs are described instead as 'non-Jewish communities', and we have seen how loaded that term became and how much it was resented. The Palestinian Arabs must have been amazed that such a document could have been formulated without any consultation with them. Throughout the document there is no sign of their interests, ambitions, or indeed their place in the new Palestine. They were expected to be satisfied with admonitions that there should be 'free exercise of all forms of worship', and that there should be no discrimination 'on the grounds of race, religion or language' (Article 15).

Even before its confirmation, in June 1922 Lord Islington introduced a motion in the House of Lords that the Palestine Mandate was 'inacceptable [sic] to this House' because it was 'opposed to the sentiments and wishes of the great majority of the people of Palestine'. He went on to warn that the Rutenberg scheme (for the electrification of Palestine) would invest the Jewish minority with wide powers over the Arab majority. Lord Islington went on to declare, 'Zionism runs counter to the whole human psychology of the age'.[182] Other peers agreed. Lord Sydenham said:

> We have dumped down 25,000 promiscuous people on the shores of Palestine ... some of them Bolsheviks ... [it] will undoubtedly, in time, transfer the control of the Holy Land to New York, Berlin, Frankfurt and other places.[183]

During this debate in the House of Lords in July 1922 there was concern expressed again about the appointment of a Jew to be high commissioner in Palestine. The archbishop of Canterbury attended, with a very anxious hope for 'elucidation on the subject' of Zionism and a Jewish home.[184] Lord Sheffield gave an answer in respect of 'national home':

> [It] might be interpreted in a harmless way, but it has also been interpreted as giving priority to a small minority of Jews over the mass of the people of Palestine. It is idle to propose that preference should be given to one-tenth who have gone to the country only lately over the nine-tenths who have been there from father to son, for generations. The Government was 'trying to smooth the way so that when things ripen the Jews can step in and take possession of their "Promised Land". That would be a thoroughly vicious principle'.[185]

This view of the Zionist cause was by no means uncommon in these elevated circles. In June 1923 this feeling was summed up, with undertones of impatience, by no less a person than the colonial secretary, the duke of Devonshire, in the House of Lords:

> Again and again it has been stated that the intention from the beginning has been to make a National Home for the Jews, but every provision has been made to prevent it from becoming in any sense a Jewish State or a State under Jewish domination.[186]

The Lords' vote was against the mandate plan with sixty voting against the Balfour Declaration and twenty-nine for.[187]

Churchill realised that this vote could end the 'Jewish Homeland', and that he would have to negate the Lords' vote in the Commons. A debate began on 4 July 1922, and once again Churchill had to counter the dominant opinion that the Arabs were being robbed of their land. A particular focus was on Pinhas Rutenberg. Rutenberg's activities provoked a crisis for Churchill and the Zionists.

Churchill had 'favoured' Rutenberg's scheme to develop electricity for Palestine in 1922. Opponents said that his 'concessions contracts had never been submitted to Parliament', and the scheme was in any case, 'grandiose but impracticable'. Arabs who had 'sought concessions' had 'been turned away'.[188] Churchill again said that Britain had pledged support to the Jews in return for their support in the war effort. Many MPs, he said, seemed to have changed their minds. 'In the crisis and heat of war' some had supported the Jews, but now 'when all is cold and prosaic' they did not. He seems to have forgotten that promises had been made to the Arabs if *they* supported the Allied war effort. The Commons overturned the Lords' vote.

Another downward step for the Palestinians was the publication, in 1922, of what has come to be known as the Churchill White Paper. It is explained in the preamble that the paper was written 'after consultation with the High Commissioner for Palestine'. Huneidi would claim that consultation is an overstatement: 'Samuel also drafted the first and official and written interpretation of the Balfour Declaration, the 1922 Statement of Policy, sometime known as the Churchill White Paper'.[189] The degree of consultation may be illustrated by a report made to John Shuckburgh by Samuel. The latter met an Arab delegation upon his arrival in May 1922.

> [He] 'derived the impression that they would not press their three demands' (abrogation of the Balfour Declaration, representative government and control over immigration).[190]

It is difficult to know which is the more likely or unlikely: whether Samuel was lying, or whether Shuckburgh could possibly believe that the Arabs had retreated from the very purpose of their visit.

The White Paper was also the result of the correspondence which took place between the secretary of state 'and a delegation from the Moslem Christian Society of Palestine, which has been for some time in England, and it states the further conclusions which have since been reached'.[191] It may be noted that it is not specified who agreed to these conclusions, and also the marked absence of any reference to acceptance of anything by the Palestinians. Arab 'apprehensions', it is claimed, 'are partly based upon exaggerated interpretations of the meaning of the Declaration'.

The general unease felt in parliamentary circles was somewhat assuaged by the publication of another claim. This stated that the government did not contemplate that Palestine as a whole should be converted into a Jewish national home. This was yet another blatant lie:

Phrases have been used such as that Palestine is to become 'as Jewish as England is English.' HMG regards any such expectation as impracticable and have no such aim in view. Nor have they at any time contemplated, as appears to be feared by the Arab Delegation, the disappearance or the subordination of the Arabic population, language or culture in Palestine.

As 'evidence' that this was consonant with Zionist policy, it is pointed out that the Zionist Congress in September 1921 passed a resolution which expressed 'the determination of the Jewish people to live with the Arab people on terms of unity and mutual respect, and together with them to make the common home into a flourishing community'.

The White Paper goes on to repeat another incessant defence: that Palestine 'as a whole' would not become a Jewish national home, 'but that such a Home should be founded in Palestine'. It deals too with the huge interference by the Zionist Commission. This organisation 'has not desired to possess, and does not possess, any share in the general administration of the country.' Rather, 'it may assist in the general development of the country, but does not entitle it to share in any degree in its Government.' Of course there must be Jewish immigration, but this must be controlled.

The promises specified in the McMahon Correspondence are dismissed in a sentence: 'The whole of Palestine west of the Jordan was thus excluded from Sir Henry McMahon's pledge.'

Another important clause was that which stated that 'persons who are politically undesirable be excluded from Palestine'. This reflected an especial difficulty with which Churchill wrestled: the exclusion of Bolsheviks. They always presented a dilemma for Churchill.

In the Churchill White Paper the political existence of Arabs is again ignored in a typically contradictory statement.

> [The Jewish National Homeland is] not the imposition of a Jewish nationality upon the inhabitants of Palestine as a whole, but the further development of the existing Jewish community, with the assistance of Jews in other parts of the world, in order that it may become a centre in which the Jewish people as a whole may take, on grounds of religion and race, an interest and a pride. But in order that this community should have the best prospect of free development and provide full opportunity for the Jewish people to display its capacities, it is essential that it should be known that it is in Palestine of right and not on sufferance ... The National Home... should be formally recognised to rest upon ancient historic connection.

This is a very forceful assertion of Zionist claims. This is not surprising when it is remembered that it was drafted by Herbert Samuel.

Shuckburgh's first hurdle in the attempt to keep the Zionist agenda in place was the presence in London during this time of an Arab delegation, which no doubt would wish to be heard. It was vital that this should not happen. And so he minuted that the delegation was 'in no sense an official body and to allow them to appear before a cabinet committee would be giving them too much importance'. In any case 'they represented "the extremist section of the Palestine Arabs, who constitute a majority perhaps, but certainly not the whole of the Arab population"'. Leaving aside the uncertain English of this sentence, Shuckburgh, as officials often did, slips in an untruth which certainly should be challenged: 'a majority *perhaps* [my emphasis]'. He also wields another familiar argument, that somehow these people are not 'real representatives'.

He had, though, to come up with some reason as to why the delegation should be deflected. After all, he believed the press was forever saying that his department was 'wholly under Zionist influence [and] accused of all kinds of Machiavellian designs to prevent any but the Zionist view on Palestinian questions reaching the Secretary of State or the Cabinet'.[192] His tactic was to respond to a wish by the delegation to give evidence 'that the committee were not hearing oral evidence and accordingly could not receive them'.[193] Sir Herbert Samuel was a sole exception from Palestine.

Shuckburgh also played another card. The Imperial General Staff was of the opinion that Palestine was of little strategic value to Britain. It may be imagined how dangerous this view was to Zionist ambition. Shuckburgh asked Meinertzhagen, in his role as military adviser, to prepare a report. This he did, listing all the reasons why Palestine was, in fact, vital. The IGS remained unimpressed, but Shuckburgh still officially, and continuously, stressed the danger of another power replacing Britain in Palestine.[194]

Weizmann went to see several influential people, notably of course Shuckburgh, who described to the colonial secretary Weizmann's 'great state of agitation' over the prospect of 'fresh concessions to the Arabs'.[195] It is to be wondered what the concessions were which had already been made. If this were to happen it would 'further whittle down the Balfour Declaration and the privileges of the Jews in Palestine'. Further it would kill 'Zionist activity in Palestine' and he, Weizmann, would feel obliged to resign.[196]

On 28 July 1923 Weizmann wrote to the colonial secretary, and referred to what he called 'an anti-Zionist petition'. This he said was full of the usual Arab propaganda ... I feel we have now reached a very serious crisis, and once more I can only turn to you with the hearty request that you may possibly say something to the Prime Minister'.[197] What happened is obscure, but it is more than likely that Balfour would do as he was asked, and this, together with pressure from Samuel, seems to have somehow swayed the committee.[198] There was to be no change in policy. Samuel tried to discourage the Arabs from sending any delegation to London, pointing out that they would not have 'official' status. He wanted to persuade them to accept a 'Palestine Order in Council', but this would be based on the declaration. The legally representative Arab Executive Committee would certainly not agree to discuss this, and so Samuel proposed setting up a 'Consultative Committee'. After a couple of meetings this committee fizzled out.

Despite opposition, the 'Palestine Arab Delegation' arrived in London. It consisted of nine members, Muslim and Christian. The first meeting they had was with Churchill. It was a pointer as to the futility of any meeting at all. Discussion was halted by two obstacles. Churchill insisted that he had 'never promised self-government', and the Arabs wanted precision about the meaning of the term 'national home'. Always in the background was Shuckburgh. In his view the group had been told that they had no official status, and that 'there was little advantage in further round table discussions with the Arab delegation'.[199]

The officials were at a loss to know how to deal with the delegation, as an important official Eric Mills wrote:

> I send you a copy of the last letter received from the Arab Delegation. You see how hopeless it all is! Anyway it is our intention to send once more an argumentative reply in order to detain them in the country until the 'nervy' season in Palestine is over. After that we shall have nothing to do with them in all probability and may send them away.[200]

There were further meetings but they were fruitless.

In February 1922 Churchill told the delegation what was to be in the new constitution. They rejected it, principally because its central premise was the Balfour Declaration. But they had detailed objection as well: for example, to the clause which established Hebrew as an official language, and to the composition of the ruling group. This would consist of the commissioner, and ten official and twelve unofficial members. A person could hardly be regarded as being unduly suspicious, if concern was expressed that the weight of the official members, added to sympathisers among the unofficial, would mean that any contentious issue could be dismissed. The next step was the appointment of a committee by the new prime minister, Stanley Baldwin, in July 1923, which was 'charged with advising the government to enable it to make a "prompt and final decision"' on Palestine.

There was still resistance to the enormous pressure exerted by the Zionists, nor was the indifference about events in Palestine universal. The committee received a petition from no fewer than 110 Conservative MPs demanding that the 'definite PLEDGES' given to the Palestinian Arabs be fulfilled and that the 'whole population of Palestine with its 93 per cent Arabs should be consulted, and a form of government agreed upon in harmony with their wishes'.[201]

Ostensibly, such a demand might be received sympathetically. The committee chairman was the colonial secretary, the duke of Devonshire, who was more balanced in his appraisal than his predecessor Churchill had been, and indeed, as has been noted, had spoken out against Zionist ambitions in the House of Lords. Lord Curzon, also on the committee, was a notable defender of the Arabs. It was to prove the case that, as often happens in British politics, civil servants proved adept at swaying process and outcome.

The report entitled 'The Future of Palestine' was submitted on 27 July 1923. It noted that:

> There are some of our number who think that the Declaration was both unnecessary and unwise, and who hold that our subsequent troubles have sprung in the main from its adoption ... But that was nearly six years ago.

The report went on to say that because of the declaration, 'Zionist cooperation in the development of Palestine has been freely given':

> Nevertheless, the alternative of a complete reversal of the policy hitherto pursued is one that, whatever the price that might have to be paid for it, we have not dogmatically refused to consider.[202]

Although 'it is difficult to blame those who ... argue that the entire Mandate is built on the fallacy of attempting to reconcile the irreconcilable', it would seem that no government could 'extricate itself without a substantial sacrifice of consistency and self-respect, if not honour'.[203]

The report is riddled with statements which any Arab delegation could have demolished, given the chance. The observation was true that 'our subsequent troubles' sprang from the declaration, as would future 'troubles', and in any case many vital changes were made in policy after much longer than six years. Quite what 'blame' is to be attached to those who saw the two sides as irreconcilable is not clear. The notion of generous Zionists helping in the development of Palestine can only be described as laughable. And if British sense of honour is to be the criterion for such momentous decisions, then the position was indeed hopeless. But, in a secret cabinet meeting on 31 July 1923, the report was accepted, with some caveats. The Jewish Agency and the Arab Agency should have 'an identical position with regard to immigration':

> Efforts should be made to induce the supporters in this country of the Arab Nationalists in Palestine to use the influence with the latter to secure their cooperation in the Government's policy.

This was the most pious of hopes.

The report not only marked the end of any prospect of a reversal of the Balfour Declaration, it was a clear indication that the opinions of Palestinian Arabs would be of no account. The overturning of the Lords' vote and the publication of the White Paper by Churchill, led to the inescapable conclusion that there was now no point whatever in any Arab delegation staying in Britain. The members returned home.

There were many indicators and warnings of trouble looming in Palestine. Brigadier-General Clayton, chief political officer of the Egyptian Expeditionary Force, advised in March 1919 that:

> Anti-Zionist propaganda has increased very considerably in Palestine lately ... there are considerable grounds for belief that anti-Jewish riots are being prepared in Jerusalem, Jaffa and elsewhere.[204]

The ever-vigilant Weizmann, confronted with such views, replied, as reported by Clayton, with a typical bizarre opinion, but one expressed with confidence:

> It does not appear to be realised that Arab national aspirations count for little in Palestine. The non-Jewish population is concerned not with national aspirations but with the maintenance in Palestine itself of a position which it considers is threatened by the advance of Zionism.[205]

A new chief administrator, Major-General H. D. Watson, reported in August 1919 that:

> The antagonism to Zionism of the majority of the population is deeply rooted—it is fast leading to hatred of the British—and will result, if the Zionist programme is forced upon them, in an outbreak of a very serious character necessitating the employment of a much larger number of troops than at present located in the territory.[206]

Many concerned British politicians were never very happy about the declaration, or the potential dangers in the mandate. Lord Derby wrote to Churchill in December 1920 expressing his concern about relations with France, but mainly because 'we are going to create a Zionist State composed of every Bolshevik Jew who will come there from the middle of Europe'.[207] He clearly did not agree with Churchill that a Jewish state would be a bulwark against Bolshevism.

Behind these developments was the phenomenal piece of luck for the Zionists: the fortuitous appointment of Churchill as colonial secretary. Although he held the post for a relatively short period (from February 1921 to November 1922), it was a critical time and he was able to make and advance key decisions. Weizmann seized his opportunity and made a number of highly advantageous suggestions. One was suggesting a person to be appointed chief administrator of Palestine. This piece of insolence was resented by Allenby who wrote that Palestine was 'under a purely military administration. Therefore, the appointment of Chief Administrator is entirely the concern of the War Office; and not one in which the Executive of the Zionist Organisation should have any voice. This does not seem to be quite clear to Dr Weizmann.'[208]

Despite Allenby's powerful position and personality, Churchill's loyalty remained intact. General Wyndham Deedes was appointed; he was Weizmann's nominee, 'and proved sympathetic to the Zionist position'.[209]

Another suggestion was that the Zionists should 'have freedom to send to Palestine a variety of experts to make a general investigation of the country and to prepare plans, so that 'when the political adjustments in Paris have been made, the Jewish people can proceed, without loss of time, with the task of reconstituting Palestine as their National Home'.[210] This would come to fruition with the appointment of a Zionist Commission.

Churchill was indefatigable, relentlessly extolling the singular contribution of Jews to culture:

> We owe to the Jews in the Christian revelation, a system of ethics which, even if it were entirely separated from the supernatural, would be incomparably the most precious possession of mankind, worth in fact the fruits of all other wisdom and learning put together. On that system and by that faith there has been built out of the wreck of the Roman Empire the whole of our existing civilisation.[211]

He rarely had reservations. Although he once pointed out to Lloyd George in 1918 when forming a cabinet: 'There is a point about Jews which occurs to me—you must not have too many of them.'[212] This was only because the wartime coalition would only succeed if the Tories supported it, and they would object to Jews getting preference.

There was, though, one potential benefit from the visit of the Arab delegation. They drew the attention of the public to the plight of the Arabs, reflected in press articles. The *Morning Post* reported that Samuel had been asked how he could justify the mass immigration of Jews. His reply was that 'if the self-determination argument were pushed to the extreme it would have prevented the colonisation of America and Australia'. The newspaper heading was: 'Crushing out the Arabs'.[213]

The visit also encouraged important figures to express sympathy. Lord Sydenham was one. He was a leading anti-Zionist in the House of Lords, and he said that the declaration was 'loaded with dynamite', and that the injustice to the Arabs 'was unprecedented in history'.[214] It is, of course, difficult to know what 'the public' thought, but Wyndham Deedes, chief secretary to Samuel, whose opinion must be respected, noted as early as August 1921 that 'one of the main objects of the Delegation was to win the sympathy of the British public and this sympathy is, it is believed, being won'.[215]

Churchill's perception was exactly the same. When he reversed the Lords' motion in which they rejected the declaration, he wrote to Samuel that it was now 'clear that the country supports His Majesty's Government in their Palestine policy'.[216]

Arab political activity was scoffed at by their opponents at the time and in the evaluative accounts by Jewish historians up to the present day. At the time of the development of systematic Arab political organisation 'some Zionists tried to discredit Arab resistance to their goals as an expression of anti-Semitism that they claimed was rooted in Islam itself.'

> Arab resistance was thus depoliticised, transposed onto a racist plane tied to religion, and robbed of moral legitimacy. However the Zionist interpretation (anti-Zionism equals anti Judaism equals anti-Semitism) misses the point: It is itself politically motivated and misses the point.[217]

We will see that, during the course of this narrative, this allegation is a persistent explanation for the expression of any doubts about Zionism, or its physical presence in the form of the state of Israel. The dismissal of any claim to seriousness in Arab political activity is well represented in the writing of Efraim Karsh. In his apologia for the Zionist cause he asks how could the Arabs be interested in politics when at the time of the declaration 'the growing Jewish presence in Palestine encountered no nationwide opposition'?[218] He quotes a British report of 1918 as noting that 'the Muslim population of Judea took little or no interest in the Arab national movement'.[219] If ever this had been the case, the 1930s saw the growth of organised political parties. Karsh describes these, but at the same time discredits them. The creation of the new parties was how 'the rival Arab factions and clans vied for political dominance'.[220] He neglects to point out that not only do politicians habitually 'vie', but the Zionists were as divided as the Arabs. This is notably expressed in the murderous split between the 'Revisionists' and the mainstream party. His remarkable conclusion is that:

> Had the vast majority of Palestinian Arabs been left to their own devices they would most probably have been content to get on with their lives and take advantage of the opportunities afforded by the growing Jewish presence in the country.[221]

As proof of the insincerity of Arab political leaders, Karsh claims that they were more interested in selling land to Jews than political progress, and sets out figures to prove it.[222]

In a parliamentary defence of his policy on 9 March 1922, Churchill said nothing new. He reiterated what he had said many times and was to say many times again. The Arab demand for majority government had to be rejected because he had to carry out government 'pledges'. He deflected any serious discussion about Jewish immigration by talking about excluding 'Bolshevist riffraff', and what good quality the immigrants would assuredly be. They were helped by the almost million pounds that the Zionist Association was spending in Palestine each year.

In the early years of the mandate, Zionist progress had been swift. Apart from widespread expressions of sympathy for the injustice of losing their land, the Palestinian Arabs had gained nothing, and were set to lose everything.

4

ESCALATION

'The Mandate ... itself had lighted the fire'[1]

The ambition to found a Jewish state in Palestine would not be resisted, and this was due in large measure to the support of powerful politicians, most especially Winston Churchill. We shall go on to see that he supported the cause of the Jews and defended them against every attack. In 1920 he wrote:

> If, as may well happen, there should be created in our own lifetime by the banks of the Jordan a Jewish State under the protection of the British Crown, which might comprise three or four million Jews, an event would have occurred in the history of the world which would, from every point of view, be beneficial, and would be especially in harmony with the truest interests of the British Empire.[2]

Since the pressure exerted by Churchill was so crucial in support of the Zionists, at this point I will explore why he was so fanatical in that support.

As was the case in respect to so much of his behaviour, Churchill followed his father's allegiances and obligations. His father was noted for his friendship with leaders of the Jewish community, such as Nathaniel, 1st Baron Rothschild, the first Jewish member of the House of Lords. The closeness of this particular relationship is exemplified by the fact that Churchill omitted to point out in his biography of his father, the 'Government business that Lord Randolph had given Rothschild's bank and the £12,758 he (Randolph) owed it on his death'.[3] For his part, Winston Churchill was close friends with the same group of elite Jews as his father, and often stayed at their homes and went on holiday with them.[4]

Churchill also was involved in business dealings with them. Sir Ernest Cassel organised his literary earnings, secured him investments with the Japanese government, and bought him bonds in the Atchison, Topeka and Santa Fe Railway. Cassel also provided money for a trip to South Africa, furnished a library for him, and when he married gave him a generous sum of money—£500.[5] This is equivalent to approximately £72,000 in 2022.

Jewish businessmen knew of Churchill's considerable influence, and sometimes brought it to bear, at some risk to Churchill's reputation. In 1923, Churchill was not an MP. During that time he was asked by Sir Robert Waley Cohen 'to act as an intermediary with the government over the merging of two [oil] companies'.[6] A senior civil servant was 'very shy of it', but Churchill needed money, and so he discussed it with the prime minister, Stanley Baldwin. Churchill reported that 'I found him thoroughly in favour of the Oil Settlement on the lines proposed. Indeed he might have been Waley Cohen from the way he talked.'[7] Churchill was paid £5,000 for his intervention, a very large sum of money.[8] In November 1928 he announced that he would withdraw from work on the merger, since he wanted to stand for parliament.[9]

Much later in his life, in late 1952, Churchill became involved in a Canadian scheme to generate electricity. He 'turned to the Rothschild bank in the City of London. [They] undertook to organise the financing of the scheme, establishing Brinco as the holding company.' At the time Churchill was prime minister, so he waited until he retired three years later before he bought shares.[10]

Churchill was often suspected of being in financial thrall to rich Jewish businessmen. Indeed he was once the centre of a libel case, famous at the time, not least because one of the people involved was Lord Alfred Douglas, the lover of Oscar Wilde. Douglas alleged that Jewish conspirators had caused the government to declare that the 1916 Battle of Jutland had been a disaster. British stock then fell. These 'conspirators' bought the depressed stock, and Churchill changed the official version of the outcome of the battle. The stock rose and fortunes were made, Churchill having been paid off.

The *Morning Post* described these allegations as 'vile insults against the Jews'.[11] Douglas sued the newspaper in July 1923, and won, but was awarded the classic, contemptuous amount of a farthing. He then published the allegations in a pamphlet, and the government brought a criminal libel action against him. He was found guilty, and sentenced to six months' imprisonment. Some would regard this as a just return for Douglas's responsibility in the ruining of Oscar Wilde.

Churchill also had very close links with individual Jews. A Hungarian Jew, Emery Reves, was his literary agent, and made a great deal of money for Churchill, as well as adding to his fame as a writer.[12] Another Hungarian Jew, Stefan Lorant, a publisher of popular magazines, played a critical part in publicising the case for Churchill's return to power at the end of the 1930s. Churchill also used his position to wield improper influence on behalf of Jews. In 1933 Albert Einstein asked him to help to bring Jewish scientists out of Germany. Churchill arranged for Frederick Lindemann to go to German universities to recruit such people. They were then given places in British universities. On another occasion, as chancellor of Bristol University, he asked the vice-chancellor to give a place in the medical school to a German Jewish student. Despite the manifest pressure of such a request, the vice-chancellor insisted the application was handled in the usual way. It was turned down.[13]

Other factors which helped support for the Zionists have been suggested. Once again Churchill was involved. As first lord of the Admiralty, he found there was a shortage of acetone, a critical component in the making of explosives. It so happened that the head of the Powder Department at the Admiralty was a Jew, Sir Frederic Nathan. He arranged for Churchill to meet Chaim Weizmann. From time to time it is claimed that in some way the Zionist cause was given validity by the contribution Weizmann made to the war effort by his success in mass producing acetone.

Another source of support was the effect of the public education in the Old Testament, which was universal in Britain. It is significant that both Lloyd George and Balfour brought to the question of Palestine the traditions and prejudices of the Christian, which in turn derived from Victorian immersion in the Bible. They were the heirs of the Christian Zionist tradition described earlier. Lloyd George expressed the lasting effect of the interminable exposure to the Bible, which was the usual experience of Welsh people of his generation:

> I was taught far more about the history of the Jews than about the history of my own people ... we were thoroughly versed in the history of the Hebrews. We used to recite great passages from the Prophets and the Psalms ... that great literature which will echo to the very last days of this old world.

Lloyd George's motives have also been attributed to his nationalism, with its sympathy for narrow nationalistic feeling. It has been said that Lloyd George was 'a product and a prophet' of Welsh nationalism.[14] Lloyd George may have expressed pride in his Welsh heritage (he was actually born in England), but it is hard to find any major expression of that nationalism in his political action in respect of Wales.

Balfour had in common with Lloyd George, a deeply biblical education. His niece points out that this was because of 'the early Scottish training which had woven the Old Testament story into the texture of his mind'.[15] Yet another crucial supporter of Zionism was Jan Smuts, a member of the war cabinet and the future long-serving prime minister of South Africa. As he himself admitted, his attitude owed a good deal to the religious traditions which so dominated Boer thinking, and which was to prove such a source of cruelty for the black population in the twentieth century:

> The Old Testament, the most wonderful literature ever thought out by the brain of man—the Old Testament has been the very marrow of Dutch culture here in South Africa. I am sure that there are thousands, tens of thousands, of Dutch

people in this country who know the Old Testament better than many Jews themselves.¹⁶

Such feelings overcame the equally strong traditions of Christian antisemitism, although there would be plenty of evidence of the latter in the debates which lay ahead.

British officials, too, were heavily influenced by their biblical education. In the case of Mark Sykes, 'the strong influence of the Bible on his world-view was critical for his unquestionable acceptance of the tenets of Zionist thought and his ever-growing embrace of Zionism as a vibrant national movement which had grown out of the deep tradition, sacred literature and mythologies of an ancient nation longing for restoration.'¹⁷

And where were the Arabs in this? Their fears about the future were kept at bay because the British government kept assuring them that they would be given independence. In this lie the British were supported by France. There was an Anglo–French Declaration of November 1918 addressed to the people of Syria and Iraq. Once again it assured them of the 'complete and definite emancipation of the peoples so long oppressed by the Turks, and the establishment of national Governments and administrations deriving their authority from the initiative and free choice of the indigenous populations'.¹⁸ Had the Arabs been more familiar with political nuance, they would have seen the danger in another phrase in the same declaration: that the West would help their ambitions which they would 'ensure by their support and adequate assistance'.

An important pillar of the argument for the 1918 Anglo–French Declaration was a deep-rooted belief, firmly held by the Victorians, that non-Caucasian peoples were inherently inferior. This, it was argued, must be true since non-Caucasians had submitted to imperial rule. They could never rule themselves, even though in the imperial age millions died attempting to prove otherwise. In respect of the Arabs, this belief in the West was held particularly firmly. In this viewpoint, T. E. Lawrence and other officers who had fought with the Arabs were exceptions.

I have quoted some of Mark Sykes' views of Arabs. Another British official, W. G. A. Ormsby-Gore, a member of parliament and an enthusiastic Zionist, expressed typical imperialist colonialist views when he made a fatuous distinction that there are different kinds of Arabs: some 'good', some 'bad'. Colonial officers and officials also divided 'natives' into 'loyal' and 'disloyal'. Ormsby-Gore wrote in August 1918 that the Arabs who supported Prince Feisal 'contained real Arabs who were real men ... The west of the Jordan the people were not Arabs, but only Arabic-speaking'. As for 'the Syrian "Intelligentzia" [sic], lawyers and traders, [they] constituted the most difficult and thorny problem of the Near East. They had no civilisation of their own, and they had absorbed all the vices of the Levant.'¹⁹ John Shuckburgh, a key civil servant, whose sympathies were entirely with the Zionists, and who had no first-hand experience of Palestine, joined in the amateur anthropological judgement. The Palestinian Arabs, he said, 'have no real sympathy with their fellow Arabs to the east and to the South. The majority of them, at any rate in the large towns and on the Mediterranean coast, are not Arabs at all.'[20]

The Peel Report challenged the myth. Palestine, 'still overwhelming[ly] Arab in character [before 1914], eked out a precarious existence mainly in the hills ... Eastwards beyond Jordan nothing remains of the Greek cities of classical times save one or two groups of deserted ruins.'[21]

This 'empty land' myth was an important part of Zionist propaganda from the beginning:

> Many First Aliya immigrants believed they were coming to a desolate, empty land and were surprised to see so many Arabs about. After all, they were returning to their Promised Land; no one else had spoken of anyone else being there.[22]

Even if there were people there, the land, according to the Zionist narrative, had been abandoned:

> [It] has become a wasteland, 'innumerable thorns and thistles cover the beautiful valleys'. The gardens and forests had vanished, the mountain slopes were lifeless. All this had occurred because it was a land without a nation. With the return of its people, its natural treasures would bloom again.[23]

This picture of inferiority is perpetuated by modern writers too. At one period the Egyptian government showed some sympathy for Zionism by their contempt for Palestinian Arabs:

> The Egyptians looked down on the rest of the Arabs, using the term 'Arab' in a derogatory fashion to denote a shiftless and uncultured nomad, someone to be viewed with contempt by a people with a millenarian tradition of settled cultivation.[24]

Churchill's disdain for the Arabs was constant. A Captain Brunton in May 1921 wrote that Churchill 'treated the Arab demands like those of negligible opposition to be put off by a few political phrases and treated like children'.[25] Churchill made clear on many occasions his contempt for Arabs:

> Left to themselves, the Arabs of Palestine would not in a thousand years have taken effective steps towards the irrigation and electrification of Palestine. They would have been quite content to dwell—a handful of philosophic people—in wasted sun-drenched plains, letting the waters of the Jordan flow unbridled and unharnessed into the Dead Sea.[26]

It was not only Arabs Churchill disliked. He hated Muslims as much as he liked Jews: 'No stronger retrograde force exists in the world far from being moribund, Mohammedanism is a militant and proselytising faith'.[27]

The supposed racial and social inferiority of the Arabs was to become a dominant theme everywhere, not least in Britain, in the battle to persuade governments to support the cause for a return to Palestine. The Jews were amongst the keenest propagandists of the portrayal of Arabs as 'backward', thus associating them with the classic colonialist view of inferiority. It was not often that Weizmann showed much understanding of Western traditions and beliefs, but in the case of the Arabs, he echoed Western prejudices. On 30 May 1918 he wrote to Balfour.[28] *The* problem, it seemed to him, was the Arabs:

> The Arabs, who are superficially clever and quick-witted, worship one thing, and one thing only—power and success. The British Authorities ... knowing as they do the treacherous nature of the Arab, they have to watch carefully and constantly that nothing should happen which might give the Arabs the slightest grievance or cause of complaint ... He screams as often as he can and blackmails as much as he can ... The first scream was heard when your Declaration was announced. All sorts of misinterpretations and misconceptions were put on the declaration. The English, they said, are going to hand over the poor Arabs to the wealthy Jews, who are all waiting in the wake of General Allenby's army, ready to swoop down like vultures on an easy prey and oust everybody from the land.[29]

The Arabs, he wrote in the same letter, could never make a success of Palestine:

> The fellah is at least four centuries behind the times, and the effendi (who, by the way, is the real gainer from the present system) is dishonest, uneducated, greedy, and as unpatriotic as he is inefficient.

He wrote of the treacherous and blackmailing nature of the Arab, whose 'Oriental mind' is full of 'subtleties and subterfuges', compared with the 'fair and clean-minded English official'.[30] Clearly Weizmann was hoping to associate Jews with these alleged virtues of the 'English official'. Fortunately for the Jews, Balfour's political character was a mixture of indifference and pragmatism, and there is no evidence that these comments annoyed him.

Weizmann was merely reflecting what other Zionists wished the West to believe about the state of Palestine and the responsibility for it. In 1935, after a visit to Palestine, a Zionist writer concluded that 'since the expulsion of this particular people, [the Jews] it is barren, deserted, and miserable, and only at the hands of this particular people.'

The Jews, like the colonialists, were contemptuous of the Arabs. The early Jewish settlers, many of whom were from semi-colonialist backgrounds, saw 'innocuous, colourful, and generous if primitive desert dwellers: "Abroad we used to believe that the Arabs are a wild desert people akin to a mule, who do not see or understand what is going on around them".[31]

It was not only immigrants who held such beliefs. Even a writer as sophisticated as Arthur Koestler indulged in such fantasies. He believed the Jews did better during the Arab Revolt (1936-39) because 'modern European Jews had a greater capacity for initiative, improvisation and coordinated action than their primitive adversaries'.[32] None of this mattered because 'the presence of the Arabs was a mere accident like the presence of some forgotten pieces of furniture in a house'.[33] If and when such derogatory remarks were made about the Jews, 'antisemitism' was the response. In any case, it was widely proclaimed there were few Arabs because 'Palestine in 1917 was an under-populated area of deserts and swamps'.[34]

Others drew a more humane picture. An early Jewish settler, Moshe Smilansky, 'recounted seeing fellah women weeping and lamenting the lands and homes they had lost, without compensation. Jewish settlers had chased them off with sticks, and then taken pride in doing so, "with shocking cynicism", he wrote.'[35]

This persistent portrayal of the Arabs as degenerate was a parody. As Kramer points out, there was an Arab elite who 'tended to see things differently, viewing themselves as aristocrats in their own society.'

> Their genealogy could easily match that of most British Colonial officials ... [They] were wealthy, if not actually rich. They were educated and, unlike most of the British residents in Jerusalem, were fluent in four or five languages, even if English was often not one of them. They were widely travelled. In short, they were cosmopolitans.[36]

The British MP Richard Crossman described an Arab society far removed from the primitive picture paraded by Jewish writers:

> It is easy to see why the British prefer the Arab upper class to the Jews ... This Arab intelligentsia has a French culture, amusing, civilised, tragic and gay. Compared with them the Jews seem tense, *bourgeois*, central European.[37]

Unusually for a British official, Brigadier Sir Gilbert Clayton, chief political officer with the Egyptian Expeditionary Force, disagreed with claims that the Arabs were degenerate. Such statements, he wrote, are not fair 'as not only are they worthy representatives of their class, but fear and dislike of Zionism has become general throughout all classes'. This 'has been greatly intensified by publication in Zionist journals and utterances of leading Zionists of a far reaching programme greatly in advance of that foreshadowed by Dr Weizmann in his discussions with Christians and Moslems here'.[38] Colonel Richard Meinertzhagen, in a briefing for Curzon in 1920, recognised this:

> The knowledge that the eventual dispossession of Arabs by Jews in Palestine is inevitable during the course of time, and that Jewish immigration spells an eventual Jewish state not only in Palestine but in Syria, very naturally frightens the Arab... It is not doubted that Zionism will and must succeed to the benefit of Palestine and all its inhabitants ... The Arabs will be compelled under Zionism to enjoy increased prosperity and security, though they will lose that delightful atmosphere of idle possession and an undeveloped wilderness.[39]

The Arabs were not as ignorant nor as stupid as the Zionists and their supporters wished people to believe. At the beginning of the twentieth century Arabic newspapers demonstrated that they knew what the Zionists were up to, and there were cultivated people who had access to the increasingly available printed material, which they discussed.

Filastin (sometimes spelt *Falastin*) was an important newspaper, so much so that Einstein wrote a letter to it on 28 January 1930, in which he pleaded for harmony between the communities. In June 1921 it published a translation of a speech by Samuel which did nothing to remove Arab fears about a takeover. The article analysed the policy of the Balfour Declaration and the subsequent deterioration of the political situation. It 'ridiculed Samuel's comment that the Arabic translation might not have conveyed the true meaning of the declaration and commented: perhaps the Arabs had missed the real meaning, but had Lord Sydenham, and all the other anti-Zionist British politicians who also condemned the Balfour Declaration also misunderstood the meaning?'[40]

In any case, what the Arabs thought seems not to have mattered. At a meeting of the Eastern Committee on 24 April 1918, chaired by Lord Curzon, Sir Percy Cox echoed a common assumption: 'nothing in the nature of a plebiscite could be arranged. It was quite unsuited to Arab thought and could excite the liveliest misgivings'.[41] Balfour expressed agreement, saying that 'surely' President Wilson 'did not mean to apply his formula [regarding the self-determination of peoples] outside Europe'.[42] Balfour followed this with an additional reason for denying the Arabs independence, especially in Palestine: 'Zionism, be it right or wrong, good or bad, is of far profounder import than the desires and prejudices of the 700,000 Arabs who now inhabit that ancient land.'[43] The use of the words 'now inhabit' implies that they have just arrived, and are there for the moment only. The use of the pejorative word 'prejudices' may also be noted.

A further factor in the Jews' favour was the slight, or total lack of interest in the future of Arabs in general, even though the exploits of T. E. Lawrence had focused on them, especially their role in the defeat of the Turks. Lawrence, it should be emphasised, wrote that although the Sykes–Picot Agreement had set out plans for independent Arab states, 'neither Sykes nor Picot had believed the thing really possible, but I knew that it was, and believed that after it the vigour of the Arab Movement would prevent the creation—by us or others—in Western Asia of unduly "colonial" schemes of exploitation.'[44]

Soldiers like Lawrence continued to express serious concern about British support for Zionism, not only because they were conscious of the role played by Arab fighters in the First World War, but because they were experiencing at first hand the way in which the Zionist Commission, which was formed in 1918, was gaining power. It was taking control, and then lying about it. This concern was dismissed by the Zionist lobby as naked antisemitism. Churchill thought so too, and advocated the dismissal of those who criticised British policy.

Smuts was an inveterate apologist for the declaration. In 1926, engaging in Churchillian hyperbole, he informed a group of Zionists that the declaration was 'one of the great causes, and one of the principal achievements of the Great War'.[45] His attitude also contained a belief, which, while negative, added to the case for supporting the Zionists. A Jewish journalist, Nathan Levi reported in 1917 that while Smuts 'wanted to see Palestine peopled with Jews ... he also wishes to prevent undue immigration into South Africa by making other countries fit to live in'.[46]

This was a recurring theme of the supporters: the desire to get rid of Jews. As Claude Montefiore, a prominent anti-Zionist said in October 1917, 'it is very significant that anti-Semites are always sympathetic to Zionism'.[47] Balfour saw the same 'benefit' in reducing the number of Jews in host societies.

> [It] will do a great spiritual and material work for the Jews, but not for them alone. For, as I read its meaning, it is, among other things, a serious endeavour to mitigate the age-long miseries created for Western civilisation by the presence in its midst of a Body which it too long regarded as alien and even hostile, but which it was equally unable to expel or to absorb.[48]

This is much nearer to the tone he used in the earlier debates about restricting Jewish immigration. As prime minister in 1905, when the Aliens Bill was being debated, Balfour's contribution had been to say:

> It would not be to the advantage of the civilisation of this country that there should be an immense body of persons, who, however patriotic ... remained a people apart, and not merely held a religion differing from the vast majority of their fellow-countrymen, but only inter-married among themselves.[49]

Smuts and Balfour were not the only national figures who saw settlement in Palestine as a solution to the reduction of their Jewish population. In 1919 Balfour had a conversation with Louis Brandeis, an associate justice on the Supreme Court of the United States. Brandeis, of Jewish birth himself, was reported to have said that, 'as an American ... confronted with the disposition of the vast number of Jews, particularly Russian Jews, that were pouring into the United States year by year … Zionism was the answer'.[50] This was a notion shared by the Zionists. Herzl believed that a Jewish homeland would 'enable them [the Great Powers] to be rid of the Jews within their borders: and, at the same time, offer a useful way of exploiting Jewish power (or potential power), wealth and skills'.

There arose another stumbling block. In the debates of the time the Revolution in Russia was paramount, and this posed a broad political problem. Where were Jewish loyalties when it came to Bolshevism and the Russian Revolution? The fear that the Revolution might spread was very real at the very time that discussion about the future of Palestine was going on. In 1918, for example, the British National Union of Police and Prison Officers called a strike. Their committee met Lloyd George, whose verdict was that the country 'was nearer to Bolshevism that day than at any time since'.[51]

The Bolshevik movement was loathed by Churchill. He explained Bolshevism as 'a worldwide conspiracy for the overthrow of civilisation' but admitted that it contained 'terrorist Jews'.[52] He was really muddled about Jews and Bolshevism. 'In view of prominent part taken by Jews in Red Terror and the regime, there is special danger of Jewish pogroms and this danger must be combated strongly.'[53] He was writing as secretary of state for war about British support for the Whites, the reactionary forces opposing Bolshevism. In 1919 he wrote that British aid would help in 'mitigating the anti-Semitism which the crimes of the Jewish Commissaries have so fearfully excited'.[54] The Jews continued to be persecuted, and Churchill wrote to Lloyd George that there was 'a very bitter feeling throughout Russia against the Jews, who are regarded as being the main instigators of the ruin of the Empire, and who, certainly have played a leading part in Bolshevik atrocities.'[55] On at least one occasion in a speech he said that Bolshevism was a 'Jewish movement'.[56]

The 'Reds' committed murders of Jews, but the White Russians committed antisemitic pogroms in greater numbers, and Churchill's way of coping with this was to make the military aid contingent upon Anton Denikin (a general in the Imperial Russian Army) 'preventing by every possible means the ill-treatment of the innocent Jewish population'.[57] This was a tall order since the Russian opponents of the revolution were convinced that it was inspired by Jews. Denikin did not stop the massacres of Jews taking place under his command.

In an article in the *Illustrated Sunday Herald* entitled 'Zionism versus Bolshevism', Churchill sought to show that the Bolsheviks were 'repudiated vehemently by the great mass of the Jewish race'. He explained Bolshevism as 'a sinister conspiracy … this worldwide conspiracy for the overthrow of civilisation.' He admitted to there being 'large numbers of Jews in the upper echelons of the Bolshevik movement', but these were 'terrorist Jews'. The Zionist cause could be used as a bulwark against Communism. This was important because—and here his enthusiasm became wild—

No thoughtful man can doubt the fact that they are beyond all question the most formidable and the most remarkable race which has ever appeared in the world ... We owe to the Jews a system of ethics, which, even if it were entirely separated from the supernatural, would be incomparably the most precious possession of mankind, worth in fact the fruits of all wisdom and learning put together.[58]

In the same article in the *Illustrated Sunday Herald* on 8 February 1920, Churchill tried to allege that the Balfour Declaration was now an integral part of British history: 'The statesmanship and historic sense of [Mr. Balfour's] Declarations ... have irrevocably decided the policy of Great Britain'.[59] It may be noted that 'Declarations' is in the plural to give added force, and that 'irrevocable' implies that the matter is finished.

On a later occasion Churchill again expressed his feelings about Bolshevism. He was angry when Samuel told him that the Arabs who had protested violently in 1921 'had been provoked by a hard core of Jewish Communists'. His response was typical:

[Samuel] should purge the Jewish Colonies and newcomers of Communist elements, and without hesitation or delay have all those who are guilty of subversive agitation expelled from the country.

But he was even more furious at Arab violence, used 'in the hope of frightening us out of *our Zionist policy* [my emphasis]'.[60] He even employed threats about what the Jews might do if they were upset:

This same astounding race may at the present time be in the actual process of producing another system of morals and philosophy, as malevolent as Christianity was benevolent, which, if not arrested, would shatter irretrievably all that Christianity has rendered possible.

By this, Gilbert says, he means Bolshevism. It was as if 'this mystic and mysterious race had been chosen for the supreme manifestations, both of the divine and the diabolical'.[61]

International and, for the most part, atheist Jews had taken 'the principal part' in the Cheka (the Bolshevik secret police). Indeed, the 'majority of the leading figures [in Bolshevism] are Jews... with the notable exception of Lenin'.[62]

Churchill saw the cause of Zionism and the establishment of a Jewish state as an antidote to Bolshevism. This would thwart Trotsky with his 'schemes of a world-wide communistic State under Jewish domination'.[63] The *Jewish Chronicle* was livid at Churchill's implication that there would be a 'world-wide communistic State under Jewish domination'.[64] This not only gave credence to a popular belief that the Jews controlled world affairs, but it was a criticism of Jews, and the *Chronicle* has never tolerated such criticism.

In a discussion in the Eastern Committee on 5 December 1918, Jan Smuts, as always spoke up for the Jews, and here he warned of the danger of upsetting them: 'It would affect Jewish *national* opinion, and *nationally* [my emphasis] they are a great people.' He was supported by General MacDonough, the director of military intelligence:

> I see a good many of the Zionists, and one suggested to me the day before yesterday that if the Jewish people did not get what they were asking for in Palestine we should have the whole of Jewry turning Bolsheviks and supporting Bolshevism in all the other countries as they have done in Russia.[65]

Lord Robert Cecil obviously thought this was such a fantastic idea that he joked, 'Yes, I can conceive the Rothschilds leading a Bolshevist mob!'[66]

The opposition from the anti-Zionist Jews to the Balfour Declaration was persistent before and after its announcement. One leading opponent was Edwin Samuel Montagu, a cabinet minister at the time. Having seen a draft of the declaration, he wrote a memorandum called 'The Anti-Semitism of the Present Government', which reiterated and summarised all the objections which Jews of his persuasion shared. He was unswerving in his beliefs that Palestine had nothing to do with the Jews, and that it was an unsuitable place for them to live. He believed that the establishment of a Jewish state would create an environment in which happily assimilated Jews would be regarded as aliens and told to go 'home'. Montagu went on to identify the emerging chronic problem of 'loyalty' when he said that Zionism could not be supported by a patriotic citizen of Britain.[67] In the war cabinet on 4 October 1917, he pointed out that in the Conjoint Committee, Anglo-Jewish support for Zionism was very slight—56 to 51 votes.[68] Nor was he happy about the fact that the Zionists were mainly foreigners. It was soon to be clear that he and other opponents were right in their predictions about what would happen.

Much of the opposition to the Zionist programme focused on a belief that the Jews would be better off improving their circumstances in the countries where they lived. Sir Philip Magnus, an influential Jewish activist and educator, thought that the idea of a 'home for the Jewish race both undesirable and inaccurate'. The president of the Anglo-Jewish Association observed that the emancipation and liberty of the Jewish race in the countries of the world were a thousand times more important than a 'home'. The chairman of the Jewish Board of Guardians rejected the implication that Jews had a separate identity from the country in which they live.[69] Prior's summary was that:

> The leadership of British Jewry, perceiving Zionism to be a threat to the well-being of British Jews, opposed it so strongly that it might prevent a British Declaration.[70]

The hope of Montagu that Jews could be assimilated into the wider society was overly optimistic. Experience has shown that assimilation means the loss of separate identity, something which most immigrant groups resist. Balfour himself recognised this resistance when he supported the attempt to prevent Jewish immigration during the debates about the Aliens Bill in 1905.

There was, in any case, opposition from non-Jews who did not believe in the cause. Despite the fact that there was tumult in the country, and the declaration seemed to be a short and certainly ambiguous statement, there were those who spotted that it was of the greatest significance. This included the distaste expressed by parliamentarians, including powerful ministers. Notable among these was Lord Curzon. He was lord president of the council, and a member of the war cabinet, and he wrote a memorandum 'The future of Palestine', dated 26 October 1917. Since the government was about to agree the Balfour Declaration almost at that moment, the memorandum infuriated the Zionists, especially Weizmann, who seemingly listed Curzon amongst 'our Jewish enemies'.[71]

In his memorandum, Curzon argued firmly against the intentions behind the declaration, listing a number of objections. These included the opinion that Palestine was unsuitable because it 'was barren and desolate... a less propitious seat for the future Jewish race could not be imagined ... Zionism was sentimental idealism, which would never be realised and [with which] His Majesty's Government should have nothing to do'.[72] Curzon wanted to avoid Jewish control of the country of Palestine, but this did not preclude Jewish immigration, or Jewish purchase of land. 'If this is Zionism, there is no reason why we should not all be Zionists.'[73] But Curzon was not sufficiently foolish to believe that this was the limit of Jewish ambition. Nor that it was simple. He wondered 'how it was proposed to get rid of the existing majority of Mussulman inhabitants and to introduce the Jews in their place?' Repatriation on a large scale he regarded as 'sentimental idealism, which would never be realised'.[74] Curzon was not to know the ruthlessness with which the foundling state of Israel would behave.

Curzon's question was a good one. How would you get rid of the existing majority? From the earliest days of Jewish settlements in the 1880s there were the glimmerings of a realisation by the Arabs of the danger their homeland faced, and the need to resist it. This took the form of an attack in March 1886 on the old Jewish settlement Petah Tikva, which had been founded in 1878. Such physical confrontation was accompanied by protests to the Ottoman government about Jewish immigration. But now, in the twentieth century, as Allenby and others had warned, 'we must prepare for outrages'.[75]

It would have been clear that failure to resist the Zionists would certainly result in 'outrages'. Nevertheless there proceeded what was the most bizarre process in twentieth-century politics, a process summed up by Arthur Koestler in a deservedly famous aphorism: 'one nation solemnly promised to a second nation the country of a third'.[76] He might have added that, in addition to this most curious of exercises, the nation who 'promised' did not even own the country it was handing over. Palestine was still part of the Ottoman empire, and in no sense would it *ever* belong to Britain. Koestler's use of the term 'second nation' might also be questioned since there was no second nation.

The commitment of the British government was reinforced by the overt duplicity of Balfour himself. At the same time as he was forcibly making the case for Zionism, he was writing:

> For in Palestine we do not propose even to go through the form of consulting the wishes of the present inhabitants of the country ... In short, so far as Palestine is concerned, the Powers have made no statement of fact which is not admittedly wrong, and no declaration of policy which, at least in the letter, they have not intended to violate.[77]

This is, of course, cynical, but it also shows once again that Balfour did not really care.

Allenby's prediction of 'outrages' was soon to be realised. It was perfectly evident that the declaration would be the cause, in a very short time, of the deaths of Arabs, Jews, and most pointless of all, of British soldiers and police officers.

There had been clashes between Jews and Arabs soon after the declaration. One, in particular, achieved some significance in Israeli history because a Jewish hero, Joseph Trumpeldor, was killed. This was in March 1920, at a Jewish farm called Tel Hai, near the Lebanese border. But it was the pilgrimage to Nebi Musa which was the scene of the first serious episode of fighting between Jews and Arabs after the end of Turkish rule.

On Sunday 4 April 1920, large numbers of Arabs had assembled in Jerusalem to celebrate at a site called Nebi Musa. It is believed to be the tomb of Moses. It coincided with the Jewish Passover and the Christian Easter. The pilgrimage had been allowed under the Turkish occupation, but it had been carefully controlled by troops, ostensibly positioned for ceremonial purposes. Previously it had always been a happy occasion. This year was different.

In his report on the disturbances, Palin offered several possible explanations for what occurred this time. Not only the causes, but even the events, were so difficult to disentangle that there can be no definitive version of what exactly happened. It would appear that this year the Arabs were especially inflamed because of the Balfour Declaration, the imperialising behaviour of the Zionist Commission, the presence of agents provocateurs, and the displaying of pictures of Emir Feisal, recently proclaimed king of Syria, which was to include Palestine. Another novel feature was the making of political speeches, which of course reflected Arab concern at the evolving political scene.

The riots started with attacks on Jews and Jewish property, with the usual concomitant looting. There was also the gang rape of a Jewish woman and a young girl. The procession had started off peaceably, but on the Sunday there was an explosion while the procession was passing through the Jaffa Gate. The chaos and confusion that followed is demonstrated by Palin's remark that 'the exact incident which caused the explosion has not been clearly ascertained—possibly there were more than one'.[78] The Jews were, naturally, terrified, and there was some retaliation. The situation had deteriorated by the Monday and martial law was proclaimed. On the Tuesday there was still violence and looting: a notable target being the Talmudic College, which was burned and looted.[79] Disorder continued, and it was not until the following Saturday that life began to return to normal. The figures of casualties reported by Palin were: Jews: 5 killed, 18 dangerously wounded, 193 wounded: total 216. Moslems: 4 killed, 1 dangerously wounded, 20 wounded: total 25.

The Zionists made many allegations against the authority, including that they should have banned the procession, that there was constant failure to protect the Jews, and that somehow prejudice against the Jews in the activities of the government had contributed. Indeed the Zionists went further by introducing the emotive word 'pogrom' to describe what had happened, a word which connotes government involvement. Allenby described a visit from Weizmann:

> He was in a state of great nervous excitement, shedding tears, accusing [the] administration of Palestine as being anti-Zionist and describing recent events as a pogrom.[80]

The Arabs, too, claimed bias, but Palin dismissed all allegations of bias. The commission concluded that 'the incidence of the attack was against the Jews and that the attack against them was made in customary mob fashion with sticks, stones and knives. All the evidence goes to show that these attacks were of a cowardly and treacherous description, mostly against old men, women and children and frequently in the back.'[81] At the same time the report laid the blame at the feet of the Zionists:

> The Zionist Commission and the official Zionists by their impatience, indiscretion and attempts to force the hands of the Administration, are largely responsible for the present crisis.[82]

With regard to the behaviour of the administration, although Palin had been critical—for example, in noting the failure to increase the establishment of police officers and the mistakes made in the disposition of troops—he concluded that:

> The Administration was considerably hampered in its policy by the direct interference of the Home Authorities... [and] that the Administration prior to the riots on the whole maintained under difficult circumstances an attitude of

equal justice to all parties and that the allegations of bias put forward by both sides, Arab and Zionist, are unfounded.[83]

One response was to impose collective fines, with Churchill reverting to his belief in 'firm' response, which had been his hallmark at the beginning of the century in all his dealings with civil disturbance. In the case of disturbances in Jaffa for example, he demanded that:

> Jaffa as well as villages should be made to realise responsibilities with least possible delay. We cannot allow expediency to govern the administration of justice.[84]

Furthermore, in a flash of Victorian imperial determination he said he would be prepared to send a warship if necessary.

The Palin Report also reflected on the behaviour of the increasingly visible Ze'ev Jabotinsky. This man is of such importance in the history of the period that he is worthy of note. He was a Russian, born in Odessa in 1880, and a journalist of distinction. He had always been active in the Zionist movement in Russia, and in Europe. He served in the British Army in the First World War, and agitated for the creation of Jewish units, which resulted in the formation of a 'Jewish Legion'. Remarkably, in the light of his subsequent activities, he was appointed to the Order of the British Empire (OBE). After the war Jabotinsky became increasingly extreme, even by Zionist standards. In 1920, in Palestine, he was sentenced to fifteen years imprisonment for the possession of weapons and preparing a riot. Others, both Jews and Arabs were also imprisoned. He had taken part in riots in which Jews and Arabs were killed, and British soldiers injured. Samuel, after his appointment in June 1920, instigated an amnesty. He was warned not to include Jabotinsky. In the view of Colonel Deedes, Jabotinsky was 'really a lunatic and should be kept under medical surveillance—if he were at large in Palestine now he would certainly cause trouble. [He] should not in any case be set at large in Palestine as he is not responsible for his actions.'[85] Nonetheless, Samuel included him in the amnesty.

During the disturbances, Jabotinsky and Pinhas Rutenberg offered the services of a Jewish force they had raised. Rutenberg was a shadowy figure, often appearing at convenient places. Weizmann 'arranged' for him to be Churchill's interpreter on his Palestine visit. The importance of this post was illustrated by the fact that Churchill talked to new Jewish arrivals from Russia about whether they were Bolsheviks. After listening to Rutenberg's interpretation, he was convinced that they were not.

Palin submitted his report in August 1920. By now Herbert Samuel was high commissioner. Allenby wrote to Lord Curzon about the publication of the report in September 1920:

> This Report has reviewed, with great ability and in extensive detail, the whole circumstances which led to the troubles in Jerusalem. Naturally, the Zionists are opposed to such publication; and Sir Herbert Samuel, in the interest of the local situation has urged H.M.G. to refrain from it. I know that you will agree with him, and, having regard to the great desirability of keeping things quiet in Palestine, I agree that it is the desirable course.

But Allenby went on to write that if 'it is to be kept secret from the public, in the interest of the Zionists—and of them alone ... the Zionists should be made to observe some restraints on their side too'.[86] This was another vivid example of the power of Samuel, and his mobilisation on behalf of the Zionists.

No doubt to the great relief of Weizmann, the report was suppressed and never published. This withholding of information is a familiar tool used by governments. As late as 1938, Antonius wrote of how the British government 'continue to withhold some of the basic documents from publication. The effect of their reticence is that their reports and statements and interpretations of policy, far from clarifying the issues and contributing to the enlightenment of public opinion, present the problem in an unreal light and a false perspective.'[87] In the particular case of Palestine, this was very much to the advantage of the Zionists.

The next serious episode of violence was not long in coming. It began on Sunday 1 May 1921, in Jaffa. May Day is, of course, a deeply significant date for the left wing of politics. By this time in Palestine the Jewish political left was split broadly into Labour and Communist, or as the authorities labelled the latter, Bolsheviks. Both wanted to hold demonstrations: the Labour party was given permission; the Bolsheviks were refused. This led to strikes and attacks against businesses and individuals who refused to cooperate with the protests. The Jewish 'Bolsheviks' also turned their attention to the Arabs and tried to convert them to their ideas of revolution, especially the attacking of the British occupation forces. Seemingly, the Arabs were alarmed by this, and the Moslem–Christian Society protested to the high commissioner. In its report on the disturbances, the Haycraft Commission observed that 'from this time onward it is not easy to follow the precise sequence of events'.[88]

As with the task facing Palin, the chaos which ensued could never be properly disentangled. An example of the difficulty of dealing with confusion, lies and rumour, was the allegation on 4 May that two Arab children had been murdered. A crowd assembled to seek revenge, only to discover that the children were unhurt. Very soon the Arabs and the Jews started fighting. The Arabs started looting and there was a great deal of trouble around Immigration House. The police not only were poorly trained and poorly staffed, and in any case lost control, but some of them colluded with the Arabs. One Arab police officer, a second inspector, left the scene and went home for lunch. On the first day the arrival of troops restored some order.

The next day there was more trouble, and something called the Palestine Defence Force, consisting of demobilised Jewish soldiers arrived and took over. The commander, a Jew named Colonel Margolin, either lost control or colluded with the Jews in the fight. A prominent casualty was Yosef Haim Brenner, a Russian immigrant, writer and an active Zionist, who was among the Jews murdered. On Tuesday martial law was declared, and a new protest emerged. Arab shopkeepers refused to serve Jews. It was decided to remove 'troublemakers' despite the appeal of a leading Muslim not to do so. Seven Arabs and three Jews were sent to Jerusalem, while fifteen non-Palestinian Jews were deported from Palestine. It was not until 18 May that the shops were operational again, although the unrest spread to the countryside around the city and there was more violence and looting. The resulting commission was asked to examine in particular the Khedera Raid, an attack on a Jewish colony near Haifa. Appendix B of the report lists the numbers killed and injured each day. Ninety-five people were killed: 48 Arabs and 47 Jews. In addition, 73 Arabs and 146 Jews were wounded. These figures, as the report points out, are not complete. 'It is known' that about twenty bodies were removed by a Bedouin tribe, and that many were treated at various out-patient facilities. The principal medical officer estimated that as many as 290 people may have been wounded.

The commission appointed to investigate these events consisted of Sir Thomas Haycraft, chief justice of Palestine, two members of the administration, and one representative each of the Jews, Muslims and Christians. The presenting cause of the disturbance, the report states, was the clash between members of the MPS (Miflagah Po'alim Sotzialistim—the Bolsheviks) and Jews who were authorised to demonstrate.[89]

The Zionists claimed that the Arabs were resentful because they wanted a return to Turkish rule where an elite had held power and made profit from the Ottoman system. The commission thought this was not true. Also, it was claimed, 'what the Arabs really want is loot'.[90] Furthermore 'Zionism has nothing to do with the anti-Jewish feeling manifested in the Jaffa disturbances ... they are primarily anti-British'.[91] David Eder, by now acting chairman of the Zionist Commission, took the opportunity to give voice to the not-so-hidden agenda of his organisation. This was summed up with his claim that there should be 'a Jewish state under Great Britain'.[92] Such a view would not have been news to Arabs since, as the report points out, they could read and were well aware of the propaganda in the European press, such as a statement in *The Jewish Chronicle* of the 20 May 1921, which hoped for a Palestine 'as Jewish as England is English'. The reaction of the commissioners to Eder's evidence was that 'he asserts on behalf of the Jews those claims which are at the root of the present unrest'.[93] The reaction of one official in London was more direct. Gerard Clauson of the Colonial Office wrote on 2 September 1921 that:

> Dr Eder in his evidence ... disclosed views which are so entirely incompatible with the policy of H.M.G. and with the professed policy of Dr Weizmann that,

if we are to make our policy a success it is urgently necessary that both we and the Zionist Organisation should publicly disavow them. The only disavowal which would be regarded as sincere by the people of Palestine would be the removal of Dr Eder from his present position [head of the Zionist Commission], a step which I think we are fully entitled to invite the Zionist Organisation, in its official position as the Jewish Agency, to take.[94]

There was some discussion about removing Eder, but John Shuckburgh, assistant secretary of state and head of the Middle East Department, blocked the proposal, ostensibly because it would upset negotiations which were then going on.[95] He was an enthusiastic supporter of the Zionists.

The commission was rather more objective in its analysis than the Zionist witnesses. There was 'no inherent anti-Semitism in the country'.[96] Rather there was objection to what was seen as discrimination against Arabs, for example in the land regulations, to which reference has been made, which was seen as a device to lower the price of land so that Jews could buy cheaply. And, as always, there was the immoveable 'obstacle' of the policy at the centre of the Balfour Declaration. There were, though, no excuses. The Arabs 'behaved with a savagery which cannot be condoned. Jews retaliated with equal savagery … but they had much to revenge.'[97]

The report made no significant change to the political direction to which the country was being manipulated. The Zionists tried to pass off the disturbances, arguing that 'the clashes were the result of deliberate agitation and did not express the Arabs' true national sentiments'.[98]

September 1928 saw the beginning of more trouble. It started with preparations for Yom Kippur, the Jewish Day of Atonement, at the Western Wall in Jerusalem. Much is made of the significance of the wall to Jews, but its totemic significance may be of recent vintage:

> The notion of the Wailing Wall as a focal point of holiness was only popularised in literary and pictorial form in the nineteenth and twentieth centuries.[99]

The Jews had set up a screen, intended to separate men and women, but some Arabs suspected that it was the beginning of an attempt to take over the wall. The British district commissioner of Jerusalem, Edward Keith-Roach, ordered that the screen be removed. The Jews prevaricated, asking for a delay, but a Constable Douglas Duff ordered his officers to destroy the screen. Unfortunately for the cause of peace, the malign influence of Jabotinsky began to make itself felt. He had just arrived in Jerusalem, and saw an opportunity to exploit the situation, especially in his fight, not with the Arabs, but with his political rival David Ben-Gurion. The screen episode provoked other protests from Arabs, including assaults on Jews.

The wall continued to be the scene of violence and in August 1929, on the occasion of yet another religious festival, this one marking the destruction of the Jewish temple in Roman times, thousands of Jews gathered at the wall. Fighting quickly spread, especially in Hebron. Later in August, thousands of Arabs went to Jerusalem from other districts to pray at the Temple Mount. Mysterious gunshots caused attacks on Jews. The situation throughout the country quickly deteriorated. Arabs murdered women and children, Jews retaliated by killing Arabs. There was looting, and Jews broke into a mosque and burned books. Such acts led the Jewish Agency to state that some Jews had 'shamefully' gone 'beyond the limits of self-defence'.[100] There was one slight consolation: 'most of Hebron's Jews were saved because Arabs hid them in their homes'. Some paid for it: 'Arabs were hurt defending their neighbours,' a Jew testified later.[101] Even this courageous behaviour has been minimised by some historians: 'a mere nineteen Arabs, [helped] compared to the thousands of rioters'.[102]

When order was finally restored, 133 Jews and 116 Arabs were dead, and 339 Jews and 232 Arabs had been injured. When it was over, charges were laid against those who had committed offences of violence and looting, including murder. About 700 Arabs were charged, including 124 with murder. Fifty-five were convicted and twenty-five sentenced to death. Some 160 Jews were charged, seventy with murder, and two were convicted and sentenced to death. The sentences of the latter were commuted to life imprisonment.[103]

The guilty Arabs presented the high commissioner, Sir John Chancellor, with yet another dilemma: whether or not to hang them. This was typical of the problems the hapless Chancellor had to deal with throughout his period in office. He could never please everyone, and often he pleased nobody. His attempt at impartiality only led to his being defined as anti-Jew by the Zionists. They were correct in that Chancellor believed that the Balfour Declaration was unworkable—'colossal blunder'.[104] In this opinion he was voicing the opinions of many, probably the majority, in the administration. He decided that three of the Arabs should be hanged, and commuted the sentences of the others. On the day of the executions a visitor found him in 'great distress'.[105]

As in previous riots the police were helpless, in part because there were not enough of them, and partly because they were substantially Arab, which meant of course that they were fearful of attacking their own people. They did what they could, thus invalidating the attempts by some Jews, notably Ben-Gurion, to label the episode a 'pogrom'. Zionists are prone to overusing the word. It is generally agreed that to qualify as a pogrom there has to be official sanction and encouragement or at least inaction.

The British government set up a commission to report 'on the Palestine Disturbances of August 1929'. It was chaired by Sir Walter Shaw, a lawyer, and he was assisted by three members of parliament: Sir Henry Betterton, Conservative; R. Hopkin Morris, Liberal; and Henry Snell, Labour. The commission's business took just over two months and heard evidence from a wide range of people.

The establishment of the commission was the source of much debate and anger from the Zionists. They did not want 'major' questions of policy to be discussed, only the causes of the riots. This was not the only time the Zionists objected to *any* inquiry into what was happening in Palestine. They were well aware that any impartial inquiry must question a situation in which the British government was arranging for the invasion and take-over of a foreign country. Sure enough, for the Zionists, the report 'confirmed all of their worst expectations'.[106]

Shaw concluded that the outbreak of violence 'was from the beginning an attack by Arabs on Jews', and that 'a general massacre of the Jewish community at Hebron was narrowly averted'. There was 'wanton destruction of Jewish property'. In respect of physical attacks and destruction of property, the Jews retaliated. One cause of the disturbances was 'the enlargement of the Jewish Agency'. There was an attempt to blame the mufti of Jerusalem for inciting disorder, but the commission rejected this: there was 'no connection' between the mufti and the rioters, and indeed he had 'cooperated with the Government in their efforts both to restore peace and to prevent the extension of disorder'. This was just one of many allegations that he had fomented trouble. The commission's rejection of the mufti's responsibility for the trouble angered the Zionists, and still does:

> This was too much for one of the Commissioners, who, in a dissenting opinion, attributed to the Mufti 'a greater share in the responsibility for the disturbances than is attributed to him in the report'.[107]

Arthur Koestler agreed. With his constant insistence that the mandatory authorities were 'anti-Zionist', he complained that they 'could have removed the Mufti from his post, dissolved his "Higher Arab Committee" and replaced it by moderate elements.'[108]

The mufti of Jerusalem, Haj Amin Al-Husseini, held a post of considerable religious and secular authority amongst his people. There is plenty of evidence that when there *was* trouble and he tried to intervene, some factions would not obey him. It is the case that until the revolt in the mid-1930s he was an advocate of peaceful negotiation rather than violence. In any case he was a nominee of the British, and had there been proof of misbehaviour, he would have been removed.

The most important sections of the report deal with Jewish immigration, and the commission's views on this outraged the Zionists. There was 'incontestable evidence' that the 'doctrine' accepted by the Zionist organisation in 1922 that immigration should be regulated by economic capacity had been subject to a 'serious departure'. Immigration policy should be clearer in purpose and administration 'with the object of preventing a repetition of the excessive immigration of 1925 and 1926'.

This matter was related to the problem of land. In a most prescient forecast, the report stated that:

> Between 1921 and 1929 there were large sales of land in consequence of which numbers of Arabs were evicted without the provision of other land for their occupation ... the position is now acute. There is no alternative land to which persons evicted can remove. In consequence a landless and discontented class is being created. Such a class is a potential danger to the country ... The feeling as it exists today is based on the twofold fear of the Arabs that by Jewish immigration and land purchases they may be deprived of their livelihood and in time pass under the political domination of the Jews.

It was logical therefore that their main recommendations included one that immigration policy should be reviewed, that non-Jewish interests should be consulted about immigration, that policy should be clearer on land, and that evictions of peasants should stop.

The Zionists now began a campaign to set up another inquiry, largely to submerge Shaw. There was pressure to appoint Smuts to lead it, but such coarseness could not be allowed, and instead Sir John Hope Simpson was sent to head a commission to examine agriculture, land settlement, and immigration. He had been a Liberal member of parliament, and served for almost twenty years in the Indian Civil Service. He reported on 1 October 1930.

His report comprises a very detailed analysis of the nature of agriculture in the country, the distribution of land, and the operation of Jewish organisations.[109] His report was published on the same day as the 'Passfield Report', to be discussed later, and both were devastatingly critical of what had happened in Palestine since the Balfour Declaration. Hope Simpson was very critical of the way in which Jews bought Arab land. They paid some of the occupants of the land much more than they were legally bound to do, which was a euphemism for saying that they were bribing sellers. The involvement of the Jewish National Fund in purchasing land meant that:

> It ceases to be land from which the Arab can gain any advantage either now or in the future. Not only can he never hope to lease or cultivate it, but, by the stringent provisions of the lease of the Jewish National Fund, he is deprived forever from employment on the land.[110]

There was a Zionist policy of not employing Arabs, which was mentioned earlier: 'the policy of the Jewish Labour Federation is successful in impeding the employment of Arabs in Jewish colonies and in Jewish enterprises of every kind'.[111] This meant, obviously enough, that displaced farmers could not find non-agricultural employment. And so 'Arab unemployment is serious and general'.

Since the activities and policies of the Jewish Labour Federation and the Jewish Agency are criticised for employing Jews in both the Hope Simpson Commission and the Passfield Report, it is necessary to explain the activities and purpose of the Jewish National Fund in particular.

The Zionists established a 'Jewish National Fund' in 1901, the principal business of which was to take possession of property in Palestine. Ever since its existence it had been the subject of worldwide controversy among Jews, with *inter alia*, allegations of fraud, forced resignations of officials, and mismanagement of funds, to which Jews contributed throughout the world. For the purposes of this account I will deal only with the impact of its activities on the displacement of Arabs.

By the end of the First World War, the Jewish National Fund owned approaching 10 per cent of the land of Palestine. This happened 'through chance, luck, improvisation, fraud, bribery, risk, violence, and vision'. But if uninhabitable land is excluded, the Zionists owned 'about 25 per cent of Palestine'.[112] The usual Zionist defence of this takeover is that the Arabs, some of whom were national figures, sold willingly: 'Arab landowners were not forced to sell. They cooperated with the Zionists against the interests of their own people.'[113]

This is no doubt true, but it did mean that those who were tenants of the owners were left without a means of subsistence, especially as the various commissions pointed out, the new owners would only employ Jews, a cornerstone of Zionist policy. Later there was set up a compensation scheme for Arabs who had allegedly been dispossessed. There were several thousand applications but 'less than seven hundred' were certified. One would not have to be a cynical Arab of the day to wonder if this figure was not influenced by the fact that the applications 'had to be vetted by officials at the Jewish Agency'.[114] As for the Jewish Labour Federation, Hope Simpson reported that it was 'successful in impeding the employment of Arabs in Jewish colonies and in Jewish enterprises of every kind'. In addition, there was an Anglo–Palestine Company, founded in London in 1902, which served the World Zionist Organisation as a credit institution.

Hope Simpson declared that the answer was to limit Jewish immigration. He also drew attention to the problem of illegal immigrants, both Jewish and Arab. These arrived with a time limit, but outstayed that limit, and 'recourse should certainly be had to expulsion'. The Passfield White Paper also recognised the urgency of curbing Jewish immigration, but it went further in trying to halt the march of Zionism. It recommended that there should be established a legislative council which would represent the Arab majority. We have seen that one assessment of the effect of the Hope Simpson Report on the Zionists, and no doubt an accurate one, is that it 'surpassed their worst expectations'.[115] For them more adversity was to come.

In October 1930 the colonial secretary, Lord Passfield, better known as Sidney Webb, issued a White Paper which declared that Britain would accord equal treatment under the mandate to Jews and Arabs.[116] The White Paper was welcomed by the British authorities in Palestine since they considered it just and hoped it would eliminate Arab attempts to stop their alienation from their land by violence. If accepted, these recommendations would have implemented the caveat in the declaration: that the rights of all the inhabitants were to be protected, and that the basic premise of democracy—the greatest good for the greatest number—would be fulfilled. Predictably though, the Zionists were outraged since the proposals threatened the end of their not-so-secret ambition for Jewish dominance and a Jewish state in Palestine. There were widespread protests from Jews around the world, including in the United States, France, Poland, Australia, Austria, and South Africa.[117] Jan Smuts himself wrote to Ramsay Macdonald, the prime minister, urging the British government to honour the Balfour Declaration.

Lloyd George quickly rallied to the cause. In a parliamentary debate on 17 November 1930 he claimed the paper was 'anti-Semitic'. He disapproved of limits on Jewish immigration and, in effect, defended Jewish restrictions on employing Arabs. There was nothing new in this. When there was discussion about Zionism he spoke in favour with what Beckerman-Boys called 'a vociferous sincerity'.[118]

Passfield also caused another explosion from Churchill. His view was that the 'obligations are totally different in character'. The Passfield White Paper 'diverged fundamentally' from the 1922 White Paper. This latter had, of course, been composed by Churchill, but he was appealing to it as though it had nothing to do with him. As always, he made claims for the declaration which were nonexistent: for example, that it contained obligations not only to the people of Palestine but 'to the Zionist Movement all over the world to whom the original promise was made'.[119] Of course the Zionists had to take care of the rights of the Arabs, 'but it did not inhibit their on-going migration and economic development, including land purchase'. Nothing different could be expected from Churchill except furious support for the Zionist objections. He also said that the Balfour Declaration had said that Jews could move from anywhere to the national home. No similar promise was made to Arabs.[120]

On 23 October 1930 *The Times* published a letter deploring the Passfield recommendations and the government's attitude:

> They have laid down a policy of so negative a character that it appears to us to conflict ... with the whole spirit of the Balfour Declaration and of the statements made by successive Governments in the last 12 years.

It was signed by Leopold Amery, a former colonial secretary, Stanley Baldwin, a former prime minister, and Austen Chamberlain, a former foreign secretary. According to Beckerman-Boys, it was Balfour's niece, Baffy, a Zionist campaigner, who pressed this powerful trio to act.[121] She drafted the letter and the three revised it. That three such powerful men should attack the government was to prove a rallying point for the Zionists, and a devastating blow to the Arab cause. This was one of several letters which the most powerful of the 'Gentile Zionists' wrote to *The Times* around this time. The reaction of the more impartial people involved is summed up by John Chancellor, the Palestine high commissioner, in a letter to O. G. R. Williams at the Colonial Office:

> Greatly concerned about the letter which Baldwin, Chamberlain and Amery have written to the Times. If all parties would accept H.M.G's. statement of policy, there would be some prospect of future peace in Palestine.[122]

On 4 November 1930 there was another letter to *The Times* written by Tory grandee Lord Hailsham and the Liberal Sir John Simon, in which they demanded that The Hague should be asked for an opinion on whether restricting Jewish immigration was counter to mandate policy. Passfield was moved to reply in a letter to *The Times* on 5 November:

> [It] is reassuring to find from their letter published in your columns ... that such high authorities as Lord Hailsham and Sir John Simon do not indicate anything in the Palestine White Paper inconsistent with the Balfour Declaration and the Mandate.[123]

Once again the Zionists were in luck: the government had much more important matters with which to deal. There was the fall-out from the stock market crash and there was the persisting furore over the future of India.

Weizmann, meanwhile, had been busy. The question was how to block the acceptance of the two reports, and once again Weizmann took the lead. Segev attributed the 'victory', that is the demolition of the recommendations, to 'charm and craftiness, his diplomatic astuteness, his conviction, audacity, and luck ... He was disappointed with the limits of British patriotism, he said gravely, and resigned from the presidency of the Zionist movement in protest.'[124]

He also resigned from the Jewish Agency. Segev's assessment of Weizmann's role is commonly expressed by Jewish historians, and is an important element in the hagiography which surrounds Weizmann. However, Beckerman-Boys attributes the growth of the somewhat mystical role of Weizmann to the version of events in his autobiography, drawn upon by historians.[125] Renton is another who questions the central role which has always been accorded to Weizmann.

> [His] contribution to the fruition of the Government's pro-Zionist policy was of minor significance. He followed rather then led the formulation and application of an effective diplomatic strategy ... His ability to secure the Declaration, which required the visible display of a united Zionist Jewry, was reliant upon the previous work of other Zionist leaders, particularly Brandeis.[126]

The government was rattled by the press discussion, and on 6 November a new sub-committee was established to review policy. Then came a series of extraordinary actions. The sub-committee was told to 'get in touch with the representative of the Zionists in the most politic and tactful manner possible in the circumstances and ... make recommendations as to the attitude to be taken up by the Government in view of the reception of the recently issued White Paper.'[127] MacDonald himself then immediately met Weizmann.

There followed meetings in which the foreign secretary, Arthur Henderson, resolutely defended the White Paper. Then, incredibly, Weizmann was shown a draft of what was to be the MacDonald letter. He was not happy with it.[128] This was followed by a number of drafts until, it seems, Weizmann got what he wanted.

The final version was approved by the cabinet on 4 February 1931. The upshot was that Ramsay MacDonald wrote a letter to Weizmann on 13 February 1931, which was 'an authoritative interpretation' of the White Paper. When it was finally finished, after protests from the Foreign Office and Colonial Office officials about the dishonesty of the opponents of Passfield, it reflected the government's weariness of the whole matter.

The letter stated that the Passfield Report never intended to attack the Jewish people or their labour organisations. The Jewish people and the Jewish Agency had always been supportive. Most important, the restrictions on immigration were wiped out as there was 'an obligation to facilitate Jewish immigration and to encourage close settlement by Jews on the land'. They could purchase land, employ only Jewish labour, and there would be no restriction on immigration. Complete submission is indicated by the statement that the final text 'had been agreed upon between representatives of the Jewish Agency and a Committee appointed by the Cabinet'. The letter did, however, restore the official stance of the Labour party, which was to support Zionism. This had been the historic position of Ramsay MacDonald himself.

MacDonald had visited Palestine in 1922, and had written a book entitled *A Socialist in Palestine*. In this book he argued that 'the Arab claim to self-determination was invalid because "Palestine and the Jews can never be separated"'.[129] The conflict for MacDonald may be gauged from the fact that he was one of the organisers of the Palestine Mandate Society, a parliamentary Zionist pressure group.[130] There was to be a serious change in the attitude of the Labour party towards Palestine when it was elected in 1945.

It is no wonder that Arabs have designated the letter as 'the Black Letter'. Their attitude was summed up later in the month when the Palestine Arab Executive wrote:

> We must give up the idea of relying on the British Government to safeguard our national and economic existence, because this Government is weak in

the face of the forces of world Jewry ... Mr. MacDonald's new document has destroyed the last vestige of respect every Arab had cherished towards the British Government.[131]

It was certainly, even by the tortuous events of Palestinian policy, an astonishing piece of behaviour by the British government. After all, the original recommendations followed careful examination of the situation on the ground by a variety of people who knew what they were talking about. Cabinet had adopted the proposed policy, and it should have been a matter of little concern that Weizmann disapproved, or that he had resigned from a position in an organisation about which most people knew nothing.

In her magisterial analysis of the government's rejection of the Passfield White Paper, Carly Beckerman-Boys explained that most accounts focus 'almost exclusively on the efficacy of Zionist lobbying'.[132] She set out some basic reasons for the *volte face*. One was that the government could not command agreement in parliament because some Labour members were supporters of Zionism. The Conservatives and the Liberals were also engaged in malicious in-fighting, and in any case there were more important problems than Palestine, notably the economy and the huge turmoil over the future of India. On the subject of the latter, Beatrice Webb, Passfield's wife, wrote 'little Palestine with its troubles—insignificant to the rest of the world—is likely to be forgotten in concern over the revolution which some say is going on in India'. Indian policy and its attendant furore is subject to lengthy discussion by Beckerman-Boys.[133]

Another important obstacle arose from the section in the Hope Simpson Report which recommended spending large sums on development in Palestine. A cabinet committee on Palestine examined the considerable proposed cost, so another financial committee was set up. This committee reported on 15 September 1930 that 'in present circumstances a proposal to spend many millions on land settlement of Jews and Arabs in Palestine would meet with serious opposition in Parliament and the country.'[134] Beckerman-Boys' summary is that:

> Rather than a Palestine policy based on a narrow interpretation of the role played by Zionist lobbying, this analysis reveals a Palestine policy based primarily on the need to maintain a modicum of unity within government and across parties, which was threatened by the strategic pro-Zionist activism of opposition leaders.[135]

The year 1931 saw an important beginning to an aspect of pressure which has been forceful ever since. This was the formation of a group which supported Zionism, and of which Churchill was a member. A Jewish Labour MP noted that the members 'made Zionism one of their parliamentary duties'.[136]

In 1929 there were attacks by Arabs when 133 Jews were killed, and there was widespread looting. Churchill, on a visit to the United States, was asked for his reaction. He listed all the achievements of the Jews: 'grown orchards and grain field out of the desert ... green, smiling fields and vineyards and delicious shady groves'.[137] He was at a loss, and always would be, to understand why the Arabs did not welcome this. He offered several explanations, none of which was the actual explanation: that they were being dispossessed. Rather, he said, 'fanaticism and a sort of envy have driven the Arab to violence'. This is why they could not appreciate 'the fruits of reason and modern science'.[138]

It can only be supposed that Churchill must have known that collective punishment went beyond fining, as this account illustrates:

> Collective punishments were imposed on villages where individual culprits could not be singled out. Arthur Lane went to one village ... to demand a fine from the muhtar. After the headman slammed the door in his face, and then his irate wife emerged brandishing a wooden spoon to chase Lane's colleague away, Lane tersely remembered what happened next: 'We burned her house down.'[139]

William Ormsby-Gore, the colonial secretary, was a dedicated Zionist, who blamed the mufti for the trouble in Palestine. In 1937 he wrote the following:

> I still feel that we shall never get on top of this murder campaign and its inevitable consequences of counter-murder by Jews whom we are unable to protect, until we have eliminated the Mufti and his gang. He was the *fons et origo* of the murders in 1929, and as long as we appear to funk dealing with this black-hearted villain, and allow him to disseminate anti-British propaganda throughout the Islamic world, and organise terrorism of any Arabs in Palestine not subservient to him and his Supreme Moslem Council, we cannot hope to maintain law and order or even be the *de facto* government of Palestine.[140]

By 1929 there were 156,000 Jews in Palestine, twice as many as in 1922, as against 794,000 Arabs, whose numbers had also increased. The rise of Hitler and the concomitant repression of 'non-Germans', led to a considerable increase in immigration to Palestine. In 1935 alone, 66,476 Jews moved to Palestine.[141] In March 1936 the Commons discussed setting up a legislative council in which the Arabs, as the majority, would have control.

Churchill, as might be expected, objected. This proposal, he said, 'would be a very great obstruction to the development of Jewish immigration into Palestine and to the development of the national home of the Jews there'.[142] But he also marshalled a new argument. He drew attention to the treatment of Jews in Germany, and he pleaded that the House would allow more to escape what was happening there. But the House was not sufficiently sympathetic to authorise an increase.

There was also a surprising piece of behaviour by the normally very pro-Zionist Shuckburgh, permanent under-secretary of state at the Colonial Office. There was in existence at the time a system of quotas for immigrants to Palestine. In December 1940 he wrote to his department suspending the issue of immigration certificates without Churchill knowing. 'Our object,' he said, 'is to keep the business as far as possible on the normal administrative plane and outside the realms of Cabinet policy and so forth.'[143]

The problem was exacerbated by the vast increase in the numbers of Jewish immigrants provoked by the rise of Nazism in Europe, the chronic antisemitism in Poland, and the reluctance of the United States to accept immigrants. This movement to Palestine was not new. We have seen that there had been a steady movement of immigrants for many years. As the question of migration was to dominate the political scene ever afterwards, I will review the salient points of its history.

As early as the seventeenth century, there was an illegal settlement in Palestine. Judah he-Hasid travelled in Europe recruiting Jews to move there. The term used was Aliya (the act of 'going up', that is going to Jerusalem), in effect the movement of Jews from the diaspora to Palestine. The attempt was not a success. Some arrived in 1700, but many died on the trip and the others were soon in debt. The chaos which followed was blamed by the Turkish authorities on the Ashkenazi Jews, even though the bulk of the Jews who were in the city before the arrival of the newcomers were Sephardic.[144, 145] There was also an Ashkenazi population of about 200 in Palestine. All Ashkenazi were banned from Jerusalem. A synagogue built by he-Hasid's followers was destroyed on several occasions, but a rebuilt building was rededicated, many years later, in 2010.

The slow movement continued throughout the nineteenth century. After the Russian pogroms, and the development of the Zionist movement in the 1880s, emigration from Russia began in earnest. Most of the Jews went to Western Europe and America. A relatively small number went to Palestine: 7,000 in 1882.[146] Quite often life there was hard, but in a tradition which would last indefinitely, rich Jews, notably the extensive Rothschild family, supported the immigrants. They were also helped financially, and of course morally, by the Zionist movement. A second Aliya started in 1904, and this resulted in the arrival of a further 33,000 Jews in Palestine. And so began the acquisition of Arab land, at this time legally. By 1914, 130,000 acres had been acquired with the help of wealthy patrons. By this time there were about 85,000 Jews in Palestine, comprising 'perhaps one-ninth of the Palestinian population'.[147]

By 1914, Jews possessed about 2 per cent of the land in Palestine, and the basic Arab demands then, as later throughout the period under study and beyond, were to end Jewish immigration and land acquisitions. However, land purchase took a new turn with the opening in 1908 of a Palestine office in Jaffa under the direction of Arthur Ruppin, assisted by a small staff of Russian Zionists. Their main purpose was to purchase every tract of fertile land available.[148] In the same way as in the countryside, competition and conflict arose in the towns, and here sophisticated protests were made against immigration. As early as 1891, Arab authorities asked their Ottoman rulers to ban the Russian influx and to stop them buying property. The rulers, probably because they were not sufficiently competent to take any action, did nothing and the movement continued.

It is not surprising that the native Arabs soon began to resent this intrusion. Not only was land falling into the possession of foreigners, but this land often comprised large estates, upon which Arabs were employed as labourers. It became a common theme of Zionist propaganda, as we have seen, that only Jews should work in Palestine. This was explained by one writer, in euphemistic terms, as a result of the Jews being 'determined to be self-sufficient'.[149]

The Farmers' Federation of Israel is an example. The federation 'hired Arab workers, who were less organised and therefore willing to work for lower wages'.[150] Nevertheless it became common practice to evict Arab labourers. This is very reminiscent of the enclosures in Britain, and the Highland clearances in Scotland. This comparison is enhanced by the claim that the locals were poor farmers, and that the Jews could do better. Force was added to this by the racist attitudes of the settlers who emphasised the backwardness of the Arabs:

> Had we permitted the squalid, superstitious, ignorant fellahin ... to live in close contact with the Jewish pioneers ... the slender chance of success ... would have been impaired, since we had no power ... to enforce progressive methods or even to ensure respect for private property.[151]

Ben-Gurion was typical of the early Zionists who wanted to replace Arab labour with that of the Jewish settlers. There were two problems. The first was that immigrant Jews often did not want to work in agriculture. One observer noted that 'you see so few Jews in work clothes, most of them are well-groomed and dressed in light suits, with Panama hats on their heads'.[152] The second problem was that 'Jewish farmers ... preferred to hire Arab labourers, who were cheaper, more experienced, less demanding, and more obedient than Jews were'.[153] But 'Ben-Gurion's primary interest remained replacing Arab labourers with Jewish ones'.[154] So 'obedient' were the Arab workers that:

> The Jewish farmers treated their Arab tenants just as they treated their farm animals ... with hostility and cruelty, commit unwarranted trespass, beat them shamefully without any good reason, and brag about doing so.[155]

Even at the time of the struggle for Palestine at the beginning of the twentieth century, this notion of 'purity' had to deal with economic reality. As time went on, a solution presented itself in the form of immigrant Jews from Arab countries, especially North Africa.

The problem of coping with 'oriental' Jews has been considerable in Israeli society. Israel has always faced huge problems in the integration of immigrants. Most of the population after the Second World War were immigrants, bound by a very slender thread: that they were Jews. They spoke many languages and came from differing cultures and various classes:

> The 'whitest' Jews from the most Westernised countries—Germany, France, England, the United States—formed the elite together with Russian and Polish pioneers of the pre-state era. Ashkenazi Jews enjoyed positions of leadership and a better standard of life in an austere country; Sephardic Jews from Mediterranean cities were cosmopolitans mostly living below the elite, followed by Jews from Muslim or Asian countries called *Mizrahi* or 'Eastern', and destined, from the government's point of view, for frontier towns.[156]

When Ben-Gurion became prime minister, he was always concerned not only about the lack of Messianic commitment of many of these immigrants, but about their social behaviour. He had to deal at one point with 'a wave of violence'... many of the rioters were Moroccan born; they were protesting discrimination'.[157] He tried various ways of developing a mood of cohesion. One was to arrange for Adolf Eichmann to be tried in Israel rather than simply to have him 'liquidated' in Argentina, where he was caught and kidnapped. Eichmann was one of the main architects of the Holocaust. Ben-Gurion's idea was to remind Israelis of the Holocaust, which would act as a binding force.[158]

Nothing, however, seemed to slow the traffic of immigrants in the 1920s and the early thirties. Despite a few attempts to intervene, such as preventing a husband's citizenship being given to his wife—a familiar racket in the culture of migration—the British administration did nothing to stem it. Once again the Zionists were lucky. The high commissioner, Sir Arthur Wauchope, was sympathetic. The result was that, 'in the short period between 1931 and 1936, the Jewish population more than doubled, from 175,000 to 370,000 people, bringing up its share of the total population from 17 to 27 per cent.'[159] Finally, the purchase of Arab land proceeded with the concomitant increase in the numbers of landless Arabs, unemployed, hungry and desperate.

For the Arabs this was clearly intolerable. As Sir John Chancellor, the high commissioner for Palestine, had predicted, after the debacle of the obliteration of the Passfield Report, the Arabs continued their resistance and expressed it through violence. The failure of the British government at this point may be regarded as one of the most important turning points in the downward regression of society in Palestine. The period also saw some of the most brutal behaviour in British imperial history. From 1936 to 1939, Arab resistance to Jewish invasion and British occupation was widespread.

Fighting began in earnest in 1930 with the establishment of an Arab military unit called the 'Black Hand'. This carried out attacks on Jewish property and

British installations until the unit's leader, al-Qassam, was killed in a gunfight in 1935. It is generally agreed that this incident was complicated by the discovery of substantial quantities of arms in Jaffa, also in 1935, intended for the Haganah, the Jewish underground force.

Izz ad-Din-al Qassam was born in Syria, and after supporting insurrection against the Italians in Libya, he moved to Palestine. On 15 April 1936 a protest began in earnest. Two Jews were killed at a roadblock, and a third died five days later of his wounds. The Jewish Irgun, the murderous band founded by Jabotinsky in 1931, carried out a revenge attack by killing two Arabs. Matters came to a head on 19 April 1936 when nine Jews were killed and several others wounded. Thus began what the Jewish community called 'the events' and the Arabs referred to as their 'rebellion'.[160] It is also called, by Arabs, 'The Great Revolt'. Karsh regards the uprising with contempt, and shows it by putting 'revolt' in inverted commas.[161] The battle calmed down after a few months, largely because of the actions of Wauchope, the high commissioner.

Did the British public care about these events? Although the fighting in Palestine may have made some hesitate, it seems that they had little interest in what was happening, excepting, that is, those few with a political interest. However, the opposition to a 'home' was so strong that it is remarkable that the idea of a return survived at all. There is still a body of Jews who do not support the idea. Considering the size and nature of the opposition to the Zionist cause, it is nothing short of astonishing that the Balfour Declaration came into being. But its mere existence did not ensure compliance.

5

THE BRITISH GOVERNMENT DISREGARDS THE LAW

'No one can give what they don't have: *nemo dat quod non habet*'[1]

On 19 April 1936 a strike began. An Arab higher committee was formed on 25 April 1936, which supported the next upheaval: a widespread demand for a general strike. The strike, which began in April, a few days before the formation of the higher committee, seems to have been only moderately successful. Certain categories of workers were exempt, while others, notably farmers, could not possibly strike. There were allegations of bullying to enforce compliance, and seemingly people were killed if they refused. Nevertheless the strike lasted for about six months. The committee had vowed to continue the strike until the British government acceded to three predictable demands: a halt to Jewish immigration; a halt to the transfer of Arab land to Jews; and the establishment of a representative government. The next step was the withholding of tax dues. On June 2 there was an attempt to blow up a train, which caused a massive deployment of troops to guard the railway. Two days later the British rounded up the leaders of the revolt and sent them to a concentration camp in the Negev desert.[2]

The next major event was the battle of Nur Shams on June 21, which was a very serious fight between the British and the rebels. The mufti of Jerusalem, Amin al-Husseini, was being forced to make a choice: either join the British, or join the struggle being mounted by his own people. He chose the latter, and became its leader. What the resistance, including the strike, made clear to both the British and the Jews was that, contrary to the feckless, thoroughly contemptible image of the Arabs promulgated by the likes of Churchill, the reality was that they would not be trifled with. It rapidly became clear that the hope that the Arabs would somehow remain unperturbed about what was happening in their country was in vain. Even Ben-Gurion conceded that there was more to Arab society than he had thought, but he still clung to the stereotype that there was a 'violent doctrine of Islam' and that 'a murderous mentality and intolerance of minorities were inherent in the Arab nature'.[3]

Even at this early stage there was a hint of the brutality to come. The British realised that this was a serious matter and the commander of the British forces in Palestine reported on how his troops and the Palestinian police were dealing with the situation:

> Village searches ... ostensibly these were undertaken to find arms and wanted persons, actually the measures adopted by the Police on the lines of similar Turkish methods were punitive and effective.[4]

Just what was meant by 'punitive' and 'effective' was described by the mayor of Nablus: 'During the last searches effected in villages properties were destroyed, jewels stolen, and the Holy Qur'an torn.' The Zionist authorities, who supported the repression, considered the punishments to be piecemeal and half-hearted. Moshe Shertok of the Jewish Agency wanted *all* the villages near an incident to be punished.[5] The view that the Arabs were being treated leniently was common amongst Zionists. Koestler was another who felt that their revolt should have been dealt with much more firmly.[6]

Between the start of the Arab uprising in 1936 and the spring of 1939, Arab attacks on the British were continuous.[7] The British officer Bernard Montgomery, then a major-general, arrived in October 1938 to take charge of units in northern Palestine. He did not have time, in army jargon, to 'square the place up', since he was ill and was sent back to England—but not before he issued an order in his usual abrupt style: 'The British Army [he believed], was to hunt down and destroy these armed gangs ... and shoot to kill.'[8]

During the 1936 rebellion, the British high commissioner, Sir Arthur Wauchope, always a reasonable man, tried to negotiate in the fight. Neighbouring Arab states were involved, and the strike was called off on October 11. Wauchope advocated for a royal commission, an action which, as might be expected, Weizmann strongly opposed. 'What was the Commission going to investigate?' Weizmann asked. By this he implied 'that there was no necessity for any investigation, only a need to subdue the riots and implement the mandate wholeheartedly'.[9]

Zionist objections to this and other inquiries were quite rational. They knew that anyone examining the situation in Palestine had to conclude that it was becoming more and more indefensible. Weizmann said as much to Ormsby-Gore: 'our experience in past years with similar reports and statements has not been very encouraging'.[10] Eventually, when the report was to be released, Weizmann was again angry because Ormsby-Gore would not let him see a copy in advance: 'We are not going to be bumped off in the dark; we shall fight you from San Francisco to Jerusalem; what you are doing is an unfriendly act.'[11]

Sir Arthur Wauchope was one of the casualties of the revolt. He had disagreed with the military commander about how the revolt should be handled. The military wanted martial law, Wauchope wanted a political solution based upon a royal commission. The verdict of the War Office was that:

> The conclusion cannot be avoided that the method adopted by the High Commissioner was entirely ineffective. Martial law and unfettered military control should have been exercised from the first. The behaviour and general conduct of the defence forces in very trying circumstances were admirable.[12]

Despite all protests, the commission arrived in November and the bulk of the disturbances stopped.

This commission was chaired by Lord Peel, and was required to enquire into the trouble and to make recommendations. Lord Peel and six distinguished members arrived in Palestine in November 1936 and reported on 7 July 1937.[13] The commission had been asked both to investigate the causes of the disturbances and how the terms of the mandate were being carried out, and to make recommendations. Their choice of language was significant. For example, they described the events as 'a rebellion'.[14]

It was a very long, detailed, somewhat repetitive report. For the most part it purveyed the truth, in so far as it was possible, in discussing what had happened. There were occasions when statements made to the commission were controversial or inaccurate, but were nevertheless included in the report. One of these was made by Lloyd George. As a former prime minister he spoke with great authority, but he was wrong. He wanted to influence the commission to believe in the goal of a Jewish 'Commonwealth'. He told the commission that:

> It was contemplated that when the time arrived for according representative institutions to Palestine, if the Jews had meanwhile responded to the opportunity afforded to them by the idea of a national home and had become a definite majority of the inhabitants, then Palestine would thus become a Jewish Commonwealth.[15]

Lloyd George may have 'contemplated' this, but it was by no means assumed by the bulk of British politicians.

Martin Gilbert has researched and published valuable material from Churchill's evidence to the Peel Commission. This evidence aptly illustrates the hopelessness of the task facing the commission when confronted with unswerving determination. It also helps to explain that as long as Churchill had any power the Zionists had little to fear. He attributed to the Balfour Declaration specific intent which was simply not there. On Jewish immigration for instance: 'The fact that we are trying to bring in as many as we can in accordance with the Balfour Declaration'.[16]

On the same subject he engaged in familiar contradiction:

> I certainly never considered they were entitled, no matter what other consequences arose, to bring up to the limit of the economic absorptive capacity. That was not intended. On the other hand, it must be made clear that our loyalty is on the side of bringing in as many as we can.[17]

At one point Churchill became positively hysterical. He foresaw 'a great Jewish State there, numbered by millions'.[18] He drew his familiar picture of the desert becoming verdant with palm and olive groves:

> Why is it injustice done if people come in and make a livelihood for more ... Why is it injustice because there is more work and wealth for everybody? ... The injustice is when those who live in the country leave it to be a desert for thousands of years.[19]

One member, Professor Reginald Coupland, was persistent, especially on the subject of the Arabs and their future. He suggested that the Jews were carrying out a 'creeping invasion'. By now it would seem Churchill was becoming not only verbose, but unintelligible, reiterating his favourite theme: the unworthiness of the Arabs.

> In 1918 the Arabs were beaten 'and at our disposition'. They were defeated 'in the open field'. It is not a question of creeping conquest. They were beaten out of the place. Not a dog could bark. And then we decided in the process of the conquest of these people to make certain pledges to the Jews. Now the question is how to administer in a humane and enlightened fashion and certain facts have emerged.[20]

Accused of 'shooting Arabs down because they dislike the Jews coming in', he replied that 'they were being killed by the British: "because we are the stronger power."'[21]

It was pointed out that Sir Horace Rumbold, formerly British ambassador to Germany when Hitler took charge, had said that the position now was that 'the indigenous population is subject to the invasion of a foreign race'. Churchill replied that the Jews were not foreigners: 'the great hordes of Islam ... broke it all up, smashed it all up ... which under Arab rule have remained a desert'.[22] He was corrected: did he not mean 'Turkish rule'. 'I do not know anything about that,' replied Churchill, adding somewhat contrary to all his contemptuous remarks: 'I have a great regard for Arabs.' Then, however, he said: 'It is a lower manifestation, the Arab.' What he had seen in Egypt as a soldier thirty-five years earlier, and what he had seen in Palestine on his two visits in 1921 and 1934, had not impressed him.[23]

Returning to the matter of immigration, Churchill calmed a little. He agreed that the speed should be controlled:

> Their well-being would be greatly enhanced if they did not quarrel. Where there is now a desert would become a really lovely place, and the Arabs would reap the benefit.[24]

Churchill then went on to make another novel claim, maintaining his belief in Arab inferiority:

The Mandate limited the development of Arab self-governing institutions as long as they do not accept the spirit of the Balfour Declaration ... It is for the good of the world that the place should be cultivated, and it will never be cultivated by the Arabs.[25]

Coupland then complained that the agency, a liaison between Jews in Palestine and the mandate, had contact with London and influence, but the Arabs, 'they have not the great engine the Jews have'. Churchill's answer was meaningless. He said there was a choice: 'It is a question of which civilisation you prefer.'[26] Churchill's evidence included unsound historical allegations.

> [He] made it clear that the Palestinian Arabs' decision to take up arms for their imperial masters the Turks and refusal to participate in the Arab Revolt had destroyed any sympathy he might have had for them.[27]

There is in fact no evidence that Churchill had ever had 'sympathy' for them. In a phrase which to Arab eyes would have been ambiguous in that it could have applied to the Roman eviction of the Jews two thousand years ago, Churchill concluded: 'I do not admit that the dog in the manger has the final right to the manger, even though he may have lain there for a very long time.'[28]

It is stated in the report that 'there was a time when Arab statesmen were willing to concede little Palestine to the Jews, provided that the rest of Arab Asia were free'.[29] It is not clear when this was said or by whom: certainly not by the most prominent of the Arabs. Later, in their evidence to the Peel Commission, the Arab Higher Committee challenged the status into which Palestine had been pushed:

> The Arabs maintain that all 'A' Mandates were or are being governed by this section with the exception of the Mandate for Palestine, and they claim that the Arabs of Palestine are as fit for self-government as the Arabs of Iraq and Syria.[30]

The report rehearsed again the longstanding causes of protest. There was nothing new or surprising in these. They included the frustrated wish of the Arabs for independence, especially since other Arab countries had achieved national status; the buying of land by the Jews; and immigration. The language of the report throughout was to the point. They wrote of 'an irrepressible conflict ... there is no common ground between them ... To pretend that Palestinian citizenship has any moral meaning is a mischievous pretence.'[31] The members realised what any impartial observer would have recognised:

> Poor and neglected though it was, to the Arabs who lived in it Palestine—or more strictly speaking, Syria, of which Palestine had been a part since the days of Nebuchadnezzar—was still their country, their home, the land in which their people for centuries past had lived and left their graves.[32]

There was a welter of grievances from the Jewish Agency. These included the administration not carrying out its 'obligation to facilitate immigration' and the complaint that restrictions on the admission of dependents 'are unduly harsh'.[33] The commission was sharp in its reply, stating that:

> It must be remembered that the Administration is faced with financial and other practical difficulties, such as inheriting an impoverished territory and the provision of the necessary services for a rapidly increasing immigrant population while, at the same time, safeguarding the position of the existing inhabitants. In our view, having regard to these difficulties, the existence at the present time of a Jewish population of 400,000 persons in Palestine is, in itself, a notable testimony to the work of the Government in discharging their obligations under the Mandate.[34]

The language of such official reports is a case study of underlying assumptions. Here the overwhelming majority, the Arabs become 'existing inhabitants' as though they are a small minority which can be expected to disappear.

There was much that is novel in the commission's opinions and recommendations. And there was a refreshing frankness about their recognition of the reality of the situation. Their underlying premise seems to have been that 'the Mandate itself ... had lighted the fire; and the Mandate itself, however applied or interpreted, was bound to keep it burning—except on the old original assumption that the two races could and would learn to live and work together.'[35]

But there could be no hope of this. The report went on to discuss the differences between the two cultures, concluding that 'the two races are entirely antagonistic'.[36] The Peel Commission effectively regarded the mandate as a failure. It had failed to hold any kind of balance between Jews and Arabs. The opening section of the report's conclusion set out an accurate assessment of the situation. It conveys the commission's central recommendation:

> Considering the attitude which both the Arab and the Jewish representatives adopted in giving evidence, the Commission think it improbable that either party will be satisfied at first sight with the proposals submitted for the adjustment of their rival claims. For Partition means that neither will get all it wants. It means that the Arabs must acquiesce in the exclusion from their sovereignty of a piece of territory, long occupied and once ruled by them. It means that the Jews must be content with less than the Land of Israel they once ruled and have hoped to rule again. But it seems possible that on reflection both parties will come to realise that the drawbacks of Partition are outweighed by its advantages. For, if it offers neither party what all it wants, it offers each what it wants most, namely freedom and security.[37]

Therefore the commission's central recommendation was partition.[38] The report discussed the details in depth. The Holy sites would remain neutral. A major problem, of course, would be that not all Arabs lived in the areas designated as theirs, nor did all the Jews live in what was to be their national home. There were 'about 225,000' Arabs in the putative Jewish area, and 'about 1,250' Jews in the Arab area. Therefore there would have to be population transfer. They considered that there had been a recent successful precedent for this, when Greek and Turkish populations had been moved at the end of a war between those countries in 1922. If what the commissioners called the 'surgical operation' was to be successful, 'the question must be boldly faced and firmly dealt with'.

The 'question' was indeed difficult. For example, the Jews moved out of Arab areas could be resettled in Jewish areas, but because of the increase in population, this would probably mean restrictions on immigration. And of course there would no longer be Jewish immigration into Arab territory. The Arabs 'constitute the major problem,' said the report. The hope lay in 'large-scale plans for irrigation, water-storage and development' in an area which would include Transjordan. As part of the plan, the latter would now include the Arab area of Palestine. All of this would cost a good deal of money—subvention was the commission's word for it—and they considered ways of meeting these costs. Notably, that the British people be asked to share the burden. The British treasury would be asked to contribute 'to an incalculable amount'.[39]

The reaction to the so-called Peel Plan was much as expected. Abdullah of Transjordan was in favour, since it meant an expansion of his country, although he wanted changes in the boundaries. Arab rivals did not like the idea of increased domination by Abdullah. There was a large and important conference of Arab states at Bloudan in Syria in September 1937, called by the Palestinian Arab High Commission in response to the Peel Report. The Arabs wanted the conference to be held in Jerusalem, but the British refused permission. The British government consul in Damascus expressed the view that there was 'little doubt that the long drawn-out deliberations over Palestine are reviving from the ashes of local jealousies, the pan-Arab phoenix'.[40]

France also disapproved of the Arab conference, and because of pressure from both France and Britain, Syria was not officially represented, although there were many Syrians present. The objectives of the conference were 'to study the duties of the Arabs in their respective countries and to agree on effective measures to resist the dangers posed by the Zionists'.[41] The conference rejected the Peel suggestion of partition in Palestine, and rejected the establishment of a Jewish state there.

Some Zionists were opposed to the central proposal of partition. At the twentieth Zionist Congress of 1937, serious reservations were expressed, but they saw some potential in some of the proposals. The opposition was forcibly expressed in *The Jewish Chronicle*:

> Partition is completely and irrevocably out of the question ... No Zionist, who *is* a Zionist will look at or touch it ... Jews will have none of it.[42]

There was the familiar Zionist historical fantasy:

> It was understood that the Jewish National Home was to be established in the whole of historic Palestine, *including Trans-Jordan* [my emphasis].[43]

There was a real danger of a split in the Zionist ranks, which Ben-Gurion and Weizmann wanted to avoid. They eventually agreed with the principle, and saw in the plan the opportunity to take the whole of what they believed to be Israel, by stealth, eventually moving the borders. So although this fell short of what the Zionists wanted, Weizmann believed that realistically this was the best they could expect. At a high-powered dinner party Churchill disagreed with his usual vehemence, which was exacerbated, or so Weizmann wrote to colleagues, by the fact that Churchill was 'under the influence of drink'.[44] Baffy Dugdale wrote how Churchill was 'in his most brilliant style, but very drunk, fulminated against HMG and in favour of Zionism for three hours'.[44] Certainly his language seems to have been intemperate. In any case, when he became prime minister he took no notice of the Peel Commission's recommendations.

The response of the government, eventually, was to be cautious. They issued another policy statement.[46] It stated that the government did not necessarily agree to 'certain features of the tentative plan of partition' and was 'in no sense committed to approval of that plan, and in particular that they have not accepted the proposal for the compulsory transfer in the last resort of Arabs from the Jewish to the Arab area'. The British government's formal response was to appoint yet another commission—the Woodhead Commission—to examine if and how Peel could be implemented. I will deal with this later.

The Jews were very much attracted by the proposal to expel Arabs since this had always been part of the Zionist programme. The Jewish claim on Palestine, as we have seen, rests on biblical myth and an assumption that the land was empty, or if it was not—that is, if it was noticed that there are Arabs there—then it could be made empty. This was clearly stated by Zionists, going back to an item in Herzl's diary entry for 12 June 1895:

> Having occupied the land and expropriated the private property, 'We shall endeavour to expel the poor population across the border unnoticed, procuring employment for it in the transit countries, but denying it any employment in our own country'.[47]

The policy was still solid some twenty years later:

> We cannot allow the Arabs to block so valuable a piece of historic reconstruction ... And therefore we must gently persuade them to 'trek' ... There is no particular reason for the Arabs to cling to these few kilometres. 'To fold their tents' and 'quietly steal away' is their proverbial habit: let them exemplify it now.

The wording is typical of Zionist writing: 'historic' emphasises the justice and inevitability of the process of 'reconstruction' that is repairing something which had existed. Then dispossession is described as a 'trek', which is reminiscent of the dignified movement of the Boers in South Africa. And finally, the Arabs do not live in the whole of Palestine, but only in a 'few kilometres'.[48]

Of course, such language covering quite false statements is to be expected from Zionists. But when powerful British political figures did the same it was very serious, because such statements in London grievously affected decisions. In 1919, when discussing the future of the Ottoman empire, Churchill wrote a memorandum for the cabinet saying: 'Lastly there are the Jews, whom we are pledged to introduce into Palestine and who take it for granted that the local population will be cleared out to suit their convenience.' Of his many dismissive remarks about the Arab population of Palestine this must be rank amongst the most contemptible, implying as it does that they are rubbish.[49]

Ben-Gurion saw in the recommendations the potential for movement forward. He became very enthusiastic about partition:

> He was overcome by a 'burning enthusiasm', he wrote. 'I see the realisation of this programme as an almost decisive stage at the beginning of our full redemption' he wrote in his diary, and the strongest possible impetus for the step-by-step conquest of Palestine as a whole ... It is a greater redemption than the days of Ezra and Nehemiah.[50]

He believed that the Peel Commission suggested the removal of the Arabs from the proposed Jewish state.[51] This he approved, since it was a cornerstone policy of the Zionists.

Ben-Gurion was a heartless fanatic, as such remarks demonstrate. He foresaw, and as it turned out quite rightly, that to establish a foothold could lead to expansion:

> Just as I do not see the proposed Jewish state as a final solution to the Jewish question, so do I not see partition as a final solution to the Palestine question.[52] ... 'Borders are not forever ... I doubt whether there is a single border on the globe that has not changed.'[53]

If there was anything constant about Ben-Gurion, it was his belief that borders could be expanded once a Jewish state was created, and that as that process was developed, the Arabs could be expelled. 'Causing the Arabs to flee as a war aim also reflected the old dream of population transfer.'[54] Ben-Gurion quite happily lied again, this time to UNSCOP, saying that 'the establishment of a Jewish state in Palestine did not require such a transfer'.[55]

Partition proposal for Palestine by the Peel Commission, 1937.

Very soon after the Peel Report was published, Palestine erupted again. This was heralded by the murder of a British official in Galilee, Lewis Andrews, which led to an increasingly strong reaction from the mandatory government. In the same month, September 1937, the Arab Higher Committee was abolished. Leading Palestinians were deported to the Seychelles and the mufti, Haji Amin al-Husseini, escaped to Lebanon.

At the outbreak of the Second World War, Haji Amin al-Husseini fled to Berlin. Arab resistance was now fragmented and the attempt by Amin to take charge failed. There was a large, ever-changing number of political societies, but all were nevertheless deadly. Arabs formed gangs and hid in the mountains. From there they ambushed and attacked British forces. The situation was complicated by the fact that Arab Christian support, not surprisingly, was slight. Another small minority, the Druze population, was important:

> Until 1936 they remained neutral in relation to Muslims and Jews. After that, most of them sided with the Jews ... their hostility, like that of the Maronite Christians, can be explained in large part by their mistrust of Arab nationalism and its heavy dose of Sunni Islam.[56]

It would seem unlikely that in a Muslim society, women should play an active part in armed rebellion, but in this uprising they did. They had certain advantages. Their dress made them difficult to identify, and of course they could certainly not be searched by British soldiers. There came into being in the late 1920s an Arab Women's Union. Young people too played their part. Rebels took over significant parts of the country, and there arose yet another complication. They tried to impose their own system of justice and social reform which included, *inter alia*, the cancellation of debt, some of which was owed to Arabs. They also persecuted, and sometimes murdered, those who would not support them. But their main business was to attack British and Jewish targets, and the British response was severe.

As part of this response there continued to develop close collaboration between the British and Jewish groups, notably the Haganah. This organised 'army' was established in 1920 to protect Jewish communities. It came to be called the Haganah, which is the Hebrew word for defence. It was not officially recognised by the British, but as in so much of the administration of Palestine, the authorities were unable, or more likely unwilling, to restrain Jewish initiatives. It is sometimes described as a militia, but strictly a militia is an official force under the authority of the government, and so the Haganah does not qualify for that designation. After the disturbances of 1929, the force became more organised, better armed, and better trained. In the late 1930s they even had aircraft. It is to be wondered how, in a turbulent area under British jurisdiction, such a large private army was tolerated:

As of April 1938, some twenty-one thousand volunteers were serving in the Haganah, including four thousand women. The vast majority were part-timers.[57]

During the course of its existence, the Haganah variously both supported and attacked the British. During the Second World War, there was included in it a group of pseudo commandos called the Palmach (strike force). The Haganah was to form the nucleus of the Israel Defence Forces, the IDF, when Israel was formed. It was suggested, especially during the Labour administration after 1945, that the Haganah be disbanded. But such was its strength that this was judged variously to be undesirable or impossible.

Settlements were fortified and 'police auxiliaries' were formed and armed. For some Jews this was not enough. By now 'Revisionist' Zionism had been founded by the extremist Jabotinsky in opposition to the official World Zionist Organisation. We have seen that it was so called because he wanted to 'revise' the mandate so that Transjordan would be included within Zionist ambition. They broke with the World Zionist Organisation in 1935 to form the New Zionist Organisation. The Irgun was its military arm. In 1937 the Irgun rejected the comparative restraint of the Haganah, and began to attack Arabs:

> In November 1937 they carried out the first terrorist attacks against Arab buses, cafés, markets, and other public places, which would be stepped up in the 1940s. In July 1938 74 Arabs were killed and 129 injured.[58]

The mayhem in the country was described by Khalil al-Sakakini, a Christian Arab and a well-known writer. 'Palestine became a battlefield,' he wrote.

> Demonstrations everywhere, attacks on police and railway stations, hundreds of dead and wounded. The hospitals are overflowing and tempers are hot with anger.[59]

As always in respect of the disturbances in Palestine, the numbers of casualties are uncertain. One generally agreed account is that more than 5,000 Arabs, over 300 Jews, and 262 British were killed, and at least 15,000 Arabs wounded. Segev points out that it is impossible to know how many were victims of attack, but records that the official account states that:

> From [1929] until the beginning of Second World War, more than 10,000 incidents were recorded, in which at least 2,000 people were killed, at least half of them Arabs. More than 400 Jews were killed in the terrorist attacks, and some 150 Britons.[60]

In March 1938, when it became clear that Arab resistance was continuing, the British high commissioner, Sir Arthur Wauchope, was replaced. He was regarded as not being hard enough on the Arabs. Previous to this, in June 1937, the death penalty was enacted for possession of weapons. Although this applied to all Palestinians, it hardly affected Jews since many Jews already had permission to carry arms. From 1937 to 1939 'more than 112 Arabs were hanged' in Acre 'mostly for the illegal possession of arms'.[61] Any family suspected of supporting terrorists had their houses blown up. This is a practice adopted by the modern state of Israel and a sure measure of the failure of the authorities to discover miscreants. There were curfews, and another British colonial practice was adopted: collective punishment.

Rebellions often produce heroes and oddities, and one of the strangest in this case was a British officer named Orde Wingate, an obsessive Zionist, who engaged with passion in the brutal suppression of the uprising. (Richard Meinertzhagen, of whom we have heard earlier, was another.) He is mostly remembered in British history for the 'Chindits', a unit he formed to fight the Japanese in Burma in the Second World War, and whose exploits became legendary. He was killed in India in an aeroplane crash later in the war, then holding the rank of acting major general.

Wingate was 'faintly unhinged', and driven by fanaticism. 'For pity's sake,' he is reported saying, 'let us redeem our promises to Jewry and shame the devil of Nazism, Fascism and our own prejudices.'[62] To the Jews in Palestine in the 1930s he was a hero. He was posted to Palestine in September 1936, and became an ardent Zionist. This can probably be attributed to his religious upbringing—he was a member of the Plymouth Brethren—and so he can be listed amongst those evangelical Christians whose beliefs are dominated, not to say distorted, by the Bible. As Mrs 'Baffy' Dugdale wrote:

> Lucky for us that Wingate's fanatical Zionism gets the better of him as an intelligence officer. He is clearly one of the instruments in God's hand.[63]

Wingate formed a virtual private army of some 200 men who made up what were called Special Night Squads. The purpose of these squads was to stop saboteur attacks on oil pipelines—a particularly damaging practice by the rebels—and generally to attack villages where, supposedly, there were rebels.

Wingate and his squads imposed severe punishment on the Arab people. On one occasion, having failed to get a prisoner to talk by choking him, he ordered one of his men to shoot him. 'Did you not hear? Shoot him,' he said. The recruit did as he was told.[64] He felt he could behave in such a way because he believed 'a Jew was worth twenty, thirty or even a hundred Arabs'.[65]

Eventually his behaviour became too extreme, and his political commitment so great, that he was removed from his post, no doubt in part because it was recognised that he was a security risk. But he was rewarded with a Distinguished Service Order. He was much admired by Jewish fighters such as the notorious Moshe Dayan. But Dayan also must have thought him slightly mad. He once reported Wingate, after an operation, sitting 'in the corner stark naked reading the Bible and munching raw onions'.[66] Several locations in modern Israel bear his name.

The British Government Disregards the Law

In February 1937 the government called a conference in London to try to negotiate a settlement. Since the Arabs would not agree to dealing directly with the Jews, separate meetings were held, but on 17 March the meetings ended in failure. The British government then set up the Woodhead Commission, mentioned earlier.[67] It was established to recommend ways of implementing the Peel proposals, specifically 'to recommend boundaries for the proposed Arab and Jewish areas and the enclaves to be retained permanently or temporarily under British Mandate'.[68] It began work in March 1938, and its report was published on 9 November 1938. It was chaired by an ex-Indian civil servant, Sir John Woodhead, and he was assisted by three members. It is generally regarded as a charade, since the evidence shows that the government did not intend to opt for partition anyway. It appears that Woodhead was encouraged to reach a 'correct conclusion' by the head of the Eastern Department.[69]

The commission went to Palestine, took evidence, although there was none from Arabs, and came up with three 'plans'. The first was based on the Peel proposals, with variations in the boundaries of each 'state'. Plan B was not much different, the major change being the inclusion of Galilee in the proposed continuation of the mandate. There would be fewer Arabs in the Jewish portion. The third plan also involved variation of the boundaries and a customs union between the Arab, Jewish and mandated territories.

Having set out the possibilities, the Woodhead Commission proceeded to object to them in varying degrees. Plan A would involve massive transfer of Arabs which would be resisted, and any voluntary transfer was unimaginable. The second plan was rejected by the majority of the commission because there was no solution to Galilee. As an Arab possession, it would be a threat to the Jewish enclave, and if it were to be part of the mandate, as proposed in Plan A, the Arabs would be deprived of an area which contained large numbers of their people. Plan C was yet another modification of borders, but it would need major financial support from the British government.

This last was a considerable objection. The government was in no position to give vast sums of money to any cause, including this one. It would be a 'very considerable financial liability'.[70] The hope of the commissioners was that some economic relationship could be established which would enable the three proposed areas to balance their financial discrepancies arising from the fact that the wealthiest Jews would be in the Arab areas and the wealthiest Arabs in the Jewish land. These difficulties were 'of such a nature that we can find no possible way to overcome them within our terms of reference'.[71]

The response to the report was much as expected from the Zionists. Weizmann wrote:

> The report was nothing but a 'piece of bare-faced cynicism ... Who had given a British official ... a disgruntled civil servant, and another civil servant the right to revise the mandate and judge the future of the Jewish people in Palestine?[72]

The government published its reaction, which was to reject the recommendations:[73]

> His Majesty's Government, after careful study of the Partition Commission's Report, have reached the conclusion that this further examination has shown that the political, administrative and financial difficulties involved in the proposal to create independent Arab and Jewish states inside Palestine are so great that this solution to the problem is impracticable.[74]

And so, for the moment, the proposal for partition disappeared. This, incidentally, removed another concern. The British government had always been concerned about repercussions from Muslim states, and especially from the huge Muslim population in India, about giving in to the Jews. India's Muslim population was the largest in the world at the time, and was itself interested in independence. It no doubt felt some solidarity with the Palestinian cause. The abandonment of partition removed this anxiety. Instead, the paper announced that the government would convene a meeting of the parties involved. The 'London Conference' was convened in February 1939. It was hampered by the fact that the Arabs would not deal directly with the Jews, and so the parties had to be dealt with separately. This fact alone led to suspicion, since MacDonald passed the views of the Arabs to the Jews and 'the Jews drew the conclusion that "the colonial secretary ... although clothing them in the form of arguments as advanced by the Arabs, conveyed the impression that in reality he was speaking the government's own mind"'.[75]

Before this there was much activity on the part of all the parties, but 'the general impression of these parleys is one of an unbridgeable gap separating Jewish and government interests'.[76] Nor was the attempted intervention by the 'Gentile Zionists' of much help. They were as extreme as they always were, and remain. Colonel J. C. Wedgwood wrote a memorandum which included the following recommendations:

> The occupation of land and refusal to leave except by force of law; going to prison; refusal to pay taxes; refusal to plead in the courts or to recognise their jurisdiction; attending demonstrations which had been banned; distributing illegal literature; assisting illegal immigration; (and) picketing and boycotting the disloyal.[77]

This was a remarkable document from a long-standing member of parliament, and sometime chancellor of the duchy of Lancaster. Reason prevailed though, and 'Chaim [Weizmann]... flung it [the memorandum] aside scornfully, and would make no use of it, indeed, hardly reading it'. The conference has been described by Tom Segev as 'a diplomatic farce'.[78] On 17 March it was pronounced a failure.

The government now seems to have somewhat lost patience with the intransigence of both sides. It issued a White Paper on 17 May 1939, written by Malcolm MacDonald of the Colonial Office, which set out firm proposals, already conveyed in essence at the conference, and which it was hoped, both sides would accept.[79] This was yet another forlorn hope, as may be gauged from the fact that it became 'known to the Jews as the Black Paper'. The main proposals were that Jewish immigration should be restricted to 75,000 over the next five years, and any further Jewish immigration would have to be approved by the Arabs. Jewish immigration would be restricted to special areas. Within ten years a Jewish national home would be set up in an independent Palestinian state.[80] There would be restrictions on the buying of land from Arabs by Jews.[81] With regard to the Jewish 'state' the White Paper emphasised that:

> His Majesty's Government believe that the framers of the Mandate in which the Balfour Declaration was embodied could not have intended that Palestine should be converted into a Jewish State against the will of the Arab population of the country ... His Majesty's Government therefore now declare unequivocally that it is not part of their policy that Palestine should become a Jewish State. They would indeed regard it as contrary to their obligations to the Arabs under the mandate as well as to the assurances which have been given to the Arab people in the past that the Arab population of Palestine should be made the subjects of a Jewish State against their will.[82]

On 22 May 1939, the House of Commons debated a motion that the White Paper was out of tune with the mandate. It was lost by 268 votes to 179. The Lords accepted the policy without voting: a reflection perhaps of support in that House for the Arab cause. Some Conservative Jewish MPs voted against their government and made clear that this proposal was a negation of Balfour. Drawing upon the fashionable political controversy of appeasement, Churchill asked, would the Arabs 'not be tempted to say: "They're on the run again. This is another Munich."'[83] For once Churchill's plea was rejected and the policy carried. Chamberlain understood the alleged dislike of Jews: 'no doubt the Jews aren't a lovable people: I don't care about them myself'.[84]

The Arabs were divided over the MacDonald paper. The Arab Higher Committee objected on a number of grounds, especially that the restrictions on migration were not enough. They wanted a complete ban, and the cancellation of the national home policy. There was an agreement with the British representative in July 1940 by the leaders of the Palestinian Arabs, accepting the paper.[85] The Zionists were very angry. Ben-Gurion labelled MacDonald 'a swindler, liar, fraudster, dissembler and traitor. He is our arch-enemy, perhaps the most dangerous enemy of the Hebrew nation after Hitler.'[86]

But their reaction was more violent than merely heaping abuse. 'Restraint was seen as weakness, and revenge as heroism and moral strength.'[87] There were attacks on government property and on Arabs:

A general strike was called for the day following its announcement, when violent and inflammatory speeches were made by Zionist leaders. In Jerusalem Arab shops were looted, the police stoned when they tried to maintain order, and a British constable was shot.[88]

An especially vicious series of assaults was mounted by Irgun in which thirty-eight Arabs were murdered and forty-four wounded. Irgun went further. Although in exile, Jabotinsky planned a full-scale revolt, and in this he was supported by Avraham Stern, who was to prove even more murderous. He planned to form a small army in Europe which would enter Palestine, and join the fight.

The White Paper was then discussed by the Permanent Mandates Commission of the League of Nations which met in Geneva in June 1939.[89] The discussion was wide-ranging: it included, for example, the news that the Jews had built new settlements in Galilee. One member asked if the Arabs had objected. The reply was that there was 'no hostility' but 'they were not received with open arms'. There was also discussion about the violence in Palestine, who was affected, and the structure of the 'gangs'.

Central to the proceedings was the appearance of Malcolm MacDonald himself, then colonial secretary. In his presentation he attributed the upsurge in violence in 1936 to the rejection of a scheme to establish a legislative council by parliament, and to the Arab conviction that Jewish influence lay behind that rejection. But the bulk of his presentation and the discussion which followed was the meaning behind, and the effects of, the Balfour Declaration. He included the following amazing claim:

> The authors of the Balfour Declaration and of the mandate who envisaged duties towards the Jews and duties towards the Arabs, which should be of equal weight, cannot have supposed that these duties would be in conflict, but that they would be mutually reconciled.

This is a clear rewriting of history: nobody in the slightest way involved could possibly have believed such a thing.

MacDonald was cautious in his opinion on such increasingly worn out questions as to the meaning of the words in the declaration, or what a national home would comprise, but his tone seems to have been aimed at emphasising the rights of the Arabs. The responses of the members of the commission were courteous but firm. Their opinion, in the main, was expressed by M. Rappard, and Count de Penha Garcia. The first observed that: 'A duty to establish a National Home for the Jews in Palestine without doing anything which might prejudice the political and social rights that a free people should be entitled to retain did not make sense.' The count summarised his view that 'the actual creation of a Jewish National Home in Palestine must be regarded as a political error and perhaps as an economic error'. There was also wide-ranging discussion over a number of possible solutions: for example, the question of some sort of federal arrangement was raised again.

There was one slight but important event associated with the debate about the conference and the White Paper. At long last the government realised the danger posed by the solid Zionism of Elliott, and his liaison with Mrs Dugdale, which had led to the Zionists having access to the detailed and secret debates about Palestine in the government. Mrs Dugdale reported to Shertok in June 1939 that Elliot believed that 'his own value to us is now at an end. He will not be consulted any more and will not form part of the inner ring which settles things.'[90]

Any opinions, and indeed any putative action arising from the White Paper, were quickly lost because of the onset of the Second World War: yet again, a fortunate event for the narrow Zionist aim in Palestine. In any case, as Ben-Gurion reported:

> Neville Chamberlain had told him explicitly that the new policy would last at most for the duration of the war: the government could hardly set itself a plan for ten years in advance.[91]

The question for the Zionists was how to proceed when once again, the world was in turmoil. For them, the initial debate was about the fate of European Jews, and how the Jews of Palestine should behave. Ben-Gurion expressed his priorities clearly:

> The world war of 1914-18 brought us the Balfour Declaration; now we must bring about the Jewish state.[92]

As to the threat to Jews in Europe:

> Ben-Gurion told the members of the Jewish Agency Executive that protecting the Jewish people throughout the world was now 'beyond human capacity' and as such they needed to focus in particular on local affairs.[93]

The onset of the Second World War posed problems for both the Arab and the Jewish populations of Palestine. What they both had in common was that their leaders saw an opportunity to breakaway from what they agreed was the stranglehold of British rule. The influx of Jews from Europe in the 1930s caused resistance on the part of Arabs, who began to attack the British Mandate authorities. The Jews responded with the increase in the activities of their own terrorist organisations, much to the confusion of ardent Zionists like Churchill. He was determined to keep a focus on Palestine, despite what was going on in Europe. He wrote in *The Daily Telegraph* on 20 October 1938 that 'the conditions in Palestine have passed into eclipse ... Jews and Arabs carry out hideous vendettas of murder and reprisal ... the spectacle is vexatious and discreditable.'[94] In what was a rare example of balance, Churchill said:

> We must give protection to the large Jewish community already established in the country; but we should also give to the Arabs a solemn assurance embodied if possible in an agreement to which Arab and Jew should be invited to subscribe, that the annual quota of Jewish immigration should not exceed a certain figure for a period of at least ten years.[95]

As Churchill predicted, there was uproar from the Jewish lobby. Churchill's own argument was hurled back at him: that Jewish immigration had improved Palestine no end. The general secretary of the Zionist federation of Great Britain wrote that Churchill's view 'is not supported by those who have played a leading part in the Palestine controversy in Parliament'.[96]

The pragmatists in both groups, Jews and Arabs, wondered which side they should support in the new world war. The attitudes of both were fluid, but in general the Palestinian Arabs could see little evidence of any British intention to give them what they wanted, whereas the German and Italians gave some indication that they were sympathetic to their cause. The Italians were an important force in the Mediterranean, and the Middle East, and did more than just utter sympathetic words:

> There is no doubt that they intervened in the Palestine rebellion. They quite certainly supplied the Arab insurgents with funds, guns and ammunition. There is at least one recorded incident of £40,000 being handed over by the Italian consulate in Jerusalem to an intermediary of the Mufti as early as April 1936.[97]

The Jews too, considering recent events, had little to expect and wondered whom they should support. They were still reeling from the White Paper, which seemed to have halted any impetus in the setting up of the Zionist state. Added to this, in February 1940 the 'Land Transfer Regulations' came into force. These stopped sales of land to Jews in most of Palestine, and 'left a paltry 5 per cent of the country fully accessible to Jews'.[98] The Italians courted them too. Mussolini himself had told Weizmann that:

> The more he watched the situation the more he felt convinced that there would be no improvement unless the Jews had a state of their own.[99]

Another important Italian assured the Jewish Agency that:

> Italy was not afraid of the Arabs and knew how to deal with them—as in Tripoli—and would aim at creating a Jewish state in Palestine.[100]

The Jews, like the Arabs, could hardly be blamed for seeking help from a major power when it was being offered. The Italian representative had discussions with Zionist officials, including Weizmann, assuring them of Italian support.[101] Naturally Weizmann had to be cautious in such double dealings, and, he claimed: 'the British government was always informed of the conversations'.[102] It is not credible that this would be done. The government would hardly condone such action.

The situation was complicated by the fact that in the beginning the Allies looked much weaker that the Axis. In the Middle East and North Africa the Italian presence seemed solid. They had established colonies in Ethiopia and Somaliland. The German Afrika Corps appeared unbeatable, and it looked as if Germany might invade Turkey. In 1940 the Italians bombed Tel Aviv and Haifa, the latter being important because it was a port, and had oil refineries. The bombing of Tel Aviv illustrated Ben-Gurion's single-mindedness. Over a hundred people were killed. 'He was appalled that the British press had not mentioned that Tel Aviv was a Jewish city, while making a point of reporting that five of the dead were Arabs.'[103]

There was further sporadic bombing of other coastal towns such as Acre and Jaffa, but the last bombing in Palestine was in June 1941. After that Palestine was relatively peaceful in respect of enemy attack. It would appear that even as early as February 1941, a city like Tel Aviv was a haven of peace:

> Tel Aviv offered a wealth of cultural events and leisure activities. Advertisements invited the public to attend sports competitions and fashion shows, end-of-year sales, plays, concerts, and other entertainments. The city's cafés and bars, hotels and dance clubs, remained crowded and lively, as if there were no world war.[104]

In Iraq there was a coup in 1941 by the pro-Axis prime minister, Rashid Ali al-Gaylani, who ordered the British to leave. An Allied force invaded from the south and regained control, with Rashid fleeing to Syria and Lebanon. Lebanon was in the hands of the Vichy French, and there was an uneasy truce with them. But it became clear that Vichy was aiding the Axis, and in June 1941, the Allies invaded. Included in the force were members of the Haganah, but for the Zionists such collaboration had advantages besides an Allied victory: 'Ben-Gurion saw it as a step towards the establishment of a Jewish army.'[105] By 14 July the Vichy forces had surrendered.

The stunning Allied victories in North Africa, especially the second battle of El Alamein, showed that the Allies were gaining the upper hand, but some Arab countries were slow to side with them. Kuwait and Transjordan declared immediately, in 1939, and the famed Arab Legion took an active part in the fighting. Iraq only declared for Britain in January 1943, and Egypt, Saudi Arabia, Syria and Lebanon only three months before the end of the war.

Some sections of Palestinian Arab society had decided that their best hope lay with supporting the Axis. This was far from universally agreed. The main rivals of the al-Husseini clan, who led the approach to the Axis leaders, were the Nashashibis, who were sympathetic to the British. About 12,000 Arabs signed up to fight for the Allies. The person who was to lead the endeavour to ally the Palestinian Arabs with the Axis was the mufti of Jerusalem, Haj Amin al-Husseini. His father, Mohammed Tahir al-Husseini, had been mufti before him, and had protested against Jewish settlement and immigration.[106]

By the beginning of the war, Amin al-Husseini was already one of the most prominent people in Palestine. He had fought in the Ottoman Army, but later became a recruiter for the Arab Revolt. In 1920 he was sentenced to ten years imprisonment for incitement in the Nebi Musa riots, but he was pardoned by the British, and in 1921 he was appointed mufti of Jerusalem by Sir Herbert Samuel, despite the fact that he had lost the election which was held to fill the post. The election had in fact been won by the rival clan, the Nashashibis, but Samuel was anxious to prevent any one clan being all powerful. This rivalry harmed the Palestinian cause for many years, but in 1936 the Arab Higher Committee was formed, and from then on there was more collaboration between the two, even though al-Husseini's title had by now been elevated to grand mufti, and he was also elected chairman of the new committee. Before this, in 1921, a Supreme Muslim Council was established, and al-Husseini was elected its president in 1922. He was regarded for some years after that as a reliable ally by the British, even though at a Haifa conference in 1921, the Arab position on Palestine changed. Previously, it was thought of as part of Syria, but now the ambition was to create a Palestinian state, a policy which the mufti supported.

By the time of the outbreak of war, therefore, the mufti was in a powerful position. He had been involved in the Arab rising, but had evaded capture in 1937 by hiding in the Haram, the neighbourhood of the Al-Aqsa mosque. From there, in October 1937, he escaped to Lebanon. In the same year he reconstituted the Arab Higher Committee. In October 1939 he fled again, this time to Iraq. In 1941 there was a coup in Iraq which was part of a protest against British rule, and he escaped yet again, with the help of the Italians, eventually to Europe. It was then that his activities began which were to earn him a reputation, in Jewish versions of history, as a supreme example of treachery. There are many claims of his villainy from Jewish writers. Zev Golan is one who exemplifies this:

> The infamous Mufti, el Husseini and his gangs were in their heyday ... the yelping marauders ... were attacking the most defenceless Jewish settlers in a war of ambush and pogrom.[107]

Karsh describes the mufti's overtures to the Nazis:

> It was indeed the Husseinis, the foremost influence in Palestinian Arab politics, who displayed the greatest enthusiasm for Nazism, going so far as to model

their youth organisation on the lines of the *Hitlerjugend* and temporarily naming it 'The Nazi Scouts'. Losing no time, the Mufti rushed to the German consul in Jerusalem to tell him that 'the Muslims in Palestine and elsewhere were enthusiastic about the new regime in Germany and looked forward to the spread of Fascism throughout the region'.[108]

However, as we shall go on to see, the possibility of dealing with Germany, was indulged, even attempted, by some Zionists too.

Al-Husseini arrived in Rome in October 1941, and in the same month met Mussolini. He offered the dictator the support of the Arabs in the course of what was apparently a friendly discussion. From Rome he moved on to Germany, where he met top Nazi leaders, including von Ribbentrop and Himmler. But his greatest prize came when he met Hitler in Berlin on 28 November 1941. He expressed solidarity with Germany, since they had the same enemies: the English, the Bolsheviks and the Jews. He offered Arab support, and suggested that he could raise an Arab Legion to fight for Germany. Hitler assured him that, in time, he would help with freeing the Palestinians from the Jews. The mufti asked if Hitler would make a public statement to that effect. But the reply was that it was too soon, since the French might think they would lose their colonies and this would increase their support for De Gaulle.[109]

On 25 November 1941 the grand mufti declared a jihad (a holy war) against the Allies. In December 1942 he made a speech at the opening of the Islamic Central Institute in Berlin. The prospects for support from both Germany and Italy must have looked good. Quite what the mufti could actually deliver is debatable. He obviously had no control over the several Arab kingdoms, or over the Arab populations of the Vichy territories. He had suggested raising a force from among Arab prisoners of war held in German camps, but this was to suppose that they would be prepared to change sides. The only certain support he had was in Palestine, and it is impossible to know how far this extended.

The mufti's ambition to bring about, not only the removal of the Zionists in Palestine, but the extermination of all Jews, has made him one of the most hated figures in Jewish writing. As the Zionists began to develop their favourite method of eliminating enemies, by targeted assassination, al-Husseini became the object of this ambition. The plot did not die with the end of the war. 'The Jewish Agency's Political Department … tried to locate [him] and kill him several times between 1945 and 1948 … all those attempts failed.'[110] Al-Husseini died of natural causes in Beirut in 1974. The venom directed at him has never stopped. An especially bizarre attempt to blacken the mufti was made by Prime Minister Netanyahu in 2015, when he alleged that it was the mufti who suggested the idea of the Holocaust to Hitler.[111]

The attitude of the Zionists to the war seemed to be firm. The Jewish Agency is often quoted as giving voice to the official position:

> The war which has now been forced upon Great Britain by Nazi Germany is our war, and all the assistance that we shall be able and permitted to give to the British Army and to the British people we shall render wholeheartedly.[112]

Weizmann wrote to Chamberlain that 'the Jews worldwide' would back Britain and there would be 'harnessing [of] Jewish manpower, technical ability, and resources to the war effort'.[113] This was an extravagant claim, and its authority is as questionable as that of the offers put by the mufti to the Axis.

There was an attempt to implement this policy. Ben-Gurion encouraged people to register for enlistment, and some 100,000 did so.[114] Weizmann went to see Churchill, and the outcome was that Weizmann was authorised to tell the chief of the Imperial General Staff that Palestinian Jews could be recruited to defend the country.[115] But this is not quite what Ben-Gurion had in mind: at least it was not his ultimate aim. What he wanted was a Jewish army. It was not enough for Jews to join the British Army. 'Why not?' was a question many people asked. Ben-Gurion's reply was that 'it was a "Jewish complex"'.[116] He saw a Jewish army as an important force to achieving independence. It can be imagined how disappointed he was when it was announced that a regiment would be established, but that it would consist of both Jews and Arabs. This was 'a slap in the face of the Jewish people'.[117] But he understood the reasoning, as was clear to everyone: 'They do not want to have Jewish soldiers because after the war they may turn against them.' But he promised to encourage enlistment 'not for the benefit of the British but for our own'.[118] In the event, the 30,000 who volunteered for military service 'constituted only a third of those who had said, at the beginning of the war, that they were prepared to enlist'.[119] Instead Ben-Gurion expanded the Haganah, and a far-reaching programme was developed. This included cultural education, 'a minimum of Hebrew' and 'books that constitute "an organic part of Jewish culture"'.[120] In the final years of the war a 'Jewish Brigade' of some five thousand was established, and no doubt Ben-Gurion would have been pleased to see that they had insignia on which was a star of David.

Although most of the Jewish terrorist bodies agreed to cease their violence, the all important Lehi, refused to do so. Their activities eclipsed any anti-British Arab activity for the rest of the war. Their leader was Avraham Stern. He was probably the most vicious of the terrorists of the day: inexplicably described by Bergman as 'the romantic ultra-nationalist', a strange adjective to apply to a professional killer.[121] His life and career was typical of many noteworthy Zionists. He was born in Poland in 1907 and aged 18 he moved to Israel. He served in the Haganah, then joined the Irgun. He returned to Poland to try to raise 40,000 men to fight the British, with the support of the Polish government, but the fall of Poland brought that adventure to an end. When most terrorists agreed to stop attacks on the British, he refused to do so and formed the Lehi—'Fighters for the freedom of Israel'. Like the mufti, he saw the potential in an alliance with Germany, and in 1940 he tried twice to put this in place:

Stern had passed a message into Vichy Syria, offering to fight for Germany if Hitler would support 'the re-establishment of the Jewish state in its historic borders, on a national and totalitarian basis, allied to the German Reich'.[122]

There was no reply.

Stern and 'his tiny band of followers employed a targeted mayhem of assassinations and bombings'.[123] They planted bombs, shot policemen, and generally deflected the attention of the British from the business of fighting the war. It is impossible to know where the loyalties of this 'tiny band' lay since their backgrounds were obscure, but it would appear that some, at least, were what would later be called mercenaries:

> Amongst the Stern Group members captured after recent attacks on railway workshops in Haifa Bay on June17, there were several recently arrived illegal immigrants who could not even speak Hebrew. Police investigation point to the large proportion of illegals recruited into the Jewish underground organisation ... former guerrilla fighters in Europe are given priority in illegal immigration transport for the sake of the use of their experience against government and security forces in this country. On arrival, several have described themselves as 'partisans'.[124]

The damage that Stern did was such that there was a price on his head. He was eventually cornered in a house in Tel Aviv on 12 February 1942, and what happened then is, for Zionists, a matter of dispute. The official version is that he was shot dead while trying to escape through a window. The senior officer present, Geoffrey J. Morton, also said that he thought Stern might detonate a bomb, which he had threatened to do. The Zionist allegation was that he was murdered in cold blood. This allegation was promulgated by four publishers, who were successfully sued by Morton. One, who published the allegation by Menachem Begin, settled out of court. Begin had written: 'after the detectives had so foully murdered the unarmed Avraham Stern'.[125]

Although it is claimed that Stern's activities were disapproved of, Stern is regarded as a hero in Israel: not only by the public, but by politicians and officials. The latter attend an annual ceremony of remembrance at his grave, the place where he was shot is now a museum, and a town is named after him. And in what seems to be the ultimate accolade in Israeli martyrology, he was commemorated on a postage stamp. His capture and death were triumphs for the Palestine police, whose skill led Arthur Koestler to describe them as 'one of the most disreputable organisations in the British Commonwealth ... with Black and Tan veterans in leading positions, riddled with former members of Mosley's Blackshirts.'[126]

Stern's followers carried on his campaign, now led in part by Yitzhak Shamir, later to become prime minister of Israel. One of their targets was Geoffrey

Morton, whom they had tried to kill on several occasions before Stern's death, because of his skill in finding terrorists. On one of the occasions they killed three policemen in the attempt, two of whom were, paradoxically, Jews. Eventually they managed to wound Morton and he returned to England.

During the war, a source of help to the terrorists was a successful partnership between the Stern gang and the Free French. By 1944, the gang and the French were in contact, and the French consul in Jerusalem received an article which read: 'the Zionist Resistance Movement and Free France have very clear common interests'.[127] It became clear that this was translated into active supply of materiel to the gang. Not only did the gang deal with the Free French, they were helped by the Vichy:

> A former member of the Stern gang confirmed that the Vichy administration in Beirut had 'gladly supplied us with arms of all kinds, knowing that they were intended to attack their British enemy'.[128]

This collaboration had much to do with the historic colonial competition between the British and the French, exacerbated at the time by rivalry over Syria and Lebanon.[129]

While the Jewish terrorists were doing as much damage as possible in Palestine, a conference was taking place in America which it is generally agreed, shifted Zionist policy away from cooperation with the British, a change which some of the leaders believed would get them what they wanted. They realised the enormous advantage they had now that Churchill was in power.

This conference was held at a famous New York hotel called the Biltmore and it became known as the Biltmore Conference. Held from 6 to 11 May 1942, it was attended by some 600 delegates from eighteen countries. The delegates included both Weizmann and David Ben-Gurion. The latter played a major role in designing the conference. A principal object was to get as many Americans as possible to support the idea of the Jewish state, since many Jews were not enthusiastic, or were plainly hostile. The implications of the resolutions passed at the conference were that the 1939 White Paper would mean the end of the Jewish 'state', and that Zionism must take a more aggressive stand.

At the end of the conference a statement was issued which set out the policies and demands of the Zionists. These were preceded by a grand statement that American Zionists 'reaffirm their unequivocal devotion to the cause of democratic freedom and international justice'.

1 Conference 'offers a message of hope and encouragement to their fellow Jews in the Ghettos and concentration camps'.
2 It sends its 'warmest greetings to the Jewish Agency Executive in Jerusalem'.
3 It explains how 'the Jewish people have awakened and transformed their ancient homeland'. Their numbers have increased 'from 50,000 at the end

of the war to more than 500,000 ... They have made the waste places to bear fruit and the desert to bloom'. It is 'a notable page in the history of colonisation'.

4. In this 'their Arab neighbours have shared'. They express 'the readiness and the desire of the Jewish people for full cooperation with their Arab neighbours'.
5. They call for 'fulfilment of the original purpose of the Balfour Declaration and the Mandate which recognises the historical connection of the Jewish people with Palestine' and to found there a Jewish Commonwealth.
6. It emphasises 'its unalterable rejection of the White Paper of 1939, and denies its moral or legal validity'. The White Paper 'seeks to limit and in fact to nullify Jewish rights to immigration and settlement in Palestine. They quote Churchill as saying that "it constitutes a breach and a repudiation of the Balfour Declaration". The White paper is 'cruel and indefensible in its denial of sanctuary to Jews fleeing from Nazi persecution'.
7. Jews must be allowed to fight in the war, as a military force, 'under its own flag'.
8. Conference urges that 'the gates of Palestine be opened, and that the Jewish Agency be vested with control of immigration' and given authority for the 'development of unoccupied and uncultivated lands'.

This is an altogether remarkable document. As ever in Zionist propaganda, it is full of blatant lies. It also exaggerates and entrenches the notion, often proclaimed by Churchill, that the Jews made 'the desert bloom'. There is talk of how the Arabs had gained so much from the loss of their land, some of which was 'unoccupied and uncultivated', and there is again the hollow claim about 'cooperation'. Neither the declaration nor the mandate recognised 'the historical connection'. Quite the contrary: as we have seen, key figures like Lord Curzon utterly rejected the claim.

A central point is true. The White Paper intended to limit immigration, and the Biltmore Conference was a warning that the Zionists would not tolerate this. But the conference and Churchill were wrong. It was not a breach of the declaration but consonant with a key provision concerning the rights of 'minorities'. The handing over of control of immigration to the Jewish Agency would have been a coup indeed. The conference also formalised what was to become an insistent theme: that Jews should be saved from the Holocaust and its aftermath. 'The fate of the displaced persons in Europe and that of the Jews in Palestine' is a vital factor in the understanding of the role played by the Holocaust in the creation of the state of Israel.[130] This is despite the fact that Ben-Gurion was never very impressed with the Jews who were forced to settle in Palestine because of the Nazis:

> He saw them as a problem, since they had come as refugees, rather than Zionists 'And they remained alien to our enterprise and our vision,' he said. 'They are different and can bring a holocaust upon us'.[131]

The right to fight in the war was an antique demand. It had been resisted because it was believed, correctly, as events were to show, that training Jews in military skills would blow up in the faces of the Palestinian authorities, as had been the case after the First World War.

The central aim of the conference was that advanced by Ben-Gurion. It was rooted in a conviction that the British had moved from support for a Jewish home to a pro-Arab stance, which would deny them that home. Therefore support had to be found elsewhere, and Ben-Gurion's belief was that it would be in America. At that time there was a strong vein of anti-Zionism among American Jews. This had several aspects: the belief that American Jews were Americans first and that any deviation from that would be construed as disloyalty or worse; that to attack British policy would undermine the united war effort; and that Palestine should form a spiritual symbol of Judaism, but no more. Whatever Biltmore may have claimed, and whatever it may have achieved, the conference 'would later come to be seen as a milestone in the struggle for the establishment of the State of Israel'.[132]

Ben-Gurion had spent a lot of the time between 1940 and 1942 in America, and had worked at developing a consciousness and an enthusiasm among American Jews for the Zionist ambitions in Palestine. And although he failed to convert all of them, especially the leaders, he had achieved enough to initiate that swing in interest which was to prove critical in the years ahead, as Britain wrestled with undoing the damage it had done by issuing the declaration. The programme which resulted from the conference was proof of that: especially in its implication, or so it was assumed by people at the time and since, that a bi-national solution (Arab and Jew) was now rejected. Morris claimed that 'the possibility that the state would be established only in part of Palestine was implicit'.[133] But he went on to show that the programme 'triggered bitter controversies within the Zionist movement, with a faction breaking away because they disagreed with the compromise implicit in Biltmore: that the state would encompass only part of Palestine'.[134]

What is certain is that the vague promise of a 'home' was now replaced with a sturdy demand for a Commonwealth. It seemed that both Zionist and non-Zionist Jews were now agreed on that. The conference also achieved a personal ambition of Ben-Gurion's, which was to unseat Weizmann. The latter had never lost his belief in the loyalty to Zionism of key powerful players in the British establishment, and as long as he believed that, he looked for 'progress'. What Ben-Gurion wanted was action, and now he would get it. Weizmann's demise was hastened by a successful conspiracy to remove him from the presidency of the World Zionist Organisation in 1946. Soon after the conference, in August 1942, Ben-Gurion saw the Biltmore programme through the inner Zionist General Council in Jerusalem, so making it 'official' policy.

It was a critical moment in the relationship between the various parts of the US government and the Zionists. Until the war, as part of its global policy, the US did not interfere with the British administration of Palestine. Beginning in 1922, however, successive governments advocated some kind of a national 'home' for the Jews. After Biltmore, the pressure became more serious:

> In 1944, under the impact of the Zionists' Biltmore programme, the Democratic party platform spoke of a 'free and democratic Jewish commonwealth' while the Republican party used the phrase 'a free and democratic commonwealth' in Palestine. In the ensuing campaign Governor Dewey indicated that the kind of commonwealth the party envisioned was a Jewish one.[135]

It is important to note the soon-to-be-standard omission of any mention of the Arabs, never mind any consideration of what would happen to them in this brave new world. The arrival of Truman in the White House was another piece of remarkable good fortune to attend Zionist history.

In 1943, Begin took command of the IZL, and it resumed a murderous campaign against the British, even though the war was still being fought. Parallel to it were the activities of the Stern gang (Lehi). It was this latter which carried out one of the highlights of Jewish terrorism, and about which some Jews agonised: the murder of the British high commissioner and secretary of state for the colonies, Walter Guinness, 1st Lord Moyne. He was gunned down in Cairo on 6 November 1944, and an Egyptian policeman eventually caught the murderers. Lance Corporal Arthur Fuller, who was accompanying Moyne, was killed immediately. The shooting of Fuller was a brutal and gratuitous murder. Apart from the horror in which the act was regarded in Britain, the debate immediately began among Zionists as to whether the murder had achieved anything.

For the Zionists the issue was simple. Any impartiality could not be tolerated. This killing fulfilled Stern's ambition that a British resident minister should be murdered. As always, any criticism had to be stifled, and someone as important as Moyne could not be allowed to express either opposition to the Zionists or support for the Palestinians. So what were the kinds of remarks that were intolerable? To a balanced observer the kinds of remarks made by Lord Moyne appear as perfectly respectable. In a speech made in the House of Lords in 1942, for example, he said:

> If a comparison is to be made with the Nazis, it is surely those who wish to force an imported regime upon the Arab population who are guilty of the spirit of aggression and domination.[136]

As well as expressing such views, Moyne was an advocate of a political solution called 'Greater Syria', which proposed the amalgamation of Palestine with Syria. This would obviously eliminate the proposed Jewish state. Therefore he had to go. His murder saw the end of debate about 'Greater Syria'. Yitzhak Shamir (at the time carrying the name Yitshak Izernitsky) and a leader of Lehi, organised the killing. In a rambling interview in 1993 with an American student Joanna Saidel, he said:

> He was an anti-Semite, Lord Moyne. And he had a hand in the White Paper, in carrying out the White Paper policy. I don't say I would have, if I had to decide, that I would decide that he ought to be shot, but once he was shot there were good reasons for him being shot ... He didn't believe that there exists such a thing as like a Jewish nation, or a Jewish people ... and therefore we decided to make this operation.[137]

The murderers were caught, due to the vigilance of the Egyptian police officer, and the two were hanged in Cairo on the 22 March 1945. Shamir later arranged for the recovery of their bodies and they were buried with full military honours.

Even the loyal Churchill was shaken by the killing of Moyne. He was a close friend, and Churchill had recently tried to persuade the Zionists that Moyne was actually sympathetic to their cause. His anger, which was short lived, was expressed in a speech to the House of Commons on 17 November 1944:

> If our dreams for Zionism are to end in the smoke of assassins' pistols and all labours for its future to produce only a new set of gangsters worthy of Nazi Germany, many like myself will have to reconsider the position we have maintained so consistently and so long in the past.[138]

Churchill wrote a letter to Weizmann, which must have come as a nasty shock:

> The Palestine position, now as concerns Great Britain, is simply such a hell-disaster that I cannot take it up again, and must, as far as I can, put [it] out of my mind.[139]

Fortunately for the Zionists, Churchill soon regained his composure, and resumed his incessant advocacy on their behalf. In Palestine, Ben-Gurion persuaded his colleagues that the dissident members should be hunted down. A 'National Guard' was formed, and a campaign mounted:

> According to the *Haganah History Book*, about seven hundred names were handed over to the British Secret police, and about three hundred people were arrested. Some thirty children were expelled from school.[140]

This 'hunting Saison', as it is termed, did not last long—only from November 1944 to March 1945—when, with the end of the war in sight, all the Jewish terrorist groups joined in the campaign against the British.

Although the Haganah held a truce, this did not include attempts to stop illegal immigration. This was a constant source of friction because the British were determined to carry out the provisions in the White Paper by restricting entry. The transport of illegal immigrants had begun some years earlier. In 1934 the first boat arrived and there had been a steady stream since.[141] The money to buy such ships came from a variety of sources, including the Hebrew Committee for National Liberation in the United States, 'and the British Government's wages train in Hadera'. This was a boast by Begin about robbery. [142]

Nor were the British authorities always to blame for the inevitable accidents and disasters. In 1940 three ships, the *Atlantic*, the *Pacific* and the *Milos* arrived in Haifa. They were carrying refugees from Europe under an arrangement made by a Jewish businessman with Nazi approval. The British refused them entry, and started to move them to another ship, the *Patria*, with the intention of sending them to Mauritius and Trinidad. The transfer was in process when a large bomb exploded, on 25 November 1940, causing the ship to sink quickly. Between 200 and 300 people died—the number is uncertain. After a number of baseless allegations about who was responsible, it eventually became clear that the Haganah had planted the bomb. Koestler made one of the more bizarre allegations that 'at 9 a.m. that day the passengers blew up their ship'.[143] Whether because of incompetence or some other reason, the first attempt had failed, and the second bomb was much too powerful. There was the usual anger in the Haganah about lack of consultation, but the incident did the Zionists a good deal of harm. The survivors were allowed to stay in Palestine, but those who had remained on the *Atlantic* went on to Mauritius. Ben-Gurion's attitude to the incident was the particularly bizarre. It was a 'Zionist action,' he said. He was in America at the time. 'Had he been in Palestine at the time he would not have prevented it ... no-one expected so many victims. It was an act of God.'[144]

In 1941 there was an especially infamous episode concerning a ship called the MV *Struma*. This ship, which was quite unseaworthy, was chartered to take Jewish illegal refugees from Romania to Palestine. She left Romania on 12 December 1941 with about 781 passengers on board, well in excess of her capacity. Repeated engine failures resulted in her being towed into Istanbul. The refugees were not allowed to disembark, because the British made it clear that they would not be allowed into Palestine, and the Turks did not want to take responsibility for them. On 23 February 1942, the Turks towed the ship out to sea, and cast her adrift. The next day she was sunk by a torpedo from a Soviet submarine. There was just one survivor. There was fury and disgust at this treatment of the refugees, and in particular at the behaviour of the British high commissioner for Palestine, Harold MacMichael, who was blamed for the deaths.

A poster appeared in Palestine stating that he was 'Wanted for Murder'. Irgun tried to murder him by ambushing his car, but the skill of his driver saved his life. The British fined the nearby settlement £500, which was probably never collected. Such a derisory amount for an attack on the most senior British officer, led to condemnation from Lord Moyne who drew parallels with the severe punishment visited upon the Arabs after the murder of Andrews in 1937.[145]

In 1945 a Labour government was elected in Britain, and the ultimate consequences for the Zionist cause were quite unexpected, but not by all. At first, many were delighted. A telegram was sent to the Labour party expressing 'Our hearty greetings at your brilliant victory ... There was even popular dancing in the streets of Tel Aviv'.[146] There was good reason for the Zionists to rejoice. The record of support from the Labour party seemed solid. There had been pro-Zionist resolutions at eleven party conferences, but it was the opinion of one Labour MP 'that the average member who attended these conferences had about as much knowledge of the Palestine question as I have of the moon. These resolutions were accepted because nobody objected.'[147] The leader, Clement Attlee, however, expressed his support, even for the ultra view that Transjordan should become Jewish.[148]

When the 1939 White Paper was issued, Herbert Morrison, a senior Labour figure had said:

> It ought to be known by the House that this breach of faith which we regret, this breach of British honour, with its policy with which we have no sympathy, is such that the least that can be said is that the Government must not expect that this is going to be automatically binding upon their successors.[149]

This was followed by a resolution at the Labour Party Conference in 1944:

> There is surely neither hope nor meaning in a 'Jewish National Home' unless we are prepared to let the Jews, if they wish, to enter this tiny land in such numbers as to become a majority. There was a strong case for this before the war. There is an irresistible case now, after the unspeakable atrocities of the cold and calculated German Nazi plan to kill all Jews in Europe.[150]

Begin and his followers were sceptical. The Irgun published its reaction:

> In Britain a Labour Party Government has taken office. Before coming to power this Party undertook to restore the Land of Israel to the people of Israel as a free State, to which all the exiles of Zion and those who long for Zion could return. This in itself is no guarantee for the attainment of our national aim ... men and parties in opposition ... have for twenty-five years made many promises and undertaken clear obligations. But on coming to power they have gone back on their word and perpetuated the policies of their predecessors.[151]

Meanwhile, during the war years, the British government wondered what to do about Palestine. They had now realised that they had created a powder keg, and that even though the war was being pursued, the day would come when reality had to be faced. A cabinet committee was set up in July 1943 to plan a policy for Palestine. In the same year a Middle East War Council was also established. In 1943 the latter recommended an increase in the numbers of troops and police to be stationed in Palestine, and also crucially expressed the opinion that any deviation from the 1939 White Paper would be fatal.

In December 1943, the cabinet committee recommended partition. This considerable reversal was deplored by the chiefs of staffs, who forecast that the Arabs would be furious. Churchill, as expected, disagreed with them, believing that if the Arabs became violent the Jews would beat them. Everyone was left wondering what might happen if there was partition: for example, whether extremist Zionists would accept it. Much of the discussion was taken up with arguments about the borders of the two putative states.[152]

By now Weizmann had protested to Churchill because it had been stated in parliament that the White Paper was 'the firmly established policy'.[153] Churchill's response was unchanged:

As promised, Churchill elaborated on his views of the [1939] White Paper before the Cabinet, emphasising that he personally remained a supporter of the Balfour Declaration, as modified by 'his own' White Paper of 1922.[154]

The cabinet committee in September 1944 was still insisting on partition. The view of the Middle East Defence Committee was unshaken. It was 'unanimous in the opinion that *the partition of Palestine would, from the military standpoint, spell irremediable disaster.*'[155]

Despite the virulent opposition of the Foreign Office, the government, at the ending of the war, seems to have drifted towards Churchill's view, and to partition. But the new Labour government, more concerned with relationships and sympathy for the Palestinians, was more guarded in decisions about the future of Palestine, and more generally the British relationship with the Arab world. It may be noted that the foreign minister in that government was Ernest Bevin, and he had serious worries about Palestine, which justified Begin's cynicism.

Bevin was one of the great figures in the powerful Labour government. He had proved himself in the wartime coalition administration as minister of labour and national service, in which post he distinguished himself. He was admired by Churchill, whose political views were very different. Bevin was the symbol of a new kind of minister. He came from a very humble background, and had limited formal education. His speech could be rough and direct. He was the sort of person with whom the Zionists were unfamiliar. His directness and his caution towards the Zionists caused them great concern. It was not long before he was defined as antisemitic by the Zionists, which, according to Richard Crossman, led to Bevin being 'convinced that the Jews were organising a world conspiracy against poor old Britain and, in particular, against poor old Ernie'.[156]

At the end of 1945, Bevin set up an Anglo–American Committee of Inquiry. Its establishment was announced at the same time by Truman and Bevin. Before this, 'a lot of negotiations—even haggling—took place'. This was after a huge amount of debate and disagreement about wording, terms of reference, and even how long the inquiry should take.[157] According to the preface to the report, it was charged with examining conditions in Palestine, what the place of Jewish immigration should be, and consulting Arab and Jewish representatives.[158] There were twelve members —six British and six American. This was an important indication that the US was becoming more involved. The setting up of the membership was one indication of how odd some of the discussion was. It was suggested that Field Marshal Smuts, a fervent Zionist, should be made president, and that Weizmann should be a member. Both suggestions were ignored. The inquiry delivered their report in Lausanne on 20 April 1946.[159]

The position of the Jews in Europe was dire. Some six million had been murdered by the Nazis and their allies, which left about 10 per cent of those remaining classified as homeless. They were often stranded in countries not of their birth and upbringing, and were put in camps while their future was argued about. They had to contend, not only with uncertainty and often wretched living conditions, but with a good deal of hostility. This arose in part because they were sometimes foreigners, and they were alleged to be uncooperative, workshy, and even criminal: 'the camp authorities complained of "depredation and banditry"'.[160] The control authorities reported that 'their past lack of discipline and black market records does not dispose us to regard them as desirable ... and the morale of our camps as a whole would benefit by their departure.'[161]

Those US troops who dealt with them at first hand, horrified Truman's special envoy, Earl G. Harrison, who reported that 'we appear to be treating the Jews as the Nazis treated them except that we do not exterminate them'.[162] An inquiry among the troops had revealed that a high proportion believed that 'Hitler was partly right in his treatment of Jews'.[163]

The members of the inquiry went to displaced persons camps in Europe, travelled to the Middle East, and heard testimony from a wide range of people. Both Jewish and Arab representatives produced a mass of documentation, each of course advancing their own agenda, neither of which had any common ground. Like all visitors to DP camps they were distressed to see the state of the people there, and anxious to discover what would be the best for their future. There were three options. The first was that they should go to Palestine. The second was that they should go to other countries. Or, thirdly, that they should be resettled in their original countries. The reaction to the third seems to have varied from country to country: some were more hopeful than others.[164]

The prospect for returning to Germany was, in the nature of things, dismal, but the least attractive place of return was Poland. Once the Soviets took Poland a civil war erupted, in which Jews were often singled out for attack. This was often for political reasons—members of one party killing another—or because of sheer lawlessness, or it was due to a resurrection of the antisemitism for which Poland was notorious. How far the last was a cause is a matter of dispute, but it could be that up to 2,000 Jews were killed in the two-year civil war. In any case neither the Soviet nor the Polish governments were helpful:

> Although Polish Jews were promised rehabilitation by the authorities, steps were taken to induce them to leave. They received passports which permitted them to leave Poland but not to return.[165]

It is not surprising that the committee found that the majority of those interviewed wanted to go to Palestine. But there had been interference in their decision making, notably by the Jewish Agency:

> People who were suspected of holding non-Zionist views were 'spirited away' from the camps before the arrival of the Committee. Other witnesses were manipulated ... 'Morrison [Lord Morrison, a committee member] asked ... to see two left-wing Jews, anti-Zionists. He had a bad conscience since he had seen only Zionist Jews all over Europe. We would appear before him and would be able to assure him that they, too, were for free immigration and a Jewish commonwealth in Palestine'.[166]

Ben-Gurion decided to visit the camps for the first time in October 1945, and he no doubt influenced the thinking of the refugees. He saw that the situation presented an opportunity for immigration. Beckoning signs in Yiddish appeared: 'the Land of Israel calls you'.[167] As Holocaust survivors, the Jewish plight was a humanitarian issue that could be used to further the Zionist cause. 'I saw that it could be a huge factor in our political struggle,' wrote Ben-Gurion.[168] This was not just a 'struggle' for the establishment of the state. The inmates were entitled to vote in the election of the Jewish Congress, and perhaps because of Ben-Gurion's personal efforts:

> More than eighteen thousand of the fifty-three thousand DPs voted for his party, making it the largest faction in the camps.[169]

The British were prepared to give out fifteen hundred immigration certificates each month, but Ben-Gurion said these should not be accepted unless the White Paper was cancelled.[170]

The matter of moving to other countries was equally problematic. An obvious place, and one which had always attracted Jews, was America. But Americans were far from enthusiastic. The new president, Truman, was unprincipled and pragmatic in respect of Jews. He is quoted making a welter of anti-Jewish remarks such as "'The Jews are not going to write the history of the United States, nor my history"... there are three groups in America who never leave him in peace ... the Italians, the Poles and the Jews'.[171] But when it came to political survival, and the Jewish vote was at stake, he changed his public tune. The American public also had serious reservations about allowing Jewish immigration:

> Post-war arrivals in the United States were described as conducting cut-throat competition with gentiles and established Jews in every field of US economic life.[172]

The inquiry made ten recommendations. These can be summarised as:

1. Palestine is an obvious destination, but 'Palestine alone cannot meet the emigration needs of the Jewish victims'. Other countries must find homes, and Governments must ensure the rights of those who remain in Europe.
2. That 100,000 visa for entry into Palestine be issued rapidly.
3. i That Jew shall not dominate Arab and Arab shall not dominate Jew in Palestine.
   ii That Palestine shall be neither a Jewish nor an Arab state.
   iii That all religious interests should be protected.
4. Because of endemic violence any attempt to set up a state will result in 'strife such as might threaten the peace of the world'. We therefore recommend that, until the hostility disappears, the Government of Palestine be continued as at present under mandate pending the execution of a trusteeship agreement under the United Nations.
5. The Mandatory authority 'should proclaim the principle that Arab economic, educational and political advancement in Palestine is equal in importance to that of the Jews'.
6. The Mandate which declares with regard to immigration that: 'The administration of Palestine, while ensuring the rights and position of other sections of the population are not prejudiced, shall facilitate Jewish immigration under certain conditions' and should therefore allow it.
7. a. The Land Transfer Regulations of 1940 should be rescinded and replaced by a 'policy of freedom' in the sale, lease or use of land 'irrespective of race, community or creed, and providing adequate protection for the interests of small owners and tenant cultivators'.
   b. There should be no 'nugatory' provisions in documents relating to land which insist that only 'members of one race, community or creed' should be employed on it.
   c. That the Holy Places should be protected from desecration.
8. Plans have been suggested for 'large scale industrial and agricultural development'. Before these can be put in place there must be peace, and 'the willing cooperation of neighbouring Arab states'.

9 'The educational system of both Jews and Arabs should be reformed, including the introduction of compulsory education within a reasonable time'.

10 'It should be made clear ... to both Jews and Arabs that any attempt from either side, by threats of violence, by terrorism, or the organisation or use of illegal armies ... will be resolutely suppressed ... the Jewish Agency should at once resume active cooperation with the Mandatory in the suppression of terrorism and of illegal immigration'.

The report had no chance of being accepted. President Truman, as always under pressure from Jewish pressure groups, cherry-picked the report, announcing he would agree to large-scale immigration into Palestine, and the reform of the land laws. The British government believed that the Jews would not accept it, and in any case believed that a preliminary was the disarming of the illegal Jewish armed groups. This would require American help, which of course was refused. So the US once again exercised power without any concomitant responsibility. It is easy to understand the unlikelihood, to put it mildly, of anyone accepting the recommendations. The Zionist extremist opinion was expressed by Begin: 'It was a shallow document full of contradictions.'[173]

The British government itself rejected the plan, and instead set up a committee. It was named after Morrison and Grady, the British and American statesmen who formed it, and it reported in July 1946.[174] It recommended that Palestine should be divided into a Jewish province and an Arab province under British trusteeship, with Jerusalem and the Negev remaining directly under British control. This was discussed at a conference in London 1946–47, attended only by the Arabs, who rejected it because it would in effect lead to partition. They proposed a unitary state. The Jews refused to attend unless their detained leaders were released and allowed to attend. The British would not agree to that. The British then proposed a 'Bevin Plan' for a five-year British trusteeship. Both sides rejected that, and so Britain, now in desperation, referred the problem to the United Nations.

It must be stressed how important the role of President Truman was in all this.

Prominent Zionists, influential Christian pro-Zionist supporters and others dissuaded Truman from supporting this solution. Most important were the warnings from politicians in New York and other areas of heavy Jewish population that this step might ruin Democratic chances in the forthcoming congressional elections. Truman soon informed the British government that the 'opposition to the Anglo–American Plan had become so intense that it was now clear that it would be impossible to rally in favour of it sufficient public opinion to give it effective support'.[175]

In the middle of 1946 Jewish terrorists stepped up their operations against the British. This included the kidnap of five British officers. This escalating violence at last exhausted British patience. On 28 June 1946, there was mounted an operation which was named 'Agatha', and is called in Jewish history, Black Sabbath, and by Ben-Gurion, the 'pogrom arranged for us by [prime minister] Mr Atlee [sic]'.[176] Ben-Gurion, as often seems to have been the case when there was serious trouble, was away from Palestine, in this case in Paris. Again, he abused the term 'pogrom'. Montgomery told the British commander what the object should be:

> Completely and utterly defeating the Jews as soon as possible ... now that the Jews have flung the gauntlet in our face, they must be utterly and completely defeated and their illegal organisations smashed forever.[177]

Although 2,718 people were caught, and documents and arms seized, the Jews had been told by a spy of the forthcoming operation, and it was only moderately successful.[178]

Since the rise of the Zionist movement the whole of the Middle East had been a centre of murderous attacks by communities, both within themselves and upon each other. This tradition was entered into by Jews, first in the years of the dying Ottoman empire before 1918, then during the British Mandate, and since the independent state of Israel was founded in 1948, by the state itself. But nothing has eclipsed the bombing of the King David Hotel in Jerusalem.

On Monday, 22 July 1946 the Zionists carved a place for themselves in the history of terrorism. They blew up part of the King David hotel in Jerusalem. Ninety-one people were murdered and forty-six were injured. They included employees of all levels, soldiers, policemen, and members of the public. A wide variety of nationals were killed, including Britons, Arabs, Jews, a Russian, an Armenian, a Greek and an Egyptian. This atrocity has been described as the worst terrorist attack in the history of the twentieth century; it was deplored throughout the civilised world, but vigorously defended by the perpetrators and celebrated by Israeli governments.

The hotel was chosen as a target because it housed a substantial part of the British administration, and it was the headquarters of the British armed forces. During 'Black Sabbath' the authorities had searched Jewish Agency offices and found documents providing incontrovertible evidence that the Haganah, itself an illegal organisation, was involved in the attacks on the British administration. This evidence now lay in the offices in the hotel, and the attack was designed in part, to destroy it. But approval had to be given by the Haganah, and that was forthcoming. The chief of the Haganah National Command, Moshe Sneh, 'ordered Begin "to carry out that little hotel thing at the earliest opportunity"'.[179] The Palmach, which was a kind of pseudo-commando unit within the Haganah, took an active part in the planning of the attack. This plan involved a number of men disguised as Arabs, placing milk cans full of explosives, in a basement under the wing of the hotel where most of the British offices were situated. These would

Right: Arthur Balfour, the colonial secretary who issued the Balfour Declaration. *Pictorial Press Ltd/Alamy*

Below: Lloyd George and Churchill: the most enthusiastic 'Gentile Zionists'. *PA Images/Alamy*

Above: Prince Feisal and Chaim Weizmann. They met several times: what exactly was said? *World History Archive/ Alamy*

Left: T. E. Lawrence 'of Arabia': a wartime legend. *Granger/Alamy*

Above left: Arthur Henry McMahon: certain areas 'cannot be said to be truly Arab'.

Above right: Sharif Hussein bin Ali: they are 'purely Arab provinces'. *Everett Collection/Alamy*

Sir Mark Sykes and François Georges-Picot: more treachery, more lies. *Paul Fearn/Alamy*

Above left: General Allenby. *Library of Congress*

Above right: General Allenby enters Jerusalem on foot as a mark of respect. It was the beginning of the end for the Arab Palestinians. *Library of Congress*

Left: Richard Meinertzhagen, military adviser, Middle East Department: a liar and a fantasist. *Paul Fearn/Alamy*

Below: The Arab delegation at the Versailles Peace Conference. Feisal is at the front, Lawrence is on the right. *IWM (Q 55581)*

Above: The Nebi Musa Disturbances, 1920: 'The Zionist Commission and the official Zionists are largely responsible for the present crisis.'

Right: Terrorist Ze'ev Jabotinsky: 'Really a lunatic.' *Paul Fearn/Alamy*

Above: Haj Amin al Husseini, the Grand Mufti of Jerusalem. He was forced to make a choice.
CBW/Alamy

Left: Avraham Stern, whose group, the Stern gang, murdered thousands of British and Arabs.
Granger/Alamy

Above left: Lord Walter Moyne. *National Portrait Gallery*

Above right: Yitzhak Shamir, the terrorist leader who arranged the murder of Lord Moyne. *CPA Media Pte Ltd/Alamy*

Right: Count Folke Bernadotte, another of Shamir's eminent victims. *Matteo Omied/Alamy*

Left: Field Marshal Montgomery: 'The Jews have flung the gauntlet ... they must be utterly and completely defeated and their illegal organisations smashed forever.' *World History Archive/Alamy*

Below: The blowing up of the King David Hotel, 1946: 'an insane act of terrorism'. *Granger/Alamy*

Above left: Menachem Begin, terrorist leader. *World History Archive/Alamy*

Above middle and right: Sergeants Martin and Paice, two of the many murdered by Begin. BPPA

Below: Sergeants Martin and Paice hanged.

The Nakba (Catastrophe): the beginning of the ethnic cleansing of the Palestinian Arabs, 1948.

The Deir Yassin Massacre, 1948.

Above: Children murdered in the Lebanon massacres of 1982. *Reuters*

Right: Ariel Sharon, facilitator of the Lebanese massacres. *Helene C. Stikkel, Civ*

Yasser Arafat, Yitzhak Rabin and President Clinton at the White House for the signing of Oslo 1, 1993. *Vince Musi*

The wall cutting off Palestinians: 'Contrary to international law.' *Jelle van der Wolf/Alamy*

Above and right: Some of the grafitti on the wall. *Philip Thomas*

Trump and Netanyahu sign the 'Peace Plan': Consigned to 'the dustbin of history?' *Official White House photo by Shealah Craighead*

be detonated at 11 a.m., when there would be no people in that area. That at least was the theory. In fact the explosives were detonated at 12:37.

There has much acrimonious debate about the sequence of events. One thing is certain: the Irgun, as it often did, displayed, in variable amounts, incompetence, inefficiency and recklessness. There was immediate furious argument about warnings, and these were especially centred upon the chief secretary, Sir John Shaw, who was in a part of the hotel which was not blown up. He was one of the targets. Menachem Begin sought to blame him for the chaos Irgun had created. Begin, as the person responsible for the bombing, had naturally to deny that the slaughter was his fault. He explained, and sought to marshal evidence, that a warning had been sent to several sources.

> [But] for some reason the hotel was not evacuated even though from the moment when the warnings had been received there was plenty of time for every living soul to saunter out. Instead, the toll of lives was terrible. More than two hundred people were killed or injured. Among the victims were high British officers. We particularly mourned the alien civilians whom we had no wish to hurt, and the fifteen Jewish civilians, among them good friends, who had so tragically fallen. Our satisfaction at the success of the great operation was bitterly marred. Again we went through days of pain and nights of sorrow for the blood that need not have been shed.[180]

Begin then asked why the warning was not heeded. He offered several explanations. These included one 'subsequently learned', that a high official ... exclaimed: 'We are not here to take orders from the Jews. We give *them* orders.' He summed up that:

> There is reason to believe that a specific order was given, by someone in authority, that the warning to leave the hotel should be ignored ... After this operation the whole world was flooded with hair-raising lies.[181]

Begin also made the claim that the British deliberately left people to be killed so that the terrorist groups would be the objects of hate. One of the more sickening features of Begin's account of terrorism is that he referred to his thugs as 'our boys', as in 'our boys captured a senior Intelligence officer', as if they were a teenage football team.[182] The phrase was common jargon amongst terrorists.

Irgun published a 'Black Paper' in 1947, in which they said that Shaw had forbidden anyone to leave the building 'while he slunk away until after the explosion'. The Zionists and their sympathisers spent a good deal of effort trying to prove Shaw's negligence. When they published their claims, Shaw took legal action.

In 1948 the *Jerusalem Post* repeated the allegations and was compelled to make an unqualified apology to Shaw. The publishers of a book entitled *The rape of Palestine* made similar allegations and they too apologised. Zionist terrorists have often tried to persuade the world that they were baffled: 'the reason for the loss of life has never been made clear'. After all, one pleads, 'one of the basic rules of Irgun operation was to avoid bloodshed whenever possible'.[183] In fact, Irgun accepted responsibility, but blamed the British for the death toll because they had neglected to evacuate the buildings. They mourned for the Jewish victims, but not for the British, nor the Arabs who had been murdered. Weizmann expressed condemnation, but only in private. In a conversation with Richard Crossman, he showed his real feelings:

> As soon as Crossman mentioned the King David, tears began streaming down Weizmann's face. When the King David Hotel bombing was mentioned, Weizmann started crying heavily. He said 'I can't help feeling proud of our boys', he said. 'If only it had been a German headquarters, they would have got the Victoria Cross.'[184]

Jewish political leaders deplored the attack as they had to, since world opinion was that of outrage, nowhere more so than in the British parliament. After all, Britain was still recovering from the world war which had finished less than a year earlier.

The new prime minister, Clement Attlee, led the protests with a speech in which he outlined what had happened. 'Of all the outrages which have occurred in Palestine,' he said, 'and they have been many and horrible in the last few months, this is the worst ... [it is] an insane act of terrorism.'[185] Churchill also criticised the attack, but loyal as ever to the Zionists, he framed it in the context of the mandate, and took the opportunity to suggest that immigration into Palestine should be increased.

The reaction of the administration in Palestine was to introduce more supervision. The GOC, Sir Evelyn Barker, immediately after the atrocity, issued an order placing all Jewish places of entertainment and private dwellings off limits. This was to draw another quite remarkable assessment of history from Begin. This was a 'notorious order to the British troops [whose] hateful contents echoed throughout the world'. This order included an admonition that 'we must not let ourselves be misled by hypocritical sympathy'. Also they should be punished 'in the manner this race dislikes most: by hitting them in the pocket, which will demonstrate our disgust for them'.[186] Later a curfew was introduced. There were a range of other measures including random home and personal searches, and mass arrests. Despite Begin's objections these were very sensible measures.

A modern Israeli government, as has been the usual practice, celebrated the massacre. In July 2006 at something called the Menachem Begin Heritage Centre, the 60th anniversary was marked by the unveiling of a plaque. This read: 'For reasons known only to the British, the hotel was not evacuated'.[187] The British objected and the wording was changed slightly to read that warning calls had been made 'to the hotel, the *Palestine Post* and the French Consulate, urging the hotel's occupants to leave immediately. The hotel was not evacuated and after 25 minutes the bombs exploded'.[188] A measure of the Zionist determination to excuse such murder can be seen from the remarks of Benjamin Netanyahu, later prime minister, that the hotel was a military target, and the bombing was not an act of terror at all. However, no amount of lying, wishful thinking, or the re-writing of history can undermine the simple truth that this was a callous act carried out by Zionists.

The years before and during the Second World War saw the most cruel visitation by the Nazi regime upon large groups of people in the policy which has come to be known as the Holocaust. This especially affected Jews. There is no need to rehearse these horrors, since they are well documented. For this account, it may be noted that one effect of the Holocaust was increasing sympathy for the case for Jews to be allowed to emigrate to Palestine. It has already been pointed out, and needs stressing, that this sympathy was an important element in the pressure to allow Jewish immigration.[189]

This merely amplified a movement which had begun in the 1930s, when German Jews began to emigrate to Palestine. This was formalised in negotiations between the Nazi government and the Zionist organisations, notably the Jewish Agency. The outcome of these negotiations was the Haavara (Transfer) Agreement, which was signed on 25 August 1933. Under this agreement, Jews could sell their possessions in Germany and buy German manufactured goods, which would then be transferred to Palestine, together with the owners. It is estimated that between 1933 and 1935, some 145,000 Jews migrated forming what 'came to be called the Fifth Aliya'.[190] The man behind this stupendous effort was Haim Arlosoroff. The Revisionists were totally against any dealings with the Nazis, and in their usual fashion showed how they felt through murder. Arlosoroff was shot in June 1933.

There were other dealings with the Nazis. It was reported that Adolf Eichmann had offered to exchange one million Jews for trucks and other goods. Romania offered to exchange Jews for cash. The matter of collaboration was to become the subject of one of the most famous trials in Israeli history: the Kastner case. Malchiel Gruenwald accused Rudolph Kastner of helping the Nazis. The Israeli government sued Gruenwald on behalf of Kastner. They could be excused for doing so because such allegations tended to seriously weaken the case for the total viciousness of the Nazis towards Jews. It was alleged that Kastner, in collaboration with Adolf Eichmann and others, had sent 1,684 Jews to Auschwitz concentration camp, having told them they were to be 'relocated'. The reward was to be the safety of Kastner's relatives and friends. The initial judgement was that Kastner was guilty. The Zionists exercised their own judgement, and Kastner was murdered by Jews in March 1957.

The expulsion of Jews suited the Zionists well, helping as it did the increase in the numbers of Jews in the population of Palestine. But the taint of collusion with the Nazis remains one of the more controversial aspects of Zionist history. Hannah Arendt, a Jewish historian, is one who has been attacked because of her expression of the truth:

It was the hope of organised Jewry in Germany that the Nazi dissimilation with the Jews would lead to emigration to Palestine. The result was an agreement between the Jewish Agency for Palestine and Nazi authorities to assist in the Zionist plans for illegal immigration into the Holy Land. Even the Gestapo and the SS were helpful for this to them was just another way of ridding Europe of the 'hated Jews'.[191]

Another demonstration of the Zionist single-mindedness was shown by Ben-Gurion as early as 1938 when the killing of Jews in Germany had just begun. Then he said:

If I knew it was possible to save all the [Jewish] children of Germany by their transfer to England and only half of them by transferring them to Eretz-Israel, I would chose the latter—because we are faced not only with the accounting of these children but also with the historical accounting of the Jewish people ... the catastrophe of European Jewry is not, in a direct manner, my business.[192]

Ben-Gurion persistently and forcibly represented the Zionist determination to take advantage of the plight of Jewish Displaced Persons, by engineering their migration to Palestine. In an inflammatory article in *The Spectator* of 22 July 1960, Erskine Childers wrote:

One of the most massively important features of the entire Palestine struggle was that Zionism deliberately arranged that the plight of the wretched survivors of Hitlerism should be a 'moral argument' that the West had to accept. This was done by seeing to it that Western countries did not open their doors, widely and immediately, to the inmates of the DP [displaced persons] camps. It is incredible ... it was done by sabotaging specific Western schemes to admit Jewish DPs.[193]

Such a not-so-hidden policy can be seen from the experience of Morris L. Ernst, a representative of President Roosevelt, who when discussing any plans for relief was told 'Morris, this is treason—you're undermining the Zionist movement'.[194] Meanwhile terrorism flourished.

Montgomery was very critical of the policies of the British government, especially the action of Creech Jones, the colonial secretary.

Towards the end of October 1946 [Creech Jones] came to the conclusion that we released from detention the leaders of the terrorist campaign whom we had arrested, and 'laid off' further searches for arms, a better atmosphere would be created; indeed, it was even stated that if we acted thus the Jewish Agency would denounce terrorism and call upon all right-minded Jews to fight it. Accordingly the detained terrorists were all released early in November, and searches for arms were suspended except after actual terrorist incidents. As a result of this concession by the Labour government, more and more restrictions were placed upon the troops in Palestine regarding their activities in the maintenance of law and order. Meanwhile, British soldiers and British members of the Palestine police continued to be killed and wounded. I became exasperated at this state of affairs.[195]

This 'exasperation' led to serious rows with the prime minister, and other ministers:

I finally said that if we were not prepared to maintain law and order in Palestine, it would be better to get out. I could not agree to a lot of young British lads being killed needlessly. This remark sparked off the devil of a row ... I then left for Palestine.[196]

This remark indicates the state of affairs when Field Marshal Montgomery, the chief of the Imperial General Staff, visited Palestine in 1946 after the King David Hotel massacre. His account shows how the British had lost control, whether through exasperation, indifference, incompetence, or political influence. He was appalled by the situation there:

I was much perturbed by what I saw and heard ... what was very definitely my concern was the action of the Army in aiding the civil power to maintain law and order, and in this respect the outlook was dismal. The High Commissioner seemed to me unable to make up his mind what to do. Indecision and hesitation were in evidence all down the line, beginning in Whitehall ... The Police Force was 50 per cent below strength and not very effective ... All this had led to a state of affairs in which British rule existed in name only; the true rulers seemed to me to be the Jews, whose unspoken slogan was—'You dare not touch us'.[197]

Montgomery wanted to 'establish effective British authority ... If this led to war with the Jews, from the army's point of view it would be a war against a fanatical and cunning enemy who would use the weapons of kidnap, murder and sabotage; women would fight as well as men, and no one would know who was friend or foe.'[198] Such was the chaotic state of affairs in Palestine in the period before the intervention of the United Nations.

6
THE ISRAELI PRIME MINISTER SETS THE GOAL

'And if dozens of Arabs get killed— that's exactly what we want'[1]

The United Kingdom referred the question of the future of Palestine to the UN on 14 February 1947, and on 14 May 1948 the mandate was ended. On this date, Palestinian Arab ambitions for freedom were doomed, as it has turned out, forever. The United Nations organisation was only a couple of years old, and could be forgiven for wondering what to do about this new responsibility for Palestine. This was insignificant when compared with the problem of the rebuilding of a shattered Europe, or the future of Japan.

After discussion came the decision to set up a United Nations Special Committee on Palestine (UNSCOP) in April–May 1947. It would consist of eleven members chaired by a Swede, Emil Sandström, and it drew its membership from representative continents. The UN Commission carried out extensive enquiries in Palestine and elsewhere, to try to understand how people felt about partition. The Jews were cooperative, and were helped by the information they received through bugging all the UNSCOP discussions.[2] The official Arab response was to place a boycott on the proceedings, but such Arab opinion as was expressed was of little use. It was voiced by a number of Arab countries who met UNSCOP in Lebanon on 22 July 1947. They proposed that there would be no political rights for Jews in Palestine, which would be an Arab state, and there should be no more immigration or Jewish purchase of land. The response of the two sides is summed up by Morris:

> The Committee members were warmly welcomed by their Jewish hosts ... The Arabs, on the other hand, everywhere greeted them with sourness, suspicion and aggressiveness.[3]

The UNSCOP report was presented to the assembly on 1 September 1947.

The majority of the members (eight) recommended the partition of Palestine into two states, one Arab and one Jewish, with some sort of economic union. Jerusalem and Bethlehem would be 'internationalised' under the UN. The minority group (three) wanted a federal set-up with power given mainly to a federal government, and some power given to the two districts. Jerusalem would be divided into Jewish and Arab districts. The federation would be supervised by an international commission. These proposals had the virtue, which no other proposals had, that they recognised the reality that Palestine had an overwhelming Arab majority.

But this recommendation for partition was a hope which could only convince indomitable optimists. Nevertheless it was the best the Zionists could hope for. The Zionist leaders constantly reminded their own doubters that if they could get an official foothold, they could eventually purloin more territory. Their argument has turned out to be sound as may be demonstrated by the annexation of the Golan Heights and the West Bank. The Zionists had everything to gain. For once, Churchill was satisfied. By 1946 he had come to see partition as the only answer: 'I am very much inclined to think that this may be the sole solution.'[4]

After all the support Churchill had given the Zionist cause, it is difficult to believe that there had been a discussion about murdering him. Gilbert, however, reported that in the late 1940s, 'within Israel and amongst Jews generally the extent to which Churchill was a friend was much debated. There were those who felt, as did several of the Zionist leaders in 1945, that he could not be trusted.[5]

The Arabs had nothing to gain, and everything to lose, from whatever was proposed. It is hardly necessary to be reminded that they were being asked to give up a portion of their land, and were to be offered in return the questionable benefits of Jewish 'progressive methods'. It was to be expected then that the Arabs would be positively hostile to the committee, and so they were. The Arab states rejected both ideas, and their official position was summed up by a statement that they would 'resist with all practical and effective means any measures which fail to ensure the independence of Palestine as an Arab state'.[6] The next stage was a familiar one. It was to set up an ad hoc committee on 25 September 1947 to study the two reports with a view to implementation.

Because this committee, in the nature of things, was quite unable to make progress, it was decided to set up a positive plethora of committees. The original committee would be divided into two: one would discuss the majority report, and the other the minority. Yet another sub-committee would then see if a compromise was possible. On 25 November 1947, the assembly rejected the minority report. The sub-committee looking at the majority report 'became the most important of the three, for the minority sub-committee was marginal and the sub-committee seeking a compromise insignificant'.[7] Pappé points out that the Jews were active in the deliberations of the majority sub-committee, but that the Arabs were not. Also significant was the active participation of the two superpowers, the United States and Russia. Britain, meantime, had largely distanced itself from the several debates.[8]

An important contribution by the superpowers was to set the British evacuation at 1 August 1948 in the hope that the British would be involved in the transition to partition. Britain maintained its distance: it simply wanted to leave Palestine. The setting up of committees was not yet finished however. The United Nations Palestine Committee began work in January 1948. It was given the task of setting up the transition of Palestine from being a mandate into two independent states, Jewish and Arab. But before its notional term had expired, 'the committee declared its failure and, like the British, left the warring parties to determine the shape and future of Palestine by force'.[9]

Before the vote was taken by the assembly there was a certain amount of behind-the-scenes negotiation about boundaries, and since the US was going through one of its periods of uncertainty about the situation, and the vote was by no means a foregone conclusion, pressure was put on the US. They in turn threatened states which were dependent on them for aid if they did not vote for partition. When these discussions and threats had been settled, 'the prospective Jewish state was to have 55 per cent of Palestine and a population of approximately 500,000 Jews with an Arab minority of close to 400,000. (Another 100,000 Jews lived in Jerusalem).'[10]

It can be seen from these figures that there was no way in which the Arabs could accept such an arrangement. Another UN committee was charged with choosing which option should be recommended to the general assembly. At the end of the British Mandate, it was proposed that a commission would monitor the process.

It is time now to deal with events on the ground in Palestine. There was terrorist murder, the scale and nature of which gives it prominence in the long history of terrorism. This was not new. Seven hundred and eighty-four British police, servicemen, crown servants and civilian staff were murdered between 1944 and 1948. Well before these events, murder was a well-established tradition in the several communities in Palestine. In the present context, on 1 March 1947, Irgun gangsters killed more than twenty British servicemen, twelve of them in a grenade attack on their officers' club in Tel Aviv, when they also injured thirty.[11]

Begin gloated over one particular incident which drew world-wide condemnation, or nearly world-wide, as we shall see. At the end of July 1947, 'The two Britons were hanged. We repaid our enemy in kind. We had warned him again and again and again. He had callously disregarded our warnings. He forced us to answer gallows with gallows.' The Britons were two army sergeants. These hangings 'broke the back of British rule'.[12]

The context of Begin's remarks, and his rejection of appeals for mercy, should be seen in the light of his hatred of 'the British', which was profound to the point of being pathological. Years later, his feelings were alive and well. In 1982 Britain fought a war with Argentina over the Falkland Islands. Even after many years Begin's hatred had not abated, and he saw a chance to damage Britain. In a book published in 2011, which drew world-wide attention, it was revealed that Begin was asked for help with the supply of arms.[13] His response, widely quoted, was: 'Is this going to be used to kill the English? *Kadima* (go ahead). Dov from up there is going to be happy with the decision'. Dov Gruner was a friend who was hanged in April 1947. Dobry writes that this agreement to supply fighter jets and other equipment was carried out 'in order to avenge its crackdown on the Irgun during the British mandate of Palestine'.[14]

The difference in the case of the two sergeants who were hanged was one which Begin could never accept. The execution of terrorists came after due process of law. But Begin's revenge was random murder. The murders to which Begin refers (the two Britons) were carried out by Irgun. They were hanged, and their bodies were suspended from trees in a eucalyptus grove, which is arguably, in the eyes of the public at the time, a most infamous episode because of its especial beastliness.

The background was that three Irgun terrorists had been sentenced to death after a mass outbreak from Acre prison. Irgun warned that if the executions were carried out there would be reprisals. This was not the first time that Jewish terrorists had been sentenced to death: for example on 16 April four were executed. However, a pattern had developed that whenever terrorists would be sentenced to death, Irgun would capture British soldiers and threaten to murder them, and the terrorists would be reprieved. But not this time: the death sentences were carried out.

At the time, UNSCOP was at work in the country, and the executions of the Jewish murderers were delayed because of their presence. Even appeals from UNSCOP, as well as from many others were rejected, and the three were executed on 29 July 1947. On the same day the British sergeants were murdered. These two were twenty year olds, and they had been held as hostages for three weeks before being hanged with piano wire. The ground around them was booby trapped. Soldiers who were cutting down the bodies, which had been mutilated, were injured when the booby traps exploded. The unusual use of piano wire recalls the chosen method of execution by the Nazis of those who plotted to kill Hitler in July 1944. Menachem Begin approved plans to display the bodies in public. He had shown his characteristic ruthlessness, not to say his heartlessness, by replying to a written appeal from the father of Mervyn Paice, one of those murdered, by saying in a radio broadcast: 'You must appeal to your government that thirst for oil and blood'. Something of an irony is the fact that Sergeant Martin's mother was a Jew.

The kidnapping led to appeals for mercy, but they too were turned down. The leaders of Haganah helped in the search because they hoped that the efforts of UNSCOP would lead to a solution favourable to the Zionist cause. Ben-Gurion was furious at the timing of the murders, since he feared that they might adversely affect the judgment of UNSCOP. He wanted to 'uproot them' and 'either kill or imprison them all ... They must be wiped off the face of the earth, this gang'. His problem was that the activities of the 'gang' were very popular, with Dov Gruner being 'metamorphosed into a national hero' after his execution.[15]

There were exceptions to the general approval. After the murders, Ben Ami of Haganah insisted 'I testify that most of our population made desperate efforts to free the kidnapped and prevent this disgrace'. But Begin in 1949 quotes the chief secretary of the British government in Israel: 'The hanging of the two British sergeants did more than anything to get us out.'[16] Two later Jewish writers seemingly deny the identity of the murderers .They write that the 'two British soldiers [were] *allegedly* [my emphasis] executed by Jewish extremists'. [17]

The murders led to widespread disturbances in Palestine and in Britain. In the former, British troops and police attacked Jews and their property. The outrage in Britain can be imagined, and the hanging of the sergeants considerably exacerbated growing anger in the country. There were attacks on Jews in several British cities, especially in Liverpool. But there were also attacks *by* Jews in Britain: for example on 7 March 1947 they bombed the British Colonies Club in central London. There were to be lasting effects in the political relationships between Israel and Britain. Over thirty years later, the British prime minister, Margaret Thatcher, no enemy of Israel, referred to the hangings. It was reported in an Israeli newspaper that 'a tearful Thatcher':

> Remarked at the G7 Summit in Ottawa in July 1981 that she would never forgive Begin for the hanging of two British sergeants during the British mandate period. Thatcher added that as a result of this episode, she would not meet with Begin in future unless it was absolutely necessary ... Number Ten refused to discuss the remarks.[18]

Many American Jews supported the terrorists. Their enthusiasm is illustrated by the writings of Ben Hecht, at the time an important figure in the Hollywood film industry. He published a letter to 'the terrorists of Palestine' in the *New York Post* on 15 May 1947 in which he assured them that:

> The Jews of America are for you. When you let go with your guns and bombs at the British betrayers and invaders of your homeland the Jews of America make a little holiday in their hearts.

There were some Jews who did not agree. Begin was attacked in a letter in *The New York Times* in December 1948, signed by twenty-nine eminent Jews, including Albert Einstein. Begin's organisation was 'closely akin ... to the Nazi and Fascist parties' which had 'boasted' of its massacre of innocents and inaugurated 'a reign of terror'.

General Jewish American support can be illustrated by the calling together of rich American and Canadian Jews by Ben-Gurion on 1 July 1945. They were 'worth in the aggregate many millions of dollars'. Ben-Gurion explained the danger of the invasion of Arab armies, and asked for support:

The Israeli Prime Minister Sets the Goal

This was the birth of what came to be called the Sonneborn Institute, a support group whose members raised money and sent to Palestine more or less everything that was needed for the war, including combat aircraft.[19]

Against this background UNSCOP carried on its work. In the same week as the murders of the sergeants, in July 1947, a ship called the *Exodus 47*, carrying illegal immigrants from Europe to Palestine was intercepted and there was fighting between the passengers and the Royal Marines. Three Jews were killed and twenty-eight injured. The British then took the ship to Haifa, removed the dead and wounded and, in other ships, took the survivors back to France. The French would not cooperate, the passengers refused to disembark, and the ships sailed to Hamburg, where the people were forced off the ship and sent to a displaced persons camp.

The Zionist propaganda machine recognised this as an opportunity to deflect attention from their outrages, and especially the murder of the sergeants. 'Nothing could have done more to promote the Zionist cause at this critical juncture,' wrote Morris.[20] So the international picture was drawn of a heartless British administration, which rather displaced the killing by Zionists—a picture apparently accepted even by UNSCOP:

> The almost simultaneous British execution of the three IZL operatives and the IZL hanging of the two sergeants apparently had a much smaller impact on the UNSCOP members.[21]

Pappé concludes that:

> In the United Nations the British, and not the Jews, were seen as the villains. The tragedy of the *Exodus* and *the overall British behaviour in Palestine* [my emphasis] resulted in UNSCOP moving another step towards a pro-Zionist position.[22]

If this analysis is correct, it shows how ineffective the British information system was, or as is more likely, how powerful was that of the Zionists. It is also no doubt the case that the members of UNSCOP, or more generally the United Nations, would have little understanding or knowledge of the history of Palestine, how angry the British were becoming at events there, or how much the whole exploit was costing Britain.

Partition plan recommended by the UN, 1947.

On 25 November 1947 the United Nations Ad Hoc Committee, looking at the alternatives, voted. The result was not enough to ensure the required two thirds in the general assembly, and so there was a struggle between the Arabs who wanted a vote without delay, and the Jews who wanted time to ensure support among their allies. In the end a three-day debate in the assembly concluded on 29 November 1947, and Resolution 181 (11) was passed. The assembly had voted for partition into the two states with an economic union, and for Jerusalem to be internationalised. The voting was 33 to 13 with 10 abstentions and one absentee. Among the abstentions, the most notable was Britain. The Palestinians walked out, and their perfectly rational anger was voiced by a Palestinian historian:

> The Palestinians failed to see why they should be made to pay for the Holocaust ... they failed to see why it was *not* fair for the Jews to be a minority in a unitary state while it *was* fair for almost half of the Palestinian population—the indigenous majority on its own ancestral soil—to be converted overnight into a minority under alien rule.[23]

The passing of this resolution was due in no small measure to the pressure wielded by the United States who 'applied every conceivable pressure to line up partition votes in favour of Israel and against the Arabs at the fateful, deciding session of the United Nations at Lake Success on 29 November 1947.'[24] It was not only the United States which influenced the votes:

> Sir Henry Gurney, the Chief Secretary of Palestine, followed and analysed the components of the Zionist' movement's propaganda carefully; his analysis was hostile, but not unintelligent. He noted that the Zionists had successfully equated anti-Zionism with anti-Semitism ... 'The pressures "the Zionist" creates', he wrote, 'makes the world hate him, but apparently he does not care. He has a suicidal urge. That was what made him so desperate and self-centred.'[25]

Within a few hours of the passing of the resolution, fighting began in Palestine. Segev's summary of consequent events is that 'December 1947 was a horrible month'.[26] The chaos caused the Haganah to propose 'a punitive response'.[27] Typical was an action in which, in two weeks, the Haganah 'had carried out fourteen actions against Arabs. Etzel and Lehi had carried out only five, but killed more'.[28] Killing was to be seen as normal, and as voiced by some, desirable. The high commissioner, Sir Alan Cunningham, was 'furious' at Jewish behaviour. To his complaints Golda Meir replied: 'and if dozens of Arabs get killed—that's exactly what we want'.[29] That an important figure should express such murderous views indicates how anarchic the situation had become.

This chaos was followed by a full-scale war involving neighbouring Arab countries. Troops from the latter invaded in May 1948, and the war continued until 10 March 1949. It is known by the Jews as the Israel War of Independence and by the Arabs as *nakba* (catastrophe). Karsh, in his insistence on the righteousness of the Jews and their cause, pours scorn upon the Arab resistance. In the *nakba*, he wrote, the Arab 'killers were hardly a shining example of unadulterated Arab patriotism: it soon transpired that they were hardened criminals driven by monetary concerns rather than a desire for national liberation'. For good measure he added that the leaders had done the same in the 1936-39 'revolt'.[30]

At first sight it appeared that the Arabs had the advantage. They vastly outnumbered the Jews, and had the backing (and expected military support of the Arab countries). But they had a number of weaknesses. They were not a cohesive entity. The Palestinian Arabs owed loyalties to family, clan and tribe, with little sense of being 'Palestinians'. There was no central command or organisation and their fighting method was to operate in small groups: very suitable for isolated guerrilla action, but quite inadequate for the large-scale onslaughts which took place in the later stages of the conflict. Their support from the surrounding countries was complicated by rivalries between several of them. The most notable of these was the well-known desire of King Abdullah to embrace Palestine as part of Transjordan, and the equally determined efforts of other groups to prevent this.

Nevertheless, in September 1947 the Arab League formed the Arab Liberation Army, consisting of Palestinians and volunteers from Arab countries. The Arabs also had the support of the Arab Legion, a British-supported experienced Transjordanian force commanded by General John Bagot Glubb, as well as the Jordanian Frontier Force. Finally, the forces of the British Mandate, including the Palestine Police Force, did not interfere in the fighting, although there were exceptions. For example, in January 1948 the Arab Liberation Army attacked the village of Kfar Szold, near the Syrian border. This was seen as an attack by foreigners on British territory, and a British armoured unit fought them off.

The Jews, although numerically weaker, had several advantages. They became better organised. The several murderous gangs put aside their differences and joined with the Haganah. Many of the settlements had good defensive systems. Although the British tried to blockade arms shipments, the Jews managed to buy arms with money raised by Americans. Golda Meir went on campaigns to solicit money in the US and in 1948 she managed to raise 100 million dollars.[31] This was despite a political development which was bound either to unnerve or make the Zionists more determined. In March 1948 the United States delegation to the UN 'introduced a motion to defer partition and establish an international trusteeship'. A few days later Truman 'egged on by Zionist lobbyists ... reiterated his support for partition'.[32] It must have been a nasty shock, but it was likely to increase Jewish determination.

It is generally agreed that an attack by Arabs on 30 November 1947 signalled the opening of the war. They attacked two buses, killing seven Jews and wounding others. This attack set the tone for what was to follow. The fighting was usually small scale, often disorganised, but lethal. The war was waged with much brutality. Jewish settlements were attacked, and so were Arab villages. There were also many British casualties. After a bombing in Jerusalem:

> Vengeful IZL [Irgun] and LHI [Stern gang] members roamed the streets and killed sixteen British troops and policemen. On February 29 a bomb planted by the LHI near Rehovot derailed a British troop train travelling from Cairo to Haifa, killing twenty-seven soldiers.[33]

The killing was indiscriminate:

> In Tel Aviv, Jaffa, Haifa and Jerusalem, in December and early January 1948, hundreds of Arab civilians were killed or wounded by IZL terror. In Jerusalem alone, 37 Arabs were killed and 80 wounded in two bombings on 13 and 29 December.[34]

The scale of the destruction of Arab villages was considerable. In April 1948 after a major battle for Kibbutz Mishmar Ha'Emek, the Haganah responded by destroying 'all ten surrounding villages. The inhabitants either fled or were expelled'. The Haganah's measures were approved, in principle, by Ben-Gurion on 8 or 9 April.[35] As presumably were the threats issued by General Yigal Allon to Arab villagers in his 'psychological campaign':

> 'If you don't flee immediately, you will be slaughtered, your daughters will be raped' and the like, and almost all the villagers fled to Lebanon and Syria.[36]

The newly formed Jewish authority for many years successfully hid the scale of their brutal eviction of Palestinians: yet another example of how they managed to keep any criticism of Israel at bay. Of course, they were only able to do this with the support of key figures in the diaspora, and because of the limp attitude of key powers. Britain by now was thoroughly bored with the trouble in Palestine, and the newly formed United Nations was to set the tone for its interventionist policies ever since: that is to say it consisted of flowery language, much demand for cessation of genocide, or attempted genocide, but very little effective action.

In recent years diligent research, combined with the successful battle against Israeli government blockages of information, has revealed the scale of the horrors visited upon the Arab population by the victors. Such revelations have been accompanied by widespread bewilderment that a people who had recently suffered studied brutality could in turn carry out the same treatment of a people who had not the slightest responsibility for what had happened in Europe.

Ilan Pappé has set out a convincing account of this treatment, and the reasons why it clearly amounts to 'ethnic cleansing'. The meaning of the Hebrew words used are explained: *tihur* 'means in Hebrew what it means in any other language: the expulsion of entire populations from their villages and towns'.[37] Ben-Gurion used a different word when he reminded the IDF that their 'principal' task was 'the cleansing of Palestine ... he used the noun *bi'ur* which means either 'cleansing the leaven' in Passover or 'root out', 'eliminate'.[38] On another occasion an order was given for a 'cleaning' operation (*nikkuy*). These are 'all terms that fit the accepted definitions of ethnic cleansing'.[39]

The studied nature of this policy can be gauged from the many years of preparation. Not only did the Jewish National Fund, founded in 1901, systematically attend to the eviction of Arabs from land purchased by Jews, it was active in a quite remarkable enterprise: the establishment of a 'cartographic department'. Its job was to prepare 'detailed files' for each of Palestine's villages. By the late 1930s this 'archive' was almost complete.[40] The details collected were exhaustive. They included the:

> Location of each village, its access roads, quality of land, water springs, main sources of income, its socio-political composition, religious affiliations, names of its muhktars [village headmen], its relationships with other villages, the age of individual men (sixteen to fifty) ... an index of 'hostility' (towards the Zionist project, that is) decided by the level of the village's participation in the revolt of 1936 ... Particular attention was given to people who had allegedly killed Jews ... in 1948 these last bits of information fuelled the worst atrocities in the villages, leading to mass execution and torture.

One of the collectors of this information from the 1940s made clear the purpose of this exercise:

> We had to study the basic structure of the Arab village. This means the structure and how best to attack it.[41]

The clearest demonstration of the purpose of this extraordinary collection of information was in in March 1948 when Plan Dalet was promulgated. The plan was 'guided' by Yigael Yadin, This was a belligerent move, with no legal authority, which was to cause considerable harm to the Arabs, especially that part called Plan D. It also made clear that one of the cornerstones of Zionism— the elimination of the Arabs—was now stated policy. It replaced previous plans about action following the establishment of a Hebrew state, and was designed to seize as much land as possible, apart from that already allocated to the Jews. The ostensible reason for the plan was that it would create defences against Arab attacks. Ben-Gurion had already restructured the Haganah, even though it still had no legal base, and introduced conscription in part to carry out the plan.

The plan ordered that areas of Jewish settlement which were outside the proposed Hebrew state would be captured and the Arabs who lived there would be evicted. Section (f) stated that these 'would be temporarily occupied', but, in complete contradiction, 'they must then be incorporated into our defensive system until operations cease'. These occupations would never cease. The 'strategy' depended upon three elements. One of these was 'cleansing' the area along the Jewish State's borders of an Arab presence. The plan established that the Arab population were 'the enemy', and set out ways in which they were to be dealt with. There would be 'operations against enemy population centres located inside or near our defensive system in order to prevent them being used by an active armed force'. This would be achieved, *inter alia,* by:

> Destruction of villages (setting fire to, blowing up, and planting mines in the debris) especially those population centres which are difficult to control continuously. Mounting search and control operations according to the following guidelines: encirclement of the village and conducting a search inside it. In the event of resistance, the armed forces must be destroyed and the population must be expelled outside the borders of the state.[42]

A Jewish 'person' will be appointed to be in charge of all villages 'which are occupied'. The action took place over about eight weeks. At the end of that time, in addition to the numbers of Arabs being killed, some 250,000 to 300,000 people had been 'displaced'.

There is a familiar controversy over the action. Apologists point to the threat of Arab invasion, and the need to connect the several parts of the country allocated to the Jews. Therefore Gelber defines it as 'a defensive scheme ... The purpose was preparing for the Arab invasion, not expelling the Palestinians. Those who disagree are wrong about Plan D':

> They have distorted its meaning by portraying it as a general order embracing all Arabs in all villages. The text, however, is clear enough: reading Plan D as it is, without deconstructing it to change its meaning, shows that there is no correlation between the actual text, and the significance, background and outcomes that the Palestinian scholars and their Israeli colleagues assign it. These paragraphs of Plan D were of marginal significance and their contribution.[43]

Morris claims that 'the plan was neither understood nor used by the senior field officers as a blanket instruction for the expulsion of the Arabs'. In any case, 'townspeople and villagers usually left their homes before or during battle, and Haganah rarely had to decide about, or issue, expulsion orders'.[44] What these apologia amount to is that there was no intention to evict Arabs, and that the government did not intend that this should be done, with a suggestion that field commanders were responsible. Morris writes that there was:

A shift from the defensive to the offensive and marked the beginning of the implementation of tochnit dalet (Plan D)—without Ben-Gurion or the HGS ever taking an in principle decision to embark on its implementation.[45]

With regard to this point it may be observed that if the soldiers were acting without orders, then they were out of control. There is no doubt about the wording or meaning of Plan D. Part of the plan says, apparently quite firmly, that this is: 'not an operation outside the borders of the Hebrew state'. But then it becomes vague:

> However, concerning enemy bases lying directly close to the borders ... these must be temporarily occupied and searched for hostiles ... and they must then be incorporated into our defensive systems until operations cease.

The plan ostensibly sets out a defensive system in the likely attack by those who were dispossessed, but it is also a licence to invade territory which was not handed over in the settlement, and to evict and kill those who resisted. The plan relied on the probable unwillingness to intervene by any credible country:

> This plan rests on the assumption that there will be no international forces stationed in the country which are capable of effective action.

The effects of the 'implementation' of the plan are in essence agreed. What is more controversial is whether those ghastly effects can be justified. A typical part of the 'plan' was to capture the city of Tiberias. The Arab population of the city was cut off, and the effect was described in the inimitable way of Zionist historians:

> The Arabs *chose to evacuate* the city and, with the assistance of units of the British Army, were transported east to Transjordan. *Thus began the great tragedy of the Arab refugee problem* [my emphasis] which was to plague the Middle East for decades after the war.[46]

Israeli historian Ilan Pappé is right in his bold assertion that 'This blueprint spelled it out clearly and unambiguously: the Palestinians had to go ... the aim of the plan was in fact the destruction of both rural and urban areas of Palestine.'[47]

The cleansing was formalised by Ben-Gurion in 1949 when he declared a 'War on Infiltration'. Havrelock explains that this was:

> A massive bureaucratic, military, and ultimately legal campaign against Palestinian return, settlement, and overall presence. For the next seven years, this campaign, more precisely named the 'War on Return', became a frightening and fate-altering staple of Palestinian daily life in Israel.[48] The assumption

promulgated by the Zionists was that Palestine was an empty land, thinly populated by a primitive people who were so traditional in the methods of cultivation they employed, that the land was, in effect going to waste. In early 1947 Ben-Gurion had talks with Bevin: Ben-Gurion maintained that a man could walk for days through the country without meeting a living soul, echoing the platitude that Palestine was a land without people for a people without a land.[49]

Such myths have been effectively shown to be baseless as a result of thorough research, by a team whose findings were edited by Walid Khalidi.[50] This published research lists in detail, and with illustrations, the destruction wrought in the 418 villages that were stolen, blown up or otherwise destroyed, and mostly repopulated by Jews in the 1948 war alone. The research also points out that at the same time there was the 'fall of more than a dozen of the major urban centres of the Palestinian people' which were either exclusively occupied by them or where they were in a majority, or where they had 'substantial pluralities'. These included Acre, Beersheba, Haifa, West Jerusalem and the seaport of Jaffa.[51] These cities are still in existence, but 'the same cannot be said of the villages.'

> They have remained altogether anonymous to the outside world and might as well never have existed. A dozen or so, though depopulated, were spared or suffered only minor damage. The rest were either totally destroyed or nearly so. They have literally been wiped off the face of the earth. The sites of their destroyed homesteads and graveyards, as well as their orchards, threshing floors, wells, livestock, and grazing grounds were all parcelled out amongst Jewish colonists that had been their neighbours or among new ones established afterwards on the erstwhile village lands ... Some hundred or so Palestinian villages in the areas conquered by Israel in the 1948 war were neither destroyed nor depopulated, and continue to exist to this day within Israel's 1967 borders. One might note, however, that over 80 per cent of the lands of these Palestinian/Israeli citizens who never left their homes have been confiscated since 1948 and put at the exclusive disposal of the Jewish citizens of the state.[52]

The fate of the inhabitants of Haifa is especially tragic, and exemplifies the scale of the cruelty. Ben-Gurion visited Haifa's Arab section on 1 May 1948. He described what he saw in his diary:

> A terrifying and fantastic sight. A dead city—a corpse of a city. In one place only we saw two old men sitting in a half-empty store, and in an alleyway we encountered an Arab woman leading her son ... how could tens of thousands of people without any sufficient reason leave their cities, homes and wealth in such a panic?[53]

It is impossible to believe that he is serious. As Segev points out:

> The last of the Arab inhabitants of Haifa had good reason to flee for their lives from their neighbourhoods in the lower city—the Haganah was bombarding them from the upper slopes of Mount Carmel with mortar fire.[54]

Ben-Gurion soon recovered from his surprise: 'It is not our job to see to the return of the Arabs... when they flee—we don't need to run after them.'[55]

With regard to the numbers of Arab refugees, the total is very unclear: perhaps between 715,000 and 780,000.[56] In the same way the number of Palestinian deaths in the war is uncertain. An average figure is 13,000.

> In the wake of the 1948 war that created the State of Israel, some three quarters of a million Palestinian refugees, over half of them villagers, took up the road for exile ... By the end of the war, hundreds of entire villages had not only been depopulated but obliterated, their houses blown up or bulldozed. While many of the sites are difficult of access, to this day the observant traveller of Israeli roads and highways can see traces of their presence that would escape the notice of the casual passer-by: a fenced-in area—often surmounting a gentle hill—of olive and other fruit trees left untended, of cactus hedges and domesticated plants run wild. Now and then a few crumbled houses are left standing, a neglected church or mosque, collapsing walls along the ghost of a village lane, but in the vast majority of cases all that remains is a scattering of stones and rubble across a forgotten landscape.[57]

Moshe Dayan, an extreme and violent Zionist, later to become a hero of 'wars' against the Arabs, boasts of the mayhem which was caused:

> Jewish villages were built in the place of Arab villages. You do not even know the names of these Arab villages, and I do not blame you because geography books no longer exist, not only do the books not exist, the Arab villages are not there either. Nahlal arose in the place of Mahlul; Kibbutz Gvat in the place of Jiba; Kibbutz Sarid in the place of Huneifis; and Kefar Yehushu'a in the place of Tal al-Shuman. There is not a single place built in this country that did not have a former Arab population.[58]

In the published listing of Palestinian villages, it is made manifest that they were peopled and thriving. There are records of numbers and of the crops which were grown. A very typical example was the village of al-Birwa in the district of Acre. The population consisted of 1,663 Muslims and Christians. There was a mosque, a church and two schools, one of which dated from the Ottoman empire. The villagers grew wheat, barley, corn, sesame and watermelons. There were olive orchards and three olive presses. In January 1949 Kibbutz Yas'ur was built on the site. All that remains of the Palestinian village are 'three houses, two shrines and a school':

> All of these landmarks stand deserted amid cactuses, weeds, and fig, olive, and mulberry trees. The debris of destroyed houses punctuates the vegetation. There are also some graves near the site that are in a state of neglect.[59]

There was constant killing and reprisals. Such happened at Balad al-Shaykh in the Haifa district. On 30 December 1947, thirty-nine Jewish workers at the Haifa oil refinery were killed by Arabs. This latter attack had been provoked by an Irgun operation which had killed six Arabs and wounded many others, including women and children. After the killings at the refinery, the Haganah attacked Balad al-Shaykh, and killed six people, including women and children. Ben-Gurion excused such action, saying that 'there was no way, during a military operation, to tell which individual Arabs were friendly and which hostile'. In this he agreed with an adviser on Arab affairs:

> A brutal and strong response is needed ... If the family is known, attack it without mercy, women and children included. Otherwise the response is not effective.[60]

We have seen that a central purpose of the Zionist programme was to remove the Arabs from Palestine. After the establishment of the mandate, the leadership of the Zionists were very much occupied in pursuing this goal. The immediacy of solving this problem gave rise to some very weird ideas, such as the solution offered by Ben-Gurion to the Arab leader Musa al-Alami in 1934 which had, for the Zionists, several advantages.

As a preliminary, Transjordan, as well as Palestine, would become part of the Jewish state. This was an idea, incidentally, which was often proposed. The Arabs would be removed from both and resettled in other Arab countries, a process in which the Jews would help. In the bizarre logic of Zionist thinking, this would mean that the problem of the sort of discrimination which happened in South Africa would be avoided because there would no longer be any Arabs to be discriminated against.[61]

Ben-Gurion *seemed* to extol the cultural and moral superiority of the Arabs. He promised that the development 'would also bring about a renaissance of its Arab inhabitants'.[62] This is an example of Ben-Gurion's lies. He was being more truthful when he said that peace with the Arabs was impossible. 'Everyone sees the difficulty of relations between Jews and Arabs,' he began, 'but not everyone sees that there is no solution to that question. There is no solution. There is an abyss and nothing can fill that abyss ... We want Palestine to be ours as a nation'.[63] There was though one constant in Ben-Gurion's thinking, if not in his public utterances: to expel the Arabs. He told the United Nations Special Committee on

Palestine, which was set up in 1947, 'that the establishment of a Jewish state in Palestine did not require such a transfer'. He assured his party, however, that he had said that for political reasons.[64]

In British government circles there had always been sympathy with this policy to evict the Arabs. As early as September 1922 Eric Mills, acting principal in the Colonial Office stated that 'Mr I. Zangwill was perfectly logical when he stated that this led to the view that the non-Jewish inhabitants of Palestine must be sent elsewhere …' He went on to say, 'however [logical] such a solution might be, in its ethical aspects, it is repugnant to all fair-minded men and of course has never been contemplated by His Majesty's Government'.[65]

The idea of a 'pure' Jewish state was not new.

> Already before the First World War, a consensus was forming in Zionist circles that Jewish colonisation of Palestine would be possible only through a 'bifurcation' of the economy, requiring the establishment of new, and exclusively Jewish structures and institutions.[66]

What did this mean in practice in the years ahead? One example of Ben-Gurion's policy can be seen from his order to demolish the 'thorns' of the villages of Ramla and Lod (Lydd) in the summer of 1948. This cleansing is just one example of the treatment of the Palestinians by the IDF.

On 10 July 1948 Lydd was attacked. After aerial bombardment, the question was raised about the disposal of the people who were left. Yitzhak Rabin, the second in command, asked what they should do:

> Ben-Gurion waved his hand in a manner that Rabin interpreted as a directive to expel them; Rabin later claimed that Ben-Gurion had given an explicit order to do so. For his part, Allon [the commander] told Ben-Gurion that the inhabitants 'were inclined to leave'.[67]

What happened was altogether a case study of 'cleansing':

> The Jewish troops went on yet another rampage of murder and pillage. 426 men, women and children were killed (176 bodies were found in the mosque).[68]

This was reported by foreign newspapers. One of them wrote that:

> Practically everything that lay in their (the Israeli forces) way died. Riddled corpses lay by the roadside.

Another told of 'the corpses of Arab men, women and even children strewn about'. An English reporter wrote how:

The Arab refugees were systematically stripped of all their belongings before they were sent on their trek to the frontiers.⁶⁹

The town of Ramla suffered the same fate:

> The people of both cities were forced to march, without food or water, to the West Bank, many of them dying from thirst and hunger on the way. As only a few hundred were allowed to stay in both towns, and given that people from nearby villages had fled there for refuge, Rabin estimated that a total of 50,000 had been 'transferred' in this inhuman way. Again the inevitable question presents itself: three years after the Holocaust, what went through the minds of those Jews who watched these wretched people pass by? ⁷⁰

The same question was asked by Count Bernadotte, and since this behaviour is still present in Israel, the question remains: how could Jews, of all people, cause such suffering? The only answer must be that the brutal traditions of Eastern Europe, and some parts of the Middle East, have persisted in Israeli culture.

The most cursory reading of Zionist policy from the beginning proclaims that this behaviour was inevitable. It is a measure of British ignorance or avoidance that this is rarely commented upon. The only part of the British government which recognised the Zionist tactics was the despised Foreign Office—despised because in the discussions about Palestine during the Second World War, it constantly supported the Arab cause. Its view was frequently expressed in terms such as these:

> The Zionists will not be deterred by the small size of the Jewish State from filling it up with immigrants beyond its capacity. They will think of the Jewish State merely as a stepping-stone towards the realisation of their wider hopes for a larger Jewish State covering the whole of Palestine and Transjordan. The Arabs will be kept in a continual state of tension. There will continually be disorders and bloodshed.⁷¹

Such a gloomy prediction was fulfilled. It happened at a notorious attack on the village of Deir Yassin on the outskirts of Jerusalem. About 600 people lived there. On the night of 9 April 1948 a mob of terrorists from Irgun and the Stern gang attacked the village. The villagers had firearms and tried to defend themselves. There was fierce fighting, with the Jews having the advantage of high explosives and hand grenades. When they left, a number of the villagers had been murdered. How many is, naturally, a matter of dispute. There is general agreement about a 100 plus figure, but some would claim that more were murdered. The killers claimed that 254 died, and the International Red Cross reported that there was 'a total of more than 200 dead, men, women and children'.⁷² Four of the attackers were killed.⁷³ It is also agreed that the villagers had entered a pact with the neighbouring Orthodox

Jewish village, Givat Shaul, that they would collaborate in avoiding conflict. This pact seems to have been effective until the attack, although some allegations are commonly made that the Deir Yassin villagers had been shooting at Jews. There is no dispute that survivors were paraded through the streets of Jerusalem.

As may be expected, there is considerable controversy about almost every aspect of the affair. The first of these is about the justification for the attack. It was supposedly necessary to help unblock the road to Jerusalem, but this is questionable. What is more likely is that it would demonstrate to the Arabs that the Jews would fight. Yehuda Lapidot, the second in command of the Irgun group attacking the village, said that orders were given to not harm women, children and the elderly, and that the villagers should be warned by loudspeaker to give them a chance to escape, but his evidence is intrinsically biased.[74] The next controversy is about the role of the Haganah. Some say that they ordered the attack, but its leadership afterwards deplored the assault. Then there are allegations, including by an Israeli historian, that there were cases of mutilation and rape.[75] There is no substance in the claim that there were Palestinian militia in the village, a claim which goes further to include the presence of Iraqi forces.

The next statement is that prisoners were butchered. A Jewish writer, Yoav Gelber supports the claim that twenty-five captured villagers were murdered and thrown into a quarry.[76] It is also claimed by one of the attackers that:

> The dissidents (Irgun and Lehi) were going about the village robbing and stealing everything: chickens, radio sets, sugar, money, gold and more ... each dissident walked about the village dirty with blood and proud of the number of people he had killed.[77]

This account by Meir Pa'il, who alleges he was one of the attackers, is dismissed by an Israeli military historian, Uri Milstein, who claims that Pa'il was not even there. This is one of a number of Milstein's assertions which is not accepted by Morris. Another of Pa'il's statements, that the Jewish residents of Givat Shaul had protested at the bloodshed and helped the Arabs is contradicted by a Haganah intelligence officer who wrote that they had 'taken part in the torture of prisoners, referring to them being kicked and shoved with rifle butts'.[78]

Allegations of rape are always fertile ground for dispute. It was reported, *inter alia*, by an assistant inspector general of the British Palestine Police Force, Richard (later Sir Richard) Catling, after extensive interviews, that 'there is, however, no doubt that many sexual atrocities were committed by the attacking Jews. Many young schoolgirls were raped and later slaughtered. Old women were also molested.'[79] Other sources deny this. Gelber explains away these allegations by defining Catling as 'an old and bitter enemy' of the Irgun and Lehi.[80] No doubt he was. Catling was described by a fellow officer as 'among the most feared CID man among the terrorists'.[81] Other main sources of the rejection of sexual attacks came from Arabs. In Arab, as in many cultures, rape, in a convoluted process of logic, is a disgrace for the woman and for the men who had failed to protect her. And so the men of the village strongly denied that there had been any rapes.[82] Not only is the evidence of rape and sexual attacks strong, but the balance of probability is that such attacks took place. It is now generally accepted that sexual attacks are the normal practice by soldiers when attacking defenceless people.

Certainly the Jewish soldiery were as likely to be as guilty as any. At the time of the War of Independence, Ben-Gurion reports:

> The bitter question has arisen of looting and rape in the conquered cities ... a shameful atrocity: Battalion 22 in Be'er Sheva apprehended an Arab man and woman. They killed the man and they (twenty two men) discussed what to do with the woman. They decided and carried out their decision—they washed her, sheared off her hair, raped her, and killed her.[83]

There was so much rape in the occupied cities that Ben-Gurion 'ordered that every Jew, and especially every Jewish soldier, caught in an act of rape ... should be shot without mercy'.[84] He seems to have been informed about each case and entered them in his diary. Every few days he has a sub-section: 'Rape Cases'.[85] There seems to be no evidence that any perpetrators were shot. Ben-Gurion was especially concerned about the behaviour of Jewish immigrants from North Africa. He expressed high hopes that the IDF would 'teach a young man from these countries to sit on a toilet like a human being, to wash himself, not to steal, not to grab an Arab girl, rape her, and murder her—that comes before everything else'.[86] There are reports of rape from Red Cross officials. One reported that 'as Palestinian men were taken away as prisoners, their women were left at the mercy of the Israelis'.[87]

There are detailed accounts which show that not much mercy was shown to Palestinian women. The British were the ultimate authority, and so Arab authorities appealed to them for help. None was forthcoming. Lieutenant-General Sir Gordon MacMillan, the GOC, said that he would only intervene and risk lives if British interests were at stake.[88]

There was widespread condemnation of the massacre. Left wing politicians in Israel deplored the way in which the reputation of Israel suffered because of this breach of something which came to be called 'the purity of arms'. The IDF have published a document called the 'Spirit of the IDF'. It calls for 'honouring the State of Israel as a Jewish ... state' and harks back to 'the tradition of the Jewish people throughout their history'.[89] This admonition was further enshrined in a document which reads in part:

> The soldier shall not employ his weaponry and power in order to hurt non-combatants or prisoners of war, and shall do all he can to avoid harming their lives, body, honour and property.

Reference was made to this 'purity' of arms after Deir Yassin. Rabbi Norman Solomon writes that the order is based on the ethical morals which are the tradition of Israel 'and the desire for moral approval and hence political support from the world community'.[90] Despite the persistent attacks and killing of civilians by the Israeli forces, especially by the Secret Services, the Israel Supreme Court has ruled that even though Arab terrorists were civilians they could not be protected by the terms of the Geneva Convention, or by extension the 'purity of arms'. This decision was criticised.[91]

In 2015 a UN Human Rights Council on Operation Protective Edge dealt with the general conduct of the IDF, this time in Gaza. The fact that the political and military leadership did not change its course of action, despite considerable information regarding the massive degree of death and destruction in Gaza, raises questions about potential violations of international humanitarian law. In 2021, the International Court of Criminal Justice recognised the state of Palestine, and it can now pursue alleged war crimes committed by Israel.

In any case, the cleaving to the myth of 'purity' is a raw case of hypocrisy. And, as Prior also notes, this 'slogan of the Haganah in early 1948—also has had to be abandoned in the face of the evidence. That Jews, too, were capable of committing atrocities has been comprehensively unmasked.'[92]

There were, and are, Jewish historians who try to variously deny, or condemn the Arabs for using the Deir Yassin massacre for propaganda purposes. Karsh, for example, describes the attack as 'a further blow to Arab morale':

> They capitalised on the *tragedy* in an attempt to gain immediate political gains ... at the time, however, the widely exaggerated descriptions of Jewish atrocities, especially of alleged rapes of women that never took place, spread panic among Palestinian society and *intensified the ongoing mass flight* [my emphases].[93]

There was widespread international horror at the attack:

> A senior British official described the atrocities at Deir Yassin as a 'beastly Holocaust'. Chief Secretary Gurney wrote that Belsen 'pales' beside the bestialities of Deir Yassin'.[94]

This could be the first time that the behaviour of the Jews was compared to that of the Nazis. It certainly would not be the last.

The reaction from the Jews was predictable. As recently as 1969 the Israeli government published a pamphlet denying that there had been a massacre, that there was an Iraqi force there, and the massacre story was 'part of a package of fairy tales for export and home consumption'. This caused outrage, even in Israel, and the pamphlet was withdrawn, but 'it remains the source of many popular accounts'.[95] Perhaps the most unrelenting defender of Jewish action was, of course the Marpasian rock, Menachem Begin. His attitude was that this was:

> A splendid act of conquest ... tell your soldiers you have made history in Israel with your attack and your conquest. Continue thus until victory. As in Deir Yassin, so everywhere, we will attack and smite the enemy. God, God, Thou has chosen us for conquest.[96]

He followed this up with denial, and with further triumphal words:

> Yet the hostile propaganda, disseminated throughout ignored the fact that the civilian population of Dir [sic] Yassin was actually given a warning by us before the battle began ... The enemy propaganda was designed to besmirch our name, in the result it helped us. Panic overwhelmed the Arabs of Eretz Israel. Kolonia village, which had previously repulsed every attack of the Haganah, was evacuated overnight and fell without further fighting. Beit-Iksa was also evacuated ... The 'Dir Yassin Massacre' lie is still propagated by Jew-haters all over the world.[97]

We are left with one certainty that, at the very least, women and children died, and that although apologists may quibble about the meaning of words, this was a massacre. We are also left with the certainty that the attackers, as volubly expressed by Begin, rejoiced in the attack. Perhaps the final irony of this aberrant behaviour is that Deir Yassin village forms part of the Kfar Shaul Mental Health Centre, an Israeli psychiatric hospital.

Then began the inevitable assurance that the Arab version was untrue, or at least exaggerated. While it may have been true that 'Lehi fighters occupied the village of Deir Yassin on the outskirts of Jerusalem, killing in the process some 100 people, including women and children' the Jewish Agency and the Haganah 'immediately expressed their disgust and regret'. This failed to satisfy the Arabs.

There were two major results of the Deir Yassin attack. The first was that it induced panic throughout the Palestinian population and led to flight to neighbouring countries: a flight which was not their fault or the result of some bizarre decision, as Karsh implies, but caused by naked fear. The second was that the fury engendered by the attack throughout the Arab world meant that Arab countries could no longer stand by. There was a meeting of the Arab League Political Committee on 10 April, and on 14 May King Abdullah fired a shot and shouted 'Forward'. The Arab invasion began at midnight.[98]

It was against this chaotic background that, on 14 May 1948, Ben-Gurion proclaimed the birth of the state of Israel. On the same day, President Truman recognised the new state against considerable advice not to, including by his own State Department, who foresaw, correctly, that it might lead to war, and a deterioration in US relations with the Arab states. Russia, too, immediately acknowledged the new state. The new Israeli government soon took over the reins of government. This had gathered speed even as the UN was dithering, and the British were solemnly carrying on their withdrawal. Ben-Gurion announced to the Jewish national assembly:

> We have to inform the world and the UN that we shall be the implementers. We ourselves, are able, capable and willing to function as a transitional government from this very moment, from the beginning of the transitional period, instead of the withdrawing British government.[99]

They were able to do this because the British were determined to have nothing more to do with Resolution 181, or its implementation, leaving power to be seized by the strongest. And so 'Jewish forces took over any government services, offices and installations they could lay their hands on'.[100] Begin of course was not satisfied. Then, as always, he was relentless: 'Israel Sovereignty had not been extended to *our capital* [my emphasis].'[101]

Ben-Gurion, while seizing power, continued to lie. He talked a lot about 'co-existence'. In a string of speeches and interviews, widely publicised by the Jewish media, he sought to dispel the pervasive scaremongering about the state, vowing that the position of this minority would, in law and in practice, be exactly the same as that of the Jewish majority counterpart. 'The Arab will enjoy full civic and political equality,' he stated time and again. 'He will have the franchise on the same terms as the Jews.'[102] And again:

> In our state there will be non-Jews as well—and all of them will be equal citizens; equal in everything without exception; that is; the state will be their state as well.[103]

He never meant that this would mean an independent Arab state. In September 1948, on his own admission, he told an American representative:

> According to my conviction we are entitled to all of Western Palestine [i.e. the whole of mandatory Palestine], since a Jewish state there hardly encroaches upon the vast Arab areas in the Middle East.[104]

In Britain, political reaction to the foundation was different from that of the two great powers: it would not acknowledge the new 'state'. This decision, was deplored by Churchill in October 1948:

> The Socialists, more than any other party in the State, have broken their word in Palestine and by incredible mismanagement have brought us into widespread hatred and disrepute there and in many parts of the world.[105]

Churchill continued his protests. In a parliamentary debate in January 1949 he spoke to 'a sceptical House of Commons', mounting an attack on Bevin. He deplored the fact that after nine months Britain still did not recognise Israel. Pointing out that Bevin had said that 'some countries had made [a mistake] in hastily recognising Indonesia [but] how absurd it is to compare the so-called Republic of Indonesia with the setting up in Tel Aviv of a government of the state of Israel.'[106] He advanced the opinion that the establishment of the state of Israel was an 'event in world history to be viewed in the perspective, not of a generation or a century, but in the perspective of a thousand, two thousand or even three thousand years. That is a standard of temporal values or time values which seems very much out of accord with the perpetual click-clack of our rapidly changing moods and of the age in which we live.'[107] Churchill is here rehearsing again his perpetual myth of long-standing Jewish rule in Palestine.

A couple of months after this speech, Churchill addressed a Jewish audience in New York and assured them of his unswerving support:

> Remember, I was for a free and independent Israel all through the dark years when many of my most distinguished countrymen took a different view. So do not imagine for a moment that I have the slightest idea of deserting you in your hour of glory.[108]

One can only guess which and whose 'dark years' he is describing. He sweeps aside the ugliness of events in Palestine when he seems to confine the 'dark years' to the Zionist struggle, and it is the foundation of Israel which is 'your hour of glory'. This was not a universal perception. Evelyn Shuckburgh, who was the head of the Colonial Office's Middle East Department, was less sympathetic to the Zionist cause than his father, John, had been:

> He considered Israel as 'the greatest irritant of all' and that 'it was founded on a false premise and in unnatural, impertinent conditions'.[109]

Another important official, Sir Alexander Helm, minister in Tel Aviv, wrote in his annual report in 1949:

> This review does not represent Israel in a very attractive light. Nor could it be otherwise ... it was born of a force applied with unscrupulous singleness of purpose by a people whose inferiority complex and sense of persecution had made them aggressive and blind to the interests of others and whose easy success facilitated by world states merely continued the belief that they could do no wrong. The nature of the Jew cannot be expected to change.[110]

In parliament too there were those not in favour. In April 1950 a Tory MP, Sir Harry Legge-Bourke, said that the recognition of Israel was 'the most hideous betrayal of all those men who fought in Palestine in the past'.[111]

The pressure on Churchill, as if he needed any, was unrelenting. In November 1948 he received a memorandum from Dorothy de Rothschild written by Marcus Sieff of the Marks and Spencer Company. Sieff had been working with Ben-Gurion, and he told Churchill that if Britain continued to refuse to recognise Israel, this might lead to Arab attacks and that Britain's stance in the United Nations was blocking good relations.[112] But Britain was adamant: it would not acknowledge Israel. Bevin set the British course:

> There are certain lines over Palestine from which I cannot deviate. I do not ... intend in the near future to recognise the Jewish State and still less to support any proposal that it should become a member of the United Nations.[113]

On a more human and personal level, the fate of Weizmann may be noted. While he may have rejoiced, he was treated abominably by Ben-Gurion. He and Ben-Gurion had always differed over policy. Ben-Gurion wanted 'action' where Weizmann believed in diplomacy. The *coup de grâce* came when, 'at the Zionist Congress of January 1946 [Weizmann] was removed from the presidency of the World Zionist Organisation. And not satisfied with victory, the vindictive Ben-Gurion was to hound him during the years that remained before his death in 1952.'

Weizmann was made president of the new state in 1949 and was thus 'politically neutered'. 'He was firmly kept away from any exercise of influence and was even prevented from signing the new state's Declaration of Independence'.[114]

By May 1948, when Israel declared independence, it should be remembered that Palestine was in a state of civil war. At this point, on 13 May, Count Folke Bernadotte was asked if he would be prepared to be considered as the UN mediator in the war which had broken out. The aim was to broker a truce. He seemed like a good choice: he was a member of the Swedish royal family, a national of a country with no recent colonial interests, and vice-president of the Swedish Red Cross. Finally, he had been closely involved in the aid given to displaced persons after the war. On 19 May 1948 he was offered the post of mediator. He kept a diary of his mission, which was published after he was gunned down by Jewish terrorists.

Bernadotte had contact with kings, soldiers, politicians, as well as ordinary people, and his diary is a valuable account of the state of Palestine and the region. The UN had received notice of failure from the UN Palestine Commission, set up to implement the partition resolution, a failure blamed in part on 'the lack of cooperation from the Mandatory Power'. It had therefore appointed another body, a Truce Commission for Palestine, on 28 April 1948, which consisted of the consuls of Belgium, France and the United States in Jerusalem. They made little or no impact on the situation.

Bernadotte arrived in the first of the countries he was to visit—Egypt—on 28 May 1948. The situation he was to find in Palestine, it goes without saying, was complicated to a degree in that it was obvious to anyone that there could be no resolution, not only for everyone, but for anyone. The most he could hope for was a truce. The problems he faced were immense. There was first the solid fact that the Jews had declared an independent state, which was moreover recognised by several countries, including the United States, but not Britain. The latter said that they were 'not for the time being prepared to take any steps against the Arabs'. There was the unswerving refusal of the Palestinian Arabs or the Arab countries to agree to an independent Jewish state in Palestine. Dominating the debate was the United Nations declaration which recommended partition. Consequent upon this recommendation, civil war had broken out. While Arabs were fleeing from Jewish violence, the Jews were pressing for more immigration. Finally there was the singular problem of 'the holy places', especially Jerusalem.

When it came to negotiations, the Jews spoke with one voice (at least to Bernadotte), whereas the Arabs were split into factions and interest groups. For example, it was generally agreed that King Abdullah would support any idea which would extend his kingdom, by including Palestine in it: a notion which was unacceptable, especially to King Farouk of Egypt. Included in this complex situation was the mufti, still active from his base in Egypt, still very influential in Palestine, and still disliked by most Arab authorities.

There is no doubt that Abdullah wished to embrace not only Palestine, but Syria too, into his domain. Arab loyalists accuse him of not giving enough support to them. Avi Shlaim has written of an interview he had with a senior official in the Jewish agency. He declared:

> We would agree to the conquest of the Arab part of Palestine by Abdullah. We would not stand in his way. We would not help him, would not seize it, and hand it over to him ... He, for his part, would not prevent us from establishing the State of Israel, from dividing the country, taking our share and establishing a state in it. Now his vagueness, his ambiguity, consisted of declining to write anything, to draft anything which would bind him ... The agreement included a provision that if Abdullah succeeded in capturing Syria, and realised his dream of Greater Syria—something we did not think he had the power to do—we would not disturb him ... but regarding the Arab part of Palestine, we did think that it was serious and that he had every chance of taking it, all the more so since the Arabs of Palestine, with their official leadership, did not want to establish a state at all.

Leaving aside this last bold assertion, this report explains why the Palestinians never really trusted Abdullah. And if this were not enough, his ambition became absurd. For he seriously proposed 'again and again':

> Perhaps you would settle for less than complete independence, and statehood, after all; under my sovereignty or within a common framework with me, you

would receive full autonomy or a Jewish canton, not a totally separate one but under the roof of the Hashemite crown.[115]

And then—a cause which began to concern Bernadotte deeply—a pitiful Arab refugee problem had been created.

Bernadotte spent some time in Paris before going to the Middle East, and while there, even before he had been to Palestine, he was told by the vice-president of the Jewish Agency that if the Arabs refused to accept a separate Jewish state then 'an agreement was impossible'.[116] On 28 May he landed in Cairo, and began a series of meetings. On 3 June, a day Bernadotte describes as 'most interesting', he met the Egyptian prime minister, the British commander of the Transjordan Arab Legion, and the Jordanian foreign minister.[117] These meetings left him 'filled with liveliest hopes that the truce question would reach a rapid solution'.[118] His next meeting with the Israeli foreign minister, Moshe Shertok, gave him a shock:

> The Jewish representatives were very unwilling to agree to any compromise, above all on the question of continued Jewish immigration into Palestine during the truce. They maintained that the Jewish interpretation of certain expressions in the Security Council's resolution was correct (which it probably was) and that consequently 'fighting personnel' must mean armed personnel, whereas 'men of military age' must mean men of military age who did not carry arms.

The Jews went on to say that immigration, 'which has begun as early as 15 May 1948' should continue, but no arms would be imported, that such men would be put in camps under Bernadotte's supervision, and he would be told when ships arrived, and the nature of the passengers. Lastly, no immigration should carry on until proper controlling mechanisms had been put in place. But in a typical sleight of hand, the Jews insisted on an exception being made 'in the case of a few ships which were expected to reach Jewish ports within the next few days'.[119]

Bernadotte realised very early on that the main obstacle to progress was Jewish obduracy:

> I recalled what I had said to my assistants on my first visit to Tel-Aviv, when I was acclaimed at the concert I had been invited to: that the friendliness that flowed towards me then would unquestionably turn to suspicion and ill-will if, in my later activities as Mediator, I failed to study primarily the interests of the Jewish party but sought to find an impartial and just solution of the problem.[120]

Bernadotte recognised that he had arrived too late and that the UN resolution was a disaster:

> The experiences I had had during the past month had gradually more and more strengthened me in my view that the resolution adopted by the United Nations General Assembly on 29 November 1947 had been an unfortunate one... in the long run it could not be lasting... The creation of a unitary State in Palestine with far-reaching rights for the Jews would in itself have been preferable ... it was of course necessary, however, to consider the circumstances of the case as they were in reality and not as one would wish them to be.

He goes on to point out that fourteen countries had recognised the state of Israel, which indeed functioned as such.[121]

Another setback came when he went to Haifa, and met the Jewish foreign minister, Shertok, on 6 June. It was, in the event, a portent of what was to come. The president of the UN Security Council had sent Bernadotte a telegram which supported a memorandum which Bernadotte had drafted, and which set out some ground rules for the mediation. Shertok's reaction was 'immediate and violent'. To Shertok the telegram was unacceptable because the president was a Syrian. Shertok objected to the suggestion that immigration should cease during a truce: 'such a provision was a violation of the self-evident right of the Jews to continue immigration'.[122] Bernadotte 'lost patience'. He said that he 'had the impression that the Israeli government did not want a truce at all', and that 'the Jewish side' rejected the views of the president 'on the grounds that he happened at the moment to be a Syrian'. He also met Azzam Pasha, secretary of the Arab League. The latter 'attracted me strongly: I felt an instinctive liking for him'.[123] He was to change his mind somewhat later: 'gradually, however, my impression changed. Azzam Pasha is a strange man.' Azzam Pasha raised the kind of question which was asked at the time and since, to which there would appear to be no answer:

> Why, he asked, must it be necessary for the approximate number of 500,000 Jews who are at present in Palestine to have a State of their own, when there are far larger numbers of Jews in other parts of the world?[124]

After many meetings the two sides agreed unconditionally to a truce. This was the first of two and would come into effect on 11 June. It was due to expire on 8 July. But the arguments never ceased. For example, Bernadotte believed that there should be no Jewish immigration during the truce. This was modified so that 'men of military age' should be excluded. But what is military age? And in any case, the Arabs claimed that the Jews were putting women, and even children, into the field.

Nothing had changed. There was sporadic violence. One of the most notable episodes was that of the ship the *Altalena*. This ship was at sea when the truce was agreed, and after arguments among the Jewish leaders, it was agreed it should land its cargo of emigrants and weaponry. There then followed serious fighting between the 'provisional' government troops and Jewish terrorists in which fifteen men were killed. Ben-Gurion rounded up some 200 Irgun members, but the organisation carried on its murderous campaign. The episode was in clear breach of the truce. The attempt by Bernadotte to discover the truth about what happened exemplifies the volume of the lies and deceit with which he had to cope.

Meanwhile the same political arguments were put forward over and over. Azzam, at a meeting with Bernadotte and representatives of the Arab states on 16 June 1948, expressed the generally held, and often repeated, Arab view:

> The historical arguments put forward by the Jews in support of their demands on Palestine are valueless and irrelevant. The Arabs controlled Spain much longer and more completely than the Jews Palestine. From a purely historical point of view, an Arab claim on Spain would be considerably stronger than the Jewish claim on Palestine ... The present situation in Palestine has its roots in the aggressiveness fostered by a minority, a large proportion of which is not even Palestinian. This aggressiveness must be met either by lawful means or by force.[125]

Bernadotte kept talking to the Jews. He saw the foreign minister, Shertok, who 'was graciousness itself', but what he said though gave Bernadotte 'little hope'.[126]

Bernadotte's prediction that the situation was hopeless was to prove correct. He had spent a huge amount of time talking to a wide range of people. He retreated to Rhodes, which was his base, to consider the situation. It did not take him long to conclude that 'the United Nations resolution of 29 November 1947 could hardly be regarded as a happy one ... The Arabs had, moreover, announced quite clearly and definitely that a solution of the kind adopted in 1947 must result in their resorting to military measures.'[127] Bernadotte was critical of the Arabs since 'they played their cards extremely clumsily, and acted too late to influence the United Nations'. He thought that perhaps it 'might be possible for Israel to retain her position as an independent state, and at the same time be associated in some way with the Arabic part of Palestine'.[128] He left Rhodes on 15 June to try once again. He held interminable discussions with all the parties, but by the end of June his optimism was at an end.

There was a related problem, already mentioned, which Bernadotte wanted to tackle. With his Red Cross background, and his post-war experience, he very soon began to notice the plight of refugees, mostly Arab. On 16 September he contacted the UN secretary-general about their wretched state. He wrote that although the two problems, the peaceful settlement, and the refugees, were separate matters, both 'require the most prompt action'.[129]

The truce made no difference to the predatory behaviour of the Israelis. Many Palestinian villages were attacked and the people driven out. One example is that of Mi'ar. An eyewitness described how, on 20 June 1948, he saw 'the approaching Israeli troops shooting indiscriminately at the villagers still busy in the fields collecting their dura. When they got tired of the killing spree, the soldiers then began destroying the houses. People later returned to Mi'ar and continued living there until mid-July when Israeli troops reoccupied it and expelled them for good. Forty people were killed in [the attack].'[130]

When the Jews captured the towns of Lydda and Ramleh, 'almost the entire population was expelled by the Israeli forces'.[131] The towns became the scene of one of the many Jewish massacres which were to be carried out over those years. Despite these crimes there were 'those who tried to stay on left after Israeli soldiers massacred about 250 people'.[132] There was another foretaste of what was, and is, Israeli policy: the annexation of land.

> Lydda and Ramleh constituted the first serious attempt to occupy areas allotted to the Arab state by evicting the resident Palestinian population.[133]

Bernadotte visited Ramallah. Even with his experience he was horrified. It may be noted that this was at an early stage in the disturbances:

> I have made the acquaintance of a great many refugee camps: but never have I seen a more ghastly sight than that which met my eyes here at Ramallah. The car was literally stormed by excited masses shouting ... that they wanted food and wanted to return to their homes. I remember not least a group of scabby and helpless old men with tangled beards who thrust their emaciated faces into the car and held out scraps of bread that would certainly have been considered quite uneatable by ordinary people, but was their only food.[134]

When he visited Transjordan:

> A preliminary examination which we carried out now in Amman showed that the refugee problem was vaster and more baffling than we had imagined. Great throngs of refugees had been herded into the old amphitheatre.[135]

After the search for a peace settlement, Bernadotte attached almost equal importance to the question of immediate action and relief for the political refugees. These were his conclusions:

A. As a result of the conflict in Palestine there are approximately 360,000 Arab refugees and 7,000 Jewish refugees requiring aid in that country and adjacent States.
B. Large numbers of these are infants, children, pregnant women and nursing mothers. Their condition is one of destitution, and they are 'vulnerable groups' in the medical and social sense.

He went on to discuss 'the destruction of their property and the loss of their assets [which] will render most of them a charge upon the communities in which they have sought refuge for a minimum period of one year (through this winter and until the end of the 1949 harvest)'.[136] Zionist apologists explain that all of this was inevitable:

> [Plan D] did envisage the possible destruction of villages and 'the expulsion of [their] population outside of the border of the [Jewish] state', that is: expulsion to the Palestinian Arab state. Yet these were ad hoc tactical measures dictated exclusively by military necessity rather than political considerations, let alone a premeditated plan of dispossession.[137]

Morris, another Jewish historian, agrees with the 'necessity':

> The pan-Arab invasion of 15 May clearly hardened Israel's resolve regarding the Palestinian civilian population, for good military and political reasons. On 16 June, the cabinet, without a formal vote, resolved to bar the return of refugees. The IDF [Israeli Defence Forces] general staff ordered its units to stop would-be returnees with live fire ... Abandoned villages were razed or mined, or, later, filled with new Jewish immigrants, as were abandoned urban neighbourhoods: fields were set alight, and landowners still in place were urged to sell out and leave.[138]

The habitual use of misleading words by apologists is once more in evidence: as in the use of 'abandoned' and 'urged to sell out', instead of 'decimated' or 'evicted'. To these may be added the description of this aggression as 'defensive'. Nor could Bernadotte foresee that the refugee 'problem' would grow to vast proportions, and become one of the most scandalous human crises created by the foundation of Israel. Because no Israeli government is going to give up territory, it will remain a source of cruelty, which must lead to continuous violence.

Official resistance to the possibility of repatriation was soon set in stone, and remains solid. During the second truce of the civil war which followed the passing of Resolution 181, 'The official Israeli committee dealing with the refugee problem decided to erase from the face of the earth some 400 Arab villages which had been declared hostile (i.e., active in the fighting) and were by then deserted.'

> Most of these were turned into agricultural land, and on the rest new Jewish settlements were built. From an Israeli point of view repatriation thereafter became an impossibility. The Israeli foreign office, in fact, informed the State Department on two occasions, once on 27 June and again a month later, that Arab refugees would not be allowed to return.[139]

Some apologists for Jewish behaviour point to the section of Bernadotte's second report submitted the day before his murder. '[It] considered the possibility of resettlement outside Palestine, with those who chose not to return being adequately compensated for their lost property.' The report read:

> It must not be ... supposed that the right of refugees to return to their former homes provides a solution to the problem ... The vast majority of the refugees may no longer have homes to return to and their resettlement in the State of Israel presents an economic and social problem of special complexity.[140]

On 28 July 1948, Shertok wrote to Bernadotte explaining the attitude of the provisional government:

> We feel convinced that any measure of repatriation undertaken solely on humanitarian grounds, in disregards of the military, political and economic aspects of the problem would prove to have been falsely conceived.[141]

In a statement that Karsh describes as 'upbeat', Ben-Gurion told the US special representative, McDonald, that 'large scale repatriation was a distinct possibility in the context of a stable and lasting peace'.[142] There was, as shown by subsequent events, no intention whatever of repatriating Arabs. The attitude of the Arab countries is described by Karsh as a 'subtler game'. This was to insist on the repatriation 'while avoiding any accompanying recognition of the Jewish state'.[143]

There is a persistent attempt by apologists to obfuscate the dismal picture of thousands of refugees desperately seeking safety from rampaging Jewish militias again by the use of neologisms. In one case the refugees are now described as 'evacuees'.[144] A former president of Israel, Chaim Herzog, explains the refugee problem as not being the fault of the Jews. After all, the Jews had dealt with their own refugees. These Jews were removed from Arab territory and relocated in Israel. The Arabs, according to Herzog, seem to have created their problem:

> The Arab governments chose to perpetuate the Arab refugee problem, to use the Arab refugees as political pawns over the years, and to allow generations to be born and to grow up in miserable refugee camps in the Middle East supported by international charity. (It is sobering to reflect that just one day's Arab oil revenues, even in 1949, would have sufficed to solve the entire Arab refugee problem. But this was not to be).[145]

The equation of Jewish and Arab refugees is taken up by other Zionist writers. In respect of Resolution 194, Karsh points out that the resolution refers to 'refugees' not 'Arab refugees'. Therefore, he argues it 'could readily apply to the thousands of Jews driven from their homes ... by the invading Arab armies. And that 'the property of those refugees not choosing to return should be made good by the governments of the authorities responsible', indicating that Arab states, as well as Israel, were seen as instigators of the refugee problem, 'be it Arab or Jewish'.[146] He goes on to claim that these clauses 'make the resolution anathema to the Arabs who opposed it vehemently and vote unanimously against it'. This showed that:

> The Palestinian leaders were [not] eager to see their hapless constituents return to their homes, lest this be interpreted as implicit recognition of Israel.[147]

In the larger matter of a settlement, time was running out. The truce was to expire on 8 July. On 29 June 1948 Bernadotte wrote to the UN with his proposals. The central, and most controversial one of these was that 'the original mandated territory of Palestine, including Transjordan, might form a Union comprising two Members, one Arab and one Jewish'. These 'Members' would *inter alia*, 'promote common economic interests' and common services 'including customs and excise'. Article 6 proposed that 'immigration within its own borders should be within the competence of its own Members' and that 'either Member would be entitled to request the Council of the Union to review the immigration policy of the other Member'. Article 9 suggested that:

> Recognition be accorded to the right of residents of Palestine, who because of conditions created by the conflict there have left their normal places of abode, to return to their homes without restriction and to regain possession of their property.

In an annex he deals with 'territorial matters'. Here he proposes that the Negev should be defined as Arab, as should Jerusalem (with conditions), and that Western Galilee should be Jewish. He also suggests discussion about the future of Jaffa, Haifa and Lydda.[148]

The reaction of the Arabs was to reiterate their basic refusal to accept anything which might look like a Jewish state. Bernadotte was not surprised, but remained remarkably optimistic: 'I had the feeling that the door to further discussions was still open.'[149] The Jewish reply was handed to Bernadotte on 6 July: 'It was sharp in tone.'[150] It was also detailed. Some of the principal objections were: that he had not taken into account the UN resolution of 29 November 1947 or the establishment of the state of Israel resulting from it. In particular:

> The Provisional Government was deeply wounded by your suggestion concerning the future of Jerusalem, which it regards as disastrous.

It went on to express the hope that the objections raised 'may cause you to reconsider your whole approach to the problem'.[151]

On 8 July the first truce ended, and the fighting began again. It lasted ten days, until a second truce was put in place on 18 July. On 13 July Bernadotte reported to the UN Security Council in New York. It was, it appears, an unfriendly reception. The president, a Ukrainian, was unsympathetic and accused Bernadotte of making proposals which were in conflict with the UN resolution. But Bernadotte retorted that he had not gone to Palestine merely to implement that resolution, and was supported in this. The Israeli speaker took the opportunity to condemn

Arab 'aggression' and demanded that the UN do something about it. The Syrian delegate refuted that. Bernadotte ended up with accusations from Russia that his proposals 'add fuel to the flames', and from the Ukrainian chairman that:

> Thanks to his mediatory activities we have slipped back not merely to the original position existing in Palestine when he was sent there as Mediator, but to an even worse position.[152]

Nevertheless, Bernadotte was authorised to return to Palestine and carry on his efforts. It is small wonder though that eventually he thought the UN was fairly useless:

> They seemed to imagine at Lake Success that once the resolution had been adopted, all would be well ... [but] without effective support I and my staff could get nowhere.[153]

Even the 'observers' sent by the UN were of no use:

> Villages which had gradually been isolated and were now easily cleansed while the UN observers, who had been sent in to supervise the truce, watched nearby.[154]

There was a further ceasefire, and at the beginning of August 1948, Bernadotte tried again. His meeting with the Jordanian ministers looked hopeful:

> They completely shared my view that there was no getting away from the fact that a Jewish State existed and would continue to exist.[155]

The Jewish response was less hopeful. After a meeting with Shertock, 'nothing that I could propose aroused any response; I got nowhere'.[156] His staff:

> Were finding it increasingly difficult to reach agreement with the Jews. Whatever questions came up, we were always met with the same passive resistance and the same lack of will to co-operate.[157]

The key figure of Azzam Pasha now took the view that the Arabs accepted the reality of the Jewish state: not that they would recognise it or desist in the efforts to destroy it.[158] Bernadotte's summary at this time was as follows:

> The Arabs had given us every possible help, particularly during the second truce. The Jews, on the other hand, constantly tried to put spokes in the wheel and did everything in their power to make our work more difficult.[159]

But he continued his efforts, and on 16 September 1948 he sent his last report to the UN, asking them to give the matter priority and to make a decision. In many respects his observations remained unchanged. For example, the Negev should belong to the Arabs, and refugees should be allowed to return. But he was firmer in recognising the existence of a Jewish state, and with regard to Jerusalem, it 'should be accorded special and separate treatment'.[160]

By this time the Zionists clearly thought that he might wield such influence at the UN that a critical resolution might be reversed to their utter disadvantage. They were also apprehensive that the Israeli government might have some sympathy with his plans, unlikely though this seemed. In a significant sign of things to come, Yitzhak Shamir ordered the assassination of Count Bernadotte. Lehi (the Stern gang) had already threatened, publicly, to kill him. They put up notices reading: 'ADVICE TO THE AGENT BERNADOTTE: CLEAR OUT OF OUR COUNTRY'. On the radio, in a reference to the assassinated Lord Moyne, they warned that 'The Count will end up like the Lord'. For good measure Shamir accused him of collaborating with the Nazis during the Second World War.[161] This slur was frequently deployed against those who seemed to be less than total in their support of the Jewish case. But here Shamir touched one of the peaks of his especial absurdities, since Bernadotte had been praised for his part in the post-war rescue of some 20,000 people, many of them Jews.

Bernadotte's murder was carried out on 17 September 1948 by the Stern gang, and was planned by a small group, the best known of whom was Yitzhak Shamir, its leader. Bernadotte's car was ambushed, and three of the murderers approached. One of them thrust a machine gun through the window and sprayed Bernadotte and a French colonel, André Sérot, with bullets. Both died. Arthur Koestler was in Israel when the murder was carried out:

> Low-voiced groups gathered at the street corners; it was strange to see women crying at the death of a man who was a stranger in Israel and politically detested by almost everybody.[162]

But not everyone was upset:

> We went to a café on the beach which is frequented mainly by Sternists and is used by them as a kind of soldiers' club. This place usually closes at about 1 p.m., but tonight, though it was much later, there was a revelling crowd there dancing Hora and Cracowiak. They are a queer, picturesque and ambitious lot of fierce-looking Yemenite gun-molls, Sephardic beauties and young men of dashing countenance ... it was all pretty disgusting.[163]

Despite this, but indicative of where Koestler's sympathies lay, he went on to make the bold claim that 'all evidence confirms that the Sternist leaders knew nothing of the Bernadotte murder'.[164]

The world condemned the murders, and the Jewish government carried out a fruitless investigation, although in such a small, tight circle it must have been known who the culprits were. In fact 'the UN was convinced the Israeli government knew who the perpetrators were and accused it of taking a lenient attitude'.[165] The mood of the Jewish public was, to judge by its reaction, sympathetic to the murderers. They might have agreed with the term 'zealots' used by Karsh, presumably to diminish the outrage.[166] A zealot, after all, can be a commendable figure, a fighter in a just cause.

The gang first denied the murders, and then admitted responsibility. There was some action taken against the gang. Three days after the murders the government passed an Ordinance to Prevent Terrorism. Some of the gangsters were arrested, some forcibly disarmed, some imprisoned, but very soon there was declared an amnesty for Lehi members and everyone was freed. In the 1950s, Ben-Gurion had a bodyguard called Yehoshua Cohen, who admitted that it was he who had fired the fatal shots. A statute of limitations prevented any action being taken against him, although there would in any case have been absolutely no chance of that happening.[167]

The liberal Shimon Peres in May 1995, at a ceremony in Tel Aviv, expressed formal regret 'that Bernadotte was murdered in a terrorist way', and mentioned his rescue of Jews. Sadly, Peres himself was gunned down by an extremist because he wanted to come to accommodation with the Palestinians. The final indication that the government approved of Lehi, despite its half-hearted protests, can be seen from the fact that in 1980 there was established an award—the Lehi Ribbon—'for military services towards the establishment of the State of Israel'.

The new Israeli government was not deterred by the condemnation heaped upon it by world opinion. Acting as though it were a perfectly proper state government, on the 22 September 1948, within days of Bernadotte's murder, it 'enacted' something called the Area of Jurisdiction and Powers Ordinance. This declared that that all territory captured during the war was now part of Israel. Furthermore, any territory captured in the future would also become part of Israel. This assumed that there would be collusion by the international community in an action without any notable precedent.

The attempts by the UN to intervene rolled on. In December 1948 it passed Resolution 194 establishing a Conciliation Commission. This was to take up the work where Bernadotte had left off. It set up an Economic Survey Mission for the Middle East. Nobody took any notice of any of their activities. This is not surprising when it was to address, for example, the problem of refugees who were the 'symbol' of the upheavals, and that they should be allowed to return home. It joined its many predecessors in the files of failed UN initiatives.

After Bernadotte, the new chief mediator was Dr Ralphe Bunche. He was a very experienced UN politician, and had been deputy to Bernadotte. For his success in negotiating a peace between Egypt and Israel he was awarded the Nobel Peace prize in 1950: the first African American to be so honoured.

The question which immediately dominated debate was what was to be done about Bernadotte's plan. There was a general hope that the two sides, and their supporters might agree to implement it. Bevin expressed a typical view when he said: 'We do not expect that either side will accept these proposals in total, but the world cannot wait forever for the parties to agree.'[168] But once again the complexities of US politics were to scupper such a swift conclusion. The unprincipled Truman was faced with a presidential election. His special counsellor on Palestine reported that it was impossible for the president to support the Bernadotte Report enthusiastically, saying that because 'the pressure from Jewish groups is mounting, the time is as bad as during the trusteeship period'.[169] Here, once again, American Jewish pressure was to prove the deciding factor in the shaping of Palestine. By now this pressure was well in place. In January 1946 Hector McNeil, liaison to Israel's envoys in London and a minister of state to Bevin, noted that:

> It is essential even when the Jews are at their most wicked and the Americans at their most exasperating not to lose sight of this point. As long as America is a major power, and as long as she is free, anyone taking on the Jews will indirectly be talking to America.[170]

In October 1948 the Security Council of the UN passed a resolution calling for a ceasefire, and called for negotiations for an armistice. In the same month Israel took the whole of Galilee, and appropriated fourteen villages *inside* Lebanon. In October, Egypt tried to negotiate a ceasefire, which was dependent on an Israeli withdrawal from certain territory, but this failed and fighting continued.

During the course of this, a very dangerous situation arose. The Israelis shot down five British reconnaissance aircraft over the Sinai desert. The two countries were on the brink of war, but inexplicably this increased the pressure for Britain to recognise Israel, and it did so three weeks later on the 30 January 1949. Despite such continued aggression, a series of armistice agreements were made in the course of 1949: with Egypt on 24 February, with Lebanon on 23 March, with Jordan on 3 April, and with Syria on 20 July. These were achieved by Dr Bunche, but only after difficult negotiations against a turbulent background in some of the Arab countries. In Egypt the government had to cope with the radical Muslim Brotherhood, and there were coups in Syria.

There were more demands from Israel for territory. They wanted what was called 'the little triangle', an area which contained fifteen Arab villages. Abdullah agreed to this, an act which was regarded as treacherous and which contributed to his assassination on the steps of the al-Aqsa mosque on 20 July 1951. There was supposed to be a peace treaty within six months but it never happened. For the moment, the argument over the West Bank ceased with it being handed over to Abdullah on 30 March 1949, and Israel agreed to withdraw from Lebanon. By the time of the ceasefire, the number of Arab refugees stood at about 700,000.

This was about half of the pre-war Arab population. During the war about 10,000 Jews were displaced.

Towards the end of 1948 the Bernadotte Report was moribund, since both sides had rejected it. The next major stage was the setting up by the United Nations of a UN Conciliation Commission for Palestine, which was established on 24 January 1949. This consisted of three members: one from France, one from the United States, and one from Turkey. The commission was to take Resolution 194 as the basis for discussion. They were to be concerned with the return of refugees, together with a two-state solution and the internationalisation of Jerusalem. After much exploratory discussion with all the parties who had an interest in the matters they were to consider, the commission met in Lausanne on 27 April, and continued their discussions until 12 September 1949. A protocol was agreed which embraced the topics to be discussed which was signed on 12 May 1949. This in itself was a considerable achievement. Regular reports on the meetings were sent back to the UN.

Like all other attempts before and since, it faced insoluble problems. There was the opposition of Ben-Gurion and King Abdullah, who were still hoping to reach accommodation over seizing chunks of Palestine themselves. The Arabs insisted on negotiating as a single unit, while the Israelis wanted to deal with each Arab state individually. The Arabs would not agree to deal with Israel in this way, but insisted they act collectively. This was because to deal with Israel directly would seem like recognition of the legitimacy of that state.

There were, effectively, two issues which were to dominate the proceedings: refugees and territory. Broadly, the Arabs wanted the matter of refugees dealt with separately, and wanted Resolution 194 (11) adhered to. The resolution was that:

> Refugees wishing to return to their homes and live at peace with their neighbours should be permitted to do so at the earliest practicable date, and that compensation should be paid for the property of those not choosing to return and for loss or damage to property which, under principles of international law or equity, should be made good by the Governments or authorities responsible.

The passing of this resolution marked two milestones. The first was the ending of the hope, still present in the resolution, that the United Nations organisation could make a difference. The second was that the Zionists, before and since, would pay no attention to any resolution that criticised their behaviour. So Israel rejected the resolution and pointed out that the Arabs were in any case responsible for causing the problem by their aggression. The Israelis were prepared to help with financing the resettlement of refugees, but that must be in Arab countries. But in general the Israelis insisted that the payment of compensation could only be discussed 'within a framework of a general peace plan'.[171] The Israelis also said that they would take back 100,000 refugees, but that they could not go back to their homes. Instead, they would be settled by the Israelis elsewhere. It emerged that this proposal was unworkable.

Ben-Gurion observed that since there was still a state of war, refugees could not be trusted. He did however agree that family members could return to a bread-winner who was still in Israel. On the whole this seems to have been successful.[172]

Members of the commission visited some camps and saw 'for themselves the deplorable material and moral situation of the refugees'.[173] In a massive understatement the commission reported that the problem could be solved 'without a considerable amount of preparatory work of a technical nature' and suggested a plan to set up a 'technical committee'.[174] One positive outcome of the commission was the establishment of an Economic Survey Mission.[175] This led in turn to the United Nations Relief and Works Agency for Palestine Refugees in the near East (UNRWA).[176]

The matter of territory was equally hopeless. The commission pointed out that the armistice agreement concluded that any 'Armistice demarcation line is not to be construed in any sense as a political or territorial boundary'.[177] The Arabs wanted, as a starting point, the territorial divisions to be those set out in Resolution 181. The Israelis brushed aside the instructions about armistice lines and summed up its position as follows:

> The Government of Israel now asserts its title to the territory over which its authority is actually recognised ... Although some of the invading Arab armies still stand on the soil of Palestine, Israel is not advancing any further territorial claims. But of the territory constituting the state of Israel, there can be no cession.[178]

Behind this lay the explanation, if one is needed, of Ben-Gurion's unyielding policy: 'The main thing is the absorption of the immigrants.'[179]

And there were other issues. Israel wanted to build a canal. But this would go through Arab territory and would necessitate the theft of several villages, and the eviction of the inhabitants. Then there was concern over the plight of Arab orange groves which lay in conquered land. These were vital, but it was likely that they would deteriorate. It was suggested that the proprietors of the groves should be allowed to return, with labourers to repair them. Members of a technical committee of the commission had seen the groves and reported that 'they were in a state of progressive deterioration'. They proposed a 'mixed group' to look after them. Israel refused, claiming that the 'Israeli custodian of Enemy Property was doing his best'.[180]

There was also the problem of refugee bank accounts and other financial complications. Israel made it clear that it would not 'suspend measures of requisition of Arab immoveable property', but it was more flexible in the matter of bank accounts and similar assets.[181] It agreed to a reciprocal agreement. This was clearly to the Israeli advantage, since numbers of Jews had moved from Arab countries to Israel, leaving financial assets behind. This too proved problematic, and at the time of the report, the process was still being worked out.[182] Associated with this issue was one of the most blatant of thefts by the Israelis. What happened in one of the wealthier areas of Jerusalem was duplicated elsewhere:

The Arabs soon fled once more; most of them left behind nearly all their belongings, from grand pianos and wedding dresses to tennis rackets and kitchen utensils and books and family photograph albums. Many of the Arab houses came into the possession of Jews who also came from the elite, among them politicians, judges and professors at the Hebrew university.[183]

Some of the latter disgraced the values of their profession. Ben-Gurion described how 'some Hebrew University faculty members entered the abandoned homes of Arab intellectuals, took their books, and deposited them in the National Library'. This he explained away as 'an outbreak of the Jewish community's most primitive instincts'.[184]

It soon became clear that the Lausanne Conference was making no progress. This fact was to have an interesting effect on US support for Israel, at least in the short term. Up to this point, and indeed for the whole of the period of the mandate, the US had distanced itself from events in Palestine, except for the occasional unhelpful interference. The Lausanne meeting, however, was a US initiative and its failure would be a humiliation. Truman and the US administration now began to understand the deadly complexities of the situation. In May 1949 the president issued the following warning:

> The US government is gravely concerned lest Israel now endanger the possibility of arriving at a solution of the Palestine problem in such a way as to contribute to the establishment of sound and friendly relations between Israel and its neighbours.

Truman's message ended in a direct warning that unless Israel changed its attitude, 'the US government will regretfully be forced to the conclusion that a revision of its attitude towards Israel has become unavoidable'.[185] Probably because Ben-Gurion could see beyond the president to the Jewish support in the US, there is no perceptible evidence of any change in the Israeli approach. The Lausanne Conference has been judged a failure.[186]

There were other occasions when US patience with Israel's stubbornness seemed to be exhausted. When peace between Israel and Syria was on the agenda in early 1949, the US ambassador in Damascus despaired:

> Unless Israel can be brought to understand that it cannot have all of its cake (and partition boundaries) and gravy as well (area captured in violation of truce, Jerusalem and resettlement of Arab refugees elsewhere) it may find that it has won Pa(lestine) war but lost the peace. It should be evident that Israel's insistence upon her pound of flesh and more is driving Arab states slowly (and perhaps surely) to gird their loins (politically and economically if not yet militarily) for long range struggle.[187]

Meanwhile, with regard to land, Israel annexed 60 per cent of the land allocated to Arabs under the partition plan. At that point Egypt controlled the Gaza Strip, and Transjordan controlled East Jerusalem and the West Bank, which led Schlaim to conclude:

> Only two parties emerged as winners from the Palestine war: Jordan and Israel. Jordan managed to defend the West Bank and East Jerusalem, and to incorporate them into its territory. Israel succeeded in extending its territory considerably beyond the UN partition borders ... The losers were the Palestinians.[188]

The UN, still officially responsible, set up a Truce Commission Organisation and a Mixed Armistice Commission to monitor events. On 11 May 1949, Israel saw another triumph: it was admitted to the UN.

The Israeli Prime Minister Sets the Goal

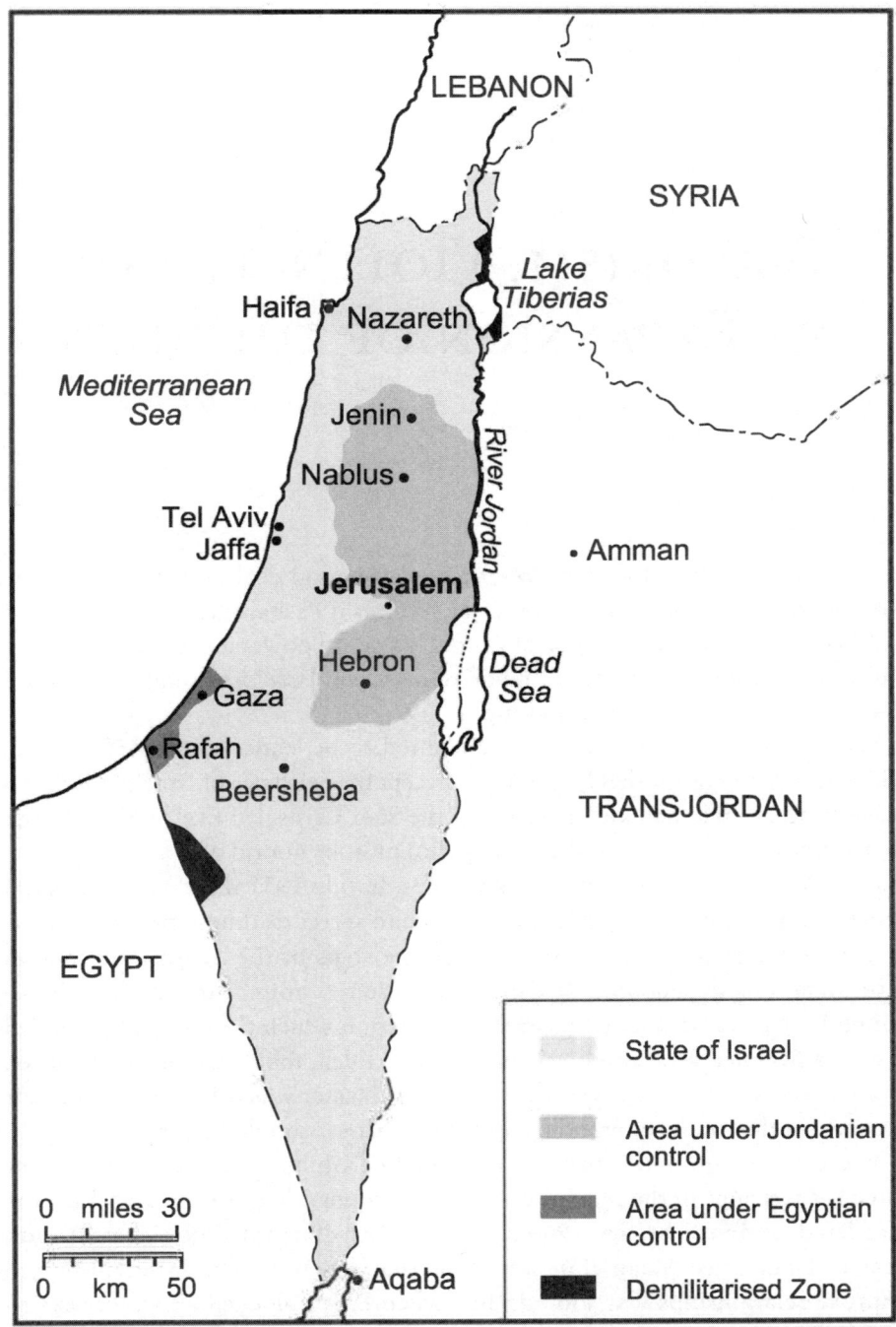

Partition proposed in the Armistice Agreement, 1949.

7

TERRORISM, VIOLENCE, AND THE EXPANSION OF THE STATE

In the years following the ceasefires, there was a good deal of turbulence in the Arab world. In Egypt the prime minister, Nokrashi Pasha, was assassinated and in 1952 a revolution saw the rise of Gamal Nasser to power and the exile of King Farouk. Ostensibly Nasser was a revolutionary, and Israel had some expectation that there might be a new relationship.

Nasser quickly made clear that he wanted to be leader of the Arab world, which *ipso facto* meant that he could not accept the existence of Israel. Indeed, his belligerence, as we shall see in respect of the Suez Crisis, led Evelyn Shuckburgh to describe him as 'a second Mussolini [who] must be got rid of'.[1]

In Syria there were frequent military coups. In July 1951 there was an especial shock. King Abdullah of Jordan, who had had secret dealings with the Israelis in a hope for peace, was assassinated on the steps of the Al Aqsa mosque in Jerusalem. His dependable British officer—some thought too dependable—Glubb Pasha, was dismissed in 1956 in an action which the colonially minded saw as a personal attack upon them. Anthony Eden, the British prime minister, was especially furious, and was convinced that Nasser was behind it. For Eden it became another of the mounting reasons why Nasser should be destroyed.

There can be no doubt that the dismissal of Glubb removed an important force for restraint in the region. In 1958, the young king of Iraq, Feisal II, was murdered, and in February 1966 a revolutionary 'Ba'athist' government took over in Damascus. Meanwhile any hope that a new regime in Egypt would improve relationships was soon dashed when Egypt blocked all waterways to Israeli shipping, including the Suez Canal. This was to be a deciding factor in Britain's further involvement in the region, and the downfall of its prime minister.

Meanwhile, there was constant fighting on the borders of the new state via incursions from the surrounding Arab countries by what came to be called 'fedayeen'. People were killed, property was stolen, and Jewish reprisals were swift. One such reprisal was a case study of Jewish reaction, and with it the began the career of a man who eventually became prime minister, and who was also to become notorious for his brutal behaviour when there was conflict. His real name was Ariel Scheinerman, better known as Ariel Sharon.

In August 1953 Sharon suggested the formation of Unit 101, a specialist group designed to operate across borders. Unit 101 has been described by Chaim Herzog, himself a general and president of the state, as 'a unit of tough, brave, dedicated young soldiers based entirely on volunteers, in which daring and sacrifice were bywords'.[4] With words like this, reputations are manufactured. Sharon trained and led the unit.

Sharon 'was imbued with a limitless and unrestrained motivation to go on operations', and he develop the tactic of avenging 'the killing of Israelis by attacking and terrorising the Arab villages from which the terrorists had set forth to harm Jews'. He drew up lists of 'punitive' raids against military and civilian targets, but 'it is an open question how many of those tasks were punitive as opposed to provocative'.[2] One of these operations was certainly punitive. It was excessive, but it illustrates Sharon's new policies.

In late 1953, fedayeen murdered a Jewish woman and her two children near Tel Aviv. Sharon decided to carry out reprisals against a village called Qibya. Two to three hundred Israelis attacked the village with grenades, mortars and gunfire. They supposedly warned people to come out of their houses, but even if this was true, there must have been so much noise of explosions and screaming that the villagers could not have heard the warning. The attackers claimed eleven had been killed. The UN commission which investigated counted about seventy Arabs killed—two thirds of them women and children—and their houses and public buildings destroyed. The world at large was appalled. Even *The Jewish Chronicle* condemned the massacre:

> By what standards is there any possible moral justification for this cruel attack on Jordanian villagers ... This was not self-defence against armed attacks, it was a reprisal of the same kind that was perpetrated by our enemies in the last war.[3]

The investigating commission sent a condemnatory report to the UN Security Council. Begin tried to lie his way out, explaining that the attack had been carried out by civilians. This explanation was widely ridiculed and it is difficult to see how this explains, much less excuse, anything. The commission's report further pointed out that not only was the Unit 101 there, but so were soldiers from the regular army (the IDF): in fact two thirds of the attackers belonged to the regular army. The United States government was furious and threatened further sanctions (some were in place already because of earlier Israeli intransigence). The US, along with others, demanded that those responsible be punished. This was ignored, but shortly afterwards Unit 101 was abolished.

There were other reprisal attacks which are worthy of note. One was known as 'Black Arrow'. In February 1955, after a gun battle, an Arab was found to have documents which, it was claimed, linked him to Egyptian intelligence. On 28 February a retaliatory raid took place which encountered Egyptian soldiers. About thirty-eight Egyptians and eight Israelis were killed. This was a significant raid because it took place inside Egypt. But Ariel Sharon went on to eminence, and it may be added, notoriety, in Israeli politics. To some people his crimes are of no significance when laid alongside his contribution to the integration of the Israeli state. Despite the fact that 'he was to be accused ... of insubordination and dishonesty ... he can best be described as a Patton-like, swashbuckling officer, who rose in the ranks of the Israel Defence Forces [and] proved himself to have an uncanny feel for battle'.[5]

The next signal failure to bring peace to the Middle East was called Project, or Operation, Alpha. It was conducted by two men, Evelyn Shuckburgh, and a US under-secretary of state, Russell. The idea was to bring to an end the dangerous situation which had continued since the end of the 1948 war. After much discussion, amendment and compromise, the outline of their proposal, delivered in 1955, was as follows: Israel should cede part of the Negev to Egypt and Jordan, so that there would be a territorial connection between them; Israel should resettle 75,000 Palestinian refugees in Palestine; and there should be established a state of non-belligerence, not peace, in the region. Both Egypt and Israel rejected these proposals.

The Egyptian response was abrupt. Anthony Eden met Nasser in Cairo on 20 February 1955. Eden adopted a 'condescending attitude', and 'made a disastrous error by announcing the conclusion of a British sponsored Iraqi–Turkish treaty, a direct snub designed to counter Egypt's aim of hegemony in the region ... Nasser's interest began and ended on 20 February.'[6]

Israel's attitude exasperated some of the British authorities. Evelyn Shuckburgh's view was that 'the Israelis are obsessed with their own national struggle. They see it in apocalyptic terms and are always in the right'.[7] John Nicholls, the British diplomat, was very insulting:

> The centre of the infection in the region is Israel and I believe we must treat the Israelis as a sick people. Their illness is psychological ... it is not reasonable to expect that a nation made up of people so psychologically unstable should be capable of a mature foreign policy, though their superior intelligence tempts one to expect it of them.[8]

There was a last attempt to salvage Alpha. In December 1955 President Eisenhower and Foster Dulles decided to approach Nasser and Ben-Gurion with proposals. This was carried out by a man called Anderson in the utmost secrecy and was a total failure.

The wonder in all of this is the naiveté of the formulators of Alpha, especially the British, with their experience of dealing with Israel. Perhaps the trouble with the British was that in spite of spending over a hundred years and more in dealing with alien people, they had learned very little. This becomes clear when they supposed that they could unseat Nasser as though he were a minor African chief, or when they started off with the premise that Britain knows best. They did not even seem to appreciate that Ben-Gurion would never, ever, give up territory that Israel had gained, nor would he ever accept the return of refugees whose land and homes he was now filling with Jewish immigrants.

It is also the case that Israel had hoped that the war of 1948 would have left Israel in control of the whole of Palestine:

> A number of politicians and generals, including Dayan, repeatedly voiced the hope that an opportunity would arise in which Israel could complete its historic mission and round out its borders (as well as expel its own, inconvenient Arab minority). Indeed, they toyed repeatedly with the idea of provoking a 'second round' and in 1955–56 they at last managed to do so.[9]

Ben-Gurion no doubt agreed, but his mind was elsewhere: 'not peace but substantially increasing Israel's population was Ben-Gurion's priority'.[10] He clearly had a choice: there could be no settlement unless there was agreement about refugees. The Arabs insisted they be repatriated to their home areas, which would thwart Ben-Gurion's ambition to flood the land with Jews.

The role of the 'Black Arrow' attack on subsequent events has been, like most of what happened at the time, a matter of dispute. Did it, for example, provoke Nasser into buying arms from the Czechs? Whatever the cause, such an arms deal took place and furthermore, Britain supplied arms to Egypt, whilst refusing to send arms to Israel. Britain justified this by saying that Israel had superiority in arms. The British government also believed that Israel was spoiling for a war. One of the few voices of reason in Israel, Sharett, believed that 'Black Arrow' was 'his greatest failure as Prime Minister'.

> [He] had never been enthusiastic about retaliation, doubting its political and military efficacy either as a punishment or deterrence. He castigated his fellow Israelis' lust for revenge under the guise of security-based reprisals.[11]

The antique rivalry between France and Britain in the Middle East was a further complication. Britain believed that its 'authority' was being threatened and France disapproved of the Baghdad Pact because it moved Iraq to centre stage, a move which could do harm to the status of Syria, which was French 'property'.

The Baghdad Pact (also called the Central Treaty Organisation) was yet another in the interminable list of failures by the British government to undo some of the mischief it had created in the Middle East. It was formed in 1955 with a membership of Britain, Iran, Iraq, Pakistan and Turkey. Its principal policy was to restrain Soviet influence in the region. The US did not join initially. Selwyn Lloyd, the British foreign secretary, thought it was, as J. Foster Dulles said, because of 'the pro-Israel lobby and the difficulty of obtaining Congressional Approval'.[12] The organisation was soon torn to pieces, because each country had its own agenda: for instance, Pakistan wanted its support in its wars with India. The pact was dissolved in 1979. There were other fruitless attempts at a settlement. For example, King Farouk indicated that one was possible, if Israel gave up part of the Negev. 'But the Israeli negotiators refused to budge'.[13] And politicians such as Selwyn Lloyd toured the Middle East, achieving very little.

By early 1956, Britain and the US seem to have agreed that Nasser had to be removed. A fatal step was the news, on 19 July, that both countries would withdraw funding for the Aswan dam, a project which was a central plank in Nasser's policy. The British and the Americans were correct in their assumption that cancellation would be a massive blow to Nasser. The US decision was heavily influenced by the Jewish lobby. William Burns explained how this was linked to another cause:

> The Israel lobby launched a two-pronged campaign on Capitol Hill, coupling a high pressure drive to secure military aid for Israel with a discreet, low key effort to block aid for the High Dam so long as Egypt continued its military build up.

Despite rallies, meetings and petitions, President Eisenhower refused to arm Israel, but he did agree to the withdrawal of aid for the dam.[14] Nasser's response came as a shock. On 26 July 1956 he announced the nationalisation of the Suez Canal. The reaction in Britain was almost universal. It ranged from serious and intelligent worries about oil supplies and transportation, to naked anger that a foreigner, especially an Arab, should dare to challenge British supremacy. Drawing upon the tired old analogy of pre-war appeasement, Nasser was defined as a latter-day Mussolini. But soon more restrained voices began to be heard, and in a very short time the issue seriously divided the country.

Planning now began for a joint attack on Egypt by Britain and France. There was much agonising about whether or not to involve Israel, because of the web of treaties which, if activated, might result in the most unlikely forces fighting, or supporting, each other. There were also the potential consequence of one of the increasing number of Israeli raids. There was an especially big one, against the town of Qalqilya in Jordan, on 10-11 October 1956. Forty-eight Jordanians and eighteen Israelis were killed. The British were then faced with a choice. They could defend Jordan, which now they nearly did, but this would mean alienating—to put it mildly—Israel, who was an ally against Nasser.

There were more discussions between Britain, France and Israel, characterised by duplicity, distrust, and mutual contempt. These culminated in the signing of the Treaty of Sèvres in October. The essential statement in it was the commitment by Israel to attack Egypt on 29 October, and this would provide a reason for French and British intervention. By now Eden had begun to act very strangely, since he arranged for the destruction of Britain's copy of the treaty and denied Britain had taken part. The Israelis had kept their copy and later it was made available, and exposed Eden as the most blatant of liars. Aneurin Bevan expressed a common opinion amongst parliamentarians, in a classical Welsh colloquialism: 'there is something the matter with him'. Whatever the political ramifications, on 29 October 1956, 'Operation Kadesh' began with the Israeli invasion of Sinai. As agreed at Sèvres, Britain and France demanded a ceasefire. Israel refused. On 5 November Britain and France invaded Egypt, Britain's invasion being given the codename 'Musketeer'.

The British now found themselves even deeper in the mire which they had created. The military were confused (the chief of the Imperial General Staff, Lord Mountbatten, wanted to resign), and Britain was the scene of mass demonstrations against the war. *The Observer*, a respected newspaper, wrote that 'we had not realised that our government was capable of such folly and crookedness ... Sir Anthony Eden must go.'[15] The ambassador to Israel was informed only partly about what was going on, Eisenhower was baffled and angry. He had insisted that the UN Security Council should call a meeting to end the fighting. At this meeting Britain used its veto. Eden's behaviour remained a matter of wonder. He said 'we are not at war, we are in armed conflict'. He continued to deny any collusion with Israel, and thus minimised the anger of the United States. In the judgement of one historian: 'Anglo–American relations sank to a lower level than at any time since 1812'.[16]

On 2 November 1956 the UN passed Resolution 997 (ES-1), which sought an end to the conflict. It called for a ceasefire, withdrawal behind the armistice lines, an arms embargo, and the re-opening of the Suez Canal. Britain and France agreed: Israel refused. By the end of November 1956 the British cabinet had had enough, and it agreed to an unconditional withdrawal. But Eden continued to lie, and said 'quite bluntly to the House, that there was no knowledge that Israel would attack Egypt'.[17] As well as the complexity of the attack on Egypt, parliament was split by the persistence of the overt support of a number of Jewish MPs for Israel. The most notable of these was Emmanuel Shinwell, an important figure in the Labour party, who now, with others, rejected his party's call for disapproval of the invasion.

In 1964 there was a conference of Arab heads of state in Cairo, at which two important decisions were made. These were the diversion of the waters of the Jordan and that the Palestine Liberation Organisation (PLO) should be founded. The PLO was committed to the obliteration of Israel. This led to further border raids and reprisals. The retaliatory attacks were sometimes excessive. In November 1966, three Israeli soldiers were killed when they ran over a mine. The Israeli response was to attack a Jordanian village called As Samu with tanks and artillery. This was despite the fact that King Hussein was talking to senior Israelis about a settlement, and that when he heard about the Israelis being killed, he expressed his regret. This may well have been an example of lack of control over the military by the Israeli government, which was to be a feature of the subsequent Six-Day War. The UN condemned Israel in Security Council Resolution 228, which had no effect. The position became more threatening when quarrels erupted in 1964 over water supplies from the Sea of Galilee and the Jordan. These led to fighting with artillery, tanks and aircraft.

In early 1967, Egypt started to move forces to the Sinai border with Israel. The area was patrolled by a UN peacekeeping force, the UNEF. As always when action was called for by the UN, none was forthcoming. The fighting escalated at the borders and reached a peak with the shooting down of six Syrian MiG-21s in April 1967. It led to all sides wondering if somebody was going to launch an attack. Then in May Egypt called for the evacuation of UN soldiers from Sinai and Gaza. The secretary-general, U Thant complied, and Nasser mobilised more forces. He announced that from 23 May the Gulf of Eilat would be closed to Israeli shipping. Israel could not be expected to tolerate this. The situation was compounded when troops arrived from other Arab countries, and Israel was surrounded by about a quarter of a million troops, more than 2,000 tanks and some 700 aircraft.[18]

The IDF mobilised its forces, and there was pressure in Israel to attack, but because the US promised a solution—forming an international fleet to break the Egyptian blockade—the Israeli government decided to wait. The US initiative was never realised. One especial fear of the Israelis was that the Egyptians would try to destroy their Dimona nuclear plant. There was much confusion and argument in the Israeli government, and much criticism of the prime minister, Levi Eshkol. The latter recruited two extremists to the government: Moshe Dayan as defence minister and Menachem Begin as a minister without portfolio. This meant that two of the most violent men in the Zionist ranks were now in two key positions. Begin's reputation for violence was well established. Dayan was a popular hero, but Segev offers a more critical assessment:

> An arrogant romantic, who sought power, women, money, and glory, he was a slave to his desires and passions. Over his lifetime he betrayed his wives and children, the law, the truth, and himself as well.[19]

There was considerable apprehension among the Israeli public about what might now happen, especially since the several Arab countries were drawing together, signing treaties and exchanging forces. It was widely announced in the Arab countries that an attack on Israel was about to happen.

President Johnson in Washington seems now to have changed his mind, and would support an Israeli attack. This change 'apparently occurred during the long Memorial Day weekend (27-31 May), which he spent on his Texas ranch with a number of Jewish friends and advisers'.[20] This removed any inhibition on the part of Israel, and on 5 June 1967, in the early morning they engaged in a pre-emptive attack. Egyptian airfields were attacked, and the Egyptian Air Force was effectively destroyed. Later on the same day the Jordanian, Syrian and Iraqi Air Forces attacked targets in Israel, while the Israelis fought back. By the end of day two of the war, 416 Arab aircraft had been destroyed for the loss of 26 Israeli aircraft.[21] Some historians give slightly different figures, but for the Arabs this was calamitous, since the Israelis now had complete command of the air.[22]

On the same day, 5 June, a ground attack began in Sinai. The Arabs faced a determined attack, with the Israelis having air support and the Egyptians none. The latter quickly retreated and were ordered to withdraw in the evening of 6 June. This order was countermanded the next day which led to utter confusion, and panic. By 8 June the Israeli Army reached the canal. Also during these few days, Jordan joined in, despite Israeli warnings, and Israeli appeals to the UN peacekeeping force commander. There was fighting in Jerusalem, and because of the collapse of Egypt, Israel made a fateful decision:

> Thought of offence began to supersede defence in Israeli thinking vis-à-vis the West Bank and East Jerusalem.[23]

By 8 June the West Bank was under Israeli occupation, and two bridges linking the West Bank with the East Bank had been destroyed. But the Israelis were still not satisfied. There remained the 'problem' of the Golan Heights. This is an area on the border of Syria and Palestine, and because of its elevation is a very important strategic position. It was allocated to Syria at the end of the mandate, and therefore at the time of the Six-Day War was still, legally, Syrian territory. Because of its position it had been used to shell Israeli communities on the border, before the war, a matter about which Israel had complained to the UN as well as engaging in retaliatory action. The Israeli attack was successful, and 12 June the Golan was under Israeli control. Thus, at the end of the war, Israel occupied Sinai, the West Bank, and the Golan Heights. The question the world asked was: what would they do now?

The popular press in Britain were enthusiastic about the Israeli victory, largely because Nasser had lost, and he had become a bogeyman in the public eye. The war was seen as a piece of military brilliance by an ancient people vastly outnumbered by its enemies, and biblical references were common. In Israel 'Religious folk spoke of a "miracle" and of "salvation"; the ancient lands of Israel had been restored to God's people.'[24] The *Haaretz* newspaper enjoined people to 'rejoice and celebrate, O dweller in Zion'. Politicians quickly referred to the West Bank as Samaria and Judea.

Somebody had to pay a price, and it was the Palestinians. When the fighting stopped the IDF 'most probably with Dayan's approval, tried to repeat the experience of 1948—to drive Palestinians into exile and demolish their homes'.[25] The numbers who were driven out from the West Bank and Gaza were between 200-300,000, with 'another eighty to ninety thousand civilians fled or were driven from the Golan Heights'.[26] Over the following months many thousands of Palestinians 'went into exile' as it was euphemistically termed by some writers. There was free transport from East Jerusalem to the Jordan border and those who left had to sign a paper saying that they were leaving voluntarily.[27] Only about 3,000 were allowed to return. The Golan Heights and West Bank were never returned to the Arabs, nor is it likely that they ever will be. There was an offer by the Israelis to return the territories, but in exchange they wanted a peace settlement, which they knew the Arabs would refuse.

The occupied territories now became the scene of what can only be described as anarchy. Settlers, government ministers, soldiers, rabbis all set up their own fiefdoms, with minimal interference from the government. Typical was the behaviour of the IDF on the Golan:

> In June 1967 the IDF—again without cabinet authorisation—had begun to raze empty villages, and that autumn the Defence Ministry decided systematically to destroy those remaining.[28]

At the centre of such activity was General Moshe Dayan. He 'emerged as the architect and then the arbiter of policy in the territories'.[29] He encouraged the maintenance of everyday economic activity by the Palestinians, but at the same time introduced rules which avoided Arab competition with Israelis. Arab schools could remain open but, at the same time, Arab school textbooks were censored—always an early step by conquerors. An early, pathetic casualty of educational restriction was the banning of Shakespeare's *The Merchant of Venice*. But the main and most cruel policy was to encourage or compel Palestinians to leave their homes and property, which was taken by Jewish settlers enabled by very favourable conditions of government support. In July 1968, Dayan made his policy clear:

> Anyone who has practical ideas or proposals to encourage emigration—let him speak up. No idea or proposal is to be dismissed out of hand.[30]

This was in accord with the way the Israelis dealt with the Palestinians. Chaim Herzog, sometime president of Israel, claimed that:

> The effectiveness of the Israeli military government (which was a very benign one) was emphasised by the fact that the Arabs were allowed to rule themselves

and live in peace and security provided that they did not in any way affect Israeli security adversely by their actions.[31]

However, Benny Morris, an Israeli historian, using Herzog's word 'benign', offers a very different summary, and one that is much more in accord with the reality:

> Israelis liked to believe, and tell the world, that they were running an 'enlightened' or 'benign' occupation, qualitatively different from other military occupations the world had seen. The truth was radically different. Like all occupations, Israel's was founded on brute force, repression and fear, collaboration and treachery, beatings and torture chambers, and daily intimidation, humiliation, and manipulation.[32]

The Israelis may have considered the war a great triumph, with land restored to its rightful owners. But it was in many ways, a Pyrrhic victory. Nasser offered his resignation, but the Egyptian public refused to accept it. So Nasser remained in place. The most dramatic reaction came from the Soviet Union. They immediately replaced the considerable amount of Egyptian and Syrian military equipment lost and destroyed. They demanded condemnation of Israel, and a withdrawal. It has also been claimed that they blocked any peace proposals.

The UN Security Council in November 1967 agreed to Resolution 242. This denied the legality of acquiring territory by war, called for a 'just and lasting peace'. Israel must withdraw from 'occupied' territories, and the Arabs had to agree to stop fighting and accept the right of all states in the region 'to live in peace within secure and recognised boundaries'. The refugee problem must also be resolved. To these ends a UN representative should be appointed to aid the process. It was a waste of time. Arab resolve had already become more determined. There was a summit in Khartoum on September 1967 at which the famous three 'noes' were agreed: no recognition of Israel, no peace with Israel, no negotiation with Israel. The stage was set for further struggle, and a shift from open warfare to a much more difficult method of attack to control: terrorism.

Israel and Egypt now faced each other across the Suez Canal and in June 1968 Egypt fired on Israeli positions. Thus began what is called 'The war of attrition'. For the next two years fighting continued which consisted of artillery assaults (especially by the Egyptians), air strikes, commando raids (mostly by the Israelis), and some naval engagement. As in the Six-Day War, ostensibly Egypt had the advantage. They had more artillery power and more manpower. There were pauses in the fighting, during one of which Israel constructed the 'Bar-Lev Line'. This was a complex of forts, barbed wire, minefields, tank and artillery positions.

The United States and Russia discussed trying to reduce the tension, but this was ineffective. In any case the Americans did not discourage the Israelis, since like the British they had a pathological hatred of Nasser. Very occasionally the

Americans expressed 'strong disapproval of deep penetration' raids, especially one on a factory in February 1970 in which some seventy civilians were killed.[33] The US did, however, come up with a peace plan which was proposed by William Rogers, the US secretary of state, in December 1969. This floated the idea of Israel withdrawing to the 1967 borders, withdrawing from the West Bank, and of Egypt agreeing to peace. All sides rejected the proposals. There was never any chance of an Israeli withdrawal, and Egypt was expecting to win. There seemed to be no resolution, and in January 1970 matters took a very serious turn.

Nasser, worried by bombing in the heart of Egypt, appealed to Russia for more help. He went in person to Moscow. This came promptly in the form of the latest surface-to-air missiles (SAM 3), and some 15,000 troops. These would be used in manning missile sites, air installations, and significantly, in actually flying aircraft. This was another unexpected by-product of the Six-Day War, for now the Soviets were to gain a place in the Middle East, and they presented Israel with a massive problem: how far to get involved in fighting Russians. As expected, the arrival of the Russians escalated the war. There were more and heavier attacks, which concerned everybody, especially the Israelis who were worried both about the extent of Russian involvement, and the commitment and loss of their limited manpower.

By the mid-1970s all parties seemed to have become weary. Gunnar Jarring, the UN ambassador, had been trying without success to bring about peace. But now Nasser accepted an arrangement based on the Rogers plan, a decision which surprised many people. Jordan followed and in July, Israel agreed. A ceasefire to last three months came into force on 8 August 1970. There was also a stipulation that neither side would try to improve their military capability during that time.

But from this another crisis erupted. Egypt took advantage of the peace to move its SAM sites nearer to the canal. Israel complained to the United States about this blatant breach of the ceasefire, but the US at first took no action. Only days after the ceasefire began, US intelligence discovered that the Israeli allegations were true. When accused, Egypt denied that it was breaching the agreement. In fact, in its turn Israel repaired and strengthened its own fortifications along the canal, including repairing the Bar-Lev line. The next dramatic event was the death of Nasser on 28 December 1970. The question arose as to whether this would make any difference.

The accounts of the war of attrition tend to be dominated by events on the Suez Canal. However the Israelis were also having to deal with the PLO and the Syrians. By the time of this war, the PLO was well established with its own policies, the principal one being the elimination of Israel and restoration of Palestinian lands to their owners. They had recruited not only from Palestine, but from other countries, and had sent their recruits for training overseas. There were offshoots of the organisation which differed on ideological grounds. The most important was the Marxist Popular Front for the Liberation of Palestine (PFLP).

The Israeli dealings with these insurgents was firm, harsh, and effective. So much so that the insurgents decided in 1967 to move their operational base to Jordan. From here they continued their raids into Israel, often killing civilians. After one such raid, the Israeli Army attacked an area around a village called Karameh near the east bank of the Jordan in March 1968. This was a considerable operation involving tanks, aircraft and paratroopers. The Israelis had not only to fight the insurgents but also a large force of the Arab Legion. A considerable battle took place, and the Israelis lost men, planes and tanks. There were Arab casualties, but the IDF, it is generally agreed, did not complete its mission, because of the resistance they met. Chaim Herzog, as a general, did not agree. Although 'a number of tactical errors had been made by the Israeli Command ... the purpose of the mission had been achieved,' he said.[34]

Once again the Israeli operation proved counter-productive. It resulted in considerable recruitment for the insurgent group which became more independent, and gained greater support from Arab states. There was a devastating result of the battle which was to have serious consequences for the Arab world. The PLO realised that to have its headquarters so near to Israel was dangerous, and so it moved into the mountains. The presence of the PLO in Jordan was to lead to civil strife in that country, and their expulsion. The PLO also decided to vary its campaign. As well as attacking targets in Israel it began attacking targets in other parts of the world.

Both sides and their supporters differ in their assessments of who won. In Israel morale had been lowered as the casualties mounted, and the peace was a relief. Yet 'the Israeli cabinet, the army, and the public believed that Israel had won'.[35] They all assumed that the situation would remain unchanged, that they could continue their occupation, and that Egyptians had shown that they could never beat the Israelis. The Egyptians' morale, remarkably, was high. They had not lost, although many had died, and they were in position for another attempt at ousting the enemy.

The Egyptians were not the only challenge to Israeli security. Chaim Herzog writes of the PLO that 'in Jordan [it] was eliminated as a military force'.[36] But he was premature. Although evicted from Jordan, it was still a considerable enemy. As to how Egypt would now behave after the death of Nasser, the new president, Anwar el Sadat, in what looked like a promising mood, dismissed the Soviet military from Egypt but maintained his military supply lines. Nevertheless, he prepared for a renewal of war, while observing the ceasefire. Thus, in the judgement of Chaim Herzog, 'Israel was lulled into a false sense of security'.[37]

During the time of this 'war of attrition', there had been constant belligerence between Israel and its neighbours. But there was also much bitterness and shame, especially in Egypt at what it saw as its failure in the Six-Day War. Sadat wanted to break the deadlock which existed, and expressed that wish publicly. He had tried to find ground for a peaceful settlement, but inevitably it foundered on familiar issues, such as the refusal of the Israelis to withdraw to the pre-1967 borders. The prime minister at the time, Golda Meir, famously said 'intransigence was to become my middle name'.[38] Sadat was left with no choice. He considered that a lightning strike would recover lost territory, and that intervention by the UN would operate to Egypt's advantage.

Full-scale war was resumed in October 1973. It is called by the Israelis the Yom Kippur War, because it began on 6 October, the Jewish Day of Atonement. Sadat believed that on that day most Jewish troops would either be at worship or at home. In the event the fact that they *were* at home made the call-up of reservists easier. It is known to the Arabs simply as the October War.

Military historians emphasise two features of the outbreak of the war. The first is that Sadat had been assiduous in his preparations for it, with massive support from the Russians, especially in the delivery of Scud surface to surface missiles. This was despite the fact that Sadat had expelled the Russian contingents. The Russians delivered supplies to Syria as well, notably SAM missiles. The second feature is, remarkably, that Israel was unprepared. This lack of readiness was caused by a profound belief that, for a number of reasons, Egypt would not go to war. This was despite obvious and sinister signs of Egyptian troop movements.

On 6 October the enormous Egyptian Army, one of the largest in the world, began its assault on the Israeli Suez Canal emplacements. Shortly afterwards, Syrian forces moved against the Golan Heights. Other Arab countries prepared contingents, but these mostly arrived too late to have any effect on the direction of the war. At first the Arabs made considerable gains, but slowly the Israelis recovered to the point where Russia began to doubt if the Arabs could win. Soviet General Secretary Leonid Brezhnev asked Henry Kissinger, the US secretary of state, to discuss an armistice, and together they submitted a peace proposal to which the UN agreed in Resolution 338.

The ceasefire should have come into effect on the evening of 22 October, but hostilities continued. On 24 October another deadline was passed, by which time Israeli forces were deep inside Egypt. The situation was extremely complicated. The armies were often not where they should have been, morale was low, and so there was no possibility of an orderly stand-down. The Israelis continued their campaign. Further UN resolutions (339 and 340) were more successful and effectively ended the war. At the end of October, UN observers were in place between the lines.

There were heavy losses of men and equipment on all sides, and the verdict is that there were no victors. After the ceasefire, the Russians continued to supply the Arabs, and the Americans restocked the Israelis with weaponry. A formal ceasefire agreement between Egypt and Israel was signed on 11 November, which included, *inter alia*, the exchange of prisoners. Prolonged discussions took place, in which Henry Kissinger was a prominent participant, and it was agreed that the IDF would leave the west bank of the Suez Canal and move back from the eastern bank. A buffer zone was established and manned by the UN.

Achieving a ceasefire with Syria was more difficult, but even this was signed on 31 May 1974. The UN would police the area between the two countries. The war had achieved very little: large parts of Arab territory were still colonised by the Israelis, and it was difficult to imagine that this position could survive for long. Further negotiation with Israel and Egypt resulted in an expansion of the buffer zone, which included oilfields now to be controlled by Egypt.

Perhaps the most remarkable outcome of the war was an initiative by Anwar Sadat to seek peace with Israel. A critical factor was the election of Jimmy Carter to the US presidency in 1976. Although he had no experience of the Middle East, he wanted to try for a settlement. He was sympathetic to the plight of the Palestinians, but he was also confused by his Christian sentiment for the mythology of Jewish history in the Bible. His ambition seemed to be doomed, however, because in May 1977 Begin formed a government. His starting position was that Israel would not give up any of the land that it had occupied as a result of the war, and that there would never be a Palestinian state. In this he was supported by the Jewish lobby in the US, which proved to be an inhibiting factor on Carter's policies. There were many futile meetings between variously, the US, Egypt, and Israel.

Then, in November 1977, in an astonishing gesture, Sadat offered to go to Jerusalem. The Arab world generally was outraged, and the Israelis deeply suspicious. Not only could they not understand such apparent flexibility, they believed that he was laying some kind of a trap. Nevertheless, on 20 November 1977, Sadat went to Israel and spoke to the Knesset. In his speech he recognised the reality of the existence of Israel, insisted that all territories occupied since the war should be returned, and that the Palestinian right to a state should be agreed. None of this was acceptable to Begin and his government, and the visit remained a gesture. In December 1977 Sadat and Begin met in Ismailia and achieved nothing.

Early in 1978 the US became more involved. In January Sadat and Carter met and afterwards issued the Aswan Declaration. This stated that any agreement should include peace, withdrawal from the occupied territories, and a resolution of the Palestinian 'problem'. Carter also worked towards the then unlikely possibility of getting the leaders to meet in the US. This was achieved, and on 5 September 1978 discussions began in Camp David in Maryland. These were marked by violent rows, threats to walk out, Sadat's frustration, and Begin's refusal to waver. However on 17 September 1978 a 'Framework for Peace in the Middle East' was signed and hailed as a great step. So much so that Sadat and Begin were awarded the Nobel Peace Prize: not the only moment of absurdity in its history.

In fact the terms of the 'Framework' were extremely vague. As far as the Palestinians were concerned, there was talk of withdrawal from the West Bank, over a period of five years and something called 'full autonomy' for the Palestinians. This 'autonomy' was something Begin had dreamed up, but what it meant can only be guessed at. Perhaps it meant something akin to the British colonial custom of allowing local 'chiefs' seemingly to be in authority, while the real power remained in the hands of the colonists. Certainly Begin insisted that the military would remain in the territories. Most of Sinai would be returned to Egypt, even though Israel had begun to build settlements there. And there was to be a resolution of the refugee crisis.

The reaction of the Arab countries was fury. They resolved both to expel Egypt from the Arab League, and to impose sanctions. For the next six months there were arguments about what had been agreed and how matters should proceed. There also developed a considerable peace movement in Israel, which at first Begin tried to ignore, but which had an influence on him. Eventually on 26 March 1979, a peace treaty was signed in Washington with all the attendant ceremony.

For Israel there were positive outcomes. Although they had given up Sinai and forcibly removed the Jewish settlers, which was much deplored by many Israelis, there was now a prospect of peace with the most belligerent of the Arab countries. The Suez Canal was reopened to Israeli shipping. For Egypt, and for Sadat personally, there was peace and the return of Sinai. The price he paid was the opprobrium of the Arab countries, and especially their allegation that he had abandoned the Palestinians. This was demonstrably true. The issue of the West Bank and the other territories had quietly been dropped. Although there were talks about the elusive 'autonomy' for Palestinians, these got nowhere. Begin instead initiated the building of more settlements in the West Bank. For both countries there was the development of normal relations: the exchange of ambassadors for example. But Sadat was to pay a heavy price for his efforts: on 6 October 1981 he was assassinated by Islamic fundamentalists.

There were radical political changes in Israel, probably caused by the war. Israeli society was very displeased at the behaviour of its government before, during, and after the war. The government's lack of preparation and its incompetence at the beginning, together with a questionable outcome, led to public protests. Not only that, but the generals started joining in the blame game. In the end there was an inquiry by a commission led by the president of the Supreme Court. It reported on 30 January 1975 and was very critical of the intelligence services and of individual senior service officers, going so far as to recommend dismissals.

But for the future of Palestinians the war caused a devastating change in the shape of Israeli politics. The general election of 1977 brought to power the Likud alliance, headed by Menachem Begin. This confirmed and encouraged a mood of nationalistic chauvinism which has dominated Israeli politics ever since. The Palestinians had always been regarded with disdain by the Israelis, and now that the government was of an ultra-right-wing persuasion, and led by a notorious extremist, their position was bound to deteriorate.

The damage done to the image of Israel in world opinion by its behaviour after the war was immense. France became much more supportive of the Arabs.

The Soviet bloc mounted a campaign against Israel: all explained away by Israeli lobbies as ideology or as naked antisemitism. The earliest signs that Israel was to be a major target of radical left hostility occurred during the 1967 Six-Day War, when left-wing politicians even in America echoed the attacks on Israel that were being levelled in the United Nations by the Soviet bloc delegates.[39] Generally, the world was not deceived. Such approval as there was in Western Europe of the Israeli victory has not lasted. As it became clear that the suffering inflicted upon the Palestinians increased, especially in recent times with the Gaza blockade, so international sympathy for the Palestinians has increased. This change began only a few years after the Six-Day War.

In 1972 a Gallup Poll by the *Jewish Chronicle* found that sympathy for Israel and its right to hold on to territory captured in the war had fallen dramatically. Forster and Epstein, in their advocacy of a belief in what they call 'new antisemitism' deplore the fact that in the same poll there was 'a clear majority of 60 per cent showing marked disinterest—in a word indifference—when it came to Israel'.[40] What the authors demand is total support for whatever Israel does. They note the 'disturbing evidence ... of clear erosion over several years in popular support for Israel'.[41] What their claim of a 'new antisemitism' seems to be founded is upon the conflation of disapproval of Israel with antisemitism. It is claimed that this is evidenced by the fact that the Soviet Union was 'supplying heavy military hardware to Israel's enemies and pouring calumny on her in the UN'.[42] Even the activities of terrorists in incidents like the Munich massacre (see below) could not negate the sympathy felt for the Palestinians. The attempts by Zionists to capitalise on Palestinian attacks were only moderately successful. Thus in September 1972, at a memorial service held in the Episcopal Catholic Cathedral in Washington DC for the Israeli athletes murdered at Munich, the dean, Francis Sayre Jr, preached that he was mourning those victims, but also 'those additional victims of the violence in Munich: those villagers in Lebanon and Syria whose lives have been extinguished by the Israeli Air Force even as the Twentieth Olympiad yet endures'.[43]

Perhaps the worst result of the war for Israel was the increase in the numbers joining the PLO. The organisation became even stronger; in Jordan it actually posed a threat to the stability of the government, and in Gaza the PLO ruled some of the refugee camps. Although many were killed or taken prisoner, substantial numbers moved to neighbouring Arab states. There was what Herzog calls 'very efficient security control'.[44] But efficiency was intermingled with brutality so that 'locals complained of numerous cases of beating and systematic humiliation at the hands of the Israeli soldiers'.[45]

From their Jordan bases, the PLO mounted raids across the River Jordan, supported by the Jordanian and Iraqi armies. The IDF responded with considerable force, and this, together with increasing resentment by the Jordanians at the behaviour of the Palestinians, resulted in fighting between the latter and the Jordanian Army. This began in May 1970. There then was a full-scale war between the two, complicated by the interference of the Syrians. There were many casualties and two attempts were made on the life of King Hussein. Hussein began to lose patience, and in July 1971 he ordered the final eviction of the PLO. On 17 September the Jordanian Army moved against the Palestinians in what became known as 'Black September'.

Gradually the PLO established bases in Lebanon and began attacks on another front. The PFLP was formed in December 1967. Although it differed from the PLO, in part because of its Marxist tendency, it was backed by various Arab states, some of whom financed their activities. In late 1968 Fatah and Al Sa'iqa, another breakaway group, began attacking Israeli targets. As these continued, the Lebanese government sent in the army and fighting broke out between it and the Palestinians. But the PLO remained in Lebanon, and in effect operated as an independent state. Israel then began not only to attack the guerrillas, but occupied a piece of Lebanese territory. The south of Lebanon became a war zone with fighting between the Israelis and the Palestinians, and between the Israelis and the Lebanese Army.

Meanwhile the PLO engaged in a new tactic: attacks on civilian aircraft. 'In all, their organisations between 1968 and 1977 hijacked or attempted to highjack twenty-nine aircraft.'[46] During these years they also forged links with other revolutionary organisations throughout the world. For example, on 30 May 1972, three Japanese 'Red Army' terrorists flew to Lydda airport, and there opened fire indiscriminately. Twenty-seven people were killed and seventy-one wounded. As well as attacking aircraft the PLO targeted hotels, Jewish community facilities, embassies outside Israel, events and individuals, including the Jordanian prime minister who was assassinated. Even President Nixon was sent a letter bomb. The impetus for most of these attacks came from a new group called 'Black September', named after the date of the PLO's eviction from Jordan.

An especially notorious attack was made upon the Israeli athletes in September 1972 in the Olympic village in Munich. Israel, following its well-advertised policy, refused the demand to release 234 Palestinian prisoners. The captors also demanded the release of Andreas Baader and Ulricke Meinof, founders of the German Red Army Faction, imprisoned in Germany. The Germans resolved on a rescue mission. They pretended that the invading party would be taken to Cairo, but instead they were taken to a site in Munich where the German police attacked them. The terrorists killed all seven Israelis. Five terrorists were killed, and three captured. The latter were later released by the Germans after a Lufthansa flight was hijacked. The Munich massacre led to massive reprisal by the Israelis. They carried out campaigns to kill those they believed responsible for Munich, notably in Syria and Lebanon.

One episode and its conclusion attracted worldwide attention. On 27 June 1976, four terrorists—two Palestinians and two Germans—hijacked an Air

France aircraft and took it to Entebbe in Uganda. In the course of the next few days more terrorists joined the original four. Ninety-four passengers, mostly Israelis, and twelve aircrew were held hostage, and the others released. The attackers demanded the release of fifty-three of their fellows imprisoned in several countries. The Israeli government was faced with a hideous dilemma. The upshot of prolonged discussion was that a rescue attempt should be mounted. Six aircraft carrying commandos were sent to Entebbe, landed and attacked the building where the hostages were being held. By 4 July the operation was over. Three of the hostages had been killed, (a fourth was murdered in a Ugandan hospital) and six wounded. Only one soldier was killed. He was the commander, Yonatan Netanyahu, the brother of the future prime minister, Benjamin Netanyahu. One other soldier was wounded. Eight hijackers as well as forty-five Ugandan soldiers were killed. The rescue, unsurprisingly, was met with rapture in Israel. It became known as a brilliant adventure, and inspired two Hollywood films.

During these same years the Israelis became involved in another conflict. When the PLO was expelled from Jordan and went to Lebanon, they once more became a focus of discontent for the local people. Lebanon was in any case an unstable country, even though compared with some other Arab countries it was quiescent. It was a country plagued by a host of mutually antagonistic religions and sects within those religions. A National Pact of 1943 sought to minimise the potentially lethal situation by arranging for a share-out of the key posts in government. There would be a Maronite (Christian) president, a Shi'ite parliamentary speaker, and a Sunni Muslim premier. This seems to have worked, despite great disparities in wealth and privilege, until 1948 and the arrival of Palestinian refugees, to whom, later on, were added the evicted PLO from Jordan. The latter brought their struggle from Jordan, and soon began to develop political influence and to arm themselves again. Fighting started in the streets, and in April 1975 this developed into a civil war.

Very broadly, on one side were the Phalangists, supported in some places by the Druze who objected to the behaviour of the Palestinians. On the other were the PLO and its various factions, both Shi'ite and Sunni. There was still a government and a Lebanese Army, which proved ineffectual. By the time peace had been restored in November 1976 some quarter of a million people out of a population of an estimated 3.2 million had been killed, wounded, disabled, and made homeless.[47]

Despite the appearance of a return to normality in the country, the civil war raged on. The Israelis were supporting the Christian Phalangists with arms. In 1981 there was an escalation of the war when the Syrians decided to attack the north, a Phalangist stronghold. The Phalangists asked Israel for help, and the prime minister, Begin, 'ordered the Israeli Air Force to lend support to the Christians, maintaining that the Christian community faced the danger of a holocaust'.[48] But it was a good deal more complicated than that.

The only way in which the Israeli invasion of Lebanon can be understood is to remember that Begin and the ultra-Zionists wanted to include in the state of Israel all the land supposedly promised to them in the Bible. So, in Lebanon, the Zionists wanted a considerable part of the south of the country to be part of Israel. In fact, when they drew a map for the 1919 Versailles Peace Conference, they had included the land up to the River Litani, well inside present-day Lebanon. The Israelis and the Maronite Christians had, for many years, dwelt upon the possibility of collaboration since they had a common enemy in the Muslims and shared much of the mystical belief expressed in the Bible. As late as 1955, the visionary and belligerent Moshe Dayan, then chief of the General Staff, saw a future where:

> The IDF will enter Lebanon, conquer the necessary territory and establish a Christian government that will be allied to Israel. The area south of the Litani will be annexed completely to Israel.

Morris goes on to quote 'an official' who:

> Spoke of the need to 'trim' Lebanon of its Muslim-populated northern, eastern, and southern fringes, with the (largely Shi'ite) population of the south (Jabal 'Amal) to be transferred to Syria and replaced by Christians with 'the aim' of achieving 'territorial continuity between Israel and the Christian community in Lebanon'.[49]

This practice of the removal of inconvenient populations, as we have seen, not only has powerful biblical authority and was reiterated in early Zionist propaganda, but it has also been put into effect by the Israeli state into the present century.

The liaison between the Zionists and the Lebanese Christians was well established. In May 1946 the Christians and the Jewish Agency had signed a treaty in which the Christians had agreed to acknowledge the Jews' right to Palestine, and in turn the Jews agreed that Lebanon was a Christian country. There was also a practical problem with which the Israelis had to deal. The build-up of Palestinian numbers in Lebanon in the 1970s, consequent upon their expulsion from Jordan, led to attacks by them from southern Lebanon upon northern Israel. These attacks naturally led to recriminatory responses, and there were many casualties on both sides.

During the Lebanese civil war, the PLO, by now almost an independent entity, sided with the Muslims, and there seemed to be no end to the war. In May–June 1976, Syria invaded and attacked the PLO, and together with the Phalangists, curbed their activity. Their invasion, named the 'Arab Deterrent Force', was legitimised by other Arab countries. Syria's interest in Lebanon was not only due to them being neighbours, but it was always because Syria had never recognised Lebanon and regarded the territory as part of a Greater Syria.

In the late 1970s the IDF established a 'Security Zone' of about six miles on the borders of Israel and Lebanon, which was dominated by Christians. In addition the UN positioned a force, the United Nations Interim Force in Lebanon, which arrived on 19 March 1978.[50] This would cover the area between the Security Zone and the River Litani, but it is generally agreed that like most UN forces it failed to stop the violence. Southern Lebanon Christians established, with IDF help, a militia which eventually was designated the South Lebanese Army. In the late 1970s the main clashes were between the Maronites and the Syrians. The latter began to make life intolerable for the Christians, and they kept up an incessant plea to Israel for help. Israel struck at Syrian forces, which led to the latter reinforcing their armaments in Lebanon.

There was a general election in Israel in June 1981 in which Begin once more became prime minister. Not only was this in itself very bad news for the Palestinians, but it was exacerbated by his appointment of Ariel Sharon to the post of defence minister. The latter had been an officer in the Israeli Army since its foundation, and we have seen an example of his brutality in the attack on the Jordanian village of Qibya in 1953. His conduct in Lebanon surpassed that.

In the months following the election, the PLO mounted serious attacks on northern Israel. As well as engaging in reprisals, Begin decided to respond by widening the scope of the assault on the PLO in other parts of Lebanon. An attempt by the US special ambassador, Philip Habib, to negotiate a ceasefire was successful in the short term, but there soon arose differences about what exactly had been agreed. The ceasefire was unlikely to be maintained in any event, because Sharon did not support it: it prevented him carrying out his ambitions to destroy the PLO and remove any stragglers from Lebanon. This was also what Begin wanted. Both also believed they could and should force the Syrians out of the country, and that they could install a Christian government led by one of the Christian oligarchy, a man called Bashir Gemayel. There was much discussion in the Israeli cabinet about the scale of an invasion. Some were apprehensive about Sharon's ambition, but preparations continued anyway. The cabinet was kept in ignorance about most of what was going on, with Sharon lying about his real intentions.

In June 1982, there was an attempt on the life of the Israeli ambassador to Britain. This was the excuse Begin and Sharon had been looking for, and on 6 June 1982, operation 'Peace in Galilee' was launched. The term was another example of Zionist eulogism, but in the event it brought no peace. The move north was attended by much death and suffering for the Palestinians in the refugee camps. The Israelis claimed that they tried to avoid civilian casualties, but the situation was such that any good intentions remained in abeyance. By 10 June the IDF had reached the outskirts of Beirut, and Syria had a choice: Should it fight?

As predicted by those who had opposed the invasion, and whose objections were swept aside by Sharon, the Syrians did fight. The situation escalated to a point when the US began to express concern and President Reagan demanded a ceasefire, but to no avail. By the middle of June, the IDF was in the suburbs of Beirut. By the end of the month the Israelis had begun a siege of the city, cutting off all supplies. The Israelis demanded that the PLO and the Syrians leave the city, and Philip Habib, continuing to seek peace, tried to encourage them to do so.

Eventually the US persuaded several countries to take in Palestinians. Sharon continued asking Begin to grant him permission to massacre the Palestinians, but the Israeli cabinet and senior soldiers refused that permission. And so the IDF continued to send assassination squads into West Beirut, where the bulk of the Palestinians lived, to look for PLO leaders. They also continued to shell and bomb the west of the city, provoking a protest from Reagan to Begin saying that the 'air raids were "unfathomable and senseless"'. Eventually the PLO agreed to leave, and on 21 August the evacuation began under the supervision of an international force.[51] By the early days of September this force left. The Christian parties led by Bashir Gemayel set out ambitions to expel the PLO and Syrian forces. His ambitions were ended with his assassination in September 1982. But the Christian determination to do something about the Palestinians remained in place.

At about the time of the expulsion of the PLO, President Reagan set out what has been called the Reagan Plan, or Initiative, which intended to settle the conflict in the region. Dated 1 September 1982, it announced that he 'was calling for a fresh start'. He proposed there should be elections to a Palestinian authority and that there should be a five-year transition after free elections for self government. This ambition was confused by his assertion that there would be no independent state in the West Bank or Gaza. But Israel should not have authority over the West Bank and Gaza. He considered that the future of Jerusalem should be negotiated. Finally he wanted an 'immediate adoption of a settlement freeze'.

Although there was firm assertion of Israel's right to exist, Begin, when he learned of the plan said it was 'the saddest day of my life'. This is not surprising since the plan torpedoed all of his political aims—the extension of settlements; the retention of the West Bank, which he now referred to by the biblical names Judea and Samaria; and the prevention of an independent Palestine. He need not have worried. Like so many US presidents before and since, Reagan found that any move to improve the situation for the Palestinians was systematically resisted by the Jewish lobby. Begin's government duly rejected the plan and, when the Palestine National Council rejected it as well in March 1983, it was dropped, like so many attempts to bring peace.

On 15 September 1982, the day after the assassination of Bashir Gemayel, the man they had marked as a puppet, the Israeli Army took over West Beirut. During discussion between IDF officers, Sharon, and the Christian leaders, it became clear that the latter wanted revenge: revenge for the disturbance brought to Lebanon and the unseating of the Christian oligarchy, and revenge for the help which the PLO had given to the Muslims. On 16 September 1982, 150 Phalangist militia men entered the Sabra and Shatilla (or Shatila) refugee camps. How this was enabled by Israeli authorities, and what happened next, was investigated by a commission of inquiry chaired by the president of the Supreme Court of Israel, Yitzhak Kahan. The inquiry held sixty sessions, took evidence from fifty-eight witnesses, and reported in February 1983.[52]

The commission stated that as darkness was falling, the Phalangists asked the IDF to illuminate the area. This they did so with mortar fire and aircraft. The Israelis set up a command post, but amazingly it gave no view of what was happening in the camps. The object of the exercise was 'searching and mopping up the camps' in an Army Order No. 6 quoted by Kahan in his report. It was claimed by the Israeli commanders that they warned the Phalangists that no civilians should be harmed. It is impossible to know how many Palestinians were in the camps. Kahan suggests an 'inexact estimate' of about 56,000 in Sabra. Kahan heard evidence that an intelligence officer said that 'there are no terrorists in the camp'. If there were it was because they had stayed behind to protect their families. The Phalangists went through the camps killing, raping and torturing men, women, and children. It is impossible to know just how many victims were slaughtered. The Palestinian Red Crescent estimated 2,000; the Lebanese Army counted 460; the Israelis between 700 and 800.

The mood of the attack is well illustrated in the evidence given to Kahan. An IDF officer heard a Phalangist officer, Kahan Elul, tell Elie Hobeika, the commander, that 'there were fifty women and children and what should we do?' He replied: 'This is the last time you are going to ask me a question like that, you know exactly what to do.' Then raucous laughter broke out among the Phalangist personnel: it was understood that the women and children were to be murdered. Kahan Elul told Brigadier Yaron about the conversation, and in his evidence to the inquiry Yaron tried to claim there was confusion over messages, but the inquiry dismissed that. A Lieutenant Grabowsky saw the murder of women and children, and one of his soldiers asked of one the murderers why they were killing civilians. The reply was because 'pregnant women will give birth to terrorists and children will grow up to be terrorists'. The situation was summed up by the Red Cross and journalists. They described how when they went into the camps they saw 'acts of barbarism'. When the news broke about these events there were protest demonstrations in Israel (including a rally which was attended by about 400,000 people) and outrage throughout the world. People demanded to know the truth.

The response of the Israeli government at first was to issue 'clarification', which amounted to denials of Israel's involvement. It was claimed in a cabinet meeting held on 19 September 1982, that 'no-one imagined that the Phalangists would commit such acts' and that the 'IDF intervened immediately'. Prime Minister Begin, at the same meeting, 'complained about accusations—in his view unfounded—which had been made against Israel'. Resorting to medieval analogy, he considered it 'a blood libel against the Jewish state'. But members of the government itself, the Israeli public, and people from around the world combined to overcome Begin's initial refusal to set up an inquiry.

Although there had been much popular demand for it, the public were not universally agreed that an inquiry was necessary. They argued that 'if Israel's direct responsibility for the atrocities is negated—then there is no place for further discussion of the problem of indirect responsibility ... we cannot accept that position'. In inquiry was demanded, however, due to Israel's 'functioning as a democratic state that scrupulously maintains the fundamental principles of the civilised world'.

The Kahn Report dismissed allegations that the IDF were actually in the camps as 'completely groundless and constitute a baseless lie'. This is one of the few positive things, if true, that the inquiry found. For the most part the members clearly did not believe the 'evidence' of the people who had been most active. They said firmly that 'the remarks of the experts on this matter were influenced to a certain extent by the desire of each of them to justify his action or lack thereof.' They found it especially unbelievable that they could not have known how the Christians would behave when they were let loose:

> Even before Bahir's assassination the possibility of the Phalangists perpetrating a massacre in the camps was not esoteric lore which need not and could not have been foreseen.

As for Begin, although he was 'not a party to have the Phalangists move into the camps ... we are unable to accept that he was absolutely unaware of such a danger [of massacre]'. In any case, two days after the entry 'he showed absolutely no interest in their actions in the camps'. As for Sharon, it 'needed no prophetic powers ... to know the concrete danger of acts of slaughter existed when the Phalange moved into the camps ... his duty would have been to prevent their entry'.

There is no doubt of two things. First the Israelis were in charge in Beirut. Instructions had been given that 'only one element and that is the IDF shall command the forces in the area'. Second that it is beyond belief that the massacre could not have been predicted, and perhaps welcomed. The inquiry heard how Mossad had heard Bashir Gemayel talk, and concluded that 'there was no room for doubt that he would resort to aberrant methods to get rid of Palestinians'.

A more personal first-hand account was published by a Chinese doctor, who was working in Beirut at the time, and who gave evidence to the Kahan Inquiry. Swee Chai Ang, in her book *From Beirut to Jerusalem*, described the murders of Palestinians she witnessed and produced evidence of rape and torture. She also pointed out that foreign medical staff were terrorised. But above all, she challenged the defence that the Israelis took little part in the abuse of the Palestinians, and she drew attention to their presence at many points in the events.

The situation was quite remarkable. What judgement could be handed down when the accused were the prime minister, the minister of defence, and senior members of the army? It may be accepted that the inquiry did not shirk facing the facts: although of course many considered it a whitewash. Of Begin it was decided that it was 'sufficient to determine responsibility'. Others, such as the director of military intelligence, it recommended for dismissal. But the fate of Ariel Sharon was the most eagerly awaited. It recommended that the prime minister should dismiss him. Sharon refused to go, but eventually he was compelled to resign. His ruthlessness was needed to carry out Israeli policy in respect of the Palestinians, and Begin kept him in the cabinet as minister without portfolio. Nor did the population disapprove of him for long. He later held several ministerial posts and from March 2001 until April 2006 he was prime minister.

The Americans now insisted that the Israelis leave Beirut, and they did. They were replaced by an international force, but the factional fighting went on. There were attacks on US installations, notably embassy buildings, on the international force, and on Israeli forces. A deadlock government was formed. This government managed to approve an exit plan, and in June 1985 the Israelis retreated to the Security Zone. Morris sums up the state of affairs at the time:

> The Israelis withdrew without having received any political or military agreements or assurances from Syria, the Lebanese government, or the various factions.[53]

The fact is that the whole attack on Lebanon was a calamity for Israel. It had been driven by hatred of the Palestinians, a wish to achieve a victory over the Syrians, and cruel territorial ambitions: it had failed to accomplish its objectives and at a cost of many Israeli casualties. The PLO had not been destroyed, although there was some consolation that they were now in Tunis, a little further away, but in the modern world this was only a minor inconvenience for them. The war also spawned a new and even more dangerous enemy for Israel, Hezbollah, the 'Party of God'.

Hezbollah was composed of Shi'ites committed to driving all foreigners out of Lebanon and setting up an Islamic state, modelled on Iran. Very soon after the war began, Iranian Revolutionary Guards made an appearance in Lebanon, and began training and fighting. They were to create huge problems for Israel in the years ahead. As for Syria, it had also suffered losses, but it was still the effective authority in Lebanon.

After the Six-Day War, the treatment of the Palestinians by the Israelis deteriorated further. They were treated as an inferior race, and were subjected to a level of abuse that can stand comparison with the excesses of any government of the twentieth century. This is summed up by Benny Morris:

> Israeli propagandists tried to project an image of an 'enlightened occupation'. But in fact it was a brutal and mortifying experience for the occupied (as well as a brutalising experience for the occupiers), involving daily, often rough, identity checks and body searches of labourers and students, accompanied by verbal abuse and, more rarely though not uncommonly, by physical abuse ... Curfews, sometimes lasting for days, were common. Soldiers and GSS [General Security Services—Shin Bet] operatives, in search of suspects, weapons, or subversive literature, broke into homes in the middle of the night, pulling whole families out of bed, overturning beds, wardrobes, and jars of oil and cereal, leaving crying mothers and babies in their wake. The men were taken off blindfolded and manacled for further interrogation ... their families learning of the whereabouts only days or weeks later.[54]

The 'exposure of grave human rights abuses ... emerged as immoral, brutal, and incompetent'.[55] The Palestinians in the occupied territories could not be expected to submit to this. Like oppressed people everywhere, including the Jews for most of their history which they seem to have forgotten, they did not want to be 'stateless inhabitants under a brutal foreign occupation'.[56]

Their anger found expression in the 'first' intifada. The word is of Arabic origin, and means 'tremor' or 'shaking off' of, say, water or fleas. The word had been used before by Arabs protesting against regimes. It was preceded by the growth of the Muslim Brotherhood and its increasing focus on Israeli injustice. It was exacerbated by the development of an even more extreme Jewish nationalism, legitimated by the success of the Likud party. A typical expression of their violence can be seen in the Jewish murder of three people, and the injury of thirty-three others at the Islamic University of Hebron in July 1983. This incident caused a good deal of reprisal and unrest, and it became clear that Jewish violence was to become a feature of everyday life.

Organisations began to appear with specific aims. One was the Faithful of the Temple Mount, who revived the historic aim, long denied by Jews, that the al-Aqsa mosque should be obliterated, and a Temple built in its place. The 'Faithful' were later, in August 1990, to cause one of the most violent clashes. Their leader, Gershon Salomon, announced the he would lay a foundation stone for a temple on the Mount. The Israeli government refused permission. However, the Arabs believed he would, and called for a defence of the Mount. It was alleged but disputed, that they brought a stock of stones and other missiles with them. The police tried to protect Jewish worshippers at the Western Wall, when the stone throwing started. Faced with tear gas and gunfire, the Arabs were forced to retreat. They came back, and the Israelis started firing live rounds. About twenty Arabs were killed more than 150 injured. Thirty-four Israelis were injured.

There was worldwide condemnation of the indiscriminate shooting and the United Nations passed Resolution 672 which authorised a mission to report. This was rejected by the Israeli government and a further resolution (673) asking them to reconsider was also rejected. Instead the government published its own report which stated that the police had acted with 'prudence', and that the fault lay with the Arabs. The Supreme Muslim Council also published a report in which it was alleged that the massacre was unprovoked and the fault lay with the Israelis. The episode led to a spate of lethal attacks by the Arabs.

The response of the Palestinians throughout the intifada was to riot, and to bring to a fine art the practice of stone throwing. The classic weapon of street protestors, the Molotov cocktail, was also used to significant effect. The Shabiba—the youth branch of Fatah—began to mount serious challenges to the IDF, even sometimes taking over the control and management of refugee camps. The unrest culminated in a series of incidents in December 1987, when Jews and Arabs attacked each other, sometimes with fatal results. This is generally agreed to be the date when the intifada started in earnest.

The intifada spread quickly and seemed to have a number of objectives. The most prominent were, one: to recover control over the lost territories; two: to encourage international debate on the plight of the Palestinians; and three: to establish an Islamic state. This last was the outcome of the establishment of Hamas ('Courage'), an offshoot of the Muslim Brotherhood.

Hamas dates from about 1987. It was led by Sheikh Ahmed Yassin and took its inspiration from the Iranian Revolution. Yassin, who was almost blind and a quadriplegic, was assassinated in March 2004. An Israeli helicopter gunship fired on him, killing him and eleven other people. The attack attracted familiar worldwide condemnation, and 200,000 Palestinians attended his funeral.

There were three notable phenomena associated with the intifada. The first was that the Israeli government took a surprisingly long time to appreciate its seriousness. The second was that it was a localised, grass-root movement and was not initiated by the PLO. And thirdly, it led not only to the establishment of Hamas as a powerful and important political force, but one which was to harry Israel until the present day. In early 1988 the intentions of Hamas (including the destruction of Israel) were specified and in the face of such evidence and their organisation of disturbances, the Israeli government realised how much of a threat they were. Another significant force in the intifada was Islamic Jihad, which was even more extreme than Hamas.

The year 1988 saw much publicity through leafleting, strikes, the withdrawal of business, refusal to pay taxes, road blockages, the burning of crops and physical confrontations: this last causing the deaths and injury of Palestinians, and injury to Israelis, mostly the IDF. Although the Palestinians had firearms, their use was discouraged. This was partly because they knew that it would excuse Israeli use of very heavy gunfire, and many more casualties, but also because the image they wanted to project to the world was themselves as 'David to Israel's Goliath'.[57] There were, however, instances when the protestors used firearms and hand grenades.

Meanwhile, the Israeli right wing began to counterattack. Among them was a group called Gush Emunim ('Bloc of the Faithful') which was determined that Jewish settlement should be increased in the occupied territories and that they should not be returned to the Arabs. In the best tradition of Zionist gobbledegook, they also said that they believed in co-existence with the Arabs. Later, a group of Gush Emunim formed an even more extreme body called Makhteret, 'The Jewish Underground'. Founded after the Camp David Accords, its objectives included the rejection of the accords, which the it believed contradicted the biblical promise of Judea and Samaria (the West Bank) for the Jews, and the blowing up the Dome of the Rock.

It was Gush Emunim which precipitated one of the ugliest incidents of the time. A group of children from one of their villages was allowed to go on an expedition in an area which was clearly Arab. They were attacked by Arab children with stones. The Jews were accompanied by three armed adults; one of these shot and killed an Arab youth, and wounded an adult. The villagers then took the Jewish children into the village and stoned the adults. The man who had killed the youth received a severe blow to the head and fired his weapon, killing two villagers and one of the Jewish party. The Arabs then protected the Jews until the IDF arrived.

The Israeli right wing went berserk. Their fury was articulated by Ariel Sharon who responded with his usual clockwork precision. He wanted the village destroyed and the villagers deported. Some villagers were arrested, and thirteen houses destroyed:

> It later emerged that several of those left homeless had taken no part in the rioting and that one of them had in fact saved hikers from the mob. Eventually the IDF paid him compensation. Six villagers were deported to Jordan.[58]

Thus the Gush Emunim, which had provoked the incident, achieved its aim: relationships would be worsened; there would be more reasons for killing Arabs; and any settlement of the uprising was made even more remote. Paradoxically, that is what Hamas wanted.

There seemed to be no end in sight. Increasing Jewish militancy and brutality led to more violent reprisals by the Arabs. Because of the increasing numbers of Arab deaths, the IDF started to use rubber bullets. These have become common with regimes trying to cope with resistance, but the weapon can be lethal and a symbol of failure. Other indications of the failure to control the Arabs was the use of imprisonment without trial, euphemistically called 'administrative detention', deportations, curfews (anyone caught breaking it would be shot), and something new: riot sticks. This 'beatings policy' was only designed to 'break [the rioters'] bones' as Defence Minister Rabin explained.[59]

Also introduced was arguably the most unjust of all penalties: collective punishment. Whole villages would be sealed off, whether or not they were guilty of anything. It will be remembered that Palestine had experience of this method of punishment during the mandate, and it was heartily approved of by Churchill, but only in Arab villages. As well as these 'legal' sanctions, there were instances of what can only be described as barbaric behaviour unworthy of any nation with pretensions to civilisation. One of these occurred in February 1988, when 'soldiers tried to bury alive four Palestinians, who were saved at the last minute'.[60] The perpetrators of such bestiality were sometimes held to account, but often were not, or received only light reprimands.[61]

All of this had a serious disruptive effect on Israeli society. Some people believed that the government should be more repressive, while a Jewish peace movement also grew up. There were some in the government who thought that there had to be negotiation, while others believed, equally strongly, that there should be no let up in the repressive measures. The IDF itself faced a problem in that some soldiers refused to beat, or in other ways abuse the Arabs. The way in which the Israelis behaved drew down international anger. There was comparison with the behaviour of the apartheid government in South Africa—not for the last time—but as is always the case, Israel took no notice of any international distaste for its behaviour, claiming—again not for the last time—that such criticism was motivated by antisemitism.

The situation was thrown into more confusion when King Hussein pronounced in July 1988 that his government was giving up any responsibility for, or claim to, the West Bank. This removed a considerable obstacle to PLO ambitions for statehood, and so created the need for Israel to develop a new policy. At about the same time there was another development. There had been some discussion in Palestinian circles about a 'two state solution'. In a speech in November 1988, Yasser Arafat himself declared a Palestine state centred on Gaza and the West Bank. He went further in December and formally renounced all forms of terrorism.

This period saw Yasser Arafat at the peak of his career. Although he had been born in Cairo in 1929, his parents were Palestinian. He was educated mainly in Cairo and it was there that he first became politically active. He co-founded Fatah, a Palestinian political party, in the 1950s. The word has great significance in Arab tradition, and means something like 'opening', 'conquering' or 'victory'. His dominance was complete when he became chairman of the PLO, which consisted of several strands of resistance, in 1969. There was a particularly brutal fight when the Israelis attacked the village of Karameh in Jordan in 1968. Arafat's image was featured on the cover of *Time* in December 1968, and his reputation soared nationally and internationally because of the publicity. But his grip began to weaken, notably among Arab leaders, when he disapproved of the invasion of Iraq in 2003. Although he lost support, after the Palestinian National Authority (PNA) was formed in 1994, he was overwhelmingly voted in as president in 1996.

At about the same time as Arafat was changing his policy in respect of the recognition of Israel, the Israeli Likud government put forward their own plan. This proposed that after a period of several months there could be elections, some form of 'autonomy', an Israeli withdrawal from some of the West Bank, and some kind of a federation of Jordan and the West Bank. There seemed to be no place for the PLO in any discussion, and certainly no consideration of an independent Palestinian state. It was inconceivable that the Likud government would have anything to do with the PLO. The 'plan' quickly died.

The next milestone was a US initiative to call a peace conference. Buoyed up by the success of the Operation Desert Storm, which ended in March 1991, President George Bush saw peace in the Middle East as his next ambition. His efforts were soured over a request by Yitzhak Shamir, then prime minister, for a substantial loan, ostensibly to help with the integration of large numbers of immigrants, especially those now arriving from the former Soviet Union. Not only were they a threat because they were settled on stolen Palestinian land, but they tended to become part of extreme right-wing political parties, such as Yisrael Ba'aliya and Yisrael Beiteinu. A flavour of the political orientation of the latter was demonstrated when the first Muslim minister was appointed in January 2007. Avigdor Lieberman, leader of Yisrael Beiteinu, resigned, calling the appointment 'a lethal blow to Zionism'.[62] In 1991 US policy was to discourage further Israeli settlements. Nobody believed that the money would be used on existing settlements: rather it would be marshalled to build more settlements.

Such problems were eventually overcome and a conference took place in Madrid from 30 October to 1 November 1991, attended by the US, the USSR, Israel, Palestinians (but not the PLO by Israeli insistence), and some Arab countries. It was followed by meetings of combinations of the parties. It achieved very little, but it did indicate that at least the warring parties were prepared to talk. It also saw the scaling down of the intifada but did not see the end of violence.

In the election of June 1992 the Labour party gained power and Yitzhak Rabin became prime minister. As far as the Palestinians were concerned, the change was not likely to mean much since Rabin seemed, like Shamir, to be in opposition to the idea of a Palestinian state. During the early part of Rabin's time in office there was unofficial contact between Israelis and Palestinians, and an Israeli academic, Yair Hirschfeld, one of those involved, persuaded the Norwegian government to become involved. A number of secret meetings were arranged. Rabin allowed these to take place, but was not keen or hopeful. For his part, Rabin bore down on Palestinian dissidents, imprisoning and deporting them. But the violence continued, especially on the Lebanese border.

The secret negotiations carried on until, in September 1993, Arafat made a number of commitments in a letter, notably that the Palestinian policies to deny Israel's right to exist 'are now inoperative and no longer valid'.[63] The secret meetings led to top level negotiations in Norway and out of these came two 'Accords' called Oslo 1 and Oslo 2. On 19-20 August 1993, after a considerable amount of discussion, a Declaration of Principles (DOP) was secretly agreed in Oslo.

The DOP, which is called Oslo 1, was signed in Washington DC on 13 September 1993 by Arafat and Rabin, with President Clinton as witness. This stated that the Palestinians recognised the right of Israel to exist and the Israel recognised the PLO as the proper negotiating body for the Palestinians. It was proposed that a Palestinian Authority with limited powers should be set up in Gaza and the West Bank. Elections would take place to that end. The Israeli military occupation of the territories would end and the withdrawal would include the area around Jericho. A Palestinian police force would be established. Israel would retain certain powers: for example for defence and for the overall security of Israelis and the settlements. There would be further negotiations about Jerusalem, the settlements, the positioning of the military, refugees, borders and foreign relations. In September Arafat stated officially that the PLO accepted that the state of Israel could exist and was entitled to peace and security, and that the denials in the Palestinian Covenant were 'no longer valid'. In the same month, Rabin recognised the PLO as representing the people of Palestine.

One effect of the DOP was that peace between Jordan and Israel became possible. For a variety of reasons relationships between the two had always been the least hostile of all the Arab states. Although the DOP raised worries for Jordan about the possible new friendship between Israel and Palestine, these eventually subsided, and on 26 October 1994 a peace treaty was signed. The significance of this for the Palestinians was that in the event of future fighting with Israel, Jordan could no longer be assumed to be on their side. This meant that two important former allies, Egypt and Jordan, were now of questionable reliability.

The reception of the DOP, when it became known in Israel/Palestine, varied from acceptance through to violent rejection. Some two thirds of the Palestinians in the territories supported the agreement, no doubt because it held out a promise of normality. Similarly, about the same proportion of Jews accepted it, probably for much the same reasons. But there was opposition in both communities. The Palestinian opposition, led by Hamas and Islamic Jihad, was determined to undo the agreement. They were to do this via terrorism. Before the end of 1993, Israeli soldiers and settlers had been murdered, and the killings were to continue for several years. The chosen method now became the suicide bomber. This was difficult to predict or stop, because the people who volunteered to kill themselves for the cause had no fear of dying.

There was violent resistance from ordinary Jews, which was among the most brutal of the time. On 24 February 1994, a settler, a doctor by profession, attacked worshippers in the mosque of the Tomb of the Patriarchs, killing twenty-nine and injuring many more. He was beaten to death: 'his grave outside Hebron becoming a place of pilgrimage for Jewish opponents of the peace plan'.[64] Palestinians too carried out attacks. Morris sums up the years 1994-96 as the 'heyday of the suicide bombers'.[65]

All of this hindered and indeed halted the movement towards a settlement, which both sets of extremists wanted to thwart. There was, however, some progress. For example, the 'Agreement on the Gaza Strip and the Jericho Area' was signed in Cairo on 4 May 1994. This formalised the arrangements whereby most of the Gaza Strip and the area around Jericho would be handed over. The shape of the new Palestinian Police Force was also set out, and those Palestinian prisoners not charged with violent offences were released. Israel duly withdrew its forces from Jericho and from large areas of Gaza in May. Gaza became the 'capital' of the Palestinian Authority, and Arafat returned to Palestine.

Part of the several agreements had always been that Arafat would restrain violence. This, however, he would not, or more likely could not, do. Since the intifada he had increasingly lost control of sections of the Arab population, and to have tried to curb the behaviour of activists would have further weakened his support.

Hamas issued a covenant which stated that 'Israel will exist until Islam will obliterate it'.[66] The suicide attacks continued, with the Israeli people becoming more and more terrified and angry, and right-wing demonstrations becoming commonplace. These were spurred on by the leaders of the Likud: Ariel Sharon and Benjamin Netanyahu.[67]

Nevertheless, the proponents of peace soldiered on, and this culminated in what is known as Oslo 2. Its full name was the 'Israeli Palestinian Interim Agreement on the West Bank and Gaza Strip', and it was signed in Washington on 28 September 1995 by Rabin, Peres and Arafat. It consisted of agreements concerning arrangements for elections in the territories, the timing of the IDF withdrawal from them, the location of Israeli forces with regard to settlements and security, access to water supplies, and the size and disposition of the new police force. It was also agreed that some Palestinian prisoners would be released. The PLO agreed again that it would change the Palestinian National Covenant, which originated in 1964, to remove references to the destruction of Israel. This was agreed by a majority in the Palestinian National Council in Gaza on 24 April 1996.

Israeli right-wing anger culminated, as it seemingly had to, in an assassination in the best Jewish terrorist tradition. A pro-peace demonstration was held in Tel Aviv on 4 November 1995. At its close a Jewish student of Yemeni origin, Yigal Amir, fired three shots, two of which hit Rabin. He died a few minutes later. The Shin Bet officer who interviewed Amir recalled what he said:

> He explained to me that Rabin had betrayed the homeland and that someone had to stop him. 'You'll see,' he said to me. 'My shots will stop the peace protest and the handing over of territory to the Palestinians.'[68]

Amir's life has always attracted media attention. He received a life sentence, married while in prison, and fathered a child during a conjugal visit. His wife registered a new political party in 2020 whose policy was to seek justice for innocent prisoners. Right wingers often call for his release.

Despite Rabin's death, the Israelis began to withdraw from the territories. By the last months of 1995 the IDF had moved out of Gaza and some of the West Bank, although some 60 per cent of it was already forbidden to Palestinians. The exit from Hebron was delayed because of terrorist activity, and did not take place until January 1997. But these moves seemed to Palestinians to fall short of what had been promised. In addition they were subjected, inevitably, to restrictions such as curfews, imposed by the Israelis in an attempt to curtail violence.

After a brief period with Shimon Peres as prime minister, there was a general election in 1996. Especially because of the assassination of Rabin, it was expected that the Labour party would win; after all, Israel had been deeply shocked by the murder. Unfortunately, the five months of his premiership coincided with major assaults by Hamas and Hezbollah, which prompted retaliation by Israel, including major assaults on Lebanon from which Hezbollah operated. This was the atmosphere in which the election took place, and it provided an opportunity for the right wing to exploit: which they did very effectively. Instead of an easy Labour victory, a right-wing government emerged.

In Gaza, Arafat won a majority, which gave him a mandate to continue the peace negotiations. The new Israeli prime minister was Benjamin Netanyahu, and his election was to be one of the great disasters in the tortured history of the Palestinians. Indeed, there are Israelis who would claim that his behaviour has been disastrous for them too. Morris writes how 'he had clearly staked out his claim to be as Israel's most incompetent—and mendacious—prime minister'.[69]

In the month after the election, Likud promulgated a sheaf of policies which effectively negated all previous agreements with the Palestinians. They included notice that the Golan Heights and Jerusalem now belonged to Israel, that there would be no 'right of return' for refugees and no Palestinian state. It became clear that there would be no prisoner amnesty, and that the settlement building would continue. The position, after a short time, is summed up by Bergman:

> Netanyahu did not abrogate the Oslo Accords, but his government heaped innumerable difficulties on the process, and for the duration of his first term, the peace process was almost completely stalled.[70]

There was nothing left for the Palestinians. As if this were not enough, Netanyahu ordered that an exit from an archaeological tunnel running along the Temple Mount should be opened. Any disruption near the Mount was likely to resurrect the old belief that the Jews were going to rebuild the Temple. Arab experience of dealings with the Jews had taught them that Jews were persistent in their determination to carry out certain ambitions, and returned to them again and again. The Arabs rioted, there was confrontation with the army, firearms were used, and after a ceasefire the dead numbered some seventy Palestinians and fifteen Israeli soldiers, as well as hundreds of people injured.

Once again the United States became involved in what had become an impasse. The parties argued over Hebron, with Arafat pointing out that agreement had already been reached about Hebron and the extent of withdrawal from the West Bank. But Netanyahu insisted that there would be no further withdrawal. The situation was saved by the intervention of King Hussein who met Arafat and Netanyahu on 12 January 1997 and arranged a series of compromises. These included a withdrawal from Hebron, and an agreement on where the IDF would remain in control of the Tomb of the Patriarchs, and the areas in which Palestinian police would patrol. The only visible result of any resolution was the withdrawal of the IDF from 80 per cent of Hebron on 17 January 1997. As to other matters, Netanyahu would not allow further withdrawals, nor the release of prisoners, nor would he allow Palestinians to establish airports and seaports. The Palestinians did not issue a new 'covenant' or stop terrorist attacks. Both leaders were constrained by the reality that they were surrounded by extremists who had no wish for a settlement.

Some blame Arafat for all the failure. Karsh is one who believes that far from inhibiting terrorism, Arafat actually orchestrated it:

> Embracing violence as the defining character of his rule, from the moment of his arrival in Gaza in July 1994 after his period of exile in Tunisia, he set out to build an extensive terrorist infrastructure in flagrant violation of the accords, and in total disregard of the overriding reason he had been brought to the territories: namely to lay the groundwork for Palestinian statehood.[71]

Such behaviour was designed 'to discredit the newly elected prime minister, Benjamin Netanyahu'.[72]

After more lengthy diplomatic moves, another summit was held in the Wye River estate in Virginia in October 1998, and a 'Memorandum' was signed in which it was agreed that the status of 13 per cent of an area of the West Bank would be changed. Twelve per cent would be under mixed Israeli and Palestinian control, and one per cent under Palestinian control. There were also the perennial promises to combat terrorism. The reaction of the Israeli right wing was horror at the concessions to the Arabs. Some of the West Bank was freed from the IDF, and some prisoners were released. Likud pressure on Netanyahu was such that he halted further developments, blaming the Palestinians for not carrying out their promises, and called an election.

In the late 1980s, there began to appear serious concern in Israeli society about the real policies of the government. Here, as a redeeming fact, should be mentioned the work of B'Tselem ['In the image of God']. Founded in 1989, the organisation 'documents human rights violations in the occupied territories; combats denial of such violations, and helps create a culture of human rights in Israel'.

B'Tselem demonstrates that there are Israelis who do not accept the dogma of their government. The organisation especially deplores the treatment of Palestinians in the Occupied Territories, and publicises abuses inflicted upon them. It describes itself as 'The Israeli Information Centre for Human Rights in the Occupied Territories'. It has attracted prestigious worldwide praise and awards for its work. Up to the present, it documents gross behaviour, especially the abuse of Palestinians and human rights. It is, naturally, accused of being subversive and disloyal to the state. Nevertheless, it seems be regarded with respect across many sections of Israeli society.

In May 1999, the elections brought another upset. Ehud Barak, the leader of the Labour party and a retired general with impeccable military credentials, was elected prime minister on a promise to bring peace. He restored talks with Arafat in September, and signed a peace deal which aimed for peace by September 2000. He also resumed talks with Syria, and after seventeen years of occupation he managed to extricate Israel from the quagmire in southern Lebanon, although a dispute continued over a small piece of land. In March 2000 more land in the West Bank and the Jericho region was returned to the Palestinians.

In July 2000, the US tried again. President Clinton arranged for Arafat and Barak to meet at Camp David. They ranged over the familiar topics with especially violent disagreement over the future of Jerusalem. Barak offered much of the eastern part of the city to the Palestinians, but Arafat insisted that the Old City and the Temple Mount should be Palestinian. He also rejected a US proposal that the city should be divided, with the Temple Mount being under the authority of the Security Council. Arafat has been much criticised for his obstinacy. Certainly Barak made the most generous offer the Palestinians had received or would ever receive again, including the offer to give up most of the West Bank. Arafat should have studied Ben-Gurion's tactic which was to take what you can, and then somehow steal the rest. The conference was pronounced a failure.

The Zionist perspective on what came next is something of a model of how to shift the blame for an event on to others. In the autumn of 1999 there broke out a second intifada, called by the Arabs the 'al Aqsa Intifada'. It was to lead to a great deal of violence. The uprising was provoked by Ariel Sharon: a seminal fact which Zionists would like to be forgotten.

On 28 September, surrounded by massive security, he visited the Temple Mount. The visit was announced beforehand and Arafat advised Barak to forbid it. There is some debate about what Sharon intended. It is difficult to see why, since he made his purpose clear:

> The Temple Mount is in our hands and will remain in our hands. It is the holiest site in Judaism and it is the right of every Jew to visit the Temple Mount.[73]

This was not the first time an Israeli leader had deliberately provoked trouble over holy sites. During the 1967 war, on 7 June, Moshe Dayan 'went to the Western Wall and declared that Jerusalem had been "liberated"':

> 'We have united Jerusalem, the divided capital of Israel. We have returned to the holiest of our Holy Places, never to part from it again'. The Zionist movement's moderate position on Jerusalem disappeared overnight.[74]

Sharon clearly felt that he was entitled to make a visit, although he would have been well aware that it would be seen as a challenge to the Arabs. It is also clear, from his usual attitude to Arabs, that he knew they would be offended, would react, and this would give him the chance to derail the peace process.

The reaction was what Sharon wanted, and immediate. There followed, over the next few days the usual attacks on the police with stones, and the police responded with rubber bullets. The situation deteriorated quickly and soon live ammunition was being used by both sides, together with stoning and the hurling of Molotov cocktails. The Israelis used tear gas. Later they would use tanks and helicopter gunships to destroy buildings which they believed were being used by the insurgents. They also singled out important Palestinian officials for assassination.

Many of the incidents on both sides horrified the international audience and the peoples of Israel/Palestine. Just two examples illustrate this. A twelve-year-old boy, Muhammad al-Dura, was shot in Gaza while he was being shielded by his father. On 12 October two Israeli reservists seem to have strayed into Ramallah. They were trapped, identified, lynched and horribly mutilated. Both sets of murders were shown around the world on television and in newspapers. The second incident led to a certainty in the Israeli leadership that Arafat did not want peace, and there was an escalation in the use of force by the IDF.[75]

Then there was an IDF attack on the town of Jenin, which the Israelis alleged was a terrorist base, which lasted from 2 to 11 April 2002. They brought in armoured bulldozers and destroyed large areas. The number of people killed on this occasion is a matter of dispute, but Amnesty International issued a critical report alleging unlawful killings, torture and ill-treatment of prisoners, and the blocking of the passage of ambulances.[76] This mayhem went on until early 2005. As always there is little agreement on the numbers of casualties. The figures hover at around 3,000 Palestinian deaths and 1,000 Israelis, as well as some foreigners. There is, naturally, furious debate about the causes of the insurgency.

The Zionist implication, and sometimes assertion, is simple and simplistic. It is that Arafat was responsible, perhaps as a result of disappointment at the failure of

Terrorism, Violence, and the Expansion of the State

the Camp David talks. Indeed it was believed that he had been carefully planning an uprising. In 2000 he launched 'his terror war shortly after Netanyahu's successor, Ehud Barak, had offered the creation of an independent state in 92 per cent of the West Bank and the entire Gaza Strip, with East Jerusalem as its capital.'[77] This, some would claim, explains the spontaneity of the response to Sharon's behaviour. But Morris writes that:

> The measure of involvement of the PA and its president, Yasser Arafat, in the initial outbreak and in the subsequent violence is not clear ... The initial rioting of 28-29 September seems to have been completely spontaneous, though the local Fatah cadres certainly were active as inciters and leaders.[78]

There is also a view that the Israeli withdrawal from south Lebanon in June 2000 was a factor. It is argued that this was seen by the Arabs as weakness, and that the massive IDF forces were not unbeatable. Morris offers a sophisticated explanation for the uprising:

> It lay in the 52-year history of marginalisation of and discrimination against the Arabs in Israeli society ... More immediately, Barak's studied indifference towards this minority and its leaders badly exacerbated existing tensions; after receiving 95 per cent of the Arab vote in the 1999 elections, Barak failed to invite the Arab leaders into his coalition or even to consult with them, let alone offer redress for their various grievances, which included high levels of poverty and unemployment, a poor education system and weak infrastructures.[79]

Morris also draws attention to the role of fundamental Islam in supporting the insurgency.

Once again, the US tried to intervene. In mid-October 2000, Clinton and Mubarak, president of Egypt, held a meeting. There Arafat and Barak agreed to try to end the violence and the US said it would send an investigative mission. This mission was led by the US senator George Mitchell, who was much involved in international affairs. Its report was published on 30 April 2001.[80]

The report can only be described as pusillanimous. It suggests that the 'catalyst for the violence' was the breakdown of the Camp David talks. It notes that the Israeli government suggested that the violence was planned by the Palestinian Authority leaders. This was rejected in the report which concluded that there was 'no deliberate plan by the Palestine Authority to initiate a campaign of violence', but there was 'no evidence on which to conclude that the PA made a consistent effort to contain the demonstration and control the violence'. Nor was there a 'deliberate plan by the [government of Israel] to respond with lethal force'. This last was in answer to the allegation that 'Israel responded with excessive and illegal use of deadly force'. And yet, paradoxically, there was no evidence that the government 'made a consistent effort to use non-lethal means to control demonstrations of unarmed Palestinians'.

The report did deal with the crucial question of Sharon's behaviour. It did not cause the intifada, it claimed, but it was 'poorly timed and the provocative effect should have been foreseen; indeed it was foreseen by those who urged that the visit be prohibited'.

The report concluded with a number of worn-out recommendations. These were that violence should cease; the Palestinian authorities should prevent terrorism; the building of settlements should stop; and peace negotiations should be resumed. Nobody took the slightest notice. What was seized upon by Zionists and their apologists was the astonishing conclusion that the role of Sharon in causing the intifada was slight, and that it would have happened anyway.

The Israeli government also issued a report on 2 December 2003. This was chaired by Theodor Orr, an Israeli supreme court judge. It was rather more specific than the Mitchell Report in identifying blame. For example, it recommended that eight police officers be reprimanded and two dismissed. It went further and recommended that the internal security minister, Shlomo Ben-Ami, be removed. As seems to be the way in Israeli politics, Ben-Ami's career was not harmed, and he later became foreign minister. The Arabs were also apportioned blame. Three prominent Arabs were accused of inciting unrest. Perhaps the most remarkable statement in the report was attributing blame to the discrimination of Arab citizens in Israel, for which it held the government responsible. Naturally, the report satisfied no one. The Arabs thought they were being unfairly blamed and the Jews felt that Orr had not been hard enough on the insurgents and their leaders.

The United States made yet another attempt to bring peace. In the last part of 2000, just before the end of Clinton's presidency, he sent proposals for a peace agreement. This was on 23 December. In the light of previous experience they were fanciful indeed. He called for most of the West Bank to be handed over, the removal of most settlements, the positioning of an international force, the disarmament of the Palestinians, the division of Jerusalem, and the return of refugees, mostly to the Palestinian areas, but some to Israel. He also mentioned the fiery matter of the 'right of return', saying both parties should recognise it. As always, nobody was prepared to accept the plan, although there were sporadic talks culminating in a meeting in Sinai in January 2001. There could be no consensus and this was the last serious attempt to achieve a settlement. On 13 June 2003, Fatah, Hamas and Islamic Jihad announced a three-month ceasefire, but the violence, although it was reduced, continued. When the intifada ended in February 2005, it was attended by more promises on both sides to return to the 'roadmap', to release Palestinian prisoners, and for the IDF to withdraw from West Bank towns.

The intifada left the Palestinian territories in a parlous state. There had been much damage to buildings. Israel also suffered economically. Israeli political opinion moved firmly, and seemingly permanently, to the right and Arafat lost his control over the Palestinians to political extremists. The most devastating outcome for the Palestinians (and for which the intifada must be held responsible) was Ariel Sharon's election as prime minister with a substantial majority on 6 February 2001. He formed a coalition government dominated by hard liners.

The power in Israel had passed to the man called by many, including Israelis, 'the butcher of Lebanon', a 'murderer' and a 'war criminal'. His stated ambition was to incorporate the East Bank of the Jordan, in fact the state of Jordan, into Israel. From that moment, the position of the Palestinians deteriorated even more, and that position has not yet changed, except for the worst.

Sharon has figured often in this book, and it will be necessary to deal briefly with him and his career. His political behaviour in any other country, and at any other time, would surely have rendered him unelectable. He had long experience in the Israeli Army, from the time of the Haganah, and as we have seen that was punctuated by excessive behaviour. In politics, he often changed his allegiance, sometimes founding new parties to retain leadership. He was the object of investigation for corruption for supporting the activities of an Israeli businessman in exchange for the payment of large sums to his son Gilad. Ariel was not charged. He was also investigated for a financial scandal in respect to the 1996 elections. This time his other son, Omi, a Knesset member, was convicted and sentenced to nine months imprisonment.

By the time of his disabling stroke in January 2006, Sharon's actions began to appear rather inexplicable. This was especially the case when he handed over complete control of Gaza to the Palestinians and removed Jewish settlements in the face of opposition from his political allies. Israel did though retain control of air space and the coast. It has been suggested that Sharon would have done the same in the West Bank if he had not been disabled, but this is not credible because when he was minister of agriculture he doubled the number of settlements, and he was well known for his ambition to flood those areas with Jewish immigrants. The rumour is more likely to have been a myth to improve his image. His career was summed up by Bergman:

> Sharon had been a political pariah for almost two decades, ever since he orchestrated the disastrous invasion of Lebanon. He'd been forced to abdicate the office of defence minister in 1983, but his misbegotten military adventure—his foolhardy plan to arrange the whole of the Middle East—dragged on for eighteen years, costing Israel 1,216 lives and more than 5,000 wounded, as well as untold Lebanese casualties ... The United States had imposed an unofficial boycott on him ... [he was] widely loathed for years.[81]

Sharon's decision in 2003, that Israel should 'disengage' from Gaza, is a matter of great speculation. What is most likely is that it was seen as a way of achieving one of the central wishes of the Zionists: to remove as many Arabs as possible from Israel. To hold on to Gaza would mean inheriting of responsibility for large numbers of them. From the point of view of the Zionists, this 'demographic' solution would remove the danger that, if all Arabs were to be enfranchised, the Jews would lose control of the government. This danger was never totally removed.

In 2015 Netanyahu appealed to the voters to be sure to vote because 'Arabs are going en masse to the polls', and again in 2020, in a desperate attempt to cling to power, he advocated that the votes of the 'Joint List' should not count in the decision to appoint the leader of a coalition government. The joint list voters were Israeli Arabs. He was giving 'Israelis another long lesson in the country's long history of racist mathematics'.[82]

For the Zionists, however, there was a dilemma in Sharon's proposal. The price of herding Palestinians away from the centre was to give up a part of the God-given land; and so there was opposition. But in September 2005, the situation was different. The settlements which had been erected in Gaza had been destroyed, and the occupying military troops had been withdrawn. Unfortunately, that was not the end of the matter.

The Israelis did not loosen their grip on Gaza. They retained control of the borders, the ports, the airspace and territorial waters. This meant that the Palestinians could not have access to one third of their arable land, or to 85 per cent of their fisheries, a critical source of livelihoods. In 2010 the UN estimated that 30 per cent of arable land had been lost in the creation of a buffer zone by Israel. In the strip in 2010, there were an estimated 1.6 million Palestinians: one of the most densely populated regions on earth. Such oppression has given rise to an interminable, and pointless debate: Is Israel 'occupying' Gaza? Discussion is pointless because, although Israeli forces are not physically present in the land, Israel is suffocating it.

There was another major complication. Contrary to all expectations, and to the horror of the Israeli and US governments, in 2006 Hamas won a majority of seats in the Palestinian legislative elections. The United States, Russia, the UN and the European Union insisted that future aid would depend on Hamas accepting previous agreements, recognising Israel, and rejecting violence. Hamas refused, and boycotts were set in place. This was not enough. The Israelis launched 'Operation Cast Lead', called by the Muslims 'The Gaza Massacre'. More generally it is simply called 'The Gaza War'. It lasted from 27 December 2008 to 18 January 2009. During the course of the war Israel launched a ground invasion, attacking military and populated areas. Palestine replied with rockets, many of which hit cities. There were between 1,000 and 1,500 Palestinian deaths, and 13 Israeli deaths. Four of these were from 'friendly fire'. Tens of thousands of people in Gaza were made homeless, with wells and hospitals destroyed.

In September 2009 a UN special commission report was presented by Richard Goldstone.[83] It accused both sides of war crimes. Israel, having refused to co-operate because of bias in the brief given to Goldstone, denied this. In 2011 Goldstone added to the confusion by changing his mind about Israel's behaviour. His co-authors of the report disagreed with him. As always, the international 'community' was divided. Nothing came of the report.

It was not long before there was more fighting. On 14 November 2012 Israel launched 'Operation Pillar of Defence'. The Zionists chose their wording carefully. Here, as in other 'operations', the words are chosen to indicate self-defence rather than belligerence. The reason for this attack was that Israel wanted to stop rocket attacks being launched from Gaza. The Palestinian explanation for their participation in what they called 'Operation Stones of Baked Clay' was that Israel was launching attacks against civilians, and they wanted an end to the blockade. They fired hundreds of rockets into Israel, even including targets like Tel Aviv. A ceasefire was mediated by Egypt on 21 November. According to the United Nations High Commission for Refugees, 174 Palestinians were killed and hundreds wounded. On the Israeli side, six were killed and 240 injured. The UN Security Council debated the operation, but failed to reach any conclusion or decision.

During the next two years there was a significant change in Palestinian politics. Al Fatah seems to have concluded that there could be no peaceable agreement with Netanyahu, and so there was a reconciliation with Hamas. A Palestinian Unity Government was sworn in on 2 June 2014. Netanyahu refused to deal with this new authority, arguing that it would 'strengthen terrorism'. In fact he was probably more worried about the strength of this new political force. Two days later, his government authorised the building of more settlements in the West Bank and East Jerusalem.

The 2012 'peace' did not last long. On 8 July 2014, Israel launched 'Operation Protective Edge', also known as the 2014 Gaza War. Once again Israel stated that its intention was to stop rocket attacks, and also to destroy a tunnel system which enabled the Palestinians to smuggle in arms. Palestinians repeated their determination to end the blockade. Once again, there are varying claims as to deaths and casualties. It is generally agree that at the end of this fight, over 2,000 Palestinians had been killed and over 10,000 wounded. In one of its reports, 'Black Flag', in January 2015, B'Tselem recorded that 1,394 of those killed (63 per cent) did not take part in the hostilities. The report went on to claim that a quarter of those killed were under eighteen. But it is also pointed out that seventeen of those children killed were participating in hostilities. The UN reported that 7,000 homes were destroyed and 87,000 damaged. On the Israeli side between sixty-two and sixty-seven soldiers were killed, and 469 injured.

Five civilians were killed with 261 injured. The B'Tselem report concluded that:

> The high number of civilian fatalities—including women, children and the elderly casts doubt on Israeli's claim that all the targets were legitimate and that the military adhered to the principle of proportionality during the attacks and took precautions to reduce harm to civilians.

Physically and economically Gaza was devastated.[84]

Meanwhile, during the second intifada, the Israelis had begun another device which was to further humiliate and restrict the freedoms of the Arabs, and draw further international condemnation. A wall was built in the West Bank. The idea seems to have originated with a proposal by Yitzhak Rabin in 1992, the same Rabin who was to be hailed as an apostle of peace. The ostensible reason for the wall was that it would control the number of suicide attacks and sniper assaults on Jews. But Rabin went on to say: 'we want to reach a separation between us and them'. The wildest reasoning was offered by Prime Minister Ehud Barak, who explained that '[the wall] is essential to the Palestinian nation in order to foster its national identity and independence without being dependent on the State of Israel'.[85]

The Israeli government claims that the wall has considerably reduced the number of attacks. It runs roughly along the 'Green Line'. This was the border agreed in the 1949 Armistice Agreement between Israel and the Arab states, although it was not intended to be a definitive mark of borders. The wall, however, does not follow the border but intrudes on the West Bank, which is, theoretically, Arab territory. Its effect has been to include West Bank Jewish settlements in the Israeli state and to divide Arab communities. It has led to the seizure of Palestinian land, the demolition of Arab homes and businesses, the separation of people from water supplies, and the massive inhibition of Arab movement from place to place. Palestinians have also been obstructed in accessing medical treatment.

There have been sustained local protests about the wall, and both Jews and Arabs have been shot in these protests. B'Tselem has been much involved, as have other Israeli groups such as the Peace Now movement, and Anarchists Against the Wall. The Israeli government rejects all protests and claims that the wall has considerably reduced the number of attacks on Jews, and that there has been greater safety for Jews, and stability for Palestinians.

The wall has attracted condemnation from a wide variety of organisations. The International Committee of the Red Cross, Amnesty International, Human Rights Watch, and the World Council of Churches are some of the more prominent groups to condemn it. There is also an especially important and detailed account by the NGO Médecins du Monde, detailing the negative effect the wall has had on the health of Palestinians.[86]

In 2004, the International Court of Justice pronounced that the wall was contrary to international law. It drew attention *inter alia* to the land confiscations, the creation of 'enclaves', to restrictions on freedom of movement, and the withholding of water, food, education and health care. Then there is the view of the United Nations. As early as 2003 the UN General Assembly overwhelmingly resolved that the wall broke international law and should be taken down. The vote was vetoed by the United States in the Security Council.

It can be seen that despite the disapproval heaped upon Israel because of its actions, the best endeavours of well-meaning presidents of the United States, and of every kind of intervention, the position of the Palestine people would appear forlorn indeed. This state of affairs is, for the foreseeable future, cemented by the grip which Likud, and especially Netanyahu and his supporters, has upon the political system.

The position of the Palestinians, and what maintains that position, is the subject of the next chapter.

8

NEW LAMPS FOR OLD?

The Treatment of Palestinians and the 'New Antisemitism'

What is the future for the Palestinians? The wretched state of the Palestinians in 2021 has been well summed up by Nathan Thrall in the context of an article which asks the question: Is Israel an apartheid state?[1] In this article he shows that in the West Bank and other occupied territories, Israelis and Palestinians, despite living in the same territory, are subject to two different legal systems, one military, the other civil:

> Palestinians ... are denied freedom of expression, freedom of assembly, freedom of movement and even the right not to be detained indefinitely without trial ... Since the 1980s, all Israeli citizens brought to trial before the military courts were Arab citizens or residents of Israel ... no judgement was found in which the request of an Arab citizen to transfer his case from a military court to a court in Israel was accepted.

The list of legal deprivation is endless:

> Israel controls all the roads leading in and out of the PA-governed areas, invades homes within them every day and night and is permitted to enter even for reasons that have nothing to do with the security of Israeli citizens, such as arresting car thieves.

An appeal against a conviction is allowed, but as Thrall points out 'the odds are not good':

> The High Court has approved nearly every internationally prohibited policy Israel has carried out in the occupied territories, including deportations,

assassinations, imprisonment without trial, demolitions, land confiscation, pillage of natural resources and collective punishments such as mass curfews, school closures and withholding electricity for an entire region.

Another assessment is made by former President Obama. It is a depressing account on the impossibility of his making any difference because of the weight of American Jewish pressure:

> Millions of Palestinians lacked self-determination and many of the basic rights that even citizens of non-democratic countries enjoyed. Generations were growing up in a starved and shrunken world from which they literally couldn't escape, their daily lives subject to the whims of a distant, hostile authority and the suspicions of every blank-faced, rifle-carrying soldier demanding to see their papers at every check point they crossed.[2]

Incidentally, with regard to the allegation that Israel is an apartheid state, the respected organisation Human Rights Watch defined Israel as such in early 2021. This is a rare example of an international body supporting Palestinians, although the Israeli government declared the denunciation to be 'preposterous'.

The present plight of Palestinians, and the likely maintenance of that plight, depend not only on the behaviour of Israelis and their government, but on the policies and interference of other nations. I have frequently referred in this book to the support given to Israel by the United States. Over the years since the First World War, this shifted from hostility, to indifference, to the unqualified financial, military, and political support which is a signal feature of US political policy today. This is kept in place by the power and expert intervention of American Jewish society, and by important members of that society. There is an organisation which is devoted to maintaining US support for Israel, regardless of whether it is right or wrong. This is the American Israeli Public Affairs Committee (AIPAC), and US politicians ignore it at their peril.

One might suppose that this 'split loyalty' must lead to some tension for American Jews, reflecting the problem, often discussed, as to where loyalties lie. Ben-Gurion expressed one view of this in 1962:

> He upbraided American Zionists 'who are reluctant to say they are not Americans and not part of the American homeland like other Americans'; declared that Israel is the basis of the whole existence of the Jewish communities everywhere, especially in the United States and predicted that the 'only thing that could save Judaism in the United States were personal ties with Israel.'[3]

Two prominent supporters of the notion of the 'new antisemitism', Forster and Epstein, describe an incident about which they write a somewhat confused assessment. It would appear to be an observation about Jewish influence. This is not likely to be true, since their stance generally is to deny any such influence. In March 1970 *Time* magazine wrote an article about the fact that New York Governor Rockefeller and Mayor Lindsay had not attended a dinner in honour of the French President Pompidou. This was because the French, after the Six-Day War, refused to sell any more 108 Mirage Jets to Israel, and there had been Jewish protests at his visit. This:

> [This] *creates an impression in the minds of some* that Washington is acting not on the basis of national interest but out of fear of Jewish wrath. When public officials of national stature, such as John Lindsay and Nelson Rockefeller, *abdicate* their ceremonial responsibilities towards a foreign leader, it is a sign that *pressure bloc politics is taking precedence over common sense and public duty*.[4]

A representative view of some key American Jews is that of Senator Charles Schumer of New York, who claimed to be acting on divine orders: 'you know, my name ... comes from the word *shomer*,' he said, '"guardian", "watcher" and I believe Hashem—God—actually gave me that name. One of my roles, very important in the United States Senate, is to be ... the *shomer Yisrael*. And I will continue to be that with every bone in my body'. Senator Booker from New Jersey also made his position clear:

> I was a supporter of Israel well before I was a United States senator ... If I forget thee, o Israel, may I cut off my right hand'. More generally, 'There was no murmur of dissent from supporters of Israel when Trump spoke to a group of American Jews and referred to Netanyahu as 'your prime minister'.[5]

Support for Israel peaked during Donald Trump's presidency in the early twenty-first century. An indication of his political illiteracy in respect of the Middle East, as in other areas, is described by Henry Siegman:

> [Trump] declared that Palestinians will have to acknowledge Israel, they're going to have to do that, entirely unaware that that is exactly what they have already done, not once, but on three separate occasions: at the request of Reagan and his secretary of state, George Schultz, in 1988; in 1993, in the context of the Oslo Accords; and again in Gaza in 1998, with Bill Clinton in attendance. Trump is probably also unaware that Netanyahu's government has never recognised the Palestinian right to national self-determination and statehood in any part of Palestine, even though this right has been affirmed repeatedly by the UN Security Council (e.g. Resolution 242 in 1967 and Resolution 1515 in 2003) and by the International Court of Justice (in 2004).[6]

In the few years of his presidency, Trump managed to destroy any hope of a settlement and consigned the Palestinians to a future as citizens of nowhere. He has done this, *inter alia*, by recognising Israel's claim to Jerusalem by moving the US embassy there; by acknowledging Israel's seizure of the Golan Heights as legitimate; and then by legitimising the building of illegal settlements. His 'peace plan' effectively took away the bulk of the West Bank from any putative Palestinian state, and he stopped financial help for refugees. It might be added that he destroyed a delicate international balance by abrogating the nuclear deal with Iran—a longstanding Israeli ambition. The enormity of these actions needs emphasising.

Because of his power, and his abuse of it, Trump's actions over Israel were devastating for the Palestinians. His bizarre antics, whilst they are a matter of rejoicing for the Israelis, have also led to further animosity towards Israel. In March 2019 he signed a proclamation which recognised Israel's sovereignty over the Golan Heights. In the process he 'tore up the international rule book'.[7] This area is the part of Syria which was occupied during the 1967 war. Israel then expelled 130,000 Syrians. In 1981 Israel announced the annexation of the region. Trump's action was tantamount to farce, except there was nothing at which to laugh. He solemnly signed away a territory which did not belong to the United States in the presence of a delighted Israeli prime minister. The United Nations, from the time of the seizure, has regarded the occupation as illegal, but Israel ignores that, confident in the knowledge that the UN will do nothing. The contrast with the US condemnation of Russia's annexation of the Crimea is glaring.

This was not the end of Trump's interference. In November 2019 the US government announced a new policy over the Palestinian/Jordanian West Bank, which is currently occupied by Israel, and upon which it has built illegal (in the view of most countries) settlements. The announcement embraced the statement that these 'settlements were no longer inconsistent with international law'. The US State Legal Department had pronounced that the settlements were a breach of international law, and so the announcement by Mike Pompeo, secretary of state, reversed four decades of US policy and distressed the international community.

There was little explanation except that the decision had been made after discussion by a White House team working on an agreement between Israel and the Palestinians. The hidden explanation lies in the fact that the team was 'led' by Jared Kushner, Trump's son-in-law, and included the US ambassador to Israel, David Friedman, whose position is summed up by his statement that 'Israeli and American supporters of a two state solution [are] worse than kapos'.[8] A kapo was an auxiliary guard, often Jewish, in the Nazi concentration camps. Kushner, as is well known, is both an Orthodox Jew and a Zionist. The reaction of Netanyahu, the Israeli prime minister, to all of Trump's actions was predictable based on an historical lie: 'Today the United States adopted an important policy that rights an historical wrong.'[9]

In early 2020 Netanyahu announced that he was going to annex parts of the West Bank. The British government and ten other European countries warned Israel not to do so, and 130 British MPs urged Prime Minister Johnson to impose economic sanctions if he did. Some Jews outside Israel objected to the proposed annexation including those described in the press as 'Prominent British Jews' and 'Leading Jewish Figures'. Over forty of these signed a letter to the Israeli ambassador to Britain 'conveying "concern and alarm"'. They describe themselves as 'committed Zionists and passionately outspoken friends of Israel':

> The signatories say their concerns are 'shared by large numbers of the British Jewish community, including many in its current leadership, even if they choose not to express them'… 'It would have grave consequences for the Palestinian people … Israel's standing would also suffer and it is incompatible with the notion of Israel as both a Jewish and democratic state'.[10]

Also in Britain, there was a Jewish Youth Petition addressed to the British Board of Deputies, pointing out that the board had supported the two-state solution, and should object. This petition was supported by the Jewish Labour Movement, and the response of the board was that the two-state solution 'remains our position'. But there was a 'counter position' and 'clear diversity of views'. It 'is not the job of the Board of Deputies to decide on the exact position of the border.'[11]

Israel has long feared the translation into action of a deep hostility from Iran. The US had negotiated a treaty with Iran which sought to limit the danger of that country in developing nuclear weapons. This Obama initiative was widely regarded as a triumph internationally. But Trump, persuaded by Israel, attacked his intelligence people for reporting that Iran was not working on a nuclear programme:

> Half of Trump's argument for exiting the agreement Obama signed with Iran in 2015, along with the UK, France, China, Russia and Germany, was that the nuclear threat was real. The other half was the fact that Iran was 'the world's leading sponsor of terror'—a misleading Israeli contribution to American political discourse.[12]

On 28 January 2020 President Trump announced a 'peace deal'. It was called 'Peace to Prosperity: a Vision to improve the Lives of the Palestinian and Israeli People'. It was announced in the presence of the Israeli prime minister, Benjamin Netanyahu. It was the result of discussions between the US—notably the US ambassador to Israel, David Friedman, and Jared Kuchner, the 'peace envoy'—on the one hand, and member of the Israeli government on the other. There was little explanation except that the decision had been made after discussion by a White House team working on an agreement between Israel and the Palestinians.

The Palestinians were not consulted, nor were they at the delivery of the 'Vision'. Cynical commentators noted the timing of the announcement. At that very moment the two heads of state, Trump and Netanyahu, were on the verge of being tried on serious criminal charges.

There is much in the plan which rehearses the history of the region and its conflicts. It is pointed out that while Israel has peace treaties with Jordan and Egypt, there are still hostilities with the Palestinians in the Gaza Strip, and these will not stop until Gaza changes its fundamental attitude to Israel. Gaza is defined as extremely dangerous, and must be demilitarised. But there would be compensations. Thus, in one of the most fanciful parts of the plan, it is proposed that something called 'Gaza Port' could be constructed on an island to be created off the coast, but only five years after all the demands in respect of neutralising Gaza have been met.[13] In fact the entire plan is dominated by concern for Israel's security. For example, an offer to the putative Palestinian state to use the ports of Haifa and Ashdod is accompanied by the condition that there must be Israeli supervision.[14]

Large tracts of the plan set out a utopian vision of the future Palestine state in considerable detail: even down to the installation of prepaid electricity meters.[15] There is a very flattering picture of the inherently positive character of the Palestinian people, and how there should be an 'unleashing' of their 'potential'. Once the new state is set up, everything will be possible: worldwide markets will be open, tourism will flourish, and so on. All to the end that the Palestinian people may be 'empowered'. Before any of this can happen, the Palestinians must agree to what the Americans and the Israelis demand. No doubt in the hope of gaining the support of the three countries for the plan, there are proposed development goals for Jordan, Egypt, and Lebanon.[16]

The heart of the plan deals with the most inflammatory issues in the country. These are the status of Jerusalem, the Israeli occupation of the West Bank, and the fate of refugees. It is accepted that the 'two state' solution is the ultimate aim. With regard to Jerusalem there is a long preamble about how sacred the city is to the three religions, how the Israelis have looked after it, and how access must be ensured. But the conclusion is that Jerusalem should be part of Israel, and should remain as the state's capital. As we have seen, this was no surprise, since on 6 December 2017, the United States, or more correctly President Trump, had pronounced that Jerusalem belonged to Israel and that the US would move its embassy there, and had passed a law to that effect. This *de facto* recognition that Jerusalem was the Israeli capital was widely condemned, including by the Pope and the kings of Jordan and Saudi Arabia. While it pleased the Israeli government and its people, the move was another factor in the increasing distaste many countries have for Israel.

Palestine had always insisted that their capital, when the state was established, would be in East Jerusalem. So, where did the plan suggest the Palestinian capital should be? After the Oslo Accords a building was erected in Abu Dis at the border of Jerusalem. This was intended as an interim solution to the question of where the capital of Palestine should be. Abu Dis is now a 'gang-ridden slum'.[17] Because the interior of Jerusalem could be seen over the security wall next to this building, the top of the offending building was demolished. It is now a pathetic sight.

With regard to the West Bank, it is proposed that all the settlements, the establishment of which have been deplored in interminable UN resolutions and by successive US presidents, should now become part of Israel. Once again this merely confirmed what the US had already decreed. In fact, 30 per cent of the West Bank would be annexed by Israel. It is declared that no alternative is possible, since any regime which controls the West Bank 'would pose an existential threat to the State of Israel'.[18] Within this area there is what is called the Triangle, situated along the Green Line, or the pre-1967 border. This contains a number of villages and towns, with an Arab population of some 350,000. This would be classified as Palestine. An advantage for Israel would be that these people would no longer be Israeli citizens, as far as any Arab can be, and so a step would be taken towards Netanyahu's ambition that only Jews are properly qualified to be citizens. A collateral problem here is that in this area there are fifteen Jewish 'enclaves', or 'Jewish enclosed communities'. These Jews would be vulnerable, as Jewish critics of the plan point out, as were those in Gaza, before it became Palestinian territory.

In respect of refugees, the 'Vision' does not set out numbers, but in 2001 it was estimated that of one third of registered Palestinian refugees, more than 1.5 million, live in fifty-eight camps in Jordan, Lebanon, Syria, Gaza and the West Bank. About 263,000 Palestinians and their descendants are displaced in Israel. The plan makes three points forcibly: that there are Jewish refugees who must be included in any compensation scheme; that refugees cannot return to Israel; and that the Arab states have treated them badly. Kuwait, for example 'began a systematic clearing of Palestinians'.[19] So, the refugees could not be allowed to return indiscriminately (nothing new here). They could be resettled only in a future Palestinian state, in third countries, or in the state in which they currently reside. The Organisation of Islamic Cooperation must play a part. Those states must take '5,000 refugees each year for up to ten years'.[20] Like everything else in the plan, the settlement of the refugee 'problem' is hedged about with conditions to protect Israel.

Another breathtaking proposal is that the fertile Jordan Valley should be defined as part of Israel. It would be impossible for Israel to vacate the valley since this 'would have significant implications for regional security in the Middle East'.[21] But the Palestinians who live and work there should feel consoled since:

> Existing agricultural enterprises *owned* or *controlled* [my emphasis] by Palestinians shall continue without interruption or discrimination, pursuant to appropriate licences or leases granted by the State of Israel.[22]

What this must mean is those who own or 'control' property will be dispossessed. On the subject of property, once the Palestinian state is in place, the long-standing Israeli practice of demolishing homes and buildings will stop, except for reasons of safety 'or punitive demolition following acts of terrorism'.[23] This must mean that the practice continues.

There are other instructions which are further impositions on any future Palestine. One is that Israel should have overall control of borders and security, so that Palestine is unable to have armed forces. The plan explains that this restriction will bring obvious advantages to Palestine since:

> The state of Palestine will not be burdened with such costs, because it will be shouldered by the State of Israel.[24]

The arrangements of borders would mean that Palestine would be spread over a wide area and would be enclosed everywhere by Israel. This would involve massive problems of movement. This would be overcome by the creation of 'an innovative network of roads, bridges and tunnels that enable freedom of movement for the Palestinians'.[25]

There are also what might be called cultural conditions. The Palestinian education system must be reconstructed so that, for instance, school curricula and text books must not contain material 'that serve to promote hatred or antagonism towards its neighbours, [and] there must be an end to the glorification of violence, terrorism and martyrdom'.[26]

Some associated proposals are extremely intrusive. The new Palestine must cease 'prisoner and martyr payments'. This refers to payments made to the families of those imprisoned, or detained, for actual or supposed terrorist offences, and the money given to the dependants of people who have been killed fighting Israel. This goal 'is to change the applicable laws in a manner that is consistent with the laws of the United States'.[27] A question arises as to why the United States legal system is nominated. In conclusion, Israel should be applauded because it has agreed to the 'transfer of sizeable territory by the State of Israel'.[28] What the US sought to do in the plan was to show that Israel was being generous in its offer, despite Palestinian intransigence, and that there were tremendous advantages for the Palestinians if they accepted the plan.

Immediate reaction to the 'Vision' was predictable. Senior Democrats in the US deplored the plan, saying that it was unfair to the Palestinians: objections dismissed by the Israelis as typical of the Democratic party. *The Times of Israel* drew upon ancient history:

> Now the US peace plan has ostensibly punished the Palestinians for their obduracy, and rewarded the Israelis by recognising our rights to further portions of this *biblically resonant territory* [my emphasis].[29]

The possibility of the achievement of a long-hoped-for Zionist ambition was spotted by the leader of Yisrael Beiteinu, Avigdor Lieberman, 'who has long espoused a population exchange, [he] issued a statement 'welcoming President Trump [for] adopting my 2004 plan'.[30] This extreme nationalist party regard themselves as the political heirs of Jabotinsky. The core of the party consists of Russian immigrants.

The Palestinians rejected the 'Vision'. Their leader Mahmoud Abbas said that it would be consigned 'to the dustbin of history'. Palestinians everywhere began protests. There were promises of political protest in the UN, despite warnings from the US ambassador to the UN, Kelly Craft, that complaints would only 'repeat the failed pattern of the last seven decades'.[31] A fair response would be that such failure was exemplified in the failure of the UN to enforce its own resolutions.

Nobody expected anything from President Trump other than a 'Vision' for the development of the Zionist project and a culmination of his studied contempt for Palestinians. He illustrated this, as well as everything else, by removing contributions to UN Relief and Works Agency for refugees, stopping financial support to the Palestinian Authority, and closing down the Palestinian diplomatic mission in Washington. His 'Vision' was to include a continuation of cruelty, deprivation and death being heaped upon Palestinians.

Next, on 13 August 2020, the White House announced a deal 'brokered' by Trump in which Prime Minister Netanyahu of Israel and Crown Prince Mohammed bin Zayed of the United Arab Emirates 'agreed to finalise a historical peace agreement after 49 years'. This would normalise diplomatic relations. It would be called the 'Abraham Accords' after the religious figure recognised by the three religions. In a series of fulsome tributes, mostly to Trump, and by Trump, he said: 'this will really change the world ... I think you'll be seeing some exciting things'. One questioner asked 'Do you support annexation of Palestinian land by Israelis at this point?' To which Trump gave a non-answer: 'Well, we're talking to Israel about that right now, actually'.[32] The central feature of the 'deal' was the future of the West Bank. It will be remembered that the peace proposals by Trump included the Israeli annexation of much of that area.

The remarkable venture with Israel was explained by the foreign minister of the UAE. He said that the UEA was trying 'to really unscrew a time bomb that is threatening a two-state solution'. He foresaw that if Israel went ahead with the latest annexation, the existence of a proper Palestinian state would be compromised. A discussion in *The Washington* Post on 13 August 2020 commented on some of the reaction to Trump's plan. It was reported that Netanyahu made it clear that the matter of the West Bank was very much alive. The words used are 'suspension' of the plan, not its end. 'He did not consider the plan "dead"':

> 'I am committed to sovereignty' he said, using the Israeli term for annexation. 'I did not give up on the settlements'.

This consoled those settlers who were at first were angry at the deal, because they wanted Israel to take the land once and for all. But soon they realised that for them, the proposals meant opportunities for commerce with the UAE, and that, because of Netanyahu's brazen caveat, they could still expect the annexation, when the new relationships were in place. Netanyahu could hardly believe his luck. He said:

> Who would ever have dreamed that there would be a peace agreement with an Arab country without our returning to the 1967 borders?

The Palestinians were of course not involved, and were very angry. As always, they got nothing. This was summed up by a spokesman in the West bank, who 'condemned the accord as a betrayal … the UAE, or any other party, has no right to speak on behalf of the Palestinian people'.

The reaction of Jared Kushner, one of the architects of the deal, to the Palestinian response was typical. He was contemptuous: 'They [the Palestinians] have a fairly predictable response that we've seen time and time again to all types of things that help make their people's lives better'. It is impossible to understand how any of the actions of the Trump government could be construed as making the lives of Palestinians better.[33]

There are Americans who object to this mindless support for all things Israeli. In 1973 a CBS White House correspondent, Robert Pierpoint 'accused the United States of a "double standard" in regard to Middle East terror—and attributed it to Israel's "formidable political and propaganda force in this country in the form of six million Jews". Pierpoint complained that the US has expressed "outrage" at the Munich slaying of Israeli athletes but "next to no outcry" at either Israeli raids against "Palestinian refugee camps" in Lebanon or the Libyan jet disaster.'[34] This disaster was the shooting down by Israel of a Libyan commercial airliner.

Relationships between Jews and African Americans in the US have also devolved into a new militancy. These relationships have changed. Gone are the days of songs about the Jordan and freedom. Now the Jews are seen as contributors to black oppression. African Americans have edged out sympathy for Jews:

> By the early seventies it appeared that major elements of the Protestant churches, both clerical and lay, had become so pre-occupied with the problems of blacks in America that they no longer considered anti-Semitism a problem at all but rather a phenomenon of the past … the pecking order of victims in need of help has changed.[35]

Even the sound assessment of the Quakers is not acceptable. In one of their documents, described by Forster and Epstein as 'allegedly "objective"', the Quakers make the following suggestion: [36]

As American Jews, most of whom have a strong sense of identity with Israel, search for ways to express their concern and support, we urge them to make special efforts to explore the variety of options available for peace in the Middle East, *to reject simplistic military solutions*, and to encourage calm and deliberate examination of all the issues. The same admonitions, of course, apply to all other groups which attempt to influence public opinion and government action towards the Middle East.[37]

It is difficult to understand how this statement qualifies as being antisemitic. The Quakers are pacifists, and their advice is extended to people other than Jews. The only thing that worries the authors must be that there is any mention of the connection at all between American Jews and Israel.

Politically aware Jews and African Americans see parallels between the latter and the Palestinians. The African Americans are widely sympathetic to Islam, with some of their organisations being, in effect, Islamic. Therefore some Jews are joining the support for far right anti-Muslim bodies. This came to the attention of Britain over the activities of the British far-right activist, Tommy Robinson. He has been imprisoned on several occasions for offences associated with the activities of extreme right-wing, racist political parties.

One of the American groups involved in supporting extreme racists is the David Horowitz Freedom Center, which is notorious for its attacks on Muslims and is a major Robinson supporter. Horowitz told *The Guardian* in an email:

Tommy Robinson is a courageous Englishman who has risked his life to expose the rape epidemic of young girls conducted by Muslim gangs and covered up by your shameful government.[38]

Another wealthy Jew, Nina Rosenwald—described as 'the sugar mama of anti-Muslim hate'—gave substantial amounts to the Middle East Forum which spent some of the money on Robinson's legal fees and on anti-Muslim demonstrations in London.[39] In general, the attitude towards Jews in the United States, it is often claimed, has deteriorated.

Britain, like America, has had to cope with the political force of Jews, even though there is only a small number in Britain. In response to a question about religion in the 2011 census, 263,346 people answered that they were Jewish. This is likely to be an underestimate, since the question was voluntary. It could be that Jews may be suspicious of questions about religion and ethnicity, and Haredi Jews have a low response rate.[40] It may also be the case that there are ethnic Jews who have no wish to be identified as such.

Ever since Britain created the mayhem which is the history of Palestine, events there have posed problems for British governments. After the fighting which led to the foundation of Israel, relationships between the two countries deteriorated.

New Lamps For Old?

This began, as we have seen, with the Suez Crisis. For Tory leaders such as Margaret Thatcher, policy towards Israel presented a number of problems. First, like most of her party, she would be inclined to support Israel against the Arabs in general, and the Palestinians in the form of the PLO, in particular. Secondly, British governments are always reluctant to deviate from the stand taken by Americans. She and other important Conservatives relied heavily on 'the Jewish vote' in their constituencies, as was expressed by the *Sunday Express* which wrote at the time of Suez:

> 'This is the fellow who relies on the Jewish vote to keep him in his shaky Willesden seat ... when the election comes in the New Year, let the Jews of Willesden recall the present performance of Mr Orbach'. In the ensuing General Election, he lost his seat.[41]

Despite the manifest support for Israel among the rulers of Britain, the Foreign Office, later the Foreign and Commonwealth Office, was often quoted as being hostile to Israel's ambition: perhaps because of the bitter memories of the mandate.

> Argov and leading members of Israel's Likud government believed that the difficult legacy of the mandate period had encouraged leading FCO officials to take a vindictive approach towards Israel ... Thatcher was no exception.[42]

But the Palestinians were not without friends. A letter written by Shlomo Argov, a distinguished ambassador to Britain, 'included a detailed report of a meeting with Robert McCrindle, a Conservative MP and CFI [Conservative Friends of Israel] member on the left of the party.'

> McCrindle revealed that Israel's friends within the Conservative party were being 'alienated' by the present Israeli government and by Begin, in particular. He mentioned that several members of the CFI had left the organisation, and that support for Israel within parliament was diminishing. The bombing of the Iraqi nuclear reactor [7 June 1981] had been a factor in this drop of support.[43]

The loyalty of parliamentarians was being tested. Margaret Thatcher was guest of honour at a dinner of the Board of Deputies in December 1981. In her speech she said:

> It was with great concern that I learned last night of the decision of the Government of Israel and the Knesset to extend Israeli law, jurisdiction and administration to occupied Syrian territory in the Golan Heights ... Mr President, the inadmissibility of the acquisition of territory by war is enshrined

in UN Resolution 242. Therefore I say with the sorrow of a friend that this latest move is harmful to the search for peace.

Such remarks are unacceptable. In a vote of thanks after a speech by Lord Carrington in autumn 1981, a former president of the Board of Deputies, said: 'I would be far from honest and less than sincere were I not to say that much of what you said made us shiver in our bones.'[44]

Once again, this reaction demonstrates the fact that the supporters of Zionism cannot accept any criticism of Israel, as reflected in these remarks by two important proponents of the 'new antisemitism':

> World Jewry would indeed be distressed to discover that some British attitudes toward Israel reflect more than a yearning for the days of empire, that despite the current security of English Jewry and its representation in all areas of British life, including Parliament, there are undercurrents of anti-Semitism in Great Britain not restricted to overt hostility to Israel ... Of course one can be unsympathetic to or oppose Israel's position on specific issues without being anti-Jewish. But many of the anti-Israel statements from non-Jewish sources, often the most respectable, carry an undeniable anti-Jewish message. Some of the public utterances that pass for legitimate discussion mask a real hostility to Jews as Jews; they are often couched in language or contain innuendo that is plainly anti-Semitic.[45]

Forster and Epstein, the authors of this statement, see the 'new antisemitism' everywhere. Russia is a particular target. In describing the discrimination against Jews in the Soviet Union, they write of 'dissemination at home and abroad of anti-Semitic propaganda under the guise of anti-Zionist criticism'.[46]

They discuss the case of a Russian Jew called Boris Kochubiyevsky. He wrote a paper 'Why I am a Zionist', which contained the phrase: 'Anti-Zionism is nothing but anti-Semitism'. He also defended the Six-Day War. In May 1969 he appeared in court charged with disseminating 'anti-Soviet slander'. He got three years.[47] The authors attribute his treatment entirely to the fact that he was a Jew, but this haphazard treatment happens, however deplorable, to other Russians who criticise the actions of the government.

Those who define the new antisemitism see its manifestation in culture and entertainment: not only in traditional texts, such as *The Merchant of Venice*, but in more contemporary work. In 1948 the Dickens novel *Oliver Twist* was made into a film, one of the central characters being the Jew Fagin. The exaggerated traits of character were still enough to provoke accusations that his portrayal was antisemitic. 'That was, I believe,' said Guinness later, 'about the only time since the war when the Russians and the Americans united in protest ... It was so ridiculous, because we fell over backwards to ensure even that the word "Jew" shouldn't be mentioned'. But in New York, where soon after the film was shown, he was playing in *The Cocktail Party*, a hostess at a party said to him, 'I wonder you dare to come. I'd rather give my children prussic acid than let them see your picture.' David Lean, the director, sent film tests to America for approval: America said 'no' to the nose. 'To hell with them', Lean responded.[48]

Forster and Epstein wanted to ban the popular musical and the film *Jesus Christ Superstar*. It is a Passion Play and is 'virtually *Oberammergau*'.[49] They refer here to the famous German Passion Play, which they would also like to see banned. They object to the portrayal of Jews as responsible for the Crucifixion, because the authors of the musical 'chose to preserve the ancient lie of an evil conspiracy by scribes, Pharisees, high priests and others whom the audiences knew to be Jewish'.[50] At the same time they 'chose to whitewash the character of Pontius Pilate'.[51]

> For Jews the rock opera was a disaster mitigated only by the facts that the lyrics were often unintelligible and that New York theatre prices might well keep many people, even those who liked rock music, away.[52]

They have other targets. One is the film version of Philip Roth's novel *Portnoy's Complaint*. This film is deplored because in it 'Jews were demeaned in a parade of anti-Semitic stereotypes'.[53] The 1967 novel, upon which the film was based, was 'a runaway best-seller, [which] could readily have been used to reinforce anti-Semitic stereotypes in some minds and create them in others'.[54] Such films are contrasted with the musical and movie *Fiddler on the Roof*. This 'spoke of the triumph of a faith, Judaism, and a people [who] surmounted extreme adversity, perpetual poverty, harassment and expulsion.'[55]

Objections to any adverse portrayal of Jews is not confined to stage and screen. On 24 June 1971 there appeared an advertisement for a book about one of the most infamous criminals in the United States. His name was Meyer Lansky. He was Jewish, and the advertisement said 'Jews control crime in the United States'. The Anti-Defamation League complained, and was told by the publishers that there were links between Lansky and Israel and that the headline had 'allegedly been run in an Israeli paper'. The president of the publishing company said that he was 'sorry to see ADL "leaping to the defence of people such as Meyer Lansky"'.[56] This assault on free speech has much wider ramifications than a few obscure objections to portrayals in plays or books. It is a by-product of the Holocaust, but because of the attendant horror of that event, the dangerous curbing of free speech is not discussed, and rarely deplored.

The Holocaust has had a malign, restricting effect on freedom of speech. Even before the war, as rumours began to circulate about the murder of Jews in Germany, there were claims that these were false. After the war, despite the wealth of evidence from victims, witnesses, including such prominent figures as

General Eisenhower, who visited camps to see for himself, and the war trials, there were those who insisted that the massacres had not taken place. Such people have come to be known as Holocaust deniers. Their denials take several forms. They claim, variously, that the whole story is a fabrication, that there were no concentration camps, no exterminations, and perhaps most pernicious and persuasive of all, that the numbers have been exaggerated. The response to these denials has been seriously damaging.

Denial has been made a criminal or civil offence in seventeen countries, and so the act of speaking has been outlawed. The British historian David Irving was the target of such a law. In 2006 he was sentenced to three years imprisonment in Austria for 'incitement to racial hatred' because he denied the existence of the gas chambers. The case of Ernst Zundel illustrates the complications of attempts to restrict free speech.

Zundel was born in Germany in 1939, and emigrated to Canada. He set up a publishing business, Samisdat Press, which *inter alia* printed neo-Nazi material. In 1983 a Holocaust survivor began a legal action, later supported by the Ontario government, which resulted in Zundel being charged with 'spreading false news and that is likely to cause mischief to the public interest in social and religious tolerance'. This was because of a book issued from his press entitled *Did Six Million Really Die? The Truth at Last* by Richard Verrall. He was tried in 1985, but acquitted on a technicality. He was tried again in 1988 and found guilty. In 1992 the Supreme Court of Canada acquitted him because the section of the law under which he had been charged was a violation of the rights of freedom of expression under the Canadian Charter of Rights and Freedoms. He then went to the United States, but was deported back to Canada because he had contravened immigration rules, and in Canada he was issued with a national security certificate because of his alleged links with neo-Nazi groups. He was deported to Germany on 1 March 2005, and there charged with inciting racial hatred, the charges actually being about his Holocaust denial. In February 2007 he was sentenced to five years, the maximum the law decreed.

Several countries, including the United Kingdom and the United States (conscious of the First Amendment) have refused to pass legislation to outlaw Holocaust denial. In those countries which have passed legislation, the effect has been traumatic for the principle of free speech. This is because these pernicious laws, derived from the Holocaust, have set a lamentable precedent. The result has been that increasingly any comment about any defined group is illegal. In Britain, although Holocaust denial is not an offence, the precedent in other countries has led to a more general prohibition. An early example of this was the passing of the Race Relations Act of 1965. This makes it illegal to make any statement which is 'likely to cause racial hatred'. Under this act in 1967 a right-wing British political activist, Colin Jordan, was sentenced to eighteen months for his public remarks, not about Jews, but about 'coloured' people.

So an important by-product of the Holocaust is the increasing amount of legislation which prevents free speech. The only way to deal with lies and absurd opinions is to draw attention to that absurdity, not to punish its expression. Refusing to let people speak does not stop any particular belief: the only way to eradicate lies is to answer them with evident fact. Any utterly absurd statement must be demonstrably absurd. The demand of those who would censor is that 'unsuitable' statements, even if true or questionable, must be replaced by more 'acceptable' versions of events. Forster and Epstein demonstrate this. They discussed the murder of a PLO official, Mahomed Hamchar (or Hamshari) in Paris. He died, they wrote, 'when a bomb exploded in his home'. This 'was immediately denounced as the work of Israeli terrorists; the charge was made by far leftists, Arabs, and less blatantly, by a large part of the French press and electronic media'—that is to say the allegation was not true.[57] Bergman, however, in his account of the workings of the Israeli security service, describes exactly what happened. Hamchari's movements were watched, and while he was out of his flat, a bomb was planted there by an Israeli team called Rainbow and when the victim answered the telephone, the bomb was detonated.[58]

It is worth mentioning at this point that Israel has won another record, which is a lineal descendant from the Days of Terror. It is for the murder of those who threaten it:

> Since the Second World War, Israel has assassinated more people than any other country in the Western world. On innumerable occasions, its leaders have weighed what would be the best way to defend its national security and, out of all the options, have time and again decided on clandestine operations, with assassination the method of choice. This, they believed, would solve the difficult problems faced by the state, and sometimes change the course of history. In many cases, Israel's leaders have even determined that in order to kill the designated target, it is moral and legal to endanger the lives of innocent civilians who may happen to find themselves in the line of fire ... Up until the writing of this book [published 2018], Israel has executed some 800 targeted killing operations, almost all of which were part of the rounds of war against Hamas in the Gaza Strip in 2008, 2012 and 2014 or Mossad operations across the Middle East against Palestinians, Syrian, and Iranian targets. By contrast, during the presidency of George W. Bush, the United States of America carried out 48 targeted killing operations, according to one estimate, and under President Barack Obama there were 353 such attacks.[59]

It is now appropriate to discuss the phenomenon of the 'new antisemitism' in more detail. A good deal of literature has accrued which seeks to claim that it does not exist and also that is does exist, and that assuming that it does, what forms it takes. It certainly is prominent in news coverage. Whatever the motives may be, one is certain: it is to deflect away the increasing world condemnation of the treatment of Palestinians, and this is its most important aim. Political and military actions have greatly increased animosity towards Israel, an animosity which began to be serious after the Six-Day War. The problem for the Israelis was in how to counter the hostility felt, and manifested by governments and individuals throughout the world. By the beginning of the twenty-first century, Israel had become virtually a pariah state:

> Abnormality is the new normal. Israel now looks like a pioneer of illiberal, ethnographic nationalism, a model for the likes of Orbán, Modi and Trump.[60]

And since allegations against Israel, notably about the treatment of Palestinians, were much stronger and more rational than such classic beliefs that Jews drank blood, for example, denigration of Israel had to be dealt with. The solution is to conflate antisemitism with contempt for the state of Israel, so that any criticism of the latter in not explained by distaste for Israeli behaviour, but is instead antisemitism in a new, yet ancient manifestation.

The 'new antisemitism' first came into public debate at the end of the twentieth century. Its advocates would claim that the establishment of the state of Israel has provoked old prejudices, and that this is based, not upon the rights and wrongs of the matter of Palestinians, but upon the naked hatred of Jews. The political right wing used to be accused of stoking antisemitism, but now everyone is accused:

> Although traditional Trotskyite ideology is in no way close to radical Islamic teachings and the shariah, since the radical Islamists also subscribed to anti-capitalism, anti-globalism, and anti-Americanism, there seemed to be sufficient common ground for an alliance. Thus the militants of the far left began to march side by side with the radical Islamists in demonstrations, denouncing American aggression and Israeli crimes ... and it was only natural that in protest demonstrations militants from the far right would join in, anti-Semitic banners would be displayed, and anti-Jewish literature such as the *Protocols* would be sold. *The Protocols of the Elders of Zion* is a book purporting to describe a Jewish plan to take over the world. Dating from the early twentieth century it is a mixture of fabrication and plagiarism. It is still widely available in many languages.[61]

Traditional political creeds and alignments have to be redefined. The result is that now the political left wing is guilty as well. The sometime foreign minister of Israel, Abba Eban, is a representative voice:

> The new left is the author and progenitor of the new anti-Semitism. One of the chief tasks of any dialogue with the Gentile world is to prove that that the

distinction between anti-Semitism and anti-Zionism is not a distinction at all. Anti-Zionism is merely the new anti-Semitism.[62]

Noam Chomsky discusses this statement, and concludes that: 'There is no sensible charge. No sensible charge. There is nothing to respond to. It's not a form of anti-Semitism. It's simply a criticism of the criminal actions of a state, period.'[63]

Some features of the new antisemitism includes advocacy of the banning of contacts with Israel in commerce and culture for instance, or Holocaust denial, or claiming that Israel is a 'racist state'. A persistent complaint is that subjecting Israel to a harsher criticism than is applied to other countries is antisemitism. It is also suggested that the anti-globalisation movement is a source of antisemitism, and that the United Nations readily condemns Israel's behaviour, but is reluctant to criticise countries which have a much worse human rights record.

Are such fears new? Or are they simply more publicised? These questions are of special concern and debate among Jewish writers. Forster and Epstein summarise their opinions thus:

> Indifference to the most profound apprehension of the Jewish people; a blandness and apathy in dealing with anti-Jewish behaviour: a widespread incapacity or unwillingness to understand and an inability to comprehend the necessity of the existence of Israel to Jewish safety and survival throughout the world. This is the heart of the new anti-Semitism.[64]

These and a number of other political trends, it is claimed, are expressed in antisemitic terms, in word and deed. Supporters of Islam, and members of 'extremist' parties, both left and right, are guilty. The main target of attacks on Jews is the behaviour of Israel, especially in its treatment of Palestinians. Attacks on one is tantamount to attacks on both, and no distinction can be made between the motives for such attacks.

The definition of a new antisemitism does not go without challenge. A commonly made criticism of the notion of a new antisemitism is that it is designed to silence criticism of Israel. This is the view of Norman Finkelstein, who has written that organisations such as the Anti-Defamation League, whose headquarters are in America, have used 'new antisemitism' 'not to fight anti-Semitism but rather to exploit the historical suffering of Jews in order to immunise Israel against criticism'.[65] Almost all of the efforts since by Jewish pressure groups has been to 'conflate'—a favourite word—the two. Earl Raab is one writer who accepts that there is a 'new antisemitism', but is critical of its confusion with criticism of Israel.[66]

A very good example of the wielding of the force of the 'new antisemitism', was the furore over the leader of the British Labour party, Jeremy Corbyn. This is an important issue, because it made an impact on British political thinking about Israel, and therefore on the future of the Palestinians. The election of Jeremy

Corbyn as leader of the British Labour party in 2015 came as a surprise, not to say shock, for the British political establishment. Worse was to come, since in the years after his election, large numbers of young people joined the Labour party, demonstrating support for Corbyn, thus increasing membership to over half a million. The next three years were to witness widespread attempts by the right wing of the Labour party, and most of the press, to discredit him mainly as being too radical, and therefore unelectable. The size of membership of the party is, of course, no guarantee of electoral success, but despite dire predictions, the election of June 2017 showed the biggest increase in Labour's share of the vote since 1945.

One of the most ferocious attacks centred on the allegation that Corbyn is antisemitic: 'The favourite—and perhaps the most persistent—of the many lines of attack employed so far is the charge of anti-Semitism.'[67] This is the matter to be addressed here, since it is a clear example of the way in which Jewish lobbies blur the distinction between antisemitism and criticism of Israel. There are two elements to this. The first is the need by lobbies to make any separation of criticism of Israel, and antisemitism, impossible, and the second is the marshalling of evidence against Corbyn and the Labour party, to reduce, or eliminate, any chance of electoral success. The process was summed up by the prominent Labour party member Ken Livingstone, a central figure in these episodes:

> Frankly, there's been an attempt to smear Jeremy Corbyn and his associates as anti-Semitic from the moment he became leader. The simple fact is we have the right to criticise what is one of the most brutal regimes going in the way it treats the Palestinians.[68]

The evidence against Corbyn was marshalled from a time before he was elected leader. This is an example from some five years before he became leader:

> Jeremy Corbyn has apologised for 'concerns and anxiety caused' after taking part in an event where the actions of Israel in Gaza were compared to the actions of the Nazis. His apology appeared on a Friday—the Jewish Sabbath—so that the issue was inflamed further, because it was widely claimed, he was advised by Jewish organisations that he should not do so, but his ignoring this advice was perceived as deliberate contempt.[69]

This went back to an event on Holocaust Memorial Day in 2010 called 'Never Again for anyone—Auschwitz to Gaza'. The main talk was given by Hajo Meyer, a Jewish survivor of that camp:

> He [Meyer] repeatedly compared Israeli action in Gaza to the mass killing of Jews in the Holocaust.[70]

After Corbyn became leader, he was under attack for another reason, once again because of his action some years earlier, this time in January 2011. In that month his colleague, John McDonnell, was the prime sponsor of early day motion 1360 in parliament, with Corbyn listed as a sponsor. There were twenty-three supporters. The motion in part read:

> Nazism targeted not only Jewish but also Roma, Jehovah's Witnesses, lesbian, gay and bisexual people and others they deemed undesirable: and [Parliament] therefore supports the call for international awareness of all communities and countries who have suffered and resisted mass extermination by renaming Holocaust Memorial Day as Genocide Memorial Day—Never Again For Anyone.

The reaction was predictable. It was widely claimed that this was certain evidence of Corbyn's antisemitism, and more generally in the Labour party, with the response including a defence that the suffering of groups other than Jews were commemorated on the Day, including for example those murdered in the Rwandan genocide. But what really upset the Jewish groups was the seeming attempt to dilute the exclusivity of the Jewish claim to be the central victims, and so there was a manifest unwillingness to share the remembrance of Nazi horror. This was summed up in the widely reported claim by Karen Pollock, chief executive of the Holocaust Educational Trust:

> The Holocaust was a specific crime, with anti-semitism at its core. Any attempt to remove that specificity is a form of denial and distortion.

At the same time, many allegations were made by members of the Labour party about fellow members. It was reported that the party had received '637 complaints about members in the past year, but only twelve have been expelled'.[71] Luciana Berger, then a Liverpool MP and chair of the Jewish Labour Movement in parliament, complained about Jeremy Corbyn's attitude to the allegations of antisemitism in the Labour party. She pointed out that Jews no longer felt welcome in the Labour party, saying 'there is no place for us in the Party anymore, and that Corbyn should do more'. Additionally, she related how she suffered a constant barrage of personal abuse.[72] Some of this abuse she alleged came from members of her own party. This was confirmed when a member wrote that Berger should be 'exposed for the disruptive Zionist she is', and that she was a member of the 'old guard'. All of this led to the proposal of a motion of no confidence in Berger:

> The moves against Berger were not motivated by anti-Semitism and accused the MP of consistently failing to represent the views of members and to support the

Labour party. Some would say this latter criticism derives from her allegedly being 'disloyal to Jeremy Corbyn'.[73]

Ms Berger was one of seven Labour MPs who resigned from the party on 18 February 2019, citing the party's failure to address antisemitism.

Another of those who resigned, Gavin Schuker, claimed in his statement that 'today the Labour Party is riddled with anti-Semitism'.[74] At the same time it became known that the Jewish Labour Movement might disaffiliate from the Labour party after ninety-nine years. On 19 February 2019, another Labour MP left the party. This was Joan Ryan, chair of the Labour Friends of Israel, and she gave as her reason that Corbyn was 'presiding over a culture of anti-Semitism and hatred of Israel'. The Labour party 'was institutionally anti-Semitic'.[75] It may be noted that Ms Ryan is here conflating antisemitism and 'hatred' of Israel. On 22 February another Labour MP, Ian Austin, resigned. He was adopted and brought up in a Jewish family, and he quoted antisemitism as one of his reasons for leaving. A common reaction in the party was expressed by a key trade unionist, Len McCluskey. He commented on the reasons for the seven leaving, and in respect of the charges of antisemitism, said:

> The party is now tackling this evil with a new energy, including expelling members. The International Holocaust Remembrance Alliance's definition of anti-Semitism has been adopted by the party. It is not clear what more Labour is expected to do.[76]

In early March, Chris Williamson, MP for Derby North, was suspended because he said that Labour had been 'too apologetic' over the allegations of antisemitism. He then apologised for his remarks, thus in a sense proving his point. The Board of Deputies of British Jews, predictably, described the suspension as 'half hearted'. There was allegedly pressure for Williamson to be dismissed from the party, and that Corbyn had intervened to lessen this to suspension: an allegation which was denied.

Margaret Hodge, a very senior figure in the parliamentary Labour party, was a leader in the attack on Corbyn. She is quoted as saying that 'if they are his mates he doesn't demonstrate zero tolerance'. She claims that he assured her that he did not intervene in disciplinary proceedings over antisemitism, but a 'whistleblower' had published a statement to the contrary.[77] According to a BBC news broadcast on 18 July 2018, she faced 'action' by the party after swearing at Corbyn and calling him an antisemite in the House of Commons. She did not confirm the words used but she wrote in *The Guardian* that she 'confronted Jeremy Corbyn in parliament and told him to his face what I and many others are feeling ... Labour was so distrusted by the Jewish community, we are the last people on earth, at this time, who should think about amending a widely accepted definition of anti-Semitism'. Her complaint is that Corbyn led Labour party objections to the acceptance of a proposed International Holocaust Remembrance Alliance, to which we will return.

'The Israel–Palestine conflict,' she said, had been 'allowed to infect the party's approach to growing anti-Semitism'. She said that she and other Jewish MPs had been receiving growing amounts of antisemitic abuse. Margaret Hodge became a rally leader for criticism of Corbyn. A full-page article she wrote in *The Guardian* is headed 'Anti-Semitism under Corbyn is growing like a cancer'.[78] He should close down branches 'that minimise the scale of the problem'. 'It has moved from individuals saying terrible things to motions being passed.' Such motions included those in which parties expressed support for Chris Williamson, the MP suspended for suggesting that Labour had been 'too apologetic' about antisemitism, or rejecting the 'internationally accepted definition of anti-Semitism'. She produced a list of forty-four cases of alleged antisemitism adding 'and I would expel most of them' (presumably without a hearing). She made the surprising statement that she 'never brought her Jewish identity into her politics'.

Allegations of antisemitism went beyond Corbyn. Several members of the Labour party were also accused, the most prominent being Ken Livingstone, a former mayor of London and a nationally known political figure. In April 2017 in a newspaper article entitled 'Eight dodgy things Ken Livingstone has said about Jews and Hitler', it was pointed out that when Livingstone was editor of the *Labour Herald* an article appeared 'alleging that Zionists prevented the rescue of European Jewry from the Holocaust'.[78] There was also a cartoon which depicted Menachem Begin, then Israeli prime minister in Nazi uniform, standing over a heap of corpses giving the Nazi salute over the heading 'The Final Solution'. In the report of a radio interview, it was recorded that Livingstone said:

> Let's remember that when Hitler won his election in 1932, his policy then was that Jews should be moved to Israel. He was supporting Zionism—this before he went mad and ended up killing six million Jews.[79]

On other occasions Livingstone denied that he had said anything as crude as Hitler was a Zionist, and drew attention to the Haavara Agreement signed by German Jews and the Nazi government in 1933. This enabled Jews to emigrate to Palestine, and by a complex arrangement, buy and export German goods and save some of their money. Livingstone drew attention to the fact that the Nazi SS set up training camps for Jews so that 'they could be trained to cope with a very different sort of country when they got there'.[80] The agreement was a matter of violent dispute among Jews, as we have seen, and one of the negotiators, Haim Arlosoroff, was murdered. The agreement did exist and it did function as Livingstone said. Not that the attacks upon him stopped, despite other attempts to defend himself and his party:

> I've heard a lot of criticism of the state of Israel and its abuse of Palestinians but I've never heard anyone say anything anti-Semitic.

And in the same interview he said:

> If I was to criticise the South African government as riddled with corruption you wouldn't say I was racist—you'd say I was being critical of that government.

As a result of the constant criticism, pressure forced his suspension in April 2016, notably because of his Zionist–Hitler equation, and in May 2018 he resigned from the party because the matter was becoming a 'distraction'. His case was not helped because of his support for another Labour MP Naz Shah. In 2014, before she became an MP, she 'shared' an image on social media which consisted of a map of Israel superimposed upon a map of the United States with a headline: 'Solution for Israel–Palestinian conflict—relocate Israel into United States: problem solved'. She was duly suspended by the Labour party and she immediately apologised on the radio, to the House of Commons, in a synagogue, and in *Jewish News*. She agreed that her language had been antisemitic—she said the 'the Jews are rallying'—and that what she had said and done was due to her 'ignorance'. She was reinstated in the party in July 2016.

When she was elected to parliament, Naz Shah ousted George Galloway in a very acrimonious campaign. But Galloway, writing in the *Herald Tribune*, emphasised the fact that here again Corbyn was the target:

> The Naz Shah affair is just another straw being laid on the back of Corbyn, and it may prove to be the last one. It is part of a bigger, wider political operation being mounted by supporters of Israel to redefine not just the political narrative but the language itself.[81]

He concluded that her comments 'are not anti-Semitic'.

Other lesser-known Labour activists have been targeted. Jenny Rathbone was a member of the Welsh Assembly. At a constituency meeting in 2018 she made remarks which were recorded and passed on to *The Jewish Chronicle*. Speaking of the increased security at a Cardiff synagogue, she said:

> The fact that the Jewish synagogue in Cyncoed is behind this fortress is really uncomfortable ... and how much of it is for real and how much of it is in their own heads is really hard for an outsider to judge. But I think siege mentality is part of this.

She went on to express the opinion that hate crimes were a reaction to 'the failure to come to a peace settlement around Palestine and Israel'. Israel's behaviour, she said, 'drives people to be hostile to the Jewish community in this country'.[82] There followed protests, a suspension from the Welsh National Assembly Labour Group, and the usual, familiar apologies. She said that her comments were 'extremely offensive', and a rabbi reported that she had been very apologetic.

Several features of this, and similar cases, may be noted. The first is that her remarks about the fortress were tinged with regret that such security was necessary. The second is that this was a fair comment on a matter of public interest. And the third is that Israel's policies towards the Palestinians are regarded by many in Britain as deplorable, and to voice these is simply to reflect commonly held opinion. Such remarks are not illegal, but are arguably in the remit of the all embracing definition of antisemitism.

It is extremely odd that a major source of the interminable attacks on Corbyn came from a Labour member of parliament, John Mann. It is from his position as chair of the All-Party Parliamentary Group Against Anti-Semitism that he mounted incessant attacks upon Corbyn and other members of his own party, notably Ken Livingstone. He deplored the fact that Corbyn 'is not prepared to make a speech exclusively, explicitly, just on anti-Semitism'.[83] This, despite the fact that Corbyn has said repeatedly that antisemitism would not be tolerated in the Labour party. A typical outburst was about Corbyn's presence at the speech by the Holocaust survivor, described earlier. Mann said it was 'extraordinary for an MP to have hosted such an event'.[84] Mann went on to attack the hesitation about agreeing to the definition of antisemitism which was being canvassed. In his view Labour 'should now adopt in full the definition of anti-Semitism accepted by the International Holocaust Remembrance Alliance.'

Lord Mann, as he subsequently became, continued his campaign after Labour's defeat at the election, a result to which he contributed so much. In his new role as 'Independent Advisor on Anti-Semitism' to the new Conservative government, he was joint author of a study associated with the rise of Covid-19. This study insists that: 'exposing the level of anti-Semitism among anti-vaxxer movements is of the utmost importance', and that antisemitic and anti-vaccination conspiracy theories will become more acute.[85]

There is an argument that the Labour party is the natural political home for Jews because of its history of tolerance. The view is constantly expressed by Jewish groups that this supposed antisemitism in the Labour party will result in Jews declining to vote Labour, and this will affect the party's prospects. There is very little evidence that more Jews vote Labour than for any other party. Laura Janner-Klausner, the senior rabbi to Reform Judaism and a long-standing Labour member, said there was 'no Jewish way to vote'.[86] Where there are Jewish Labour voters, their support for the party can, it seems, be easily shaken. When Ed Miliband was leader, Maureen Lipman, a well-known public figure in entertainment, announced she would not be voting Labour, in part because of antisemitism in the party, but also because Miliband's support for recognising the state of Palestine 'sucks'. She goes on to claim that 'the Jewish community is preparing to break with Labour's first Jewish Leader', and that Miliband 'needs to ask why'.[87]

The main attack on Corbyn centred on the issue of the International Holocaust Remembrance Alliance (IHRA) guidelines. He was reluctant to support these and his refusal became a major weapon to be wielded against him. Because of this controversy, and because of the claims and counter-claims about the meaning of some of its contents, it is set out below. Its source was the EU Monitoring Centre on Racism and Xenophobia, later the EU Agency for Fundamental Rights. In 2005 it formulated a 'working definition of anti-Semitism', later the International Definition of Anti-Semitism. Several governments and agencies accepted it. These included, as examples, the European parliament, the US Department of State, the UK College of Policing, and the British government. But it has also been pointed out that some of the agencies which have 'accepted' the document have somewhat bowdlerised the content:

> What I did not appreciate then was, first, that the IHRA text was not original but had been retrieved from the files of two other bodies which had never adopted it; second, that the 'examples' had been added to the adopted text; and, third, that the content of the versions adopted by UK institutions and bodies (and by governments such as those of Austria and Romania) has itself been variable.[88]

The definitions include 'but are not limited to' the following:

- Calling for, aiding, or justifying the killing or harming of Jews in the name of a radical ideology or an extremist view of religion.
- Making mendacious, dehumanising, demonising, or stereotypical allegations about Jews as such or the power of Jews as collective—such as, especially but not exclusively, the myth about a world Jewish conspiracy or of Jews controlling the media, economy, government or other societal institutions.
- Accusing Jews as a people of being responsible for real or imagined wrongdoing committed by a single Jewish person or group, or even for acts committed by non-Jews.
- Denying the fact, scope, mechanisms (e.g. gas chambers) or intentionality of the genocide of the Jewish people at the hand of National Socialist Germany and its supporters and accomplices during the Second World War (the Holocaust).
- Accusing the Jews as a people, or Israel as a state, of inventing or exaggerating the Holocaust.
- Accusing Jewish citizens of being more loyal to Israel, or to the alleged priorities of Jews worldwide, than to the interests of their own nations.
- Denying the Jewish people their right to self-determination (e.g. by claiming that the existence of a State of Israel is a racist endeavour).

- Applying double standards by requiring of Israel a behaviour not expected or demanded of any other democratic nation.
- Using the symbols and images associated with classic anti-Semitism (e.g. claims of Jews killing Jesus or blood libel to characterise Israel or Israelis).
- Drawing comparisons of contemporary Israeli policy to that of the Nazis.
- Holding Jews collectively responsible for actions of the state of Israel.

Several opinions were sought as to the legality of the contents of this document, whether it contradicted other accepted policies, and whether the contents could be married up with existing law. The Campaign Against Anti-Semitism sought, and promulgated, the opinion of two lawyers, David Wolfson and Jeremy Brier.[89] They expressed the opinion that: 'Criticism of Israel, even in robust terms, cannot be regarded as anti-Semitic *per se* and such criticism is not captured by the Definition'.[90] But they go on to make a *caveat* which effectively negates this last remark:

> However, criticisms of Israel in terms which are channels of expression for hatred towards Jewish people (such as by particular invocations of the Holocaust or Nazism) will in all likelihood be anti-Semitic.[91]

Their overall conclusions are supportive:

> The Definition is a clear, meaningful and workable definition [and] there is no danger or disadvantage for public bodies or universities in adopting this Definition. It does not seek to stifle free expression or free speech and poses no issue as regards compliance with Article 10 of the European Convention on Human Rights para 14... On the other hand, adopting such comprehensive and modern definition would appear to serve a very useful purpose and be an important tool in the fight against anti-Semitism and hatred towards Jews.[92]

Opponents of the adoption of the definition would not accept such uncritical glossing over of the restrictive implications in it. A coalition of organisations, sympathetic to the plight of the Palestinians, asked a lawyer, Hugh Tomlinson, for his legal opinion. He gave it in March 2017. He was very critical of much of the wording, both for its potential danger to civil freedom, and more simply because it is badly written. He notes that: 'The definition is unusual and therefore potentially confusing' and that the IHRA definition is 'unsatisfactory'. His conclusion in his last sentence is definite:

> Properly understood in its own terms, the IHRA Definition does not mean that activities such as describing Israel as a state enacting policies of apartheid, as practising settler colonialism or calling for policies of boycott investment or

sanctions against Israel can properly be characterised as anti-Semitism. A public authority which sought to apply the IHRA Definition to prohibit or sanction such activities would be acting unlawfully.[93]

It can be seen that such a view is diametrically opposed to the whole intent of the definition.

Another very distinguished lawyer who has grave doubts about the definition is Stephen Sedley. He is Jewish, and a British ex-appeal court judge. In his article he began by confirming a truism: 'endeavours to conflate the two by characterising everything other than anodyne criticism of Israel as anti-Semitic are not new'. He went on to point out, and in this he echoed Tomlinson, that: it 'fails the first test of any definition: it is indefinite'. Sedley seemed to be especially dissatisfied with the attempt to protect Israel from claims of bad behaviour which would not be made against similar states. Israel is different. The clauses about comparison of Israel with other countries result in:

> Placing the historical, political, military and humanitarian uniqueness of Israel's occupation and colonisation of Palestine beyond permissible criticism.

Sedley then dealt with the question of stifling public criticism and debate:

> It can readily be seen why it may be contrary to law in the UK to bar a speaker or an event because of anticipated criticism of Israel's human rights record, or of its policies and practices of land annexation. If so, the bar cannot be validated by a policy, much less one as protean in character and as open-ended in shape as the IHRA definition.

More seriously, there can be pressures which are successful in preventing discussion:

> In recent times a number of institutions, academic, religious and social, have stood up to pressure to abandon events critical of Israel. What are less easy to track are events which failed to take place because of such pressure, or for fear of it; but the IHRA definition offers encouragement to pro-Israel militants whose target for abuse and disruption in London have recently included the leading American scholar and critic of Israel Richard Falk, and discouragement to university authorities which do not want to act as censors but worry that the IHRA definition requires them to do so.[94]

In the *London Review of Books*, a letter from Karl Sabbagh gives an example of the fear of attack. The author of the book *State of Terror*, Thomas Suàrez, was invited to speak at a Palestine Solidarity Campaign meeting in Portsmouth. On the advice of the local MP, the location was changed three times because 'there might be some trouble from people who were opposed to [his] visit.' The meeting was eventually held in a third location.⁹⁵

Sedley might have added that such militancy is unlikely to reduce criticism of Israel, nor to improve Jewish/Gentile relations. He is one of many who wonder why the Labour party is under such attack because of its supposed antisemitism:

> It may be worth asking why now? How is it that the use of live rounds to shoot unarmed protesters on the Gaza–Israel border (38 of them fatally at the time I write: without much question a major crime) has been pushed off the front pages by the continuing accusation that the Labour Party is riddled with anti-Semitism about which Corbyn can or will do nothing?

Sedley offers one explanation which is that there is an 'undeclared war going on inside the Labour Party' between pro-Israeli groups and pro-Palestinian groups locked in battle.⁹⁶ This is no doubt true, but the main factor in the press onslaught is that alleged antisemitism is as good a reason as any to attack a Labour leader whose policies seem so unnerving. Writers commonly say the same thing:

> While Israel was completing its transition from *de facto* to *de jure* apartheid state by enshrining Jewish only settlements in law. The attention of the British media was [constantly] focused on Corbyn and the Labour Party.⁹⁷

The 'definition' by the IHRA caused enormous controversy, especially since Jeremy Corbyn demurred about signing it. Corbyn was one of many who saw considerable danger in the acceptance of this document, and its incorporation into organisational rules, with the attraction of sanctions in the event of the commission of a very wide definition of antisemitism. There is also the likelihood that pressure groups will try to establish such 'offences' as statute law. If this were to happen this would be a further step in the diminution of free speech, a further progress down the path of censorship which began with the concept of 'Holocaust denial'. This is a development which is well under way.

The objections set out by some members of the Labour party centred on four of the 'examples'. These were that there should be no comparison of Israeli policies with Nazi policies; that it should not be alleged that the creation of the Jewish state was a racist endeavour; that it must not be said that Jews were more loyal to Israel than to their home country; and that Israel should not be expected to have higher standards than any comparable democratic country. Instead of simply accepting the examples, the party set out its own document which, it was claimed, was even firmer in deploring antisemitism. Jon Lansman, a virulent opponent of accepting the IHRA document, wrote:

> Far from lowering the bar for what constitutes anti-Semitism, this code lifts it. It requires a higher standard of behaviour than the IHRA examples do. Labour's code should be seen as the new gold standard.[98]

Lansman goes into some detail about why some members object to the IHRA document. For example with regard to Israel being 'racist':

> This is the one that runs the greatest risk of prohibiting legitimate criticism of Israel. It cannot possibly be anti-Semitic to point out that some of the key policies of the Israeli state, observed since its founding days, have an effect that discriminates on the basis of race and ethnicity.

The essence of the objections set out by Lansman is that the clauses to which exception is taken stifle criticism of Israel. People, he said, should have the right to criticise, including 'other oppressed groups, who have suffered at the hands of discriminatory Israeli state policies'.

> The Palestinians have experienced decades of occupation, gross human rights violations, and war crimes. The Bedouins have had their homes destroyed, the latest example being the demolition of Khan al-Ahmar. And ethnic minorities within Israel have been treated appallingly, such as the Sudanese and Eritrean refugees who have been detained and deported, and questions over the treatment of Ethiopian women, including allegations that they were given birth control without their consent.[99]

Accepting the new Labour code with its rejection of some clauses would imply that the examples set out by Lansman have basis in fact, and justified criticism of Israel. Predictably, therefore, this was totally unacceptable to Jewish parliamentarians, Jewish pressure groups and the Jewish press. There were acrimonious disputes and hyperbolic pronouncements were made:

> One Jewish MP told The *Jewish Chronicle* the decision was one of the worst ever made by the Labour Party ... This is a decision the leadership of the Labour Party will come to regret.[100]

Another senior Labour source added: '"This is a classic fudge"... this is utterly pathetic'. Joan Ryan, chair of the Labour Friends of Israel, was critical:

> The NEC has decided to prioritise the rights of those who wish to demonise and delegitimise the state of Israel over the struggle against anti-Semitism.[101]

The chair of another pressure group, the Jewish Labour Movement, the Labour MP Luciana Berger, whose position has been discussed above, demanded that the definition should be accepted: 'no "ifs" or "buts". It must be adopted in full without any caveats.'¹⁰² In a familiar threat about votes, Barry Rawlings, Labour leader of Barnet Council in London, considered that the episode: 'could be interpreted as institutional racism'. The *Jewish Chronicle* went on pointedly to explain that: 'Barnet has the most Jewish residents of any council in Europe. Labour failed to win control of its council at the local elections in May.' The chair of The Campaign Against Antisemitism (CAA), Gideon Falter, presents the most hysterical blanket condemnation: 'The problem is not one man but an entire movement which has hijacked the anti-racist Labour party of old and corrupted it with a racist rot.'¹⁰³

The response of the Labour party was to appoint Ms Shami Chakrabarti to carry out an 'Inquiry into anti-Semitism and other forms of racism in the Labour Party'. The Shami Chakrabarti Report was published on 30 June 2016. Since the terms of the report included 'other forms of racism' it was unlikely to satisfy the several Jewish interest groups, as this deflected from their only concern, which was antisemitism. The report was summarised, probably fairly, as characterised by her 'warmth and her frequent invocations of Labour values of universalism and human rights [which] suggest an appeal to decency, calmness and common humanity'.¹⁰⁴ Khan-Harris goes on to say that Shami Chakrabarti,

> Doesn't offer an unambiguous definition of anti-Semitism and its relationship to anti-Zionism. She does not point the finger at particular individuals for particular crimes ... some may well be aghast at her rejection of lifetime bans.

The demand for punishment by Jewish lobbies seems infinite. But the problem for them, and their supporters, was that some of the report was taken up with what, to them, was beside the point. Thus Chakrabarti related a story of how she once shared a platform with a former detainee of the notorious Guantanamo Bay, and how she was attacked for it. She discussed the plight of 'refugees drowning in the Mediterranean'. ¹⁰⁵ She recommended 'clear rules, guidance and training and the insertion of a legally qualified panel into the disciplinary process [in the party]' and that 'the largely unchecked power of regional staff should be much more closely supervised'. ¹⁰⁶ A fair amount of the report was focused on training, education, and even language skills.

None of this was likely to commend itself to Jewish groups. They were unsatisfied with references to allegedly parallel minorities and her modest proposals. 'I recommend that the use of racist epithets has no place in the Labour Party'— Zio and Paki are examples.¹⁰⁷ She advised that the term 'Zionist' should be used 'advisedly, carefully and never euphemistically or as part of personal abuse'. This wording is strange—how is the term used euphemistically?—and the result must be that the word should not be used at all. Nor were such groups likely to be satisfied with the broad nature of some of her remarks: 'Whilst my remit is racism, I believe the recommendations that I make here are of wider applicability to all aspects of discipline'.[108] There was also dissatisfaction with the restraint in her observation that 'there is already legislation on "hate speeches or offences"'.[109]

It was certain that the various Jewish groups would not regard the report as adequate. The Parliamentary Select Committee on Anti-Semitism was of the opinion that the inquiry was 'compromised'. Labour's failure lends 'force to allegations that elements of the Labour movement are institutionally anti-Semitic'. Yet this damaging allegation was modified by the opinion that 'there exists no reliable, empirical evidence to support the notion that there is a higher prevalence of anti-Semitic attitudes within the Labour Party than any other political party'.[110]

Further ammunition was available when Ms Chakrabarti was made a life peer shortly after the publication of the report. For the Jewish pressure group, the Community Security Trust, this was 'a shameless kick in the teeth for all who put hope in her now wholly compromised inquiry into anti-Semitism', while the Board of Deputies of British Jews summed the matter up as a 'whitewash for peerages scandal'.[111] Lord Mitchell, a Jewish Labour peer, in discussing Chakrabarti's 'anaemic report on anti-Semitism', said that 'the peerage smacks of a reward for preparing the report that the leadership wanted'.[112] In a withering attack on Corbyn he explains that 'I'm Jewish and I'm very strongly Jewish and I make no bones about it'. The leader, he alleged, was surrounded by allies who were 'hostile to Jews, so in my view, they're pretty bad guys'. Mitchell echoed another familiar complaint when he said that 'when Corbyn mentions it [antisemitism] he combines it with other forms of racism, so he will never specifically deny it'.[113] Mitchell resigned from the Labour party in September 2016.

The question is raised: is there an increase in antisemitism in Britain? In a case which centred on a dispute over the fact that the Agudas Housing Association in London would only rent houses to Orthodox Jews, Lord Sales, a supreme court judge, ruled that this action did not breach the Equality Act of 2010 in respect of race because the charity 'discriminated on religious grounds'. The court accepted that '"because of widespread and increasing overt anti-Semitism", many Haredi Jews faced barriers to renting privately'.[114] Furthermore, the CAA alleges on its website that because of increasing antisemitism,

> 1 in 3 British Jews has considered leaving Britain in the past two years due to anti-Semitism with concern mounting over failures to tackle anti-Semitic crime and anti-Semitism in politics.

Some high profile Jews have recently publicly made such a promise. As well as several Jewish MPs who left the party, some public figures left as well. Lord Alan Sugar, a businessman and television personality, was a Labour supporter. He resigned in May 2015 giving as his ostensible reason the party's 'negative business policies and general anti-enterprise concepts'. However there is an indication of another reason. In the House of Lords he 'continues to be outspoken on Mr Corbyn, especially about his approach to the anti-Semitism crisis'.[115] He went further, threatening to leave the country if a Corbyn government was elected. His distaste for Corbyn was also illustrated when he posted an image of Corbyn's face next to an image of Hitler: anyone it seems is capable of promulgating distasteful images. Even the former general secretary of the Labour party, Lord Triesman, a Jew, argued that the party was 'plainly institutionally anti-Semitic'.[116]

Simon Sebag Montefiore, another eminent Jew, reflected on this putative exodus in an interview reported in *The Times*.[117] In this, Montefiore states:

> I would not stay in England and see my children living in an environment hostile to Jewish people ... It might surprise non-Jewish people to know that virtually every Jewish family I know has discussed leaving Britain because of Labour's anti-Semitism.

He clearly believes in the force of antisemitism in the Labour party, since he talks of 'this vomiting of anti-Semitic venom'. The reporter challenged Montefiore's motives for leaving England, writing that:

> The conversation soon turns to the possibility of removing his family from their 'gilded establishment niche' and fleeing England ... defenders of the Labour leader might consider that Sebag's view on the anti-Semitism row must have a political dimension given his friendships with Cameron, Michael Gove and the like.

When it comes to the question as to where he might go to seek refuge: 'Europe or New York or California'. The choice of America as a haven might seem obvious. But in October 2018, eleven Jews were killed and several injured in one of many shooting sprees in the US. Described as the worst attack on Jews in American history, this may lead him to wonder about his choice. British antisemitism is child's play by comparison.

Montifiore says that he is a critic of Israel, but says, 'I don't use anti-Semitic tropes to do it'. He develops this theme in the interview in the *London Evening Standard*:

> He finds 'deeply evil the oft-aired comparison' of Israeli defence of its own security with the (actions of the Nazis)' ... I don't think for a moment that anyone who criticises Israel is an anti-Semite. I do it myself. However a lot of the criticisms of Israel do derive from a new anti-Semitism which is extremely unpleasant. During the Israeli war in the Lebanon (2006) it really reached a fever pitch which was just absurd.

The use of the word 'war' to describe the butchery in Lebanon may safely be described as a euphemism. And the term 'new antisemitism' should be noted.

Corbyn was under attack throughout his time as leader by many powerful British Jews. The former chief rabbi exemplified the excess of such attacks when he said:

> Mr Corbyn has given support to racists, terrorists and dealers of hate who want to kill Jews and remove Israel from the map.[118]

The campaign against the Labour party reached a new stage in October 2020. In that month there appeared a report by the British Equality and Human Rights Commission (EHRC). It was entitled 'Investigation into anti-Semitism in the Labour Party'. The commission was able to act because the Equality Act of 2010 rules that there must be no discrimination against, harassment or victimisation of its members on the basis of a number of protected characteristics, including race and religion, in political parties.[119]

In 2016 there were three reports on antisemitism: one by a Home Office Select Committee, one by Jan Royall, and one by Shami Chakrabarti.[120] The Chakrabarti Report I have discussed. The Home Office Report looked at the broad issue of alleged antisemitism in the UK, and was much occupied with the awkward question of what the term means. It also debated the question of the International Holocaust Remembrance Alliance document on antisemitism, and illustrated the unpleasantness of material which has appeared on social media. It also quoted the views of some leading Jews, such as Sir Mick Davis, chairman of the Jewish Leadership Council, who 'told us that criticising Zionism is the same as anti-Semitism'. The Home Office committee recommended that the definition should include these clauses:

> It is not anti-Semitic to criticise the government of Israel without additional evidence to suggest anti-Semitic intent.
> It is not anti-Semitic to hold the Israeli government to the same standards as other liberal democracies, or to take a particular interest in the Israeli government's policies or actions, without additional evidence to suggest anti-Semitic intent.

These recommendations were rejected by the British government.

The Royall Report is on alleged antisemitism in the Oxford University Labour Club. This came about because one of the joint chairs resigned because he claimed that its members have 'some kind of a problem with Jews'. Central to this seems to be the support for 'Israel Apartheid Week'. Royall expresses some general opinions (presumably her own) such as 'anti-Semitism often hides behind the rhetoric of anti-Zionism', but her actual conclusion based on the evidence is expressed thus:

> From the weight of witnessed allegations received ... there have been some Incidents of anti-Semitic behaviour ... however, it is not clear to me to what extent this behaviour constituted intentional or deliberate acts of anti-Semitism.[121]

These reports did not satisfy Jewish complainants, and they demanded another. Their dissatisfaction is reflected in the EHRC Report, when it states that the recommendations made in those three reports had not been implemented 'to a satisfactory standard'. This latest action arose from complaints made by the campaign against antisemitism and the Jewish Labour Movement.[122] There were produced 'more than 220 allegations of anti-Semitism within the Labour Party dating back to 2011'.[123] The essential conclusion of this report was that there had been a 'serious failing of leadership'.[124] The commission drew attention to the contrast with procedures for dealing with sexual harassment complaints which were 'far better in several important ways'.[125] The final verdict was:

> We have concluded that there were unlawful acts of harassment and discrimination for which the Labour Party is responsible.[126]

Also that: There is 'a clear breakdown of trust between the Labour Party, many of its members and the Jewish Community.

Perhaps the commission made this conclusion in part because 'over 20 elected representatives ... resigned from the Party in 2018 and 2019 citing a failure to tackle anti-Semitism in their reasons'.[127] On the other hand 'the Labour Party has recently made significant improvements'.[128] It must be supposed that the expulsion of forty-five members of the party in 2019 is considered as part of these 'improvements'.[129]

The consequence of this is that the commission has served 'an unlawful notice act'.[130] This rehearses the commission's findings, singling out 'its agents' Ken Livingstone and Pat Bromley. It demands that the Labour party prepare an 'action plan' to redress the complaints. What evidence does the commission produce for such allegations?

They give examples, such as a complaint from a member of the party that another member said that '[the member] should be held responsible for the actions of the Israeli government'.[131] The offending member was suspended, but did not receive the prescribed 'training'. The commission paid special attention to allegations of antisemitism in social media. Of the seventy complaints they investigated, 'fifty-nine involved conduct on social media'.[132] The commission is notably deficient in making clear to the reader exactly what is in the complaints, but in this case they relate two. These are Holocaust denial and 'Rothschild conspiracy theories'.[133]

Much of the report focuses on poor complaints procedures. The commission found that complaints were not handled properly or were ignored, or when an offence had been confirmed, that the penalties were not heavy enough. Also record keeping was poor. Another substantial part of the report deals with the solution offered to every organisation which is supposed to be defective: education and training. There must be both 'before any individual is allowed to be involved in any stage of the anti-Semitism complaints process'.[134] There had been a failure of 'adequate practical training'. It will be interesting to see what such education might comprise, since it will be directed at mature, experienced, intelligent adults.

There is substantial discussion about 'political interference' in the complaints process. Out of seventy files investigated, in twenty-one there were 'instances of political interference', and they give examples.[135] They paid particular attention to the role of staff in the Leader of the Opposition's Office (LOTO), especially their involvement in decisions on suspension. They found that the office had been much involved and that this 'indirectly discriminated against Jewish members and was unlawful'.[136]

Three individuals were singled out for especial censure by the commission: Naz Shah, Pat Bromley and Ken Livingstone. Pat Bromley, a borough councillor, wrote on Facebook remarks that were drawn to the attention of the commission. The following were included in the report:

> Fake accusations of anti-Semitism. This what, despite international condemnation, Israel does to its neighbour Palestine... all hidden behind a fog of fake accusations of anti-Semitism.[137]

The following was given as an example of a 'trope':

> Had Jeremy Corbyn and the Labour Party pulled up the drawbridge and nipped the AS (anti-Semitism) in the bud in the first place ... the fifth column in the Labour Party would not have managed to get such a foothold.[138]

She was expelled from the Labour party in 2020.

Naz Shah, an MP, was criticised for remarks made in April 2016 deemed to be unacceptable, including one to which reference has already been made:

> Israel should be relocated to the United States, with the comment 'problem solved', and a post in which she appeared to liken Israeli policies to those of Hitler.

She apologised in the House of Commons, but she was expelled from the Labour party.[139] Livingstone expressed the opinion, widely, that her remarks were:

Merely criticism of Israeli policy at a time of conflict with the Palestinians [and] was part of a campaign by the 'Israeli lobby' to stigmatise critics of Israel as anti-Semitic.[140]

This, and other opinions expressed by Livingstone created a furore amongst Jewish organisations and individuals, and there was 'shock and anger' amongst Jewish Labour party members. His comments caused 'immeasurable damage'.[141]

The verdict of the commission in respect of the remarks made by all three was that they constituted 'unlawful harassment'. None of the remarks was protected by Article 10 of the European Convention of Human Rights. The comments made 'went beyond legitimate criticism of the policies of the Israeli government'.[142] For example, Pat Bromley was not protected under Article 10 because of her 'repeatedly saying that the allegations of anti-Semitism were fabricated'.[143] The commission set out the contradiction which any expression of opinion faces.

> [Leaders of parties] should uphold and defend their rights to speak freely, but they also have a responsibility to conduct debate responsibly, and to lead others in doing so.[144]

This goes to the very heart of the notion of free speech, which is assaulted if the hearer or reader insists on deciding what is 'responsible', since the law, in this case, increasingly supports Jewish pressure groups who demand the right to make that decision. The report recounts some very few crude and puerile examples of clear antisemitism, such as:

> How can we not have empathy with the Palestinians when they are up against these murdering Zionest [sic] bastards. Their NAZI masters taught them well.[145]

But generally it would seem that the conclusions of the report perfectly exemplify the truism that the task facing Jews is to conflate the criticism of Israel with antisemitism, since all of the complaints which are dealt with at length are to do with criticism of Israel.

The reaction to the report showed little promise of conclusion. Jeremy Corbyn proclaimed that the 'problem was dramatically overstated for political reasons', which led to his suspension from his own party.[146] Jewish reaction was that the report was satisfactory, but for many commentators, Corbyn's remarks rather eclipsed other feelings. On 17 November 2020, it was announced that Jeremy Corbyn would be reinstated as a member of the Labour party. This led to uproar from the Jewish lobby, which felt that he had not been punished enough, despite the humiliation of being suspended from the party of which he had been leader. The feeling was that his apology was a non-apology, and the apparent expedition of his case, in the opinion of three leaders of Jewish organisations, adds 'insult to injury'.[147]

Returning to the matter of the future of the Palestinians, from which the campaign against antisemitism is designed to deflect attention, there seems to be little hope. As part of the colonising process the Zionists changed Palestinian place-names. This process involved alleging that places originally had Hebrew names, and that these should be restored. These were not just villages, but included mountains, streams, wadis and other natural features. An authoritative account of this matter was catalogued by Meron Benvenisti in his book *Sacred Landscape: The Buried History of the Holy Land since 1948*. He points out the absurdity which permeated this activity: for example, in the rush to claim ownership, a site would be identified with somewhere in biblical or Jewish tradition, only for it to be found later that the association was inaccurate.

Early in the Jewish takeover, the practice accompanying the establishment of new settlements was carried out by a body curiously called the 'Jewish Naming Committee', set up in 1925. On this committee there were archaeologists 'whose job it was to Hebraize Palestine's geography'.[148] The practice is to allege that a Palestinian village was, in fact, historically Jewish:

> The archaeological zeal to reproduce the map of 'Ancient' Israel was in essence none other than a systematic, scholarly, political and military attempt to de-Arabise the terrain—its names and geography, but above all its history.[149]

Just one example is the Arab village of Mujaydil, which has been transmuted into the Hebrew town of Migdal-Ha-Emek. The Jewish National Fund also buries former Palestinian villages under a network of forests and parks. Palestinian refugees can only contemplate their 'own houses [which] lie entombed under these trees and playgounds'.[150] The Jewish Naming Committee was joined by the 'Negev Naming Society' in 1950 in the obsessive endeavour by Ben-Gurion to thoroughly 'Hebraize' the Negev. All of this was crowned in 1951 by the establishment of the 'Governmental Naming Committee'.

The stealing of Palestinian land continues unabated. The taking of territory during the Six-Day War led to international condemnation, supported by the fact that the United Nations had defined such action as breaking international law. In 2020, for example:

> In the biggest demolition in years, excavators escorted by military vehicles tore down shacks, tents, animal shelters, toilets and solar panels in the Bedouin settlement of Khirbet Humsa in the Jordan Valley. Some 73 people were left homeless, the UN said.

The area is to be used as a firing range. The UN described the demolition as a 'grave breach' of the Fourth Geneva Convention. The Israeli government claimed the action was 'legal'.[151] Such encroachment on Palestinian land is accompanied by the destruction of swathes of communities. Central to Israeli policy is not only the killing and eviction of Palestinians, but the wholesale destruction of their villages and neighbourhoods, and especially their erasure, as people from history. Occasionally there are feeble noises from parts of the Israeli government, but on the whole this is, in effect, government policy. The theft of Palestinian land, and renaming, continues:

> 46 Palestinian Bedouin villages, home to some 8,000 people, have been targeted by the Israeli authorities for 'relocation' to a number of designated sites. This includes 18 communities Israel reportedly intends to demolish as part of the E1 settlement plan, aimed at creating a continuous built-up illegal settlement area.[152]

We have seen how the forced removal of Palestinians from their land has always been such a commonplace of Israeli policy that it rarely attracts comment in the world press. Often when the Israelis destroy a building, they justify the action by saying that the building has been put up without a permit:

> But it is virtually impossible for Palestinians to obtain such permits. Between 2009 and 2016 Israeli authorities approved less than 3 per cent of Palestinian applications.[153]

Typical is the experience of a community called Khan al Ahmar-Abu al Helou, which was put on a list for eviction in 2018. One of the residents gave an account of life there:

> I am unable to support my family in the way I was taught and was passed down generationally. With the few livestock I have left, my kids are afraid to herd, because we are constantly under settler violence. They have guns ... Night terrors? Is there something that can be prescribed for my daughter who won't leave my side for fear that she will be shot at by an Israeli settler? [154]

So how can the behaviour of the state of Israel be summed up in the early twenty-first century? And how is it continuing to affect the Palestinians? From the beginning the Zionists tried to convince the world that the Palestinian Arabs would be well off under Zionist rule. This began with fiction. In his book *Altneuland,* Herzl puts these words into the mouth of a character Reshid Bey. A 'Muslim Arab protagonist':

> Jewish immigration was a blessing for all of us. Naturally first of all for the landowners who either sold their acres to the Jewish company at high prices, or kept them waiting for even higher ones. As regards myself, I've sold my land to the New Society [Herzl's Utopia] because I find myself better off.

He goes on:

> These people [Arabs] are far better off than before; they are healthy, they have better food, their children go to school. Nothing has been done to interfere with their customs or their faith—they have only gained by welfare.[155]

For Karsh this piece of fiction has become fact. He would have us believe that the Arabs are well off because of the Jewish invasion. The theme of Arab happiness consequent upon the invasion of Palestine has to become a well-developed theme in Jewish apologetic literature.

In the 1920s and '30s, the Arab population grew 'owing to the substantial improvement in socio-economic conditions attending the development of the Jewish National Home'.

> No less remarkable were the advances in Arab social welfare ... This can be explained only by the decisive Jewish contribution to mandatory Palestine's socio-economic well-being ... This massive contribution to state revenues was accompanied by the Yishuv's extensive public health provision which benefited a substantial part of the country's Arab population ... Had the vast majority of Palestinian Arabs been left to their own devices they would most probably have been content to get on with their lives and take advantage of the opportunities afforded by the growing Jewish presence in the country.[156]

Karsh states that:

> Within less than a year of the establishment of the PA in Gaza, more than half of the Strip's residents claimed to have been happier under Israeli rule than under the Arafat-controlled administration.[157]

He draws upon opinion polls of 1995 and 1996 which, he claims, show that '78 per cent of Palestinians in the West Bank and Gaza rated Israeli democracy as very good or good ... only 6.9 per cent had a negative opinion of Israeli democracy'.[158]

There can be no argument that the influx of Jewish money made a difference. But that is quite a different matter from the claim that the Arabs should have been grateful to see their land purloined in exchange for physical comfort. That is perilously close to the classic defence of slavery: that slaves are worse off when they are free. Such claims are reminiscent of statements made about the Uighur people of China. The president of China said in a speech in September 2020 that 'The sense of gain, happiness, and security among the people of all ethnic groups has continued to increase.'[159] All the credible evidence is that the land of the Uighurs is more like a gulag.

A more accurate assessment than that forwarded by Karsh, is that of Morris:

New Lamps For Old? 321

In the course of the twentieth century the Arabs of the Levant were repeatedly to be humbled by the Jews, and none more so than the Palestinians, ultimately transformed into a weak minority in their own land. Such slights the Muslim world found difficult to countenance: such a situation could not be allowed to endure.[160]

The true position of the Palestinian people means that they are, in the phrase of Frantz Fanon, among 'the wretched of the earth'. Any examination of that position reveals the hopes, or absence of them, of any amelioration of the situation. And we have seen how, in the propagation of the theory of 'new antisemitism', Israel tries to cope with, and deflect, the worldwide condemnation of its treatment of the Palestinians.

Most of the Palestinians who live outside Israel, in the Middle East, do so in refugee camps. These are in Jordan, Lebanon, Syria, Saudi Arabia and Egypt. There are people from the Palestinian diaspora in many other countries. It is estimated that there are about one and a half million of these, but the figures are difficult to calculate. The situation has been worsened in recent times because of the upheavals in Syria, Iraq and Lebanon. There are 7.2 million Palestinian refugees throughout the world and 4.3 million are registered as recipients for UN aid. There are also refugee camps in Israel, and two thirds of the two million people of Gaza are refugees.

These camps vary in quality, but it must be *de facto* that they are not, to put it at its most restrained, comfortable. Just how desperate the situation can be for refugees may be judged from the experience of attempts to provide medical provision in Gaza, and in countries which also have large numbers of refugees, and whose regimes have become chaotic, such as Lebanon.

An example of the treatment of Palestinians is the medical facilities in Gaza. These are very sparse and difficult to improve because of the Israeli blockade. Such provision as there is has to be supplemented by charitable organisations. The picture is dire, and is complicated by the excessive use of force if the people of Gaza mount any kind of protest. It was reported in 2018 that 'health workers trying to reach, treat and evacuate wounded demonstrators have also come under fire'.

Scores have been shot with live ammunition, directly hit with tear canisters or have suffered tear gas inhalation. Dozens of ambulances have also been damaged. By September [2018] three health workers had been killed and 428 injured by Israeli forces while carrying out vital and often life-saving work. They were in uniform … In earlier military offensives 39 health workers have been killed.[161]

Here is an account of one such killing:

21 year old medical volunteer Razan al-Najjar was fatally shot while trying to reach injured demonstrators close to Israel's perimeter fence in Khuza'an in the south of Gaza. Witnesses said Razan approached the fence wearing a white medic's vest with both of her arms raised to show Israeli forces about 100 metres away that she posed no threat.[162]

In 2016 the UN Security Council promulgated Resolution 2286, which condemned attacks on health services in conflict and asked states to pursue perpetrators of such crimes. Israel took no notice. A British barrister, Lady Helena Kennedy, in an appeal to her government to act, wrote:

Impunity is contagious. Silence is collusion. If the UK and others fail to act, I'm afraid any hope of peace and justice also lies in critical condition.[163]

One personal account, by a well-educated Palestinian, born, living, and working in Jerusalem for Medical Aid for Palestinians, gives a flavour of life there:

I lived in constant fear of being killed, detained, or losing my family. There are Israeli soldiers on every street, watching, waiting for the smallest 'suspicious move' to shoot you. The recent killing of Eyad Hallaq [an autistic man with learning disability shot by police on his way to an occupational training centre] is not exceptional; he was the second Palestinian killed by Israeli forces in East Jerusalem since the start of the year and the seventeenth Palestinian killed in Palestine during 2020 ... Our homes are under the constant threat of being demolished, our Jerusalem Government's threat to annex more Palestinian land looms further over our dignity.[164]

In 2018 the US cut all funding to UNRWA, nearly a third of their budget, making a bad situation worse. This 'jeopardised vital services, including health clinics, social services and education and undermining the protected status of Palestinian refugees ... In September the US State Department withdrew $25 Million budgeted for Palestinian hospitals in East Jerusalem.'[165] One of the latest inhumane acts inflicted upon the Palestinians is the discrimination arising from the Covid-19 pandemic from 2020 onwards. There was much cover in the international media about the brilliant way in which the Israeli government was vaccinating its people. What was not proclaimed, a significant political fact in itself, is that 'Israel [was] withholding vaccines from the approximately five million stateless Palestinians living under its rule'.[166]

The convoluted justification for this is that the 'the Oslo Accords ... give the Palestinian Authority oversight of public health'. This apparently trumps Article 56 of the Geneva Convention which states the 'the Occupying Power' has the duty of maintaining health provision 'with particular reference to the adoption and application of the prophylactic and preventative measures necessary to combat the spread of contagious diseases and epidemics'. As is often the case with the ill-treatment of Palestinians, the situation is worse than appears at first sight. Although the PA had bought vaccines from the Russians, Israel refused 'to allow the transfer of two thousand vaccine doses to the Gaza Strip', arguing that this 'was waiting for a political decision' from Israel.

Another flavour of the treatment of Palestinians in Israel is the way in which Israel conducts its prison system. How a country treats its prisoners is a certain indicator of the humanity, or lack of it in that country. Dostoyevsky said that 'the degree of civilisation in a society can be judged by entering its prisons'. Applied to Israel, what does this show?

> At the end of 2017 there were 5,881 Palestinian security detainees and prisoners in Israeli prisons. Another 730 were locked up for being in Israel illegally. All of these are classed as criminal.[167]

> Since 1967 more than a quarter of Palestinians have been imprisoned on political grounds.[168]

Hundreds have been locked up 'under administrative detention', that is without having a trial, not to say a chance to defend themselves. This is a practice which is used in those countries threatened by serious political opposition, where that opposition has no chance of success against a government which they see as illegitimate. Examples are plentiful: Nazi Germany, Tsarist Russia, and Britain in Northern Ireland in the 1970s.

But Israeli 'administrative detention' has another dimension. It is often the case that 'political' prisoners are held under less oppressive condition than criminals. Even in pre-communist Cuba, under an extremely repressive Batista regime, there was a decree (3688) that political prisoners or detainees had to be kept separate from criminal prisoners, 'and will not be subjected to any kind of work or other penal regulations applied to common prisoners'.[169] Not so in Israel. In the first place, they are not classed as 'prisoners of war' or political prisoners. Secondly, they are *more* repressed than criminals. Thus, unlike criminals they are not allowed access to telephones, they are not allowed conjugal visits, which are allowed in Israeli prisons, and they are given no release date.[170] To arrange a visit means facing a 'monstrous bureaucracy'.

> [It requires] three permits—a permit from the military to enter Israel, a permit from the Civil Administration to pass through the Seam Zone, a permit from the Israeli Prison Service (IPS) to hold the specific visit, and the involvement of the General Security Service (GSS) and the Israeli Police in the process of clarifying entitlement to all these permits.[171]

Not only is there widespread condemnation of the use and abuse of administrative detention, such behaviour is contrary to the anchor point of the treatment of prisoners laid down in the Geneva Convention. Article 49 rules that such prisoners should be imprisoned in their own country:

> Individual or mass forcible transfers, as well as deportations of protected persons from occupied territory to the territory of the Occupying Power or to that of any other country, occupied or not, are prohibited, regardless of their motive.

As well as all of this:

> Physically, Palestinian female prisoners are also subject to all forms of torture during interrogation, including beating, shaking, suspension, segregation and forced nakedness ... Rasmiya Odeh's tale of rape was strongly documented by defence lawyer Felicia Langer in the *Sunday Times* report of 19 June 1977 which concluded that 'torture of Arab prisoners is so widespread and systematic that it cannot be dismissed as "rough cops" exceeding orders. It appears to be sanctioned as deliberate policy'. In Rasmiya Odeh's case, her father was brought to prison and was ordered to rape his daughter. When he refused, prison officials forced a stick into Rasmiya's vagina and left her to bleed, while her father lay unconscious on the floor.[172]

The Israeli government constantly condemns the Palestinian for their use of force. This raises the question of any conceivable hope for Palestinians from the actions of politicians. There seems to be none from Israeli mainstream parties. Elections in the early twenty-first century were not fought over the plight of Arabs: rather they were devoted to the desperate wish 'to get rid of Netanyahu'.[173]

In the Israeli elections of 2019, the man to challenge him was Benny Gantz, a former chief of the General Staff who had been in charge during the Pillar of Defence and Protective Edge attacks on Gaza. This is an example of the widely admitted absence of any opposition to the classic Zionist, one-dimensional extremism of modern Israel. Here was as a man who talked of rejecting talks of Palestinian statehood, that Israel should never give up the West Bank, and there should be no giving up over Jerusalem: a very unlikely person to champion Arabs.[174]

The Likud leader Benjamin Netanyahu is an unashamed racist. During the course of the 2020 elections he came up with the suggestion that the Joint List, 'a group of parties representing most of the 1.6 million Palestinian citizens of Israel, which won 15 seats shouldn't count. In his words: "As the Joint List denigrates our soldiers".'[175]

The Jewish nation state was enacted in 2018 and Netanyahu said on Instagram:

> According to the nation-state law we passed [in July 2018], Israel is the nation-state of the Jewish people—and not anyone else.¹⁷⁶

The 'nation state law' was enacted in 2018. Its formal title is 'Basic Law: Israel as the Nation-State of the Jewish People'.¹⁷⁷ Amjad Iraqi points out that this law was not the first to discriminate. 'Since the state's establishment in 1948, more than 65 laws have been used to restrict the rights of Palestinians with more being passed every year'. Palestinians are restricted in their purchase of property. Palestinian history is not taught. If a Palestinian marries someone from the Occupied Territories that someone cannot become a citizen. What this means in practice is that human rights are confused with national rights, and in Israel such rights belong only to Jews.

The Palestinians can expect help from very, very few people. Each new outrage referred to the UN either draws rejection, or at best an anodyne response, such as that of a UN envoy when answering protests about the building of almost 5,000 houses in the West Bank in October 2020: 'The significant number and location of advancements is of great concern'.¹⁷⁸ The same is the case with the EU, where that organisation's foreign policy spokesman said of the Trump plan: 'we recognise [its] merit'.¹⁷⁹ Almost the only international body which has acted decisively in favour of the Palestinians is the International Criminal Court (ICC).

In 2021 the ICC ruled that it had jurisdiction over the territories occupied by Israel. This means that Palestinian charges of crimes committed against them by the Israeli authorities can be heard by the court. Netanyahu proclaimed that this was 'pure anti-Semitism'.¹⁸⁰ Israel does not recognise the jurisdiction of the court for the very good reason that, as major state criminals, they would have been prosecuted on many occasions. The certainty is that Israel will ignore any findings by the ICC, and will be happy to increase its legal and moral isolation.

It is clear that the Palestinians can expect no help from US governments. Even Democratic presidents and congresses have not been able to make any difference to what Israel does. In any case, even such a radical politician as Barack Obama was cautious about disturbing Jewish opinion. He notes that he has sympathy for the Palestinians, even though, as a child, he was 'infected by Exodus'. But he was up against the fact that when he took office the bulk of Republicans in Congress 'had abandoned any pretence of caring about what happened to the Palestinians. During his presidency the amount of armament sent to Israel increased, and he drew parallels between the Zionist and the Civil Rights movement. He did however express disapproval of settlements in Arab sectors of East Jerusalem. But it has made no difference. Even a president as courageous and liberal as Obama had to cave in. He wrote that having visited Cairo, he thought of going to Tel Aviv:

> But in deference to the Israeli government's wishes that I not make the Palestinian question the primary focus of my speech—nor feed the perception

that the Arab–Israeli conflict was the root cause of the Middle East's turmoil—we had settled instead on a tour of one of the epicentres of the Holocaust to signal my commitment to the security of Israel and the Jewish people.[181]

Obama's presidency finished in January 2017. The arrival of Trump saw the end of even the slightest protest.

The election of President Biden in 2021 started with an important gesture. It was announced that he was going to restore aid to the Palestinians to the amount of $200 million to enable them to have enough food and clean water. He proposed restoring $150 million to UNRWA, which will support 5 million refugees. Predictably the forces of reaction moved quickly. Israel deplored the move since UNWRA was 'a bloated, flawed group'. The Israeli lobby in the United States Congress made clear that it would try to stop the aid. The aid would appear to be a preliminary to Biden's wish to resurrect the 'two state' idea. It will be interesting to see if he manages to achieve any of this.

In Israel there are pressure groups which sometimes object to government policy, such as B'Tselem and Yesh Din, but they make little impact. There are individuals who try to show that they disapprove of Zionist ideology. One such is Daniel Barenboim, who, together with the distinguished Palestinian Edward Said, formed an orchestra of Jews and Arabs—the West-Eastern Divan Orchestra—in a personal show of peace. But such people are usually ignored, and are sometimes subject to serious threats.

The Israeli public offers little hope. In the matter of the proposed annexation of the West Bank, for example, 'the public didn't care much about the issue'.[182] Such indifference, together with active support, encourages actions such as that of Netanyahu, who appointed Pinchas Wallerstein to head a new government committee to legalise illegal settlements in the West Bank.[183] In June 2021, at last Netanyahu lost his position as prime minister to Naftali Bennett. The change offers no hope for the Palestinians since Bennett is the leader of what is usually described as an ultra-nationalist right-wing party.

As for successive British governments, they have always supported the Israeli government, apart from the occasional symbolic protest, such as objecting to Netanyahu's proposed annexation of the West Bank. Leaving aside the attempt by the post-Second World War Labour government to be balanced, most governments have allowed Israel to do what it wants. Of Margaret Thatcher, for instance, Netanyahu said: 'She was a staunch friend of Israel and the Jewish people.'[184]

There was a time when there might have been a better world for Jews and Palestinians. Such a hope was expressed by George Antonius:

> Once the fact is faced that the establishment of a Jewish state in Palestine, or of a national home based on territorial sovereignty, cannot be established without forcibly displacing the Arabs, the way to a solution becomes clearer. It is not

beyond the capacity of British, Jewish and Arab statesmanship to devise one. There seems to be no valid reason why Palestine should not be constituted into an independent Arab state in which as many Jews as the country can hold without prejudice to its political and economic freedom would live in peace, security and dignity, and enjoy full rights of citizenship.

There could be ensured the 'inviolability of the Holy Places of all faiths, for the protection of all minorities and minority rights, and affording the Jewish community the widest freedom in the pursuit of their spiritual and cultural ideals'.[185] But this was never what the Zionists would consider. The result causes expressions of remorse from some Jews, condemnation of Israel, and a forlorn hope that the relationship would change. One Israeli, Nathan Chofshi, wrote:

> Only an internal revolution can have the power to heal our people of their murderous sickness of baseless hatred [for the Arabs]. It is bound to bring eventual ruin upon us. Only then will the old and the young in our land realise how great was our responsibility to those miserable wronged Arab refugees in whose towns we have settled Jews who were brought from afar; whose homes we have inherited, whose fields we now sow and harvest; the fruit of whose gardens, orchards and vineyards we gather; and in whose cities that we robbed, we put up houses of education, charity and prayer, while we babble and rave about our being the 'People of the Book' and the 'Light of the Nations'.[186]

This is an echo of a biblical prophecy (Deuteronomy 6) quoted at the beginning of this book.

Moshe Sharett, who was prime minister of Israel from 1954 to 1955, was one of the more restrained and balanced members of the Israeli hierarchy. In a diary entry of 11 January 1955, he expressed his hope for his country, but without much hint of optimism:

> I wonder about the nature and fate of this nation, capable of such fine spiritual sensitivity, of such profound love of humanity, of such honest yearnings for the beautiful and the sublime, while at the same time it produces from amongst the ranks of its youth boys who are capable of murdering people with a clear mind and in cold blood by thrusting knives into the flesh of young, defenceless Bedouin. Which of the two souls that run around in the pages of the Bible will overcome its rival within this nation?[187]

Experience has eliminated the first of his expectations. The hatred of both towards each other runs deeper than the classic class differences, as Ben-Gurion quickly recognised:

The national element overwhelms the class element, and a powerful hatred of Jews is lit in the hearts of the masses of Arab workers.[188]

Ben-Gurion also notes 'the huge might of Arab hostility'.[189] The British chief of the Imperial General Staff put it in blunter language. In Palestine there are 'two peoples living in a small country hating each other like hell'.[190] It was once written of the Japanese and the Koreans: 'no two people on earth liked each other less'.[191] That unenviable state of affairs has been equalled, or even surpassed, by the relationship between Jews and Arabs.

In mid-2021 serious violence erupted again. This was caused by Netanyahu's government announcing its intention to evict Palestinians from their homes in East Jerusalem, and to move Jewish settlers into the area. Protests by the Palestinians led to the police using rubber bullets near the al-Aqsa mosque, and from there the Israelis started to bomb and shell Gaza, and the Palestinians retaliated by firing rockets into Israel. There followed communal violence in the form of street fighting between Jews and Arabs. At the end of May 2021, after some eleven days of violence, 'more than' 240 Palestinians had been killed, including sixty-six children and about 2,000 wounded. There is usually uncertainty about the number of Palestinian casualties. There was massive destruction of homes and building in Gaza. Twelve Israelis including two children were killed.

Israeli brutality takes many forms. Eyal Weizman discusses the tortured logic and the cruel action derived from it of the Israeli military leader Aviv Kochavi. The tactic is to break into a line of Palestinian houses, with concomitant destruction. The effect is described by a Palestinian woman:

> Imagine it—you're sitting in your living room that you know so well, this is the room where the family watches TV together after the evening meal ... And suddenly, that wall disappears with a deafening roar, the room fills with dust and debris, and through the wall pours one soldier after another, screaming orders. You have no idea if they're after you, if they've come to take over your home, or if your house just lies on their route to somewhere else. The children are screaming, panicking ... Is it possible to even begin to imagine the horror experienced by a five-year-old child as four, six, eight, twelve soldiers, their faces painted black, submachine guns pointing, antennas protruding from their backpacks, making them look like giant alien bugs, blast their way through that wall?[192]

As a result of such behaviour, there seems to be a move towards sympathy for the Palestinians internationally. This was symbolised by parallels drawn between the murder by a police officer in Minnesota of George Floyd in 2020, which led to the spreading of a campaign called BLM—Black Lives Matter. Campaigners for Palestine carried placards reading PLM—Palestinian Lives Matter. There was also a suggestion that the new president, Joe Biden, might look again at his long-standing support for Israel. This is questionable when it is borne in mind that his first reaction was to defend Israel's 'right to defend itself' and blocking UN Security Council resolutions. The fact is that this episode was a reminder, if one is needed, that the situation is hopeless, and the ceasefire does not presage a settlement: only a pause before mayhem resumes. [193] Is there any hope? Raja Shehada, a distinguished Palestinian writer and activist, believes that there may be, but that 'Our only hope is in the next generation'.[194]

There are four persisting justifications made for the seizure of Palestine. They are the promises in the Bible, that the Jews settled and developed the land, that the international community granted it, and that the territory was won in war. None of these reasons is valid excuse, or sufficient reason, for one of the great injustices of the twentieth century.

Glossary

Aliya:	Literally 'going up' that is, to Jerusalem. The term is used to describe phases of immigration into Palestine.
Askenazi:	Broadly, Jews from Northern Europe.
Bar Giora:	The first Jewish terrorist group, founded in 1907, committed to armed insurrection and the establishment of a Jewish state in Palestine.
B'Tselem:	Literally 'in the image of' [God]. An organisation which tries to create a culture of human rights in Israel, and documents violations of human rights in the Israeli-occupied territories.
Chalukka or Chalukah or Halukka:	Charitable donations by Jews in the diaspora for Jews in colonial Palestine.
Diaspora:	The dispersal of a group from their original homeland to other countries, in this case Jews.
Eretz Israel:	The Jewish name for the claimed land by Zionists in Palestine and its vicinity
Irgun Izvai Leumi or IZL or Etzel:	'The national military organisation in the land of Israel'. A terrorist group established in 1931.
Lohamei Herut Yisrael or Lehi or Stern Gang:	'Fighters for the freedom of Israel'. The most extreme terrorist group. It split from Irgun in 1940 because of latter's support for Britain.

Glossary

Haganah:	'The Defence'. The principal paramilitary force of the Jews in Palestine from 1920 to 1948.
IDF:	Israel Defence Forces.
Kristallnacht:	German words meaning 'Night of Broken Glass'. This was the attack on Jews which happened in Germany on 9 and 10 November 1938.
Mossad:	The Israeli 'Intelligence and Special Operations' organisation.
Nakba:	Arabic word meaning disaster or catastrophe. It is used to describe the period between 1947 and 1949, when approximately 80 per cent of Palestinians were driven from their homes.
P.A.:	Palestinian National Authority. Broadly, the governing body of Gaza and the West Bank.
Palmach or Plugot Mahatz:	'Strike Force'. A sub group of the Haganah.
PFLP:	Popular Front for the Liberation of Palestine. A Marxist group founded in 1967.
Pogrom:	Official, publicly approved attacks on minority groups.
Sephardic:	Jews of Iberian, Middle Eastern, or North African origin.
UAE:	United Arab Emirates.
UNSCOP:	United Nations Special Commission on Palestine.
Yishuv:	The Jewish population of Palestine before 1948.

ENDNOTES

Chapter 1

1. Angela Saini, *Superior: The Return of Race Science* (4th Estate: London, 2019), p. 191.
2. Tom Segev, *One Palestine Complete: Jews and Arabs under the British Mandate* (Abacus: London, 2001), p. 401.
3. Review by Adam Shatz of *We are Conquerors* in *London Review of Books*, 24 October 2019.
4. Rachel Havrelock, *The Joshua Generation: Israel Occupation and the Bible* (University of Chicago Press: Chicago, 2011), p. 106.
5. *Ibid.*, p. 17.
6. Joshua 10:19 (Authorised King James Version).
7. Havrelock, *op. cit.*, p. 155.
8. James Renton, *The Zionist Masquerade: The Birth of the Anglo-Zionist Alliance 1914-1918* (Palgrave Macmillan: London, 2007), p. 87.
9. Menachem Begin, *The Revolt* (W. H. Allen: London, 1951).
10. *Ibid.*, p. 30.
11. *Ibid.*, p. 31.
12. *Ibid.*, pp. 87-88.
13. *Ibid.*, p. 30.
14. Genesis 12:1-2.
15. Deuteronomy 30:5.
16. Genesis 15:18.
17. *Ibid.*, 17:8.
18. *Ibid.*, 28:13.
19. Deuteronomy 1:7-8.
20. Numbers 34:2-13.
21. Deuteronomy 19:8-9.
22. *Ibid.*, 8:9.
23. Exodus 23:29-31.
24. Tom Segev, *A State at Any Cost: The Life of David Ben-Gurion* (Apollo: London, 2019), p. 418.
25. Genesis 21:12-13, quoted in Sami Hadawi, *Bitter Harvest: A Modern History of Palestine* (Scorpion Press: Essex, 1989), pp. 23-24.

26 Numbers 34:53 and 34:55.
27 Deuteronomy 6:10-11.
28 *Ibid.*, 7:1-2.
29 Joshua 6:21.
30 *Ibid.*, 8:25.
31 *Ibid.*, 8:27.
32 A. Forster and B. Epstein, *The New Antisemitism* (McGraw-Hill: New York, 1974), p. 240.
33 Gudrun Kramer, *A History of Palestine from the Ottoman Conquest to the Founding of the State of Israel* (Princeton University Press: Princeton, 2008), p. 21.
34 Deuteronomy, 7:3.
35 Ronen Bergman, *Rise and Kill First: The Secret History of Israel's Targeted Assassinations* (John Murray: London, 2018), p. 135.
36 William G. Dever, *Who Were the Early Israelites and Where Did They Come From?* (William B. Eerdmans: Grand Rapids, 2006), pp. 4-5.
37 Ibid.
38 *Ibid.*, p. 47.
39 *Ibid.*, p. 45 ff.
40 *Ibid.*, p. 39.
41 *Ibid.*, p. 72.
42 *Ibid.*, p. 226.
43 Segev (2001), *op. cit.*, p. 40, quoting Chaim Weizmann, *Trial and Error* (Hamish Hamilton: London, 1949), p. 391.
44 Quoted in Segev (2001), p. 144.
45 Tim Mackintosh-Smith, *The Arabs: A 3,000-Year History of Peoples, Tribes and Empires* (Yale University Press: New Haven, 2019), p. 441.
46 Renton, *op. cit.*
47 Quoted in Renton, pp. 85-86.
48 Robert S. Wistrich, 'Theodor Herzl, Myth-Maker and Social Utopian' in *Israeli Affairs* (1995), vol. 1, no. 3, p. 32.
49 Joseph Heller, 'The Zionist Right and National Liberation: from Jabotinsky to Avraham Stern' in *Israel Affairs* (1995), vol. 1, no. 3, p. 85.
50 Wistrich, *op. cit.*, p. 32.
51 Yael Zerubavel, 'The Multivocality of a National Myth: Memory and Counter-Memories of Masada' in *Israel Affairs* (1995), vol. 1 no. 3, pp. 113.
52 As Yael Zerubavel wrote in *Israeli Affairs*, p. 114: 'It has even been claimed that Josephus' description of the mass suicide at Masada was a literary fabrication.'
53 *Ibid.*, p. 112.
54 *Ibid.*, pp. 122-23.
55 *Ibid.*, p. 123.
56 Segev (2019), *op. cit.*, p. 105.
57 Ze'ev Tzahor, 'Ben Gurion's Mythopoetics' in *Israel Affairs* (1995), vol. 1 no. 3, p. 66.
58 *Ibid.*, p. 67.
59 *Ibid.*, p. 75.
60 Havrelock, *op. cit.*, p. 36.
61 Tzahor, *op. cit.*, p. 68.
62 Mel Scult, *Jewish Liberties: a Study of the Effort to Convert the Jews in Britain, up to the Nineteenth Century* (EJ Brill: Leiden, 1978), p. 16.
63 *Ibid.*, p. 19.
64 *Ibid.*, p. 18.
65 Daniel 12:7 reads, 'When he shall have accomplished to scatter the power of the holy people, all these things shall be finished'.

66 Simon Sebag Montefiore, *Jerusalem: The Biography* (Phoenix: London, 2011), p. 301.
67 Scult, *op. cit.*, p. 31.
68 *Ibid.*, p. 62.
69 *Ibid.*, p. 60.
70 *Ibid.*, p. 63.
71 Quoted in Scult, p. 69.
72 See Scult p. 111 for a discussion of some English beliefs.
73 Quoted in Scult, p. 140.
74 *Ibid.*, p. 111.
75 *Ibid.*
76 Quoted in Martin Gilbert, *Churchill and the Jews* (Simon and Schuster: London, 2007), p. 95.
77 A. J. P. Taylor, *English History 1914-1945* (Oxford University Press: Oxford, 1965), p. 128.
78 Darrell G. Young, 'Focus on Jerusalem Ministry' in *The Bible and Palestine* (2006), vol. 97, no. 1.
79 *Ibid.*, p. 3.
80 *Ibid.*, p. 8.
81 *Ibid.*, p. 3.
82 *Ibid.*, p. 5.
83 *Ibid.*, p. 7.
84 Michael Prior, *Zionism and the State of Israel: A Moral Enquiry* (Routledge: London, 1999), p. 142.
85 Barack Obama, *A Promised Land* (Viking: London, 2020), p. 628.
86 *Ibid.*
87 *Ibid.*, p. 632.
88 Prior, *op. cit.*, p. 142.
89 Young, *op. cit.*, p. 5.
90 For details see N. A. Rose, *The Gentile Zionists: A Study in Anglo-Zionist Diplomacy 1929-1939* (Frank Cass: London, 1973), chapter 4.
91 *Ibid.*, pp. 73-74.
92 Segev (2001), *op. cit.*, pp. 89-90.
93 'Report of the Court of Inquiry Convened by the Order of H.E. The High Commissioner and Commander-in-Chief' (The Palin Report), 12 April 1920, p. 9.

Chapter 2

1 Ze'ev Tzahor, 'Ben Gurion's Mythopoetics' in *Israel Affairs* (1995), vol. 1, no. 3, p. 70.
2 *Ibid.*, p. 71.
3 For details of Dreyfus see Armand Charpentier's *The Dreyfus Case* (1935).
4 Sami Hadawi, *Bitter Harvest: A Modern History of Palestine* (Scorpion Press: Essex, 1989), p. 215.
5 *Hansard Debates*, fifth series, vol. 347, col. 1967, May 1939.
6 George Antonius, *The Arab Awakening: the Story of the Arab National Movement* (Hamish Hamilton: London, 1969), p. 388.
7 N. Rose, *The Gentile Zionists A Study in Anglo-Zionist Diplomacy 1929-39* (Frank Cass: London, 1973), p. 4.
8 Novitch quoted in Ian Hancock, 'Romanies and the Holocaust: A Re-evaluation and Overview' in Dan Stone (ed.), *The Historiography of the Holocaust* (Palgrave MacMillan: London, 2004), p. 383.
9 *Ibid.*, pp. 388-89.

10 *Ibid.*, p. 392.
11 *Ibid.*, pp. 384-85.
12 *Ibid.*, p. 384.
13 *Ibid.*, p. 385.
14 Tom Segev, *One Palestine Complete: Jews and Arabs under the British Mandate* (Abacus: London, 2001), p. 71.
15 *Ibid.*
16 Gudrun Kramer, *A History of Palestine: From the Ottoman Conquest to the Founding of the State of Israel* (Princeton University Press: Princeton, 2008), p. 103.
17 Leonard Stein, *The Balfour Declaration* (Simon and Schuster: New York, 1961), p. 193.
18 *Ibid.*, p. 172.
19 *Ibid.*, p. 176.
20 *Ibid.*
21 Arthur Koestler, *Promise and Fulfilment: Palestine 1917-1949* (Macmillan: London, 1949), p. 333.
22 *Ibid.*, p. ix.
23 *Ibid.*, p. 334.
24 Stein, *op. cit.*, p. 163.
25 Michael Prior, *Zionism and the State of Israel: A Moral Enquiry* (Routledge: London, 1999), p. 8.
26 Tom Segev, *A State at Any Cost: The Life of David Ben-Gurion* (Apollo: London, 2019), p. 18.
27 Prior, *op. cit.*, p. 8.
28 Koestler, *op. cit.*, p. 37.
29 Stein, *op. cit.*, p. 33.
30 *Ibid.*, 30.
31 Martin Gilbert, *Churchill and the Jews* (Simon and Schuster: London, 2007), pp. 154-55.
32 *Ibid.*, p. 249.
33 Erik Cohen, 'Israel as a Post-Zionist Society' in *Israel Affairs* (1995), p. 204.
34 Count Folke Bernadotte, *To Jerusalem* (Hodder and Stoughton: London, 1951), p. 190.
35 Quoted in Andrew Roberts, *Churchill: Walking With Destiny* (Allen Lane: London, 2018), p. 759.
36 'Report of the Court of Inquiry Convened by the Order of H.E. The High Commissioner and Commander-in-Chief' (The Palin Report), 12 April 1920, p. 13.
37 Segev (2019), *op. cit.*, p. 462.
38 Editor's note, *Israel Affairs* (1995), vol. 1, no. 3, p. xii.
39 Quoted in Benny Morris, *Righteous Victims: a History of the Zionist–Arab Conflict 1881-2001* (Vintage Books: New York, 2001), p. 459.
40 Segev (2019), *op. cit.*, p. 104.
41 *Ibid.*, 103.
42 *Ibid.*, 104.
43 *Ibid.*, 563.
44 Hadawi, *op. cit.*, p. 57.
45 Segev (2019), *op. cit.*, p. 246.
46 Quoted in Stein, *op. cit.*, p. 35.
47 *Ibid.*, p. 36.
48 *Ibid.*, p. 33.
49 Joseph Finn, *A Voice From the Aliens* (Twentieth Century Press: London, 1895), p. 1.

50 *The Daily Mail*, 3 February 1900.
51 Colin Holmes, *Antisemitism in British Society 1876-1939* (Routledge: London, 1979), p. 27.
52 David Rosenberg, *Rebel Footprints: a Guide to Uncovering London's Radical History* (Pluto Press: London, 2015), p. 94.
53 David Rosenberg, *Battle for the East End: Jewish Responses to Fascism in the 1930s* (Five Leaves Publications: Nottingham, 2011), p. 114.
54 *The Times*, 31 May 1904 59, quoted in Andrew Roberts, *Churchill: Walking with Destiny* (Allen Lane: London, 2018), p. 95.
55 *Ibid.*
56 Quoted in Roberts, p. 352.
57 *Ibid.*, p. 415.
58 *Ibid.*, p. 367.
59 *Ibid.*, p. 64.
60 Gilbert, *op. cit.*, p. 22. For a full account of Churchill's repressive methods see Gilbert, p. 19 ff.
61 Segev (2001), *op. cit.*, p. 44.
62 Stein, *op. cit.*, p. 155.
63 *Ibid.*, p. 154.
64 Simon Sebag Montefiore, *Jerusalem: The Biography* (Phoenix: London, 2011), p. 354.
65 Quoted in Stein, *op. cit.*, p. 15.
66 *Ibid.*, p. 157.
67 A. G. Gardiner, *Prophets, Priest and Kings*, quoted in Stein, *op. cit.*, p. 105.
68 Jonathan Schneer, *The Balfour Declaration: The Origins of the Arab-Israeli Conflict* (Bloomsbury: London, 2011), p. 125.
69 *Ibid.*, p. 126.
70 Stein, *op. cit.*, p. 110.
71 Quoted in Schneer, *op. cit.*, p. 136.
72 Stein, *op. cit.*, p. 111.
73 Quoted in Stein, p. 583.
74 *Ibid.*, p. 190.
75 Quoted in Stein, p. 509.
76 *Ibid.*, p. 608 ff.
77 See chapter 12 of Stein for a full discussion of American Jewish attitudes.
78 Stein, *op. cit.*, p. 203.
79 James Renton, *The Zionist Masquerade: The Birth of the Anglo-Zionist Alliance 1914-1918* (Palgrave Macmillan: London, 2007), p. 46.
80 *Ibid.*
81 Stein, *op. cit.*, p. 191.
82 *Ibid.*, 197.
83 *Ibid.*, 227.
84 Elie Kedourie, *In the Anglo-Arab Labyrinth: The McMahon–Husayn Correspondence and Its Interpretations* (Cambridge University Press: Cambridge, 1976), p. 35.
85 *Ibid.*
86 *Ibid.*, pp. 21-22. He points out that this would have disappeared had a copy of the proclamation not been found in the archives of the Cairo embassy.
87 Quoted in Schneer, *op. cit.*, p. 57.
88 Kedourie, *op. cit.*, p. 100 ff. for a discussion.
89 Letter to the Sharif, quoted in Michael Prior, *Zionism and the State of Israel: A Moral Enquiry* (Routledge: London, 1999), p. 11.

90 Antonius, *op. cit.*, p. 416.
91 *Ibid.*
92 *Ibid.*, p. 419.
93 *Ibid.*
94 Quoted in Antonius, p. 423. The complete correspondence is set out in Antonius, Appendix A.
95 Walter Reid, *Empire of Sand: How Britain Made the Middle East* (Birlinn: Edinburgh, 2011), p. 71.
96 Doreen Ingrams, *Palestine Papers 1917-1922: Seeds of Conflict* (John Murray: London, 1972), pp. 48-49.
97 *Ibid.*, p. 40.
98 *Ibid.*, p. 43.
99 Kedourie, *op. cit.*, p. 210.
100 See for example Arnold Toynbee and Isaiah Friedman, 'The McMahon-Hussein Correspondence' in *Journal of Contemporary History* (1970), vol. 5, no. 4, pp. 185-201.
101 Rachel Havrelock, *The Joshua Generation: Israel Occupation and the Bible* (Princeton University Press: Princeton, 2020), p. 231 ff.
102 Kedouri, *op. cit.*, p. 297.
103 Sahar Huneidi, *A Broken Trust: Herbert Samuel, Zionism and the Palestinians 1920-1925* (IB Tauris: London, 2001), p. 65.
104 *Ibid.*
105 Kedouri, *op. cit.*, p. 262.
106 Gilbert, *op. cit.*, p. 48.
107 Rachel Havrelock, *River Jordan: The Mythology of a Dividing Line* (University of Chicago Press: Chicago, 2011), p. 7.
108 *House of Lords Debates*, 27 March 1923, vol. 53, col. 639-69.
109 *Ibid.*, 20 July 1937, vol. 106, col. 599-665.
110 *Ibid.*, 27 March 1923, vol. 53, col. 639-69.
111 Quoted in Kedourie, *op. cit.*, p. 119.
112 James Barr, *A Line in the Sand* (Simon and Schuster: London, 2011), p. 29.
113 'Correspondence between Sir Henry McMahon, His Majesty's High Commissioner at Cairo, and the Sherif Hussein of Mecca, 1939', Cmd. 5957.
114 Segev (2001), *op. cit.*, p. 438.
115 Stein, *op. cit.*, p. 267.
116 *Ibid.*
117 *Ibid.*, p. 269.
118 Efraim Karsh, *Palestine Betrayed* (Yale University Press: New Haven, 2011), p. 41.
119 T. E. Lawrence, *The Seven Pillars of Wisdom: A Triumph* (Jonathan Cape: London, 1952), p. 24.
120 Kedourie, *op. cit.*, p. 3.
121 Lawrence, *op. cit.*, p. 57.
122 Benny Morris, *Righteous Victims: A History of the Zionist–Arab Conflict 1881-2001* (Vintage Books: New York, 2001), p. 68.
123 Quoted in Barr, *op. cit.*, p. 8.
124 *Ibid.*, p. 68.
125 Quoted in Stein, *op. cit.*, pp. 246-247.
126 *Ibid.*, 620.
127 Segev (2001), *op. cit.*, p. 42.
128 Schneer, *op. cit.*, p. 80.
129 *Ibid.*, p. 82.
130 Ingrams, *op. cit.*, p. 30.

131 Renton, *op. cit.*, p. 8.
132 *Ibid.*, p. 17.
133 Quoted in Stein, *op. cit.*, p. 575.
134 The Palin Report (1920), p. 14.
135 Morris, *op. cit.*, p. 23.
136 Stein, *op. cit.*, p. 576.
137 Herzl, *The Jewish State*, quoted in Kramer, *op. cit.*, p. 108.
138 Ingrams, *op. cit.*, pp. 7-8.
139 Alfred M. Lilienthal, *The Other Side of the Coin: An American Perspective of the Arab-Israeli Conflict* (The Devon-Adair Company: New York, 1965), p. 65.
140 Quoted in Stein, *op. cit.*, p. 476.
141 Ingrams, *op. cit.*, p. 7.
142 Renton, *op. cit.*, p. 46.

Chapter 3

1 The Palin Report (1920), paragraph 7.
2 Leonard Stein, *The Balfour Declaration* (Simon and Schuster: New York, 1961), pp. 511-12.
3 Quoted in Stein, pp. 464-65.
4 *Ibid.*, p. 470.
5 *Ibid.*, p. 664.
6 *Ibid.*, p. 548.
7 Michael Prior, *Zionism and the State of Israel: a Moral Inquiry* (Routledge: London, 1999), p. 13.
8 Benny Morris, *Righteous Victims: A History of the Zionist–Arab Conflict 1881-2001* (Vintage Books: New York, 2001), p. 75.
9 Doreen Ingrams, *Palestine Papers 1917-1922: Seeds of Conflict* (John Murray: London, 1972), p. 13.
10 Prior, *op. cit.*, p. 13.
11 'Palestine Royal Commission Report' (The Peel Report), 1937, Cmd. 5479, pp. 108-109.
12 Karsh, *op. cit.*, p. 5.
13 Ingrams, *op. cit.*, p. 81.
14 See Martin Gilbert, *Churchill and the Jews* (Simon and Schuster: London, 2007), pp. 58-61.
15 *Ibid.*, p. 62.
16 Efraim Karsh, *Palestine Betrayed* (Yale University Press: New Haven, 2011), p. 22.
17 Quoted in Sahar Huneidi, *A Broken Trust: Herbert Samuel, Zionism and the Palestinians 1920-1925* (IB Tauris: London, 2001), p. 14
18 Ingrams, *op. cit.*, p. 54.
19 *Ibid.*
20 Prior, *op. cit.*, p. 75.
21 Quoted in Prior, *op. cit.*, p. 75.
22 PRO FO.800/217, quoted in Ingrams, *op. cit.*, p. 72.
23 Robert Wistrach and David Ohana, *The Shaping of Israel Identity: Myth, Memory and Trauma* (Frank Cass: London, 1995), p. 5.
24 Ingrams, *op. cit.*, p. 66.
25 Barr, *op. cit.*, p. 85.
26 *Ibid.*
27 Ingrams, *op. cit.*, p. 21.

28 Huneidi, *op. cit.*, p. 30.
29 Ingrams, *op. cit.*, pp. 23-24.
30 Tom Segev, *One Palestine Complete: Jews and Arabs under the British Mandate* (Abacus: London, 2001), p. 65.
31 CO733/5 Minute by Clauson, 2 September 1921, quoted, Huneidi, *op. cit.*, p. 135.
32 Segev, *op. cit.*, p. 69.
33 *Ibid.*, p. 70.
34 *Ibid.*, p. 71.
35 *Ibid.*, p. 70.
36 *Ibid.*, p. 88. See this reference for examples.
37 The Palin Report (1920).
38 *Ibid.*, p. 15.
39 *Ibid.*, para. 21.
40 *Ibid.*, para. 24.
41 *Ibid.*, para. 26.
42 *Ibid.*, p. 30.
43 Segev, *op. cit.*, p. 95.
44 N. Rose, *The Gentile Zionists A Study in Anglo-Zionist Diplomacy 1929-39* (Frank Cass: London, 1973), p. 1.
45 The Palin Report (1920), sections 19 and 26.
46 Segev, *op. cit.*, p. 66.
47 Gudrun Kramer, *A History of Palestine: From the Ottoman Conquest to the Founding of the State of Israel* (Princeton University Press: Princeton, 2008), p. 104.
48 *Ibid.*, p. 106.
49 *Ibid.*, pp. 119-120.
50 *Ibid.*, p. 120.
51 *Ibid.*, p. 111.
52 *Ibid.*, pp. 111-112.
53 Tom Segev, *A State at Any Cost: The Life of David Ben-Gurion* (Apollo: London, 2019), p. 479.
54 Jonathan Schneer, *The Balfour Declaration: The Origins of the Arab-Israeli Conflict* (Bloomsbury: London, 2011), pp. 11-12.
55 Ingrams, *op. cit.*, pp. 109-110.
56 This was a cornerstone of Ben-Gurion's policy.
57 Walid Khalidi, *All That Remains: the Palestinian Villages Occupied and Depopulated by Israel in 1948* (Institute for Palestine Studies: Washington DC, 1992), pp. 595-96.
58 See for example Ben-Gurion on their 'thirst for blood'; Segev (2019), *op. cit.*, p. 217.
59 Gilbert, *op. cit.*, p. 68.
60 *Ibid.*, p. 71.
61 Segev (2001), *op. cit.*, p. 45-46.
62 Ingrams, *op. cit.*, p. 12.
63 Huneidi, *op. cit.*, p. 156.
64 Tim Mackintosh-Smith, *The Arabs: A 3,000-Year History of Peoples, Tribes and Empires* (Yale University Press: New Haven, 2019), p. 442.
65 Segev (2019), *op. cit.*, p. 135.
66 Stein, *op. cit.*, p. 561.
67 Rose, *op. cit.*, p. 101.
68 Huneidi, *op. cit.*, p. 246.
69 Ingrams, *op. cit.*, p. 66.
70 Huneidi, *op. cit.*, p. 29.
71 Ingrams, *op. cit.*, p. 47.

72 Huneidi, *op. cit.*, p. 32.
73 Sami Hadawi, *Bitter Harvest: A Modern History of Palestine* (Scorpion Press: Essex, 1989), p. 46.
74 *Ibid.*, 45.
75 Ingrams, *op. cit.*, p. 84.
76 *Ibid.*, p. 45.
77 Huneidi, *op. cit.*, p. 52.
78 *Ibid.*
79 *Ibid.*, p. 87.
80 *Ibid.*, p. 52.
81 T. E. Lawrence, *The Seven Pillars of Wisdom: A Triumph* (Jonathan Cape: London, 1952), p. 136.
82 *Ibid.*, pp. 282-83.
83 Morris, *op. cit.*, p. 75.
84 Lawrence, *op. cit.*, p. 283.
85 CO 733/17, minute by T. E. Lawrence, 29 June 1921, quoted in Huneidi, *op. cit.*, p. 52.
86 Lawrence, *op. cit.*, p. 283.
87 George Antonius, *The Arab Awakening: the Story of the Arab National Movement* (Hamish Hamilton: London, 1969), p. 319.
88 Gilbert, *op. cit.*, p. 46.
89 Lawrence, *op. cit.*, pp. 22-23.
90 Ingrams, *op. cit.*, p. 62.
91 Quoted in Stein, *op. cit.*, p. 564.
92 Brian Garfield, *The Meinertzhagen Mystery: The Life and Legend of a Colossal Fraud* (Potomac Books: Washington DC, 2007), p. 25.
93 *Ibid.*, p. 5.
94 *Ibid.*, p. 8.
95 Lawrence, *op. cit.*, p. 393.
96 The Palin Report (1920), para. D.
97 Garfield, *op. cit.*, p. 12.
98 Ingrams, *op. cit.*, p. 115.
99 Wasserstein, *The British in Palestine*, quoted in Huneidi, *op. cit.*, p. 77.
100 Huneidi, *op. cit.*, p. 74, quoting Mark Cocker, *Richard Meinertzhagen: Soldier Scientist and Spy* (1989), pp. 152-155.
101 Segev (2001), *op. cit.*, p. 397.
102 *Ibid.*, pp. 397-98.
103 *Ibid.*, p. 475.
104 Antonius, *op. cit.*, p. 270. It should be pointed out that Antonius's experience was first hand. He was a Lebanese-Egyptian Christian and worked for the British Mandate.
105 *Ibid.*, p. 433.
106 *Ibid.*, pp. 433-34.
107 *Ibid.*, p. 273.
108 *Ibid.*, p. 271.
109 Quoted in Antonius, pp. 435, 436.
110 *Ibid.*, p. 255.
111 *Ibid.*, p. 258.
112 *Ibid.*, pp. 267-68.
113 *Ibid.*, p. 268.
114 Ingrams, *op. cit.*, p. 88.
115 *Ibid.*

116 *Ibid.*, p. 89.
117 Barr, *op. cit.*, p. 39.
118 Ingrams, *op. cit.*, p. 90.
119 *Ibid.*, pp. 90-91.
120 Kramer, *op. cit.*, p. 162.
121 Ingrams, *op. cit.*, p. 91.
122 *Ibid.*, pp. 92.
123 *Ibid.*, p. 93, quoting *The Beduin* [sic] *Chiefs of Transjordan*.
124 Huneidi, *op. cit.*, p. 19.
125 Ingrams, *op. cit.*, pp. 56-57.
126 *Ibid.*, p. 57.
127 *Ibid.*, p. 94.
128 *Ibid.*, p. 95.
129 *Ibid.*, p. 96.
130 Joshua 9:21.
131 Ingrams, *op. cit.*, p. 96.
132 Huneidi, *op. cit.*, pp. 20-21.
133 Ingrams, *op. cit.*, p. 60.
134 *Ibid.*, p. 61.
135 *Ibid.*, p. 97.
136 *Ibid.*, p. 98.
137 *Ibid.*
138 *Ibid.*, p. 99.
139 *Ibid.*, p. 100.
140 *Ibid.*, p. 101.
141 *Ibid.*
142 *Ibid.*, p. 19.
143 James Renton, *The Zionist Masquerade: The Birth of the Anglo-Zionist Alliance 1914-1918* (Palgrave Macmillan: London, 2007), p. 77.
144 *Ibid.*, p. 78.
145 Segev, (2001), *op. cit.*, p. 245.
146 Lawrence, *op. cit.*, p. 464.
147 Stein, *op. cit.*, pp. 605-606.
148 Ingrams, *op. cit.*, p. 76.
149 Rachel Havrelock, *River Jordan: The Mythology of a Dividing Line* (University of Chicago Press: Chicago, 2011), p. 7.
150 Rachel Havrelock, *The Joshua Generation: Israel Occupation and the Bible* (Princeton University Press: Princeton, 2020), p. 168.
151 Stein, *op. cit.*, p. 622.
152 Karsh, *op. cit.*, p. 22.
153 Stein, *op. cit.*, p. 622 ff.
154 Huneidi, *op. cit.*, p. 32.
155 Quoted in Stein, *op. cit.*, p. 634.
156 Ingrams, *op. cit.*, p. 67.
157 Stein, *op. cit.*, p. 645 ff.
158 *Ibid.*, p. 648.
159 *Ibid.*, p. 649.
160 Ingrams, *op. cit.*, p. 102.
161 *Ibid.*, p. 103.
162 *Ibid.*, pp. 103-104.
163 *Ibid.*, p. 105.
164 *Ibid.*, p. 106.

165 Huneidi, *op. cit.*, p. 44.
166 Ingrams, *op. cit.*, p. 107.
167 Gilbert, *op. cit.*, p. 46.
168 Karsh, *op. cit.*, p. 15.
169 'Report on Middle East Conference Held in Cairo and Jerusalem, 12-30 March 1921'. British Colonial Office, June 1921 (CO 935/1/1).
170 Huneidi, *op. cit.*, p. 125.
171 Ingrams, *op. cit.*, p. 117.
172 'Report on Middle East Conference Held in Cairo and Jerusalem, 12-30 March 1921', Appendix 23.
173 *Ibid.*
174 Gilbert, *op. cit.*, p. 56.
175 'Report on Middle East Conference Held in Cairo and Jerusalem, 12-30 March 1921', Appendix 23.
176 Gilbert, *op. cit.*, p. 57.
177 *Ibid.*, p. 49.
178 Morris (2001), *op. cit.*, p. 100.
179 Ingrams, *op. cit.*, p. 117.
180 Karsh, *op. cit.*, p. 24.
181 Gilbert, *op. cit.*, pp. 127-28.
182 *Ibid.*, p. 76.
183 *Ibid.*, pp. 76-77.
184 Huneidi, *op. cit.*, p. 45.
185 *Ibid.*, pp. 45-46.
186 Stein, *op. cit.*, p. 556.
187 Gilbert, *op. cit.*, p. 77.
188 *Ibid.*, p. 78.
189 Huneidi, *op. cit.*, p. 11.
190 *Ibid.*, p. 159.
191 'Correspondence with the Palestine Arab Delegation and the Zionist Organisation' (Churchill White Paper), 1922, Cmd. 1700.
192 Quoted in Huneidi, *op. cit.*, p. 73.
193 *Ibid.*
194 *Ibid.*, p. 73-74.
195 CO 733/54, 25 July 1923, quoted in Huneidi, p. 74.
196 *Ibid.*
197 *Ibid.*, p. 74-75.
198 *Ibid.*, p. 75.
199 *Ibid.*, p. 153.
200 *Ibid.*, pp. 154-55.
201 *Ibid.*, p. 73.
202 *Ibid.*, p. 75 (CO 733/58 Secret Cabinet Report CP 351, July 1923).
203 *Ibid.*
204 Ingrams, *op. cit.*, p. 65.
205 *Ibid.*, p. 44.
206 *Ibid.*, p. 81.
207 Gilbert, *op. cit.*, p. 44.
208 *Ibid.*, p. 34.
209 *Ibid.*, p. 35.
210 *Ibid.*, p. 34.
211 *Ibid.*, p. 38.
212 *Ibid.*, p. 29.

213 Huneidi, *op. cit.*, 159.
214 *Ibid.*, p. 154.
215 *Ibid.*, p. 162.
216 *Ibid.*, p. 161.
217 Kramer, *op. cit.*, 268.
218 Karsh, *op. cit.*, 10.
219 *Ibid.*
220 *Ibid.*, p. 30.
221 *Ibid.*, p. 14.
222 Karsh, *op. cit.*, *passim.*

Chapter 4

1 The Peel Report (1937), chapter 11.
2 'Zionism versus Bolshevism', *Illustrated Sunday Herald*, 8 February 1920, quoted in Andrew Roberts, *Churchill: Walking with Destiny* (Allen Lane: London, 2018), p. 278.
3 Roberts, *op. cit.*, p. 101.
4 *Ibid.*, p. 95.
5 Martin Gilbert, *Churchill and the Jews* (Simon and Schuster: London, 2007), pp. 4-5.
6 *Ibid.*, p. 88.
7 *Ibid.*, p. 89.
8 *Ibid.*, p. 88.
9 *Ibid.*, p. 90.
10 *Ibid.*, pp. 284-85.
11 Quoted in Gilbert, p. 87.
12 For details, see Gilbert, p. 138 ff.
13 *Ibid.*, p. 101.
14 John Grigg, *The Young Lloyd George* (Eyre Methuen: London, 1973), p. 297.
15 Leonard Stein, *The Balfour Declaration* (Simon and Schuster: New York, 1961), p. 158.
16 Quoted in Stein, p. 483.
17 James Renton, *The Zionist Masquerade: The Birth of the Anglo-Zionist Alliance 1914-1918* (Palgrave Macmillan: London, 2007), p. 22.
18 The Peel Report (1937), p. 25.
19 Doreen Ingrams, *Palestine Papers 1917-1922: Seeds of Conflict* (John Murray: London, 1972), p. 33.
20 Sahar Huneidi, *A Broken Trust: Herbert Samuel, Zionism and the Palestinians 1920-1925* (IB Tauris: London, 2001), p. 61.
21 Quoted in Gudrun Kramer, *A History of Palestine: From the Ottoman Conquest to the Founding of the State of Israel* (Princeton University Press: Princeton, 2008), p. 166.
22 Benny Morris, *Righteous Victims: A History of the Zionist–Arab Conflict 1881-2001* (Vintage Books: New York, 2001), p. 42.
23 Tom Segev, *A State at Any Cost: The Life of David Ben-Gurion* (Apollo: London, 2019), p. 140.
24 Efraim Karsh, *Palestine Betrayed* (Yale University Press: New Haven, 2011), p. 47.
25 CO 733/13 secret report by Captain Brunton, 13 May 1921, quoted in Huneidi, *op. cit.*, p. 128.
26 Quoted in Roberts, *op. cit.*, p. 284.
27 Gilbert, *op. cit.*, pp. 53-54.
28 As always, Weizmann assumed that Balfour shared his prejudices.

29 Ingrams, *op. cit.*, p. 31.
30 *Ibid.*, pp. 31-32.
31 Quoted in Morris, *op. cit.*, p. 43.
32 Arthur Koestler, *Promise and Fulfilment: Palestine 1917-1949* (Macmillan: London, 1949), p. 74.
33 *Ibid.*, pp. 33-34.
34 *Ibid.*, p. 22.
35 Segev, *op. cit.*, p. 77.
36 Kramer, *op. cit.*, p. 35.
37 Tom Segev, *One Palestine Complete: Jews and Arabs under the British Mandate* (Abacus: London, 2001), pp. 469-70.
38 Ingrams, *op. cit.*, p. 63.
39 *Ibid.*, 83.
40 Huneidi, *op. cit.*, p. 132.
41 Quoted in Jonathan Schneer, *The Balfour Declaration: The Origins of the Arab-Israeli Conflict* (Bloomsbury: London, 2011), p. 84.
42 *Ibid.*, p. 86.
43 *House of Lords Debates*, 21 June 1922, vol. 50, col. 1118. Quoted in Segev (2001), *op. cit.*, p. 45.
44 T. E. Lawrence, *The Seven Pillars of Wisdom: A Triumph* (Jonathan Cape: London, 1952), p. 136.
45 Quoted in Stein, *op. cit.*, p. 481.
46 *Ibid.*, p. 478.
47 *Ibid.*, p. 526.
48 *Ibid.*, p. 163.
49 Walid Khalidi quoted in Michael Prior *Zionism and the State of Israel: a Moral Inquiry* (Routledge: London, 1999), p. 18.
50 Stein, *op. cit.*, p. 161.
51 G. W. Reynolds, and A. Judge, *The Night the Police Went on Strike* (Weidenfeld and Nicolson: London, 1968), p. 70.
52 Roberts, *op. cit.*, p. 278.
53 Gilbert, *op. cit.*, p. 31.
54 *Ibid*.
55 *Ibid.*, pp. 32-33.
56 *Ibid.*, p. 37
57 Roberts, *op. cit.*, p. 275.
58 *Illustrated Sunday Herald*, 8 February 1920, quoted in Roberts, *op. cit.*, p. 278.
59 Quoted in Gilbert, *op. cit.*, p. 42.
60 *Ibid.*, p. 73.
61 Quoted in Gilbert, p. 38.
62 *Ibid.*, p. 40.
63 *Ibid.*, p. 42.
64 *Ibid.*, p. 43.
65 Ingrams, 50.
66 *Ibid*.
67 Michael Adams and Christopher Mayhew, *Publish it not... the Middle East Cover-Up*, quoted in Prior, *op. cit.*, p. 13.
68 Ingrams, *op. cit.*, p. 11.
69 *Ibid.*, pp. 15-16.
70 *Ibid.*, p. 14.
71 Stein, *op. cit.*, p. 545.
72 Quoted in Schneer, *op. cit.*, p. 339.

Endnotes

73 Quoted in Segev (2001), *op. cit.*, p. 45-46.
74 Ingrams, *op. cit.*, p. 12.
75 *Ibid.*, p. 105.
76 Koestler, *op. cit.*, p. 4.
77 Ingrams, *op. cit.*, p. 73.
78 The Palin Report (1920), para. 56.
79 *Ibid.*
80 Ingrams, *op. cit.*, p. 86.
81 The Palin Report (1920), para. 66.
82 *Ibid.*, para. 69.
83 *Ibid.*
84 Gilbert, *op. cit.*, p. 73.
85 'A Report by Brigadier Wyndham Chief Secretary to the Palestine Government 1920-1922' quoted in Huneidi, *op. cit.*, p. 40.
86 *Ibid.*, p. 41.
87 Antonius, *op. cit.*, pp. 387-88.
88 'Palestine. Disturbances of May 1921: Reports of the Commission of Inquiry with Correspondence Relating Thereto' (The Haycraft Report), Cmd. 1540, p. 24
89 The Haycraft Report (1921), part 11, conclusion.
90 *Ibid.*, p. 13.
91 *Ibid.*, p. 43.
92 *Ibid.*, p. 22.
93 *Ibid.*, p. 57.
94 Ingrams, *op. cit.*, p. 135.
95 *Ibid.*, 136.
96 The Haycraft Report (1921), p. 54.
97 *Ibid.*, p. 44.
98 Segev (2001), *op. cit.*, p. 180.
99 Kramer, *op. cit.*, p. 25.
100 Segev (2001), *op. cit.*, p. 327.
101 *Ibid.*, 325-26.
102 Karsh, *op. cit.*, p. 20.
103 Segev (2001), *op. cit.*, p. 329.
104 Segev (2001), *op. cit.*, p. 334, quoting Chancellor's letter to his son.
105 *Ibid.*, p. 330.
106 Rose, *op. cit.*, p. 7.
107 Karsh, *op. cit.*, p. 277.
108 Koestler, *op. cit.*, p. 19.
109 'Report on Immigration, Land Settlement and Development' (The Hope Simpson Enquiry), 1930, Cmd. 3686.
110 *Ibid.*, p. 56.
111 *Ibid.*, p. 133.
112 Segev, (2001), *op. cit.*, pp. 273-74.
113 *Ibid.*, p. 275.
114 *Ibid.*, p. 379.
115 Rose, *op. cit.*, 17.
116 'The Passfield White Paper', 20 October 1930, Cmd. 3692.
117 *Jewish Daily Bulletin*, USA, 26 October 1930.
118 Carly Beckerman-Boys, 'The Reversal of the Passfield White Paper, 1930-31: A Reassessment'. *Journal of Contemporary History* (2016), vol. 51, no. 2, pp. 226.
119 Gilbert, *op. cit.*, p. 94.
120 *Ibid.*

121 Quoted in Beckerman-Boys, pp. 224-25.
120 Beckerman-Boys, *op. cit.*, p. 227.
121 *Ibid.*, p. 228.
124 Segev (2001), *op. cit.*, p. 336.
125 Beckerman-Boys, *op. cit.*, p. 214-15.
126 Renton, *op. cit.*, p. 70.
127 Beckerman-Boys, *op. cit.*, p. 229-30.
128 *Ibid.*, p. 231.
129 Quoted in Beckerman-Boys, p. 219.
130 *Ibid.*
131 Quoted in Morris (2001), *op. cit.*, p. 122.
132 Beckerman-Boys, *op. cit.*, pp. 213-33.
133 *Ibid.*, p. 221 ff.
134 *Ibid.*, p. 217.
135 *Ibid.*, p. 214.
136 *Ibid.*, p. 94.
137 *Ibid.*, p. 92.
138 *Ibid.*
139 James Barr, *A Line in the Sand: Britain, France and the Struggle that Shaped the Middle East* (Simon and Schuster: London, 2011), p. 186.
140 Michael J. Cohen, *Palestine: Retreat from the Mandate: The Making of British Policy 1936-1945* (Paul Elek: London, 1978), p. 53.
141 Gilbert, *op. cit.*, p. 108.
142 *Ibid.*
143 *Ibid.*, p. 180.
144 These were Jews of European origin.
145 The word means Spanish but is also applied to Jews from the Islamic world.
146 Schneer, *op. cit.*, p. 10.
147 *Ibid.*, pp. 11-12.
148 Huneidi, *op. cit.*, p. 4.
149 Schneer, *op. cit.*, p. 12.
150 Walid Khalidi, *All that Remains: the Palestinian Villages Occupied and Depopulated by Israel in 1948* (Institute for Palestine Studies: Washington DC, 1992), pp. 595-96.
151 Schneer, *op. cit.*, p. 12-13.
152 Segev (2019), *op. cit.*, p. 74-75.
153 *Ibid.*, p. 73.
154 *Ibid.*, p. 78.
155 *Ibid.*, p. 76.
156 Havrelock (2020), *op. cit.*, p. 101.
157 Segev, (2019), *op. cit.*, p. 621.
158 For a detailed discussion, see Segev (2019), p. 621 ff.
159 Kramer, *op. cit.*, p. 240.
160 Segev, (2001), *op. cit.*, p. 366
161 For example see Karsh, *op. cit.*, p. 101.

Chapter 5

1 Legal rule about theft.
2 Edward Horne, *A Job Well Done: A History of the Palestine Police Force 1920-1948* (Book Guild: Leicester, 2003), p. 213.

Endnotes

3 Tom Segev, *One Palestine Complete: Jews and Arabs under the British Mandate* (Abacus: London, 2001), p. 376.
4 Abdul Wahhab Kayyali, *Palestine: A Modern History* (Routledge Croom Helm: London, 1978), p. 196.
5 Segev, *op. cit.*, p. 423.
6 See his chapter 2.
7 Martin Gilbert, *Churchill and the Jews* (Simon and Schuster: London, 2007), p. 157.
8 James Barr, *A Line in the Sand: Britain, France and the Struggle that Shaped the Middle East* (Simon and Schuster: London, 2011), 194.
9 N. Rose, *The Gentile Zionists A Study in Anglo-Zionist Diplomacy 1929-39* (Frank Cass: London, 1973), p. 125.
10 *Ibid.*, p. 137.
11 *Ibid.*, p. 136.
12 Michael Cohen, *Palestine: Retreat from the Mandate: The Making of British Policy 1936-1945* (Paul Elek: London, 1978), p. 15.
13 The Peel Report (1937).
14 *Ibid.*, p. 363.
15 The Peel Report, chapter 11, p. 24.
16 Gilbert, *op. cit.*, p. 111.
17 *Ibid.*
18 *Ibid.*, p. 113.
19 *Ibid.*
20 *Ibid.*, p. 115.
21 *Ibid.*
22 *Ibid.*, pp. 115-16.
23 *Ibid.*
24 *Ibid.*, p. 117.
25 *Ibid.*, pp. 117-18.
26 *Ibid.*, p. 119.
27 Andrew Roberts, *Churchill: Walking with Destiny* (Allen Lane: London, 2018), p. 414.
28 *Ibid.*, p. 415.
29 The Peel Report, chapter 13, p. 395.
30 *Ibid.*, chapter 4, p. 108.
31 *Ibid.*, chapter 20, p. 370.
32 *Ibid.*, chapter 26.
33 *Ibid.*, chapter 10, p. 293.
34 *Ibid.*, chapter 10, p. 294.
35 *Ibid.*, chapter 3, p. 77.
36 *Ibid.*, chapter 8, p. 320.
37 *Ibid.*, chapter 10–conclusion, p. 394.
38 *Ibid.*, chapter 22, 'A plan of Partition'.
39 *Ibid.*, chapter 20, pp. 373-74.
40 Raghid El-Solh, *Lebanon and Arabism: National Identity and State Formation* (IB Tauris: London, 2004), pp. 69-70.
41 *Ibid.*, p. 67.
42 Rose, *op. cit.*, p. 135.
43 Zionist Peel Conference Resolution in Wikisource.
44 Gilbert, *op. cit.*, p. 122.
45 Rose, *op. cit.*, p. 148.
46 'Policy on Palestine. A Despatch of 23 December, 1937, from the Secretary of State for the Colonies to the High Commissioner for Palestine', Cmd. 5634.

47 Translation from Michael Prior, *Zionism and the State of Israel: a Moral Inquiry* (Routledge: London, 1999), p. 9.
48 Zangwill, *Israel, The Voice of Jerusalem*, quoted in Prior, *op. cit.*, p. 192.
49 Gilbert, *op. cit.*, p. 35.
50 Tom Segev, *A State at Any Cost: The Life of David Ben-Gurion* (Apollo: London, 2019), p. 264.
51 *Ibid.*, p. 270.
52 *Ibid.*, p. 264.
53 *Ibid.*, p. 267.
54 *Ibid.*, pp. 418-19.
55 *Ibid.*, p. 419.
56 Kramer, 287.
57 Segev (2019), *op. cit.*, p. 276.
58 *Ibid.*, p. 291.
59 Segev, (2001), *op. cit.*, p. 350-51.
60 *Ibid.*, p. 367.
61 Gudrun Kramer, *A History of Palestine: From the Ottoman Conquest to the Founding of the State of Israel* (Princeton University Press: Princeton, 2008), p. 29.
62 Barr, *op. cit.*, p. 187.
63 Rose, *op. cit.*, p. 111.
64 Barr, *op. cit.*, p. 189.
65 *Ibid.*, p. 187.
66 Simon Sebag Montefiore, *Jerusalem: The Biography* (Phoenix: London, 2011), p. 453.
67 'Palestine Commission Report' (The Woodhead Report), 1938, Cmd. 5854.
68 *Ibid.*, p. 7.
69 For a detailed discussion see Michael J. Cohen, *Palestine: Retreat from the Mandate: The Making of British Policy 1936-1945* (Paul Elek: London, 1978), pp. 44-47.
70 The Woodhead Report (1938), p. 246.
71 *Ibid*
72 Rose, *op. cit.*, p. 171.
73 'Palestine: Statement by His Majesty's Government in the United Kingdom in November 1938', Cmd. 5893.
74 *Ibid.*, para. 4.
75 Rose, *op. cit.*, p. 184.
76 *Ibid.*, p. 186.
77 *Ibid.*, p. 185.
78 Segev (2019), *op. cit.*, p. 284.
79 'White Paper of 1939. Palestine: Statement of Policy' (The MacDonald Paper), Cmd. 6019.
80 MacDonald White Paper (1939), section 11.
81 *Ibid.*, section 111.
82 *Ibid.*, section 1.
83 Gilbert, *op. cit.*, p. 159.
84 *Ibid.*, p. 162.
85 Marwn Buheiry, *The Formation and Perception of the Modern Arab world*. Edited by Lawrence I Conrad. (Darwin Press: Princeton, 1989), p. 177.
86 Segev, (2019) *op. cit.*, p. 285.
87 *Ibid.*, p. 279.
88 Sami Hadawi, *Bitter Harvest: A Modern History of Palestine* (Scorpion Press: Essex, 1989), p. 54.

Endnotes

89 League of Nations Permanent Mandates Commission: 'Minutes of the thirty-sixth session held at Geneva from 8-29 June 1939, including the Report of the Commission to the Council.'
90 Rose, *op. cit.*, pp. 195-96.
91 Segev, (2001), *op. cit.*, p. 449.
92 Segev, (2019), *op. cit.*, p. 287.
93 *Ibid.* p. 286.
94 Gilbert, *op. cit.*, p. 141.
95 *Ibid.*, p. 143.
96 *Ibid.*
97 Rose, *op. cit.*, p. 104.
98 Efraim Karsh, *Palestine Betrayed* (Yale University Press: New Haven, 2011), p. 60.
99 Rose, *op. cit.*, p. 105.
100 *Ibid.*
101 *Ibid.*, p. 106.
102 *Ibid.*, p. 105.
103 Segev (2019), *op. cit.*, 294.
104 *Ibid.*, p. 303.
105 *Ibid.*, p. 311.
106 Ilan Pappé, *The Making of the Arab-Israeli Conflict 1947-51* (Macmillan and St. Anthony's Press: New York, 1992), p. 2.
107 Zev Golan, *Free Jerusalem: Heroes, Heroines and Rogues Who Created the State of Israel* (Devora Publishing: Israel, 2002), p. 9.
108 Karsh, *op. cit.*, p. 30.
109 *Documents on German Foreign Policy 1918-1945*, Series D, vol. xiii, London, 1964.
110 Ronen Bergman, *Rise and Kill First: The Secret History of Israel's Targeted Assassinations* (John Murray: London, 2018), pp. 22-23.
111 *Time* magazine, 22 October 2015, quoted in Bergman.
112 Benny Morris, *Righteous Victims: A History of the Zionist–Arab Conflict 1881-2001* (Vintage Books: New York, 2001), p. 161.
113 Karsh, *op. cit.*, p. 60.
114 Segev (2019), *op. cit.*, p. 288.
115 *Ibid.*, p. 297.
116 *Ibid.*, p. 315.
117 *Ibid.*, p. 332.
118 *Ibid.*
119 *Ibid.*, p. 346.
120 *Ibid.*, p. 288.
121 Bergman, *op. cit.*, p. 3.
122 Barr, *op. cit.*, p. 268.
123 Bergman, *op. cit.*, pp. 3-4.
124 Arthur Koestler, *Promise and Fulfilment: Palestine 1917-1949* (Macmillan: London, 1949), p. 18.
125 Begin, *The Revolt* (W. H. Allen: London, 1951), p. 106. A later edition (1979) changed the wording to: 'After the death of the unarmed Abraham Stern'.
126 Koestler, *op. cit.*, 15.
127 Barr, *op. cit.*, 265.
128 *Ibid.*, p. 270.
129 *Ibid.*
130 Pappé, *op. cit.*, p. 10.
131 Segev (2019), *op. cit.*, p. 308.

132 *Ibid.*, p. 321.
133 Morris, *op. cit.*, p. 168.
134 *Ibid.*, 169.
135 Alfred M. Lilienthal, *The Other Side of the Coin: An American Perspective of the Arab-Israeli Conflict* (The Devon-Adair Company: New York, 1965), p. 273.
136 *Hansard House of Lords*, col. 208, 9 June 1942.
137 *The Times, of Israel*, 10 May 2020.
138 Roberts, *op. cit.*, p. 846.
139 Nathan Aridan, *Britain, Israel and Anglo-Jewry 1949-1957* (Routledge: London, 2004), p. 93.
140 Segev (2019), *op. cit.*, p. 383.
141 *Ibid.*, p. 274.
142 Begin, *op. cit.*, p. 182.
143 Koestler, *op. cit.*, p. 60.
144 Segev (2019), *op. cit.*, p. 300.
145 Barr, *op. cit.*, pp. 273-74.
146 Begin, *op. cit.*, p. 180.
147 Amikam Nachmani, *Great Power Discord in Palestine: The Anglo–American Committee of Inquiry into the Problems of European Jewry and Palestine* (Frank Cass: London, 1987), p. 46.
148 *Ibid.*, p. 45.
149 'House of Commons Debate on the White Paper', May 1939, quoted in Koestler, *op. cit.*, p. 109.
150 Quoted in Koestler, *op. cit.*, p. 110.
151 Begin, *op. cit.*, p. 180.
152 For a detailed discussion, see Cohen, *op. cit.*, p. 169.
153 *Ibid.*, p. 152.
154 *Ibid.*, p. 162.
155 *Ibid.*, p. 160.
156 Richard Crossman, *A Nation Reborn* (Hamish Hamilton: London, 1960), p. 69.
157 For details see Nachmani, chapter 4.
158 *Ibid.*, 61.
159 'Report of the Anglo–American Committee of Inquiry regarding the Problems of European Jewry and Palestine 1946', Cmd. 6808.
160 Nachmani, *op. cit.*, p. 10.
161 *Ibid.*, p. 14.
162 *Ibid.*, p. 1.
163 *Ibid.*
164 Anglo-American Committee Report, chapter 2, para. 12.
165 Nachmani, *op. cit.*, p. 11.
166 *Ibid.*, p. 143.
167 Segev (2019), *op. cit.*, p. 375.
168 *Ibid.*, p. 370.
169 *Ibid.*, p. 389.
170 *Ibid.*, p. 370.
171 Nachmani, *op. cit.*, p. 56.
172 *Ibid.*, p. 57.
173 Begin, *op. cit.*, p. 200.
174 'Proposals for the Future of Palestine' (The Morrison–Grady Plan), 1946, Cmd. 7044.
175 Truman's memoirs quoted in Lilienthal, *op. cit.*, p. 278.
176 Segev (2019), *op. cit.*, p. 385.

177 Barr, *op. cit.*, p. 321.
178 *Ibid.*, pp. 321-22.
179 Segev (2019), *op. cit.*, p. 386.
180 Begin, *op. cit.*, p. 220.
181 *Ibid.*, pp. 221-22.
182 *Ibid.*, p. 245.
183 Shmuel Katz, *Days of Fire* (Doubleday: Garden City, 1968), p. 93.
184 Thurston Clarke, *By Blood and Fire: The Attack on the King David Hotel* (Hutchinson: London, 1981), p. 286.
185 *Hansard House of Commons*, 23 July 1946.
186 Begin, *op. cit.*, p. 221.
187 Tom Segev, 'The Spirit of the King David Hotel', *Haaretz*, 23 July 2006.
188 Ned Parker and Stephen Farrell, 'British anger at terror celebration', *The Times*, 20 July 2006.
189 Ilan Pappé, *The Making of the Arab-Israeli Conflict 1947-51* (Macmillan and St. Anthony's Press: New York, 1992), p. 12.
190 Segev (2019), p. 244.
191 Lilienthal, p. 19.
192 Morris, *op. cit.*, p. 162.
193 Quoted in Hadawi, *op. cit.*, p. 42.
194 *Ibid.*
195 Bernard Law Montgomery, *The Memoirs of Field-Marshal the Viscount Montgomery of Alamein* (Collins: London, 1958), pp. 466-67.
196 *Ibid.*
197 *Ibid.*, p. 423.
198 *Ibid.*

Chapter 6

1 Golda Meir quoted in Tom Segev, *A State at Any Cost: The Life of David Ben-Gurion* (Apollo: London, 2019), p. 10.
2 Benny Morris, *Righteous Victims: A History of the Zionist–Arab Conflict 1881-2001* (Vintage Books: New York, 2001). 182.
3 *Ibid.*
4 Martin Gilbert, *Churchill and the Jews* (Simon and Schuster: London, 2007), p. 251.
5 *Ibid.*, p. 281.
6 Efraim Karsh, *Palestine Betrayed* (Yale University Press: New Haven, 2011), p. 87.
7 Ilan Pappé, *The Making of the Arab-Israeli Conflict 1947-51* (Macmillan and St. Anthony's Press: New York, 1992), p. 38.
8 *Ibid.*
9 *Ibid.*, p. 53.
10 Morris, *op. cit.*, p. 184.
11 *Ibid.*, p. 181.
12 Menachem Begin, *The Revolt* (W. H. Allen: London, 1951), p. 290.
13 Hernan Dobry, *Operation Israel: The Rearming of Argentina During the Dictatorship of 1976/1983*.
14 *Haaretz*, 21 April 2011; *The Mail Online*, 20 April 2011.
15 Segev, *op. cit.*, pp. 401-402.
16 Begin, *op. cit.*, p. 290.
17 Arnold Forster and Benjamin Epstein, *The New Anti-Semitism* (McGraw-Hill: New York, 1974), p. 260.

18 Azriel Bermant, *Margaret Thatcher and the Middle East* (Cambridge University Press: Cambridge, 2016), p. 67.
19 Segev, *op. cit.*, p. 368.
20 Morris, *op. cit.*, p. 183.
21 *Ibid.*
22 *Ibid.*
23 Walid Khalidi, quoted in Morris, *op. cit.*, p. 186.
24 Alfred M. Lilienthal, *The Other Side of the Coin: An American Perspective of the Arab-Israeli Conflict* (The Devon-Adair Company: New York, 1965), p. 280.
25 Tom Segev, *One Palestine Complete: Jews and Arabs under the British Mandate* (Abacus: London, 2001), p. 497.
26 *Ibid.*, p. 409.
27 Segev (2019), *op. cit.*, p. 410.
28 *Ibid.*
29 *Ibid.*
30 Karsh, *op. cit.*, p. 101.
31 Morris, *op. cit.*, p. 193.
32 *Ibid.*, p. 205.
33 *Ibid.*, p. 201.
34 *Ibid.*, p. 198.
35 *Ibid.*, p. 210.
36 Quoted in Morris, p. 213.
37 Ilan Pappé, *The Ethnic Cleansing of Palestine* (One World Publications: Oxford, 2006), p. 72.
38 *Ibid.*, p. 128.
39 *Ibid.*, p. 155.
40 *Ibid.*, p. 18 ff.
41 *Ibid.*, p. 19.
42 Dalet: section 3, part 4.
43 Yoav Gelber, *Palestine 1948: War, Escape and the Emergence of the Palestinian Refugee Problem* (Sussex Academic Press: Eastbourne, 2006), p. 306.
44 Benny Morris, *The Birth of the Palestinian Refugee Problem* (Cambridge University Press: Cambridge, 1987), p. 165.
45 Benny Morris, *1948: A History of the First Arab-Israeli War* (Yale University Press: New Haven, 2009), p. 116.
46 Chaim Herzog, *The Arab-Israeli Wars: War and Peace in the Middle East From the War of Independence to Lebanon* (Arms and Armour Press: London, 1985), p. 33.
47 See Pappé (2006), *op. cit.*, pp. 86-126.
48 Rachel Havrelock, *The Joshua Generation: Israel Occupation and the Bible* (Princeton University Press: Princeton, 2020), pp. 102-103.
49 Segev (2001), p. 493.
50 Walid Khalidi, *All that Remains: the Palestinian Villages Occupied and Depopulated by Israel in 1948* (Institute for Palestine Studies: Washington DC, 1992).
51 *Ibid.*, p. xxxii.
52 *Ibid.*, p. xxxii.
53 Segev, (2019), *op. cit.*, p. 416.
54 *Ibid.*, p. 417.
55 *Ibid.*
56 Khalidi discusses the various totals in *All that Remains*, p. 282.
57 Khalidi, *op. cit.*, p. xv.

Endnotes

58 Moshe Dayan, 'Address to the Technion (Israel Institute of Technology), Haifa' as quoted in *Haaretz*, 4 April 1969, quoted in Khalidi, *op. cit.*, p. xxxi.
59 *Ibid.*
60 Segev (2019), *op. cit.*, p. 412.
61 Nur Masalha, *Expulsion of the Palestinians: the Concept of Transfer in Zionist Political Thought 1882–1948*, (Institute for Palestine Studies: Washington, 1992), pp. 22-23, quoted in Michael Prior, *Zionism and the State of Israel: a Moral Inquiry* (Routledge: London, 1999), p. 193.
62 Segev (2019), *op. cit.*, p. 132.
63 *Ibid.*, p. 158.
64 *Ibid.*, p. 419.
65 Quoted in Sahar Huneidi, *A Broken Trust: Herbert Samuel, Zionism and the Palestinians 1920-1925* (IB Tauris: London, 2001), p. 12.
66 Gudrun Kramer, *A History of Palestine: From the Ottoman Conquest to the Founding of the State of Israel* (Princeton University Press: Princeton, 2008), p. 114.
67 Segev (2019), *op. cit.*, pp. 438-39.
68 Pappé, (2006), *op. cit.*, p. 167.
69 *Ibid.*, p. 168.
70 *Ibid.*, p. 169.
71 Quoted in Michael J. Cohen, *Palestine: Retreat from the Mandate: The Making of British Policy 1936-1945* (Paul Elek: London, 1978), p. 177.
72 David Hirst, *The Gun and the Olive Branch* (Faber and Faber: London, 2003), pp. 252-53.
73 Yoav Gelber, *op. cit.*, p. 310.
74 See Yehuda Lapidot, *Besieged Jerusalem 1948: Memories of an Irgun Fighter* (Yehuda Lapidot: Israel, 1992) for one version of events.
75 Morris, (1987), *op. cit.*, p. 113.
76 Gelber, *op. cit.*, p. 312.
77 Quoted in Morris (1987), *op. cit.*, p. 238.
78 Quoted in Morris (1987), *op. cit.*, p. 238.
79 Quoted in Dominique Lapierre and Larry Collins, *O Jerusalem* (Simon and Schuster: London, 1972), p. 276.
80 Gelber, *op. cit.*, p. 316.
81 Horne, *op. cit.*, p. 563.
82 See Susan Slyomovics, *Nakba: Palestine 1948 and the Claims of Memory* (Columbia University Press: New York, 2007).
83 Segev (2019), *op. cit.*, p. 449.
84 *Ibid.*
85 Pappé (1992), *op. cit.*, p. 209.
86 Segev (2019), *op. cit.*, p. 465.
87 Pappé (2006), *op. cit.*, p. 209.
88 Gelber, *op. cit.*, p. 316.
89 The 'Doctrine' by the IDF can be retrieved on www1.idf.il/dover/site/mainpage.asp?sl=EN&id=32.
90 Norman Solomon, 'Judaism and the Ethics of War', *International Review of the Red Cross* (June 2005), issue 87, p. 858.
91 See Kristen Eichensehr, 'On Target? The Israeli Supreme Court and the Expansion of Targeted Killings', *Yale Law Journal* (June 2007), vol. 116, no. 8.
92 Prior, *op. cit.*, pp. 208-209.
93 Karsh, *op. cit.*, p. 122.
94 Segev (2001), *op. cit.*, p. 507.

95 Benny Morris, 'The Historiography of Deir Yassin', *The Journal of Israeli History* (2005), vol. 24, no. 1, pp. 79-107.
96 Lawrence Wright, *Thirteen Days in December: The Dramatic Struggle for Peace* (Doubleday Publishing Group: London, 2014), p. 271.
97 Begin, *op. cit.*, p. 163 ff.
98 Benny Morris Benny, *1948: A History of the First Arab-Israeli War* (Yale University Press: New Haven, 2009), p. 209.
99 Quoted in Pappé, (1992), *op. cit.*, p. 53.
100 *Ibid.*, p. 55.
101 Begin, *op. cit.*, p. 159.
102 Karsh, *op. cit.*, p. 111.
103 *Ibid.*, p. 235.
104 Pappé (1992), *op. cit.*, p. 166.
105 Gilbert, *op. cit.*, p. 272.
106 *Ibid.*, p. 274.
107 Andrew Roberts, *Churchill: Walking with Destiny* (Allen Lane: London, 2018), p. 912.
108 *Ibid.*
109 Nathan Aridan, *Britain, Israel and Anglo-Jewry 1949-1957* (Routledge: London, 2004), p. 94.
110 *Ibid.*, 20.
111 *Ibid.*, p. 23.
112 Gilbert, *op. cit.*, pp. 272-73.
113 Aridan, *op. cit.*, p. 2.
114 Morris, (2001), *op. cit.*, p. 170.
115 Avi Shlaim, *Lion of Jordan: The Life of King Hussein in War and Peace* (Allen Lane: London, 2007), pp. 29-30.
116 Count Folke Bernadotte, *To Jerusalem* (Hodder and Stoughton: London, 1951), p. 9.
117 *Ibid.*, p. 46.
118 *Ibid.*, p. 51.
119 *Ibid.*
120 *Ibid.*, p. 107.
121 *Ibid.*, p. 118.
122 *Ibid.*, pp. 59-60.
123 *Ibid.*, p. 32.
125 *Ibid.*, pp. 100-101.
126 *Ibid.*, p. 105.
127 *Ibid.*, p. 94.
128 *Ibid.*
124 *Ibid.*, p. 71.
129 *Ibid.*, p. 235.
130 Pappé (1992), *op. cit.*, p. 150.
131 *Ibid.*, p. 154.
132 *Ibid.*
133 *Ibid.*
134 Bernadotte, *op. cit.*, p. 200.
135 *Ibid.*, p. 196.
136 *Ibid.*, p. 243.
137 Karsh, *op. cit.*, pp. 235-36.
138 Morris (2001), *op. cit.*, pp. 256-57.
139 Pappé (1992), *op. cit.*, p. 157.
140 Karsh, *op. cit.*, p. 226.

141 *Ibid.*, p. 223.
142 *Ibid.*, p. 224.
143 *Ibid.*, p. 227.
144 For example, Karsh, *op. cit.*, p. 215.
145 Chaim Herzog, *The Arab-Israeli Wars: War and Peace in the Middle East From the War of Independence to Lebanon* (Arms and Armour Press: London, 1985), pp. 105-106.
146 Karsh, *op. cit.*, p. 226.
147 *Ibid.*, p. 227.
148 Bernadotte, *op. cit.*, p. 126 ff.
149 *Ibid.*, p. 145.
150 *Ibid.*, p. 149.
151 *Ibid.*, p. 151-52.
152 *Ibid.*, p. 170 ff.
153 *Ibid.*, p. 193.
154 Pappé (2006), *op. cit.*, p. 174.
155 Bernadotte, *op. cit.*, p. 196.
156 *Ibid.*, p. 199.
157 *Ibid.*, p. 199-200.
158 *Ibid.*, p. 228.
159 *Ibid.*, p. 208.
160 *Ibid.*, p. 238-39.
161 Ronen Bergman, *Rise and Kill First: The Secret History of Israel's Targeted Assassinations* (John Murray: London, 2018), p. 28.
162 Arthur Koestler, *Promise and Fulfilment: Palestine 1917-1949* (Macmillan: London, 1949), p. 279.
163 *Ibid.*, p. 279-80.
164 *Ibid.*, p. 281.
165 Pappé (1992), *op. cit.*, p. 163.
166 Karsh, *op. cit.*, p. 226.
167 Bergman, *op. cit.*, p. 842.
168 Quoted in Pappé (1992), *op. cit.*, p. 165.
169 Quoted in Pappé (1992), *op. cit.*, p. 166.
170 Aridan, *op. cit.*, p. 10.
171 'General Progress Report 11 December to 23 October 1950': General Assembly Official Records: Fifth Session Supplement No 18 (A/1367/Rev. 1) New York 1951, chapter 111, para. 44.
172 *Ibid.*, para. 8.
173 *Ibid.*, chapter 11, para. 4.
174 *Ibid.*, para. 9.
175 *Ibid.*, para. 38.
176 *Ibid.*, para. 41.
177 *Ibid.*, chapter 4, para. 17.
178 *Ibid.*, chapter 4, para. 20.
179 Morris (2001), *op. cit.*, p. 263.
180 'General Progress Report 11 December to 23 October 1950', para. 33.
181 *Ibid.*, para. 32.
182 *Ibid.*, paras 35-37.
183 Segev (2019), *op. cit.*, p. 451.
184 *Ibid.*, p. 449.
185 Quoted in Pappé (1992), *op. cit.*, pp. 218-219.
186 Pappé (1992), *op. cit.*, passim; Morris (2001), *op. cit.*, p. 262.

187 Quoted in Morris (2001), *op. cit.*, p 264.
188 Avi Shlaim, *Lion of Jordan: The Life of King Hussein in War and Peace* (Allen Lane: London, 2007), p. 31.

Chapter 7

1 Nathan Aridan, *Britain, Israel and Anglo-Jewry 1949-1957* (Routledge: London, 2004), p. 161.
2 Ronen Bergman, *Rise and Kill First: The Secret History of Israel's Targeted Assassinations* (John Murray: London, 2018), p. 44.
3 *The Jewish Chronicle*, 23 October 1953, quoted in Aridan, *op. cit.*, p. 236.
4 Chaim Herzog, *The Arab-Israeli Wars: War and Peace in the Middle East From the War of Independence to Lebanon* (Arms and Armour Press: London, 1985), p. 120.
5 *Ibid.*
6 Aridan, *op. cit.*, p. 140-41.
7 *Ibid.*, p. 139.
8 *Ibid.*, p. 141.
9 Benny Morris, *Righteous Victims: A History of the Zionist–Arab Conflict 1881-2001* (Vintage Books: New York, 2001), p. 261.
10 *Ibid.*, p. 263.
11 Aridan, *op. cit.*, p. 162.
12 Selwyn Lloyd, *Suez 1956: A Personal Account* (Jonathan Cape: London, 1978), p. 54.
13 Morris, *op. cit.*, p. 265.
14 William J. Burns, *Economic Aid and American Policy toward Egypt 1955-1981*. (State University of New York Press: Albany, 1985), p. 49.
15 *The Observer*, 4 November 1956, quoted in Aridan, *op. cit.*, p. 186.
16 Aridan, *op. cit.*, p. 182.
17 Quoted in Aridan, *op. cit.*, p. 182.
18 Herzog, *op. cit.*, p. 149.
19 Tom Segev, *A State at Any Cost: The Life of David Ben-Gurion* (Apollo: London, 2019), p. 565.
20 Morris, *op. cit.*, p. 310.
21 Herzog, *op. cit.*, p. 153.
22 Note for example, Morris, *op. cit.*, p. 318.
23 Morris, *op. cit.*, p. 323.
24 *Ibid.*, p. 329.
25 *Ibid.*, p. 327
26 *Ibid.*
27 *Ibid.*, p. 328.
28 *Ibid.*, p. 333.
29 *Ibid.*, p. 337.
30 *Ibid.*, p. 339.
31 Herzog, *op. cit.*, p. 203.
32 Morris, *op. cit.*, p. 341.
33 *Ibid.*, p. 356.
34 Herzog, *op. cit.*, p. 205.
35 Morris, *op. cit.*, p. 362.
36 Herzog, *op. cit.*, p. 222.
37 *Ibid.*, p. 223.

38 Morris, *op. cit.*, p. 389.
39 Arnold Forster and Benjamin Epstein, *The New Anti-Semitism* (McGraw-Hill: New York, 1974), p. 11.
40 *Ibid.*, pp. 255-56.
41 *Ibid.*, p. 255.
42 *Ibid.*, p. 15.
43 *Ibid.*, pp. 83-84.
44 Herzog, p. 203.
45 Morris, (2001), p. 371.
46 *Ibid.*, p. 377.
47 *Ibid.*, p. 558.
48 Herzog, *op. cit.*, p. 349.
49 Morris, *op. cit.*, p. 498.
50 UN Security Resolutions 425/426.
51 Morris, *op. cit.*, p. 537.
52 'Report on the Events at the Refugee Camps in Beirut', 3 February 1983.
53 Morris, *op. cit.*, p. 557.
54 *Ibid.*, p. 568.
55 *Ibid.*, p. 569.
56 *Ibid.*, p. 562.
57 *Ibid.*, p. 580.
58 *Ibid.*, p. 583.
59 *Ibid.*, p. 589.
60 *Ibid.*, p. 590.
61 *Ibid.*, p. 593.
62 *Haaretz*, 11 January 2007.
63 Quoted in Morris, *op. cit.*, p. 621.
64 Morris, *op. cit.*, p. 624.
65 *Ibid.*, p. 626.
66 Efraim Karsh, *Palestine Betrayed* (Yale University Press: New Haven, 2011) p. 254.
67 Bergman, *op. cit.*, p. 425.
68 *Ibid.*, p. 43.
69 Morris, *op. cit.*, p. 645.
70 Bergman, *op. cit.*, p. 448.
71 Karsh, *op. cit.*, p. 251.
72 *Ibid*.
73 Suzanne Goldberg, *The Guardian*, 29 September 2000.
74 Avi Shlaim, *Lion of Jordan: The Life of King Hussein in War and Peace* (Allen Lane: London, 2007), p. 258.
75 Bergman, *op. cit.*, p. 489.
76 AI Index MDE 15, (149) 2002. Human Rights Watch also made allegations of the same kind. May 2002, vol. 14, no. 3, (E).
77 Karsh, *op. cit.*, p. 251.
78 Morris, *op. cit.*, p. 666.
79 *Ibid.*, p. 661.
80 The full title of the report is the 'Sharm el-Sheikh Fact Finding Committee Report', (2001).
81 Bergman, *op. cit.*, p. 490.
82 Yonatan Mendel, 'Covid-19 in the Time of Netanyahu', *London Review of Books*, 7 May 2020, vol. 42, no. 9.
83 'United Nations Fact Finding Commission on the Gaza Strip.'

84 The quotations are from the B'Tselem report: 'Black Flag: The legal and moral implications of the policy of attacking residential buildings in the Gaza Strip' (summer 2014). The figures may be seen in many publications from the UN, in journals, and in newspapers, for example the *Jerusalem Post* of 28 August 2014.
85 David Makovsky, 'How to Build a Fence' and 'The Wayback Machine' in *Foreign Affairs,* March/April 2004, vol. 83, Issue 2, p. 53.
86 'The ultimate barrier: impact of the Wall on the Palestinian health care system.' Médecins du Monde, 2005.

Chapter 8

1 Nathan Thrall, 'The Annexation Delusion' in *London Review of Books*, 21 January 2021.
2 Barack Obama, *A Promised Land* (Viking: London, 2020), p. 628.
3 Alfred M. Lilienthal, *The Other Side of the Coin: An American Perspective of the Arab-Israeli Conflict* (The Devon-Adair Company: New York, 1965), pp. 29-30.
4 Arnold Forster and Benjamin Epstein, *The New Anti-Semitism* (McGraw-Hill: New York, 1974), p. 118.
5 Adam Shatz, 'Trump's America, Netanyahu's Israel' in *London Review of Books*, 9 May 2019.
6 Henry Siegman, 'The Ultimate Deal' in *London Review of Books*, 30 March 2017, vol. 39, no. 7.
7 *The Week*, 6 April 2019.
8 Henry Siegman, 'The Ultimate Deal' in *London Review of Books*, 30 March 2017, vol. 39, no. 7.
9 Widely reported, including in *The New York Times*, 19 November 2019.
10 *The Guardian*, 6 June 2020.
11 *The Jewish Chronicle*, 18 June 2020.
12 'House-Cleaning: David Bromwich on Trump's Latest Moves' in *London Review of Books*, 7 March 2019, vol. 41, no. 5.
13 'Peace to Prosperity: a vision to improve the lives of the Palestinian and Israeli people' (The Trump Peace Plan), 2020, p. 33.
14 *Ibid.*
15 *Ibid.*, p. 119.
16 *Ibid.*, pp. 135, 137, 139 ff.
17 *The New York Times*, 31 January 2020.
18 The Trump Peace Plan, p. 12.
19 *Ibid.*, p. 35.
20 *Ibid.*, p. 36.
21 *Ibid.*, p. 49.
22 *Ibid.*, p. 12.
23 *Ibid.*, p. 43.
24 *Ibid.*, pp. 25, 54.
25 *Ibid.*, p. 11.
26 *Ibid.*, pp. 39, 40.
27 *Ibid.*, p. 43.
28 *Ibid.*, p. 12.
29 *The Times, of Israel*, 2 February 2020.
30 *The Times, of Israel*, 1 February 2020.
31 *Haaretz*, 1 February 2020.

32 'The Abraham Accords', Supra, Note 13. See also the White House Statement, 13 August 2020.
33 All the above discussion is taken from *The Washington Post*, 13 August 2020.
34 Forster and Epstein, *op. cit.*, p. 123.
35 *Ibid.*, p. 16.
36 *Ibid.*, p. 87.
37 *Ibid.*, p. 88.
38 *The Guardian*, 8 December 1918.
39 *Ibid.*
40 Graham Davi and Stanley Waterman, 'Underenumeration of the Jewish population in the United Kingdom' *in Population, Space and Place*, March/April 2005, pp. 89-102.
41 Aridan, *op. cit.*, p. 239.
42 Azriel Bermant, *Margaret Thatcher and the Middle East* (Cambridge University Press: Cambridge, 2016), p. 66.
43 *Ibid.*, p. 67.
44 *Ibid.*, pp. 78-79.
45 Forster and Epstein, *op. cit.*, pp. 267-68,
46 *Ibid.*, p. 223.
47 *Ibid.*, p. 231 ff.
48 Garry O'Connor, *Alec Guinness: Master of Disguise* (Hodder and Stoughton: London, 1995), p. 99.
49 Forster and Epstein, *op. cit.*, pp. 91.
50 *Ibid.*, p. 93.
51 *Ibid.*, p. 94.
52 *Ibid.*, pp. 93-94.
53 *Ibid.*, p. 104.
54 *Ibid.*, p. 106.
55 *Ibid.*, p. 91.
56 *Ibid.*, p. 103.
57 *Ibid.*, p. 259.
58 Bergman, *op. cit.*, pp. 161-62.
59 *Ibid.*, p. xx.
60 'Trump's America, Netanyahu's Israel' in *London Review of Books*, 9 May 2019.
61 Walter Laqueur, *The Changing Face of Anti-Semitism: From Ancient Times to the Present Day* (Oxford University Press: Oxford, 2006), p. 186.
62 Abba Eban, 'Anti-Zionism is Merely the New Anti-Semitism', Congress Bi-weekly, American Jewish Congress (1973), vol. 40, issues 2-14, p. xxv.
63 Noam Chomsky, 'Transcript of Amy Goodman interview of Noam Chomsky', (*http:www.democracynow.org/2014/11/27/Noam Chomsky at United Nations*).
64 Forster and Epstein, *op. cit.*, p. 324.
65 Norman Finkelstein, *Beyond Chutzpah: On the Misuse of Anti-Semitism and the Abuse of History* (University of California Press: California, 2005), pp. 21-22.
66 Raab Earl, 'Is there a New Antisemitism?', *Commentary* (May 1974), pp. 53-54.
67 Lorna Finlayson, 'Corbyn Now' in *London Review of Books*, 27 September 2018, vol. 40, no. 18.
68 *The Independent*, 28 April 2016: a report of an interview on Radio London.
69 *Ibid.*
70 *Metro*, 25 February 2019.
71 *The Sunday Mirror*, 1 September 2018.
72 *The Guardian*, 9 February 2019.
73 *The Guardian*, 19 February 2019.

74   *The Jewish Chronicle*, 20 February 2019.
75   *The Guardian*, 19 February 2019.
76   *Mail Online*, 5 March 2019.
77   *The Guardian*, 9 March 2019.
78   *The Daily Telegraph*, 5 April 2017.
79   *The Independent*, 28 April 2016.
80   *The Guardian*, 30 March 2017.
81   *Herald Tribune*, 27 April 2016.
82   *The Jewish Chronicle*, 15 November 2018.
83   *The Jewish Chronicle*, 30 June 2017.
84   *The Guardian*, 2 August 2018.
85   *The Jewish Chronicle*, 21 October 2020.
86   *The Guardian*, 3 June 2017.
87   *The Daily Telegraph*, 30 October 2014.
88   Stephen Sedley, Letter to the *London Review of Books*, 8 February 2018, vol. 40, no. 3.
89   David Wolfson and Jeremy Brier, 'The opinion of the IHRA Definition of anti-Semitism by the Government of the United Kingdom', July 2017.
90   *Ibid.*, para. B4.
91   *Ibid.*
92   *Ibid.*, para. B3 (1) and para. 15.
93   *Ibid.*, para. 25.
94   Stephen Sedley, 'Defining Antisemitism' in *London Review of Books*, 4 May 2017, vol. 39, no. 9.
95   Karl Sabbagh, *London Review of Books*, 1 June 2017, vol. 39, no. 11.
96   Stephen Sedley, 'Short Cuts' in *London Review of Books*, 10 May 2018, vol. 40, no. 9.
97   Lorna Finlayson, 'Corbyn Now' in *London Review of Books*, 27 September 2018, vol. 40, no. 18.
98   *The Guardian*, 12 July 2018.
99   *Ibid.*
100 *The Jewish Chronicle*, 17 July 2018.
101 *Ibid.*
102 *Sunday Mirror*, 1 September 2018.
103 *The Guardian*, 12 July 2018.
104 Keith Khan-Harris in *The Guardian*, 30 June 2016.
105 'The Shami Chakrabarti Report on Antisemitism and Other Forms of Racism in the Labour Party', 30 June 2016, p. 13.
106 *Ibid.*, p. 1.
107 *Ibid.*, p. 9.
108 *Ibid.*, p. 15.
109 *Ibid.*, p. 7.
110 *The Observer*, 16 October 2016.
111 *The Jewish Chronicle*, 7 August 2016.
112 *The Guardian*, 8 August 2016.
113 ITV Report, 25 September 2016.
114 *The Guardian*, 17 October 2020.
115 *The Jewish Chronicle*, 12 December 2018.
116 *The Guardian*, 10 July 2019.
117 Interview by Damian Whitworth in *The Times*, 10 October 1918.
118 *The Daily Telegraph*, 28 August 2018.
119 'Investigation into anti-Semitism in the Labour Party', p. 16.

120 These are: 'House of Commons Home Affairs Committee: Antisemitism in the UK: Tenth Report of Session 2016-17', HC 136, 13 October 2016 and 'Allegations of anti-Semitism Oxford University Labour Club', by Baroness Jan Royall, 2016.
121 Royall Report, p. 11.
122 EHRC Report, p. 118.
123 *Ibid.*, p. 16.
124 *Ibid.*, p. 100.
125 *Ibid.*, p. 58.
126 *Ibid.*, p. 6.
127 *Ibid.*, p. 17.
128 *Ibid.*, p. 82.
129 *Ibid.*
130 *Ibid.*, Annex 1.
131 *Ibid.*, p. 81.
132 *Ibid.*, p. 85.
133 *Ibid.*, p. 86.
134 *Ibid.*, p. 14.
135 *Ibid.*, p. 43.
136 *Ibid.*, p. 56.
137 *Ibid.*, p. 109.
138 *Ibid.*, p. 28.
139 *Ibid.*, p. 105.
140 *Ibid.*
141 *Ibid.*, p. 106.
142 *Ibid.*, p. 108.
143 *Ibid.*, p. 110.
144 *Ibid.*, p. 16.
145 *Ibid.*, p. 79.
146 *The Guardian*, 29 October 2020.
147 *The Jewish Chronicle*, 18 November 2020.
148 Ilan Pappé, *The Ethnic Cleansing of Palestine* (One World Publications: Oxford, 2006), p. 226.
149 *Ibid.*
150 *Ibid.*, p. 229.
151 *The Week*, Issue 1305, 14 November 2020.
152 'Witness: Medical Aid For Palestinians', winter 2018.
153 *Ibid.*
154 *Ibid.*
155 Robert Wistrich, 'Theodor Herzl: Zionist Icon, Myth-maker and Social Utopian'. *Israel Affairs* (1995), vol. 1, no. 3, p. 26.
156 Efraim Karsh, *Palestine Betrayed* (Yale University Press: New Haven, 2011), pp. 12-13, 14.
157 *Ibid.*, p. 253.
158 *Ibid.*
159 *The Guardian*, 17 October 2020.
160 Benny Morris, *Righteous Victims: A History of the Zionist–Arab Conflict 1881-2001* (Vintage Books: New York, 2001), p. 13.
161 'Witness: Medical Aid For Palestinians', winter 2018.
162 *Ibid.*
163 'Witness: Medical Aid For Palestinians', winter 2018.
164 *Ibid.*
165 *Ibid.*

166 Mouin Rabbani, 'Short Cuts' in *London Review of Books*, March 2021, vol. 43, no. 6, p. 18
167 'Israeli Information Centre for Human Rights in the Occupied Territories.' www.btselem.org/statistics/detainees_and_prisoners
168 Esmail Nashif, *Palestinian Prisoners: Identity and Community* (Routledge: London, 2008), introduction.
169 J. E. Thomas, *Voices from Captivity: Incarceration from Siberia to Guantanamo Bay* (Jessica Kingsley Publishers: London, 2018), p. 355.
170 Alon Harel , '*Who is a Security Prisoner and Why? An Examination of the Legality of Prison Regulations Governing Security Prisoners*' in Abeer Baker, and Anat Matar, (eds.) *Threat: Palestinian Political Prisoners in Israel* (Pluto Press: London, 2011), p. 37.
171 Michael Sfard, 'Devil's Island: The Transfer of Palestinian Detainees Into Prisons Within Israel', in Baker and Matar, *op. cit.*, p. 189.
172 Abdo Nahla, 'Palestinian Women Political Prisoners and the Israeli State', in Baker and Matar, *op. cit.*, pp. 63, 65.
173 Yonatan Mendel, 'Covid In the Time of Netanyahu' in *London Review of Books*, 7 May 2020.
174 *The Guardian*, 6 April 2019.
175 Mendel, *op. cit.*
176 Iraqi Amjad, *The Guardian*, 13 March 2019.
177 Ibid.
178 Nathan Thrall, 'The Annexation Delusion' in *London Review of Books*, 21 January 2021.
179 Ibid.
180 *The Week*, 13 February 2021, issue 1318.
181 Obama, *op. cit.*, pp. 627, 628, 368.
182 Thrall *op. cit.*
183 *Israel National News*, 26 October 2017.
184 *The New York Jewish Week*, 8 April 2013.
185 George Antonius, *The Arab Awakening: the Story of the Arab National Movement* (Hamish Hamilton: London, 1969), p. 410.
186 Translated from the Israeli-Hebrew-language Magazine *Ner*, January–February 1961 issue, and published in the American Council for Judaism magazine, *Issues*, Fall 1961, p. 19, quoted in Sami Hadawi, *Bitter Harvest: A Modern History of Palestine* (Scorpion Press: Essex, 1989), pp. 5-6.
187 Bergman, *op. cit.*, p. 46.
188 Segev (2019), *op. cit.*, p. 79.
189 *Ibid.*, p. 97.
190 James Barr, *A Line in the Sand: Britain, France and the Struggle that Shaped the Middle East* (Simon and Schuster: London, 2011), p. 101.
191 Lawrence Olson, *Japan in Post-War Asia* (Praeger: Westport, 1970), 102.
192 Eyal Weizmann, 'Tunnel Vision' in *London Review of Books*, 16 December 2021, vol. 43, no. 24.
193 Reports and Commentary appeared in *The Guardian*, 22 May 2021, *London Review of Books*, 3 June 2021, and *The Week*, 29 May 2021.
194 Raja Shenadeh, *Going Home* (New Press: New York, 2019), p. 48.

BIBLIOGRAPHY

British official documents

British National Archives
Documents on German Foreign Policy 1918-1945, Series D, volume xiii, London, 1964
Hansard's Parliamentary Debates

British official commissions and reports in chronological order

Royal Commission on Immigration, 1903, Cmd. 1741.
'Report of the Court of Inquiry Convened by the Order of H.E. The High Commissioner and Commander-in-Chief' (The Palin Report), 12 April 1920. This report was suppressed and never published. It has been retrieved from the British National Archives (BNA FO 371/5121) by Brendan McKay and published online at users.cecs.anu.au/~bdm/yabber/yabber_palin.html.
'Report on Middle East Conference Held in Cairo and Jerusalem, 12-30 March 1921'. British Colonial Office, June 1921 (CO 935/1/1).
'Palestine. Disturbances of May 1921: Reports of the Commission of Inquiry with Correspondence Relating Thereto' (The Haycraft Report), Cmd. 1540.
'Correspondence with the Palestine Arab Delegation and the Zionist Organisation' (Churchill White Paper), 1922, Cmd. 1700.
'League of Nations Mandate for Palestine with a note by the Secretary General relating to its application to the territory known as Trans-Jordan under the provision of Article 25', December 1922, Cmd. 1785.
'Report of the Commission on the Palestine Disturbances of August 1929' (The Shaw Report), Cmd. 3530.
'Report on Immigration, Land Settlement and Development' (The Hope Simpson Enquiry), 1930, Cmd. 3686.
'Passfield White Paper', 20 October 1930, Cmd. 3692.
'Palestine Royal Commission Report' (The Peel Report), 1937, Cmd. 5479.
'Policy on Palestine. A Despatch of 23 December, 1937, from the Secretary of State for the Colonies to the High Commissioner for Palestine', Cmd. 5634.
'Palestine Commission Report' (The Woodhead Report), 1938, Cmd. 5854.

'Palestine: Statement by His Majesty's Government in the United Kingdom in November 1938', Cmd. 5893.
'White Paper of 1939. Palestine: Statement of Policy' (The MacDonald Paper), Cmd. 6019.
'Correspondence between Sir Henry McMahon, His Majesty's High Commissioner at Cairo, and the Sherif Hussein of Mecca, 1939', Cmd. 5957.
'Report of the Anglo–American Committee of Inquiry regarding the Problems of European Jewry and Palestine 1946', Cmd. 6808.
'Proposals for the Future of Palestine' (The Morrison–Grady Plan), 1946, Cmd. 7044.
'Palestine: Termination of the Mandate, 15 May 1948: Statement prepared for public information by the Colonial Office and Foreign Office', HMSO.
'House of Commons Home Affairs Committee: Antisemitism in the UK: Tenth Report of Session 2016-17', HC 136, 13 October 2016.

Other British reports

Documents on German Foreign Policy 1918–1945, Series D volume xiii, London 1964.
'The Shami Chakrabarti Report on anti-Semitism and other forms of racism in the Labour Party', 30 June 2016.
'Allegations of anti-Semitism, Oxford University Labour Club', by Baroness Jan Royall 2016.
Wolfson, David and Jeremy Brier, 'The opinion of the IHRA Definition of anti-Semitism by the Government of the United Kingdom', July 2017.
Report by the British Equality and Human Rights Commission (EHRC): 'Investigation into anti-Semitism in the Labour Party', October 2020.

League of Nations reports

League of Nations Permanent Mandates Commission: 'Minutes of the thirty-sixth session held at Geneva from 8-29 June 1939, including the Report of the Commission to the Council.'

United Nations reports

'UN Fact Finding Mission on the Gaza Conflict.' Report by Richard Goldstone September 2009.
'General Progress Report 11 December to 23 October 1950': General Assembly Official Records: Fifth Session Supplement No 18 (A/1367/Rev. 1) New York 1951.

Israel reports

Commission of Inquiry chaired by the president of the Supreme Court of Israel, Yitzhak Kahan. 'Report on the Events at the Refugee Camps in Beirut'. The report was published on 3 February 1983.
Report of the Commission of Inquiry into the clashes between security forces and Israeli citizens in October 2000 by Theodor Or, 2 December 2003.

US reports

King–Crane Commission Report 'Suppressed Official Document of the United States Government', 1922.
Reagan Ronald W., The Reagan Plan, 1982.
Sharm el-Sheikh Fact Finding Committee Report'. 30 April 2001, (The Mitchell Report).
'Peace to Prosperity: a vision to improve the lives of the Palestinian and Israeli people' (The Trump Peace Plan), 2020.
Agreements between Israel and the United Arab Emirates and the United States (The Abraham Accords), 13 August 2020.

Humanitarian reports

'The ultimate barrier: impact of the Wall on the Palestinian health care system.' Médecins du Monde, 2005.
Human Rights Watch. May 2002, vol. 14, no. 3 (E).

Newspapers

Daily Mail
Daily Mirror
The Manchester Guardian
Daily Telegraph
Metro(UK)
Evening Standard
Morning Post
The *Guardian*
The New York Jewish Post
The New York Times
Haaretz
The Observer
Herald Tribune
Sunday Express
The Independent
The Sunday Mirror
The Jewish Chronicle
The Times
The Jewish Daily Bulletin
The Times of Israel
London Review of Books
The Mail Online
The Manchester Guardian
Time Magazine
The Washington Post
Medical Aid for Palestinians
The Week (UK)

Books

ANG SWEE CHAI, *From Beirut to Jerusalem* (Grafton Books: London, 1989).
ANTONIUS, George, *The Arab Awakening: the Story of the Arab National Movement* (Hamish Hamilton: London, 1969).
ARIDAN, Nathan, *Britain, Israel and Anglo-Jewry 1949-1957* (Routledge: London, 2004).

BAKER, Abeer, and Anat MATAR (eds) *Threat: Palestinian Political Prisoners in Israel* (Pluto Press: London, 2011).
BARR, James, *A Line in the Sand: Britain, France and the Struggle that Shaped the Middle East* (Simon and Schuster: London, 2011).
BEGIN, Menachem, *The Revolt* (also published under other titles) (W. H. Allen: London, 1951).
BENVENISTI, Meron, *Sacred Landscape: The Buried History of the Holy Land Since 1948* (University of California Press: California, 2002).
BERNADOTTE, Count Folke, *To Jerusalem* (Hodder and Stoughton: London, 1951).
BERGMAN, Ronen, *Rise and Kill First: The Secret History of Israel's Targeted Assassinations* (John Murray: London, 2018).
BERMANT, Azriel, *Margaret Thatcher and the Middle East* (Cambridge University Press: Cambridge, 2016).
BUHEIRY, Marwn R., *The Formation and Perception of the Modern Arab world. Edited by Lawrence I Conrad.* (Darwin Press: Princeton, 1989).
BURNS, William J., *Economic Aid and American Policy toward Egypt 1955-1981.* (State University of New York Press: Albany, 1985).

CARROLL, Robert, and Stephen PRICKETT (eds), *The Bible: Authorised King James Version* (Oxford University Press: Oxford, 1997).
CHAMI, Joseph G., *Days of Tragedy: Lebanon 75-76* (Shoushan: Beirut, 1977).
CHARPENTIER, Armand, *The Dreyfus Case.* Translated by J. Lewis May (Geoffrey Bles: London, 1935).
CLARKE, Thurston, *By Blood and Fire: The Attack on the King David Hotel* (Hutchinson: London, 1981).
COCKER, Mark R., *Meinertzhagen: Soldier Scientist and Spy* (Martin Secker and Warburg: London, 1989).
COHEN, Michael J., *Palestine: Retreat from the Mandate: The Making of British Policy 1936-1945* (Paul Elek: London, 1978).
CROSSMAN, Richard, *A Nation Reborn* (Hamish Hamilton: London, 1960).

DEVER, William G., *Who Were the Early Israelites and Where Did They Come From?* (William B. Eerdmans: Grand Rapids, 2006).

EBAN, Abba, *Voice of Israel* (Horizon Press: New York, 1957).
EL-SOLH, Raghid, *Lebanon and Arabism: National Identity and State Formation* (IB Tauris: London, 2004).

FINKELSTEIN, Norman, *Beyond Chutzpah: On the Misuse of Anti-Semitism and the Abuse of History* (University of California Press: California, 2005).
FINN, Joseph, *A Voice from the Aliens* (Twentieth Century Press: London, 1895).
FORSTER, Arnold, and Benjamin EPSTEIN, *The New Anti-Semitism* (McGraw-Hill: New York, 1974).

Bibliography

GARFIELD, Brian, *The Meinertzhagen Mystery: The Life and Legend of a Colossal Fraud* (Potomac Books: Washington DC, 2007).
GELBER, Yoav, *Palestine 1948: War, Escape and the Emergence of the Palestinian Refugee Problem* (Sussex Academic Press: Eastbourne, 2006).
GELBER, Yoav, *Propaganda as History: What Happened at Deir Yassin* (Sussex Academic Press: Eastbourne, 2006)
GILBERT, Martin, *Churchill and the Jews* (Simon and Schuster: London, 2007).
GOLAN, Zev, *Free Jerusalem: Heroes, Heroines and Rogues Who Created the State of Israel* (Devora Publishing: Israel, 2002).
GRIGG, John, *The Young Lloyd George* (Eyre Methuen: London, 1973).

HADAWI, Sami, *Bitter Harvest: A Modern History of Palestine* (Scorpion Press: Essex, 1989). Originally published 1967 by New World Press.
HAVRELOCK, Rachel, *River Jordan: The Mythology of a Dividing Line* (University of Chicago Press: Chicago, 2011).
HAVRELOCK, Rachel, *The Joshua Generation: Israel Occupation and the Bible* (Princeton University Press: Princeton, 2020).
HERZOG, Chaim, *The Arab-Israeli Wars: War and Peace in the Middle East From the War of Independence to Lebanon* (Arms and Armour Press: London, 1985).
HIRST, David, *The Gun and the Olive Branch* (Faber and Faber: London, 2003).
HOLMES, Colin, *Antisemitism in British Society 1876-1939* (Routledge: London, 1979).
HORNE, Edward, *A Job Well Done: A History of the Palestine Police Force 1920-1948* (Book Guild: Leicester, 2003).
HUNEIDI, Sahar, *A Broken Trust: Herbert Samuel, Zionism and the Palestinians 1920-1925* (IB Tauris: London, 2001).

INGRAMS, Doreen, *Palestine Papers 1917-1922: Seeds of Conflict* (John Murray: London, 1972).

KARSH, Efraim, *Palestine Betrayed* (Yale University Press: New Haven, 2011).
KATZ, Shmuel, *Days of Fire* (Doubleday: Garden City, 1968).
KAYYALI, Abdul Wahhab, *Palestine: A Modern History* (Routledge Croom Helm: London, 1978).
KEDOURI, Elie, *In the Anglo-Arab Labyrinth: The McMahon-Husayn Correspondence and its Interpretations 1914-1939* (Cambridge University Press: Cambridge, 1976).
KHALIDI, Walid, *All that Remains: the Palestinian Villages Occupied and Depopulated by Israel in 1948* (Institute for Palestine Studies: Washington DC, 1992).
KOESTLER, Arthur, *Promise and Fulfilment: Palestine 1917-1949* (Macmillan: London, 1949).
KRAMER, Gudrun, *A History of Palestine: From the Ottoman Conquest to the Founding of the State of Israel* (Princeton University Press: Princeton, 2008).

LAWRENCE, T. E., *The Seven Pillars of Wisdom: A Triumph* (Jonathan Cape: London, 1952).
LAPIDOT, Yehuda, *Besieged Jerusalem 1948: Memories of an Irgun Fighter* (Yehuda Lapidot: Israel, 1992).
LAPIERRE, Dominique, and Larry COLLINS, *O Jerusalem* (Simon and Schuster: London, 1972).
LAQUEUR, Walter, *The Changing Face of Anti-Semitism: From Ancient Times to the Present Day* (Oxford University Press: Oxford, 2006).
LLOYD, Selwyn, *Suez 1956: A Personal Account* (Jonathan Cape: London, 1978).
LILIENTHAL, Alfred M., *The Other Side of the Coin: An American Perspective of the Arab-Israeli Conflict* (The Devon-Adair Company: New York, 1965).

MACKINTOSH-SMITH, Tim, *The Arabs: A 3,000-Year History of Peoples, Tribes and Empires* (Yale University Press: New Haven, 2019).
MONTEFIORE, Simon Sebag, *Jerusalem: The Biography* (Phoenix: London, 2011).
MONTGOMERY, Bernard Law, *The Memoirs of Field-Marshal the Viscount Montgomery of Alamein* (Collins: London, 1958).
MORRIS, Benny, *The Birth of the Palestinian Refugee Problem* (Cambridge University Press: Cambridge, 1987).
MORRIS, Benny, *Israel's Border Wars 1949-1958: Arab Infiltration, Israeli Retaliation and the Countdown to the Suez War* (Clarendon Press: Oxford, 1993).
MORRIS, Benny, *Righteous Victims: A History of the Zionist–Arab Conflict 1881-2001* (Vintage Books: New York, 2001).
MORRIS, Benny, *The Birth of the Palestinian Refugee Problem Revisited* (Cambridge University Press: Cambridge, 2004).
MORRIS, Benny, *1948: A History of the First Arab-Israeli War* (Yale University Press: New Haven, 2009).

NACHMANI, Amikam, *Great Power Discord in Palestine: The Anglo–American Committee of Inquiry into the Problems of European Jewry and Palestine* (Frank Cass: London, 1987).
NASHIF, Esmail, *Palestinian Prisoners: Identity and Community* (Routledge: London, 2008).

OBAMA, Barack, *A Promised Land* (Viking: London, 2020).
O'CONNOR, Garry, *Alec Guinness: Master of Disguise* (Hodder and Stoughton: London, 1995).
OLSON, Lawrence, *Japan in Post-War Asia* (Praeger: Westport, 1970).

PAPPÉ, Ilan, *The Making of the Arab-Israeli Conflict 1947-51* (Macmillan and St. Anthony's Press: New York, 1992).
PAPPÉ, Ilan, *The Ethnic Cleansing of Palestine* (One World Publications: Oxford, 2006).
PRIOR, Michael, *Zionism and the State of Israel: a Moral Inquiry* (Routledge: London, 1999).

REID, Walter, *Empire of Sand: How Britain Made the Middle East* (Birlinn: Edinburgh, 2011).
RENTON, James, *The Zionist Masquerade: The Birth of the Anglo-Zionist Alliance 1914-1918* (Palgrave Macmillan: London, 2007).
REYNOLDS, G. W., and A. JUDGE, *The Night the Police Went on Strike* (Weidenfeld and Nicolson: London, 1968).
ROBERTS, Andrew, *Churchill: Walking with Destiny* (Allen Lane: London, 2018).
ROSE, N., *The Gentile Zionists A Study in Anglo-Zionist Diplomacy 1929-39* (Frank Cass: London, 1973).
ROSENBERG, David, *Battle for the East End: Jewish Responses to Fascism* (Five Leaves Publications: Nottingham, 2011).
ROSENBERG, David, *Rebel Footprints: A Guide to Uncovering London's Radical History* (Pluto Press: London, 2015).

SAINI, Angela, *Superior: The Return of Race Science* (4th Estate: London, 2019).
SCHNEER, Jonathan, *The Balfour Declaration: The Origins of the Arab-Israeli Conflict* (Bloomsbury: London, 2011).
SCULT, Mel, *Jewish Liberties: A Study of the Effort to Convert the Jews in Britain, up to the Mid Nineteenth Century* (EJ Brill: Leiden, 1978).

SEGEV, Tom, *One Palestine Complete: Jews and Arabs under the British Mandate* (Abacus: London, 2001).
SEGEV, Tom, *A State at Any Cost: The Life of David Ben-Gurion* (Apollo: London, 2019).
SHEHADEH, Raja, *Going Home* (New Press: New York, 2019).
SHLAIM, Avi, *Lion of Jordan: The Life of King Hussein in War and Peace* (Allen Lane: London, 2007).
SIMENON, Georges, *The Krull House* (Penguin: London, 2018). Written in 1939.
SLYOMOVICS, Susan, *Nakba: Palestine 1948 and the Claims of Memory* (Columbia University Press: New York, 2007).
STEIN, Leonard, *The Balfour Declaration* (Simon and Schuster: New York, 1961).
STONE, Dan (ed.), *The Historiography of the Holocaust* (Palgrave MacMillan: London, 2004).

TAYLOR, A. J. P., *English History 1914-1945* (Oxford University Press: Oxford, 1965).
THOMAS, J. E., *Voices from Captivity: Incarceration from Siberia to Guantanamo Bay* (Jessica Kingsley Publishers: London, 2018).

WEIZMANN, Chaim, *Trial and Error* (Hamish Hamilton: London, 1949).
WINSTONE, H. V. F., *The Illicit Adventure: The Story of Political and Military Intelligence in the Middle East from 1898 to 1926* (Jonathan Cape: London, 1982).
WISTRICH, Robert, and David OHANA, *The Shaping of Israel Identity: Myth, Memory and Trauma* (Frank Cass: London, 1995).
WRIGHT, Lawrence, *Thirteen Days in December: The Dramatic Struggle for Peace* (Doubleday Publishing Group: London, 2014).

Articles

BECKERMAN-BOYS, Carly, 'The Reversal of the Passfield White Paper, 1930-31: A Reassessment'. *Journal of Contemporary History* (2016), vol. 51, no. 2, pp. 213-33.
BROMWICH, David, 'House-Cleaning: On Trump's Latest Moves'. *London Review of Books* (7 March 2019), vol. 41, no. 5.

CHOMSKY, Noam, 'Transcript of Amy Goodman interview of Noam Chomsky' (2014). http:www.democracynow.org/2014/11/27/Noam Chomsky at the United Nations.
COHEN, Erik, 'Israel as a Post-Zionist Society'. *Israel Affairs* (1995), vol. 1, no. 3.

DAVID, Graham, and Stanley WATERMAN, 'Underenumeration of the Jewish population in the United Kingdom'. *Population, Space and Place* (March/April 2005), vol. 12, no. 2, pp. 89-102.

EBAN, Abba, 'Anti-Zionism is merely the new anti-Semitism'. *American Jewish Congress* (1973), vol. 40, pp. 2-14.
EICHENSEHR, Kristen, 'On Target? The Israeli Supreme Court and The Expansion of Targeted Killings'. *Yale Law Journal* (8 June 2007), pp. 116.

FINLAYSON, Lorna, 'Corbyn Now'. *London Review of Books* (27 Sept. 2018), vol. 40, no. 18.

HELLER, Joseph, 'The Zionist Right and National Liberation: From Jabotinsky to Avraham Stern'. *Israeli Affairs* (1995), vol. 1, no. 3, pp. 85-109.

HUGHES, M., 'The Banality of Brutality: British Armed Forces and the Repression of the Arab Revolt in Palestine 1936-39'. *English Historical Review* (2009), vol. 124. no. 507, pp. 313-354.

IRAQI, Amjad, 'Netanyahu is Right: Israel Has No Interest In True Equality'. *The Guardian* (13 March 2019).

MAKOVISKY, David, 'How to Build a Fence'. *Foreign Affairs* (2004), vol. 83, no. 2.
MEANEY, Thomas, 'In Whose Interest?' *London Review of Books* (Dec. 2018), vol. 40, no. 23.
MENDEL, Yonatan, 'Covid in the time of Netanyahu'. *London Review of Books* (7 May 2020).
MORRIS, Benny, 'The Historiography of Deir Yassin'. *The Journal of Israeli History* (2005), vol. 24, no. 1, pp. 79-107.

PARKER, Ned, and Stephen FARRELL, 'British Anger at Terror Celebration'. *The Times* (20 July 2006).

RAAB, Earl, 'Is there a New Antisemitism?' *Commentary* (May 1974).

SEDLEY, Stephen, 'Letters'. *London Review of Books* (8 Feb. 2018), vol. 40, no. 3.
SEDLEY, Stephen, 'Defining anti-Semitism'. *London Review of Books* (4 May 2017), vol. 39, no. 9.
SEDLEY, Stephen, 'Short Cuts'. *London Review of Books* (10 May 2018), vol. 40, no. 9.
SEGEV, Tom, 'The Spirit of the King David Hotel', *Haaretz* (23 July 2006).
SHATZ, Adam, 'Trump's America, Netanyahu's Israel'. *London Review of Books* (9 May 2019).
SHATZ, Adam, 'Review of *A State at Any Cost: The Life of David Ben-Gurion* by Tom Segev'. *London Review of Books* (24 Oct. 2019).
SIEGMAN, Henry, 'The Ultimate Deal'. *London Review of Books* (30 March 2017), vol. 39, no. 7.
SOLOMON, Norman, 'Judaism and the Ethics of War'. *International Review of the Red Cross* (June 2005), vol. 87, no. 858, pp. 53-54.

THRALL, Nathan, 'The Annexation Delusion'. *London Review of Books* (21 Jan. 2021), vol. 43, no. 2.
TOYNBEE, Arnold, and Isaiah FRIEDMAN, 'The McMahon-Hussein Correspondence'. *Journal of Contemporary History* (1970), vol. 5, no. 4, pp. 185-201.
TZAHOR, Ze'ev, 'Ben Gurion's Mythopoetics'. *Israel Affairs* (1995), vol. 1, no. 3.

WEIZMANN, Eyal, 'Tunnel Vision'. *London Review of Books* (16 Dec. 2021), vol. 43, no. 24.
WISTRICH, Robert S., 'Theodor Herzl: Zionist Icon, Myth-maker and Social Utopian'. *Israel Affairs* (1995), vol. 1, no. 3.

YOUNG, Darrell G., 'Focus on Jerusalem Ministry'. *The Bible and Palestine* (2006), vol. 97, no. 1.

ZERUBAVEL, Yael, 'The Multivocality of a National Myth: Memory and Counter-Memories of Masada'. *Israel Affairs* (1995), vol. 1 no. 3, pp. 110-128.

Index

Abbas, Mahmoud 290
Abdullah, Emir 57, 289
   'given' Transjordan 99, 11, 112
   meets Churchill 111
   prepares to fight French in Syria 111
   territorial ambitions
      wishes to include Palestine in his country 111, 162, 206, 223
      wishes to include Syria in his country 223
   supports Peel Plan 162
   opposition of Farouk to his ambition 223
   Palestinian opposition to his ambition 223
   Jewish support for his ambition 223
   agrees to Jewish takeover of villages 234
   agrees to sharing Palestine with the Jews 235
   allocated the West Bank 234
   assassinated 240
African Americans 291
Alexander III, Tsar 48
Aliens Bills/Acts 1904/1905 49-51, 132
'Aliyas' 45-46, 85
Allenby, Edmund 94, 128
   objects to power of Weizmann and Zionist interference 100-01, 106, 121-22, 129, 138
   assured by Curzon that Zionists would be contained 88-89
   blamed by Weizmann for 1920 riots 91
   removes Arab flag 96
   supports Feisal as king of Syria 99
   publicly rebukes Picot 105
   warns of trouble in Palestine 100, 136-37

   recommends suppression of Palin Report 140-41
   opposes appointment of Samuel as high commissioner 109
Amir, Yigal 270
Anglo-American Committee of Inquiry (1946)
   origin 188
   visit to displaced persons camps 188
   recommendations 190 ff
   reaction 191
Anglo-Jewish Association
   establishment 41
   Montefiore made president 41, 93
   opposition to Balfour Declaration 93, 135
Anti-Defamation League 295, 299
Arab Higher Committee
   establishment 186
   evidence to Peel Commission 73
   Koestler demands abolition 151
   objects to MacDonald Paper 171
   Mufti's role 176
   abolished 166
Arab Revolt (1916) 91 ff
Arab Revolt (1930s)
   Jewish denial of significance 91, 130, 163, 160
   claim of Jewish superiority 130
   not dealt with firmly 165
   high commissioner removed 157
   leaders imprisoned 56
Arab Women's Union 166
Arafat, Yasser 267 ff

Area of Jurisdiction and Power Ordinance 233
Asquith, Herbert 54
  Israeli record of assassination 282
Aswan Dam 244
Aswan Declaration 253
Attlee, Clement 51, 186, 194

Baghdad Pact (Central Treaty Organisation) 243 ff
Balfour, Arthur 11, 52
  and the Bible 32, 34, 66, 126
  deplores exclusivity of Jews 132
  meets Weizmann 26, 52-53
  Weizmann's influence on 71, 84, 103 ff., 108, 118, 129, 173
  opposition to Jewish immigration into Britain 49, 51, 132
  support for Aliens Bill (1905) 49, 51
  asks for a draft of a declaration 69, 71
  'Jews the most gifted race' 53
  belief in Jewish influence 69
  agrees there should be a Jewish homeland 66, 78, 131
  concern about Zionist behaviour 88
  accused of ignoring Zionist ambitions 93
  alarmed by the appointment of King-Crane Commission 79
  niece a Zionist spy 95
Balfour Declaration 76, 80, 98, 103, 105, 108
  ambiguity of 73, 101
  celebration of promulgation 17
  contribution of Jewish Bureau 26
  alleged contribution of Christian Zionists 34
  Arab opinion and reaction 35, 74, 81, 87, 97, 101, 116, 119, 131, 137
  attempt to force Arabs to accept 108, 131, 137
  'Declaration to the Seven' 96
  British parliamentary support 38
  Jewish lobbies 39, 56, 67 ff, 73, 86, 110, 18 ff
  President Wilson's opinion 56, 108, 131
  Curzon's opinion 60, 100, 103, 108, 136
  Daily Mail demands cancellation 61
  Edward Grey's opinion 63
  role of American bankers in 69
  Samuel's role in formulation 120
  the text of 72
  Zionist demand for a Jewish state 73, 110, 173
  Jewish opposition to Zionism 104, 135-136, 155
  Zionists insist on getting all of Palestine 73
  demands by Brandeis 78
  Balfour agrees with Brandeis 79, 132
  Balfour alarmed by establishment of King-Crane Commission 80
  American Congress approves of a 'national home' 80
  cause for unrest 97, 108, 121
  Churchill's opinion 86, 134, 147, 158, 160, 187
  Hogarth placates Hussein 97
  becomes British policy 97
  Weizmann objects to whittling down of 86, 118
  Smuts urges government to press ahead with 147
  see also King Crane Commission *and* Biltmore Conference
Bar-Giora
  Jewish leader 83
  illegal Jewish armed force 83
Begin, Menachem
  background 44
  definition of 'Eretz Israel' 17, 220, 258
  basis of Jewish claim to Palestine 17, 18
  on British policy 18
  on death of Stern 179
  commands IZL (Irgun) 183
  sources of money for illegal immigration 185
  reaction to 1945 election of Labour government 187
  blames British for deaths in King David Hotel 192 ff
  delights over the murder of the two British sergeants 201 ff
  sends military aid to Argentina during the Falklands War 200 ff
  Thatcher's refusal to excuse role in murder of sergeants 202
  Irgun 'closely akin to Nazi and Fascist parties' 202
  delight at Deir Yassin massacre 218-19
  lies about Qibya massacre 241
  appointed to government post 246
  head of Lifud 46, 254
  leads government 253, 259
  failed meeting with Sadat 253
  awarded Nobel Peace Prize 253
  'full autonomy' for Palestinians 253-54
  attitude to Peace Movement 254
  orders air force to support Christians in Lebanon 258

Index

Reagan deplores bombing in Lebanon 260
policy in Lebanon 259, 260
'Peace in Galilee' 259
US disapproves of his bombing in Lebanon 260
disapproves of Reagan Plan 260
denies Israel's part in Lebanon massacres 262
condemned by Kahan Inquiry over Lebanon 262, 263
refuses to dismiss Sharon over Lebanon 263
alienates British Conservatives 293
portrayal as Nazis in cartoon 303
Ben-Gurion, David
background 44, 85
belief in biblical authority for taking Palestine 16, 21, 28, 37
changes his name 28
as mythmaker 16, 17, 28
limited historical vision 29
depiction of Herzl 36
distress at the idea of an alternative to settling in Palestine 42
proposes fighting for the Turks 47
on immigration 154, 189, 196
concern about behaviour of IDF troops 154, 217, 228, 229
Jews in the British Army 175, 178
Jewish immigration benefits Arabs 75
must 'absorb' immigrants 236
blames British commanders for 1920 disturbances 91
praise for Meinertzhagen 94
dealings with Blanche 'Baffy' Dugdale 95
rivalry with Jabotinsky 142
calls 1929 disturbances a 'pogrom' 143, 192
hatred of Arabs 327-28
calls Arabs 'murderous' 156
approves destruction of Arab villages 207, 213, 214
on stealing of Arab land 235, 243
distrust for Arab refugees 236
claim that Arabs will be equals 213, 220
on Arab virtues 213
expects Arabs will be expelled 37, 208
repatriation of Arabs 229, 243
shocked by damage done to Haifa's Arabs 211
deplores theft of Arab property by Jewish academic staff 237
cleansing of Palestine 164, 208, 210, 214
claims that Palestine is empty 28, 211
takes Palestine by stealth 153, 163, 164, 173, 235
attacks MacDonald 171
expands and restructures Haganah 178, 208
on Second World War 173, 175, 178
on 'Plan D' 210, 220
criticises American Jews 283
appeals to rich North Americans for funds 202-03
Alpha Peace Proposals 242
at the Biltmore Conference 180-82
persecution and removal of Weizmann 182, 222
on the 'Hunting Saison' 184
immigrant ships 185
visits displaced persons camps 189
on not saving Jewish children 196
angry at murder of British sergeants 201
suggests Transjordan becomes part of a Jewish state 213
proclaims birth of Israel 219-20
influence on Marcus Sieff 222
rounds up Irgun members 225
bodyguard murders Bernadotte 233
plan to 'Hebraize' the Negev 318 ff
Bernadotte, Count Folke
background and appointment 222
arrives in the Middle East 222
surprise at Jewish lack of sympathy for Arabs 44, 215
negative attitude of Jews 224, 225, 226, 229, 230, 231
cooperation of Arabs 224, 231
opposes Jewish immigration during truce 225
on refugees 224, 226-29
UN Resolution unworkable 224, 226, 231
recommendations to UN 227, 228, 230-31
murder of 232
aftermath of murder 233 ff
Bevin, Ernest
policy towards Palestine 187, 188, 221-22, 234
sets up Anglo-American Committee of Enquiry 188
accused of antisemitism 187
the Bevin Plan 191
discussion with Ben-Gurion 211
refuses to recognise Israel 220-22
Biden, Joe 326
Biltmore Conference (1942) 180-82
'Black Arrow' reprisal (1955) 16, 242, 243
Board of Deputies of British Jews
foundation 31, 41
opposes Zionism 41

thanks Churchill for support 51
attitude to 'two state' solution 286
on Thatcher's criticism of Israel 293
opinion of Labour's response to
    antisemitism 302
criticises Chakrabarti Report 312
Brandeis, Louis D. 40, 78, 89, 132, 149
British Brotherhood League 48-49
Bromley, Pat 315, 316, 317
B'Tselem 273, 279, 280, 326
Bunche, Dr Ralphe 233, 234
Bush, George W. 268, 297

Canaan and Canaanites
    Jews 17
    land given to Jews 19, 21, 24, 30, 33, 41
    Jews superior to 28
Cairo Conference (1921) 92, 110
Carter, Jimmy 33, 235
Catholic Church 84, 102, 103, 255
Catling, Sir Richard 216
Chakrabarti Report (2016) 311, 312, 314
Chamberlain, Austen 147, 148
Chamberlain, Joseph 42, 43, 48
Chamberlain, Neville 171, 173, 178
Churchill, Winston
    and the Bible 31, 34, 35, 122
    dislike of Arabs 86, 128, 129, 151, 156,
        160, 164, 171, 267
    support for Jewish immigration into Britain
        49 ff
    suggestion for country of resettlement 43
    warns against Russian 'barbarism' 45
    appointed home secretary 51
    appointed colonial secretary 88, 121
    1922 White Paper 62, 63, 116, 117, 121,
        147, 187
    appointed to War Office 87
    support for appointment of Samuel as high
        commissioner 109-10, 111
    support for Zionism 53, 75, 84, 89, 90, 92,
        111, 112, 116, 119, 120, 122, 132, 134,
        147, 150, 151, 158, 163, 181, 184, 187,
        194, 221
    relationship with T. E. Lawrence 94-96, 114
    appoints Meinertzhagen 93-94
    appoints Feisal as king of Iraq 99
    Abdullah and Transjordan 111, 112
    on partition 187, 199
    at Cairo Conference (1921) 10 ff
    rejects suggestion for Transjordan to
        become part of Jewish state 111
    friendship with British Jews 124 ff
    shaken by murder of Lord Moyne 184
    on Jabotinsky 113, 114
    on Rutenberg 110, 115, 116, 139
    attacks Bevin over policy towards Israel
        220-221, 222
    Shuckburgh suspends immigration without
        Churchill's knowledge 152
    meets Weizmann 121, 122, 126, 178, 187
    quoted at Biltmore Conference 181
    Jewish discussion about murdering him
        199
Clinton, Bill
    witnesses Oslo 1 269
    arranges Camp David meeting 273
    arranges meeting with Arafat and Mubarak
        275
    proposes peace agreement 276
    witnesses Arafat's agreement to recognise
        Israel 284
Communism/Bolshevism
    in Russia 133, 135
    in Palestine 117, 121, 123, 133, 134, 139
    in Britain 133
Community Security Trust 312
Corbyn, Jeremy
    elected Labour leader 299-300
    accused of antisemitism
        by Luciana Berger 301-02
        by chief rabbi 314
        by Margaret Hodge 302-03, 320-21
        by John Mann 305
        by Lord Mitchell 312
        by Joan Ryan 302
        by Lord Alan Sugar 312
    advocates change of name of Holocaust
        Memorial Day 40, 301
    unwilling to support the International
        Holocaust Remembrance Alliance
        guidelines 303, 306 ff
    suspended from and reinstated to the
        Labour party 317
'Cousinhood' Group of elite British Jews 40-41
Creech Jones, Arthur 196
Cromwell, Oliver 26, 29
Curzon, Lord George 108
    chairman of Eastern Committee 131
    supports Palestinian Arabs 60, 86, 89,
        100-02, 114, 120, 136, 181
    objects to wording of Mandate 103,
        108-09, 120
    opposes Jewish immigration 60

warning from Meinertzhagen about Jewish reaction 130-31
objects to influence of Weizmann 84, 103, 109
advised not to publish Palin Report 140
contact with Weizmann 97, 109, 136
contact with Samuel 99
supports appointment of Samuel 109
Zionists block changes 83

Damascus Protocol 57, 59
Daniel, book of 29-30
Dayan, Moshe
  opinion that Israel should include biblical Palestine 38, 106, 243
  visits Western Wall 274
  on destruction of Palestinian villages 212, 248
  assessment of 246
Declaration of Principles (DOP) *see* Oslo Accords
Delamere, Lord 43
Deir Yassin massacre (April 1948)
  course of 215 ff
  Jewish reactions 218-219
  British reactions 218
Department of Information 'Jewish Section', UK 26, 104
Deuteronomy, book of
  promise of land to Jews 19, 20, 327
  exhortation to kill 21
diaspora
  definition of 25, 36, 152
  alleged British sympathy for 26
  cultural stagnation 85
  Ben-Gurion's contempt of 27, 29
  influence exaggerated 68, 207
disturbances in Palestine (1929)
  Shaw Report 143 ff
  Mufti accused of responsibility 144
Douglas, Lord Alfred 125
Dulles, John Foster 242, 244
Dreyfus, Alfred 37
Druze 166, 257
Dugdale, Blanche 'Baffy'
  drafts letter deploring Passfield Report 147
  no small assistance (to Zionists) 9

Eban Abba 298
Eden, Anthony 240
  anger over dismissal of Glubb 240
  meets Nasser 242
  denies arranging destruction of Treaty of Sèvres 245
  lies about Suez invasion 245
  call for resignation of 245
Eder, David
  as chairman of Zionist Commission 43, 81, 84
  recommendation for removal of 81, 141-42
  insists on exclusively Jewish state 141
Eisenhower, Dwight
  attempts to negotiate peace 242
  refuses to arm Israel 244
  anger at invasion of Suez 245
  visits concentration camps 296
Eretz Israel
  meaning and claims to 17, 18, 23, 33, 73, 196, 219
ethnic cleansing
  meaning in English and Hebrew 207-08
  Israeli policy of 209-10, 214
Evangelical Christians
  support for Zionism 31, 34
  role in the election of Reagan 33
  support for Republican party in the US 33
  Orde Wingate 168
Exodus, book of
  promise of land to Jews 21
  importance in mythology 24, 28
  Obama 'infected by' 325
Exodus (ship) carrying illegal immigrants 203
expulsion of Jews advocated 195
  by Louis Brandeis 132-33
  by Balfour 49, 132
  by Herzl 133
  by Smuts 132
  in Hungary 79

Farouk, King 223, 240, 244
Fatah 256, 265, 267, 275, 276, 279
Feisal, Emir and King 57, 61
  Turkish approach after Sykes–Picot 97 ff
  opinion that he should be king of Syria 79
  declared king of several countries 99
  pronounced by Churchill to be king of Iraq 99, 111
  allegation that gave up claim to Palestine 92
  discussion with Weizmann 108
  Arab support 127, 137
  Paris Peace talks 92, 111
  deposed by France 99
Feisal II 240

France
- ambitions in Palestine 31, 37, 66, 67, 76, 100
- ambitions in Syria 52, 60, 65, 66, 76, 98, 107, 162, 243
- lies about future of Arab independence 95, 127
- disputes with British 54, 121, 243
- British claim to France stronger that Jewish claim to Palestine 103
- French Jews an elite in Israel 154
- French Jews object to Passfield recommendations 147
- collaboration with Jewish terrorists 180
- Truce Commission 222
- UN Conciliation Commission for Palestine 235
- attack on Suez 244, 245
- support for Arabs 254
- Sèvres 245
- Obama and the agreement with Iran 286
- French Revolution and the Jews 31

Gantz, Benny 324
Gemayel, Bashir 259, 260, 262
'Gentile Zionists' 35, 148, 170
Goldstone Report 279
Golan Heights
- Arabs driven out 248
- Syrian attempt to recapture 252
- Jewish claim to include in their state (1919) 37
- seizure by Israel 37-38, 19, 247, 248, 271
- Thatcher objects to seizure 294
- Trump approves of seizure 285

Grey, Sir Edward 54, 58, 63, 66
Guinness, Alec 295
Gush Emunim 266

Haavara Agreement 195, 303
Haganah
- formation 166
- expansion and training 155, 167, 175, 178, 208
- espionage 95
- links with Avraham Stern 178
- links with Ariel Sharon 277
- atrocities committed by 184, 185, 192, 201, 205, 206, 207, 209, 212, 213, 216, 218, 219

Hamas 265, 266, 269, 270, 271, 276, 278, 279, 297
Hamchari (Hamshari) Mahomed 297

Haycraft Report 81
- membership 141
- on events 140 ff
Hecht Ben 202
Henry VII 16
Herzl, Theodor
- background 26, 36
- as a mythmaker 26
- draws attention to Dreyfus case 37
- *Der Judenstaat* 37
- *Altneuland* 319
- attempts to influence
  - Chamberlain 42, 43
  - Kaiser Wilhelm II 47
  - King Victor Emmanuel III of Italy 42
  - Sultan Abdul Hamid II of Turkey 37, 47, 69
- on expulsion of Arabs 107, 163, 319 ff
- on expulsion of Jews from Europe 133
Herzog, Chaim
- praises unit 101, 241
- criticises IDF 251
- on Israel's 'efficient security control' 255
- on Arab refugees 229
- claims elimination of PLO 251
Hezbollah 263, 271
Holocaust *see also* Nazis
- influence on decisions about the future of Palestine 12, 17, 27, 181, 195
- Jewish refusal to include Roma in definition of 39
- survivors 44, 215
  - Begin regards as alien 45, 182
  - Begin regards as useful pawns 189
  - Biltmore Conference demands for 181
- Begin alleges danger of a Christian holocaust in Lebanon 258
- role of Adolf Eichmann 154
- Netanyahu alleges that the Mufti gave Hitler idea of 177
- Palestinians protest no involvement in 205
- comparison with Deir Yassin massacre 218
- comparison with Israeli behaviour in Gaza 300
- allegation that Zionists prevented the rescue of victims 303
- Obama obliged to visit memorial 326
- Holocaust Memorial Day 300
- Corbyn suggests renaming of Holocaust Memorial Day 301
- Corbyn accused of rejecting the 'Remembrance Alliance' 302, 303, 305, 306-07, 314

Index

Jewish insistence on monopolising the term 40, 301
  denial of 296-97, 299, 314
  effect on free speech 295, 305, 309, 315
Hope Simpson Report 145 ff
House, 'Colonel' 55, 105
Human Rights Watch 280-83
Hussein, Grand Sharif and King 57, 111
  joins Allies 57, 111
  the McMahon Letters 58 ff, 96
  learns of Sykes–Picot 96
  asks for clarification of Balfour Declaration 97
  refuses treaty of friendship with Britain 112
  end of kingship 112
Hyamson, Albert 26, 104, 105-06

Ibn Saud 112
Intifada
  meaning of the word 264
  the first 27, 265, 268, 270
  the second 273, 276-77, 280
Irgun Zvai Leomi
  meaning 113, 167
  members 46
  role of Avraham Stern 178
  reaction to election of British Labour government in 1945 186
  attacks and murders of Arabs 155, 167, 172, 213, 215, 217
  murders of British soldiers 200 ff, 207
  King David Hotel murders 193 ff
  attempted murder of high commissioner 185
  Begin rounds up members 226
  Begin's revenge on Britain 201
Irving, David 296
Israel, state of
  foundation (1948) 219
  reactions to foundation
    in Britain 220-22
    in United States 219
    in the USSR 219
  admitted to the United Nations 238
Israel Defence Forces (IDF) 246, 255, 265, 274
  foundation 167
  tasked to 'cleanse' Palestine 208, 214, 228, 248, 251
  invades Lebanon 260, 261-62
  sets up 'security zone' between Israel and Lebanon 259
  helps in the Lebanon massacres 261 ff
  atrocities committed by 218, 241, 248, 279
  attack on Jenin 274
  some members refuse to abuse Arabs 267
  Ben-Gurion's concern over behaviour 46, 217
  use of rubber bullets 266
  the Lavi Plan 46
  'Spirit of the IDF' 217
  evacuates
    Gaza 270-271
    south Lebanon 275
    most of Hebron 272
    part of the West Bank 270-72, 279
Israel War of Independence (1948) see Nakba
Israeli nuclear defence 246

Jabotinsky, Ze'ev 27, 56, 70, 104, 113
  background 113, 139, 290
  terrorist activities 139, 142, 155
  criticised in Palin Report 139
  founds 'Revisionist' opposition 99, 113, 167, 172
  'really a lunatic' 139
Jarring, Gunnar 250
Jewish Labour Federation 145-46
Johnson, Lyndon 247
Jordan, Colin 296
Joshua, book of 16-17, 22, 24, 28, 36, 106
Judea 23, 27, 32, 33, 123, 247, 260, 266

Kahan Report on Lebanon massacres 261, 263
King-Crane Commission 79
King David Hotel attack 192-95, 197
Kissinger, Henry 252
Kushner, Jared 285, 291

Labour government's policy on Palestine 149, 150, 167, 186-87, 197
Lansky, Meyer 295
Lausanne Inquiry and Conference 188, 235, 237
Lawrence, T. E. 57, 108, 127
  on McMahon 65, 91
  on Sykes 65
  on Sykes–Picot Agreement 91, 131
  on Meinertzhagen 94
  reports Picot–Allenby verbal exchange 105
  attends peace talks 92, 111
  fails to persuade Hussein to accept Treaty of Friendship with Britain 112
  appointed political adviser to the Middle East Department 93

on the outcome of the First World War 92, 98, 132
League of British Jews 104
League of Nations
commission on mandates 55, 172
adopts mandate system 75
Blanche 'Baffy' Dugdale's British delegate to 95
Curzon apprehensive about the mandate 102
Curzon objects to Weizmann seeing draft of mandate 109
House of Lords disapproves mandate 115
House of Commons debates mandate 171
approves Britain holding the mandate for Palestine 99, 113
British Mandate ends 12, 198
Lipman, Maureen 305
Livingstone, Ken
accused of antisemitism 300, 303 ff
Lloyd George, David 34, 42, 52, 53, 54, 122, 133
and the Bible 32, 53, 126
support for Zionism 68, 86, 147, 158
support for Jewish immigration 147
discusses American involvement in Palestine 105
considers where borders of the Jewish state should be 105
fear of Bolshevism 133
Lloyd, Selwyn 244
London Society for the Promotion of Christianity amongst the Jews 38

MacDonald letter 88
MacDonald, Malcolm 170
issues White Paper (1939) 170-171
gives evidence to the Permanent Mandates Commission 172
Ben-Gurion likens him to Hitler 171
MacDonald, Ramsay 147
supports Zionism 149 ff
urged by Smuts to implement the Balfour Declaration 147
sends controversial letter to Weizmann 149, 150
May 1, 1921 Disturbances *see* Haycraft Commission
McMahon, Arthur Henry 58
McMahon Letters 58 ff, 96
inclusion of Palestine in promises to Arabs 60-64, 66
and Sykes–Picot 66

opinion of T. E. Lawrence 65, 91
opinions of Jewish historians 65, 67, 117
Meinertzhagen, Richard 90
background 93-94
appointed as military expert to the Middle East Department 93, 97
Zionist supporter 90, 95, 118, 130-31
criticised in Palin Report 94
Merchant of Venice, The 248, 294
Middle East Department
composition of 93 ff, 221
refusal to dismiss Dr Eder 142
criticism of 94
Mitchell Report 275, 276
Montefiore, Claude 41, 93, 132
Montgomery, Bernard
appointed to Palestine 157
policies 192
disagrees with government policies 196-97
Montagu, Edwin 41, 135
Morrison-Grady Report ('Proposal for the Future of Palestine', 1946) 191 ff
Morton, Geoffrey 179, 180
Moslem Christian Society of Palestine 116, 140
Moyne, Lord 183, 184, 186, 232
Mufti of Jerusalem (Haj Amin Al-Husseini)
background 144, 156, 174, 176, 177
blamed for 1929 disturbances 144, 176
role in 1930s revolt 151
escapes to Lebanon 166
overtures to Mussolini and Hitler 176, 177, 178
declares *jihad* against Allies (1942) 177
accused of suggesting Holocaust to Hitler 177
later influence of 223
Munich attack in Olympic Games (1972) 255, 256, 291
Mussolini, Benito 24, 43, 174, 177, 240

Nakba (Catastrophe) 206
Nasser, Gamal Abdel 240
nationalises the Suez Canal (1956) 244, 246
reaction in Britain 240, 243, 244, 245, 247, 249
reaction in USA 242, 244, 249
reaction in USSR 249, 250
dealing with Anthony Eden 242
appeals to Moscow 250
death of 20, 251

'Nation State Law' (Israel) 324, 325
Nazis 39, 152, 168, 181, 188, 195, 301, 303
   Arabs' negotiation with 176-77
   capture and execution of Eichmann 195
   Jewish treatment of Palestinians compared with 39, 40, 183, 218, 232, 300, 307, 313
Netanyahu, Benjamin 257, 270, 271, 272, 275, 281, 284, 324, 325, 326
   settlements 34, 272, 286, 326, 328
   excuses the King David Hotel atrocity 195
   accuses the Mufti of responsibility for Holocaust 177
   negative dealings with Palestinians 278, 279, 284, 288, 324
   opposes jurisdiction of the International Criminal Court 325
   Trump's 'Peace Plan' 285, 286 ff, 290-91
   assessment of 271
'New antisemitism'
   meaning of 12, 255, 297
   example of 22, 283-84, 294, 299
   used to deny fact 314
   denial of existence of 299
Newton, Isaac 30
Nokrashi Pasha 240
Numbers, book of 19
Nur Shams, battle of 156

Obama, Barack
   on the support of American politicians for Israel 33
   deplores Palestinian deprivation 283
   achieves nuclear treaty with Iran 286
   'targeted killings' 297
   'infected by Exodus' 325
   persuaded not to speak out about Palestine 325-26
   presidency ends 326
October War *see* Yom Kippur War
Oliver Twist 294
Operation Cast Lead' ('The Gaza Massacre' and 'The Gaza War') 278
'Operation Protective Edge' 218, 279, 324
Operation Stones of Baked Clay 279
'Oriental Jews' 46, 154
Orr Commission Report (2003) 276
Oslo Accords 271, 287, 322

Palestine Police
   demand by Zionist Commission to be involved in recruitment 83
   targeted for murder 95
   attacks on and murders of 137, 167, 172, 179, 180, 192, 197, 200, 207
   shortage of 138, 140, 143, 187, 192, 197, 200
   alleged collusion with Arabs 140
   behaviour of 157, 179, 206
   killing of Stern 179
   provide evidence of rape 216
Palestinian Liberation Organisation
   foundation 246, 250
   move to Jordan 251 ff
   expulsion from Jordan 256, 257
   move to Lebanon 256, 257, 259, 260
   leave Lebanon 260, 263
   in Tuns 263
'Palestinian Lives Matter' 328
Popular Front for the Liberation of Palestine 250, 256
Palin Commission Report (1920)
   set up to investigate Nebi Musa disturbances 87
   causes of Nebi Musa disturbances 137
   difficulties in discovering what happened 137-38, 140
   list of casualties 138
   rejects allegations of bias towards Arabs 138-39
   Arabs unable to understand Jewish attitudes 35
   Arabs note that East European Jews were more politically ambitious 45
   describes Jewish spying 63
   deplores interference by Zionist Commission 82, 145, 184
   criticises Jabotinsky 137
   criticises Meinertzhagen 94
   suppression of 140
Palmach unit of Haganah 167, 192
Parliamentary Select Committee on Antisemitism (2016) 312, 314
Paris Peace Conference (1919) 37, 61, 77, 97
Passfield, Lord (Sidney Webb)
   White Paper (1930) 39, 84, 145, 146, 147, 149, 150 154
      Churchill reaction 147
      Lloyd George reaction 147
      Zionist reaction 147
      letters to *The Times* 147-48
'Peace to Prosperity' (Trump's 'Peace Deal') 286 ff
Peel Report (Royal Commission, 1937) 128, 166

origins 158
evidence submitted by Churchill 158
Ben-Gurion 16
Arab evidence 73, 160
conclusions 161
recommends partition 161 ff
reaction to 162, 163, 164, 165, 169
'Pillar of Defence' 279, 324
Phalangists 257, 258, 261, 262
Picot, François Georges- see Sykes–Picot Agreement
Plan Dalet 208, 210
Project (Operation) Alpha 242, 243
pogroms
  misuse of word 138, 143, 176, 192
  in Russia 48, 50, 84, 133, 152
Popes 70, 73, 287
Popular Front for the Liberation of Palestine (PFLP) 251, 256
Priestley, Joseph 31
Provisional Executive Committee (USA) 40, 55, 56

Rabin, Yitzhak
  claims that Ben-Gurion ordered forcible removal of Arabs 214
  numbers evicted 215
  explains 'beating policy' 267
  becomes prime minister 268
  role in Oslo Accords 269
  recognises PLO 269-70
  role in the creation of the separation wall 280
  murdered 270
Reagan, Ronald
  attempt to intervene in Lebanon 274
  resistance by Zionists to his 'peace plan' 260
  witnesses Arafat's acceptance of Israel 284
Red Cross and Red Crescent
  evidence of atrocities by IDF 215, 217, 261
  condemns separation wall 280
Refugees
  from Europe to Britain 48-49, 311
  Arab 215, 227, 228, 229, 232, 233, 235, 236, 237, 243, 257, 269, 318, 327
  numbers 212, 229, 235, 242, 288, 321
  Bernadotte's concern 232, 226-228
  in Lebanon 257, 321
  UN demands return 235
  Project (Operation) Alpha recommendation 242

  Clinton proposes allowing return 276
  Israeli view that the problem is caused by Arab governments 229
  Israeli governments refuse to allow return 228-229, 235, 237, 241, 271, 288
  treatment of ethnic minorities in Israel 310
  UN Relief and Works Agency for Palestine (UNRWA) 236, 322, 326
  sympathy by some Israelis 327
  future of refugees in Trump's 'Peace Plan' 285, 287, 288
  Trump stops aid 290, 322
  Biden promises to restore aid 326
Jewish
  and the Holocaust 12, 43, 181
  in Palestine 185, 189, 227, 229, 288
  illegal immigration to Palestine 146, 152, 170, 179, 185, 191, 196, 203, 224
Roma (Gypsy) people and the Holocaust 29 ff
Roosevelt, Franklin D. 38, 196
Rothschild family 26, 135
  wealth of 31, 41
  influence of 42, 88, 101, 222
  help given to Jews in Palestine 42, 69, 85, 152
  submission of proposals for a Jewish homeland 41, 71 ff
  relationship with Winston Churchill 112, 124-25
  'conspiracy theories' 316
Royall Report on Antisemitism 314 ff
Ruppin, Arthur 153
Rutenberg, Pinhas 110, 115, 116, 139

Sabra massacre (Lebanon) 261 ff
Sadat, Anwar
  Yom Kippur war 252
  dismisses Soviet military 251-52
  initiates peace talks 46, 251-52
  offers to go to Jerusalem 293
  peace talks with Begin fail 253
  issues Aswan Declaration with President Carter 253
  Camp David talks 253, 266, 273, 275
  awarded Nobel Peace Prize 253
  assassinated 254
San Remo Conference 97, 99, 100
Samaria 23, 248, 260, 266
Samuel, Herbert
  background 41, 53

Index

canvasses for Jewish state 54, 76, 99
appointed high commissioner 90, 109, 111
criticism of his appointment 109-10, 115
receives letters from Balfour expressing concern about Zionist behaviour 88
the King/Crane Commission 79
letter from Weizmann about tactics in dealing with Colonial Office 94
asked to justify mass immigration of Jews 122
influence on dismissal of senior British official 84
appoints Hyamson as head of immigration 105
favourable treatment of Rutenberg 110
amnesty includes Jabotinsky 139
makes Hebrew an official language 110
arranges arming of colonists 110
claim made of British sympathy for Zionists 122
proposes abolition of Zionist Commission 110
proposes Arab Consultative Committee 119
criticised by Zionists 86, 110
appoints Mufti 176
opposition to Arab ambitions 86, 131
on the McMahon Letters 63
dislike of British military 90
tries to include Transjordan in Jewish state 111
drafts Churchill White Paper (1922) 116, 118
encouraged by Churchill to treat Jewish Communists harshly 134
Scott, C. P. 42, 52, 55, 67
Sebag Montefiore, Simon 30, 313
Shah, Naz 304, 316
Shamir, Yitzhak
  background 44
  succeeds Stern as leader of Lehi 179
  arranges murder of Lord Moyne 183 ff, 232
  registers delight at the murder of Moyne 184
  attempts to extract money from President Bush 268
  opposes establishment of a Palestinian state 268
Sharett, Moshe 243, 327
Sharon, Ariel 241, 259, 270, 277, 278
  suspected of corruption 277
  forms unit 101, 241
  massacre in Qibya 241
  Lebanon and Lebanese massacres 259-63

his demand for reprisal 266
assessment 241, 242
Shatilla massacre (Lebanon) 261 ff
Shaw Report (1929) on Yom Kippur disturbances 143 ff
Shertok, Moshe
  friend of Blanche 'Baffy' Dugdale 95, 173
  Bernadotte's experience of 224-26, 229
Shuckburgh, Evelyn
  disapproves of Zionism 221, 242
  describes Nasser as 'a second Mussolini' 240
  member of Project (Operation) Alpha 242
Shuckburgh, John 61, 62, 93, 116
  support for Zionism 90, 116, 118, 119, 127, 142
  keeps information from Churchill 152
Schumer, Charles 284
Six-Day War (1967)
  lack of Israeli government control over military 246 ff
  Soviets gain a foothold in the Middle East 249-50, 255
  Golan Heights annexed 247
  deterioration in treatment of Palestinians 248-49
  effect of world opinion 255
Smuts, Jan
  and the Bible 32, 34, 126
  notes that the Arabs were powerless 39
  supports Zionism 126, 132, 135, 147
  declares that Balfour Declaration would 'rally Jewry' to support Allies 69-70
  credited with idea of mandates 75
  wishes to reduce Jewish immigration into South Africa 132
  failed attempts to be made leader of inquiries 145, 188
Sokolow, Nahum 70-73
Solutrean Hypothesis 15
Sonneborn Institute 203, 207
Spies, Zionist 84, 94, 95, 97, 192
Stern, Avraham
  background 27, 45, 172
  leader of Lehi 178, 183
  offers to support Germany and Vichy French 179, 180
  death 179, 190
  regarded as Israeli hero 179
Stern Gang atrocities 179, 183, 215, 232
Sykes, Sir Mark 65
  and McMahon Letters 66

and the Bible 127
reports complaints about military in
 Palestine 90
assessment by T. E. Lawrence 65
Sykes–Picot Agreement
 origins 65
 Weizmann becomes aware of 67
 existence kept from Arabs 66
 Sharif Hussein becomes aware of 96 ff
 and McMahon 66
 misquoted by Balfour 66-67
 T. E. Lawrence's opinion 91
 recommendations set aside 74, 76, 96, 131

Temple Mount 143, 264, 271, 273, 274
Thatcher, Margaret 202, 293, 326
Titus, Emperor 25
Toynbee, Arnold 60-61
Truman, Harry
 commission of enquiry 188
 horrified at American troops' treatment of
  Jews 188
 attitude to Jews 190
 rejects Anglo-American Enquiry 191
 support for partition 206
 recognises Israel 219
 rejects Bernadotte plan 234
 threatens Israel 237
Trump, Donald 284, 285

United Arab Emirates 290
United Nations
 Goldstone report received 279
 takes over from British in Palestine 12, 44,
  190, 197-98, 207
 agrees to partition 205, 223, 225, 226
 Britain refuses to support Israel's
  membership of 225-26
 condemns annexation of Palestinian land 318
 condemns annexation of Golan Heights
  285
 condemns separation wall 281
 receives recommendations of
  Anglo-American Inquiry 201
 states refugees should be allowed to return
  249
 Israel rejects criticism of 38, 235
 criticised for persistent condemnation of
  Israel 255, 299
United Nations Ad Hoc Committee (1947) 205
United Nations Commission on Qibya
 massacre (1953) 241

United Nations Conciliation Commission
 (1949) 235
United Nations Human Rights Council on
 Operation Protective Edge 218
United Nations Mixed Armistice Commission
 238
United Nations Special Committee on Palestine
 (UNSCOP) 203, 213-14
United Nations Relief and Works Agency
 for Palestinian Refugees in the Near East
 (UNRWA) 236, 290 322, 326
United Nations Interim Force in Lebanon
 (1978) 259

Wailing Wall 18, 82, 142-43, 264, 274
 see also Shaw Report
Wedgwood, J. C. 37, 170
West Bank
 definition 37
 Jewish claims 37, 106, 266
 annexation by Israel 38, 199, 247, 248,
  254, 260, 266, 286, 320, 324, 325-26
 Abdullah's perception 111, 234
 Israeli withdrawal from 250, 252, 254, 268,
  269, 270, 272, 273, 275, 279
 Hussein gives up claim 267
 and McMahon 117
 Arab refugees 215, 248
 Arafat claims as part of Arab state 248, 267
 Clinton calls for handing back 276
 Trump's proposals 21, 285, 287-88, 290,
  291
 UN attitude 325
West Bank wall of separation 280-81
Weizmann, Chaim
 background 52
 influence on
  Balfour 26, 53, 84, 86, 101, 108, 109
  Churchill 43, 121-122, 126, 139,163,
   178, 184, 187
  Scott, O. A. 52, 55, 67
  Lloyd George 52, 53, 80
  Allenby 138, 140
  Sykes 71
  American Jews 55
 use of spies 94, 95, 97
 MacDonald and the White Paper 88, 148,
  149, 150, 170
 praises Meinertzhagen 94
 praises Blanche 'Baffy' Dugdale 95
 dealings with Mussolini 174-75
 Curzon's criticism of 84, 100, 101, 103, 109

letters to Curzon, 97, 100
Curzon 'one of our Jewish enemies' 136
asked to submit proposals for a Jewish state 41, 73, 148
expansionist policy of 68, 71, 103, 107, 112, 130, 163
opposes any investigation into events in Palestine 148, 157, 169
organises Biltmore Conference 180-82
Lausanne Report 188
attitude to Arabs 37, 81, 107-08, 118, 121, 129
expresses pride at King David Hotel bombing 194
behind decision to establish the Zionist Commission 80-81
expresses delight at declaration 87
letters expressing concern about weakening support for declaration 97-98, 118
operation of the Zionist Commission 81-82, 84, 94
support for allies in Second World War 178
rejects Wedgwood's advice 170
threatens to resign 148
describes operation of the Zionist Commission 80-81
removal from political power 182, 222
White Paper of 1939 see MacDonald, Malcolm
Wilson, Woodrow
promises to support Zionism in return for electoral support 57
mixed support for Zionism 56
Jewish pressure 57
does not endorse Sykes–Picot 69
petition by Reform Jews rejecting Zionism 78
advocates that local people should be consulted 67, 79
view on Paris Peace Conference 99
Balfour disagrees about self-government 131

Wilhelm II, Kaiser 47, 69
Wingate, Orde
background 168
enthusiastic Zionist 168
forms 'Special Night Squads' to attack Arabs 168
orders murder of prisoner 168
Wolf, Lucien 56, 70
Woodhead Commission (1938)
purpose 164, 169
reactions to 169 ff
World Wars see First and Second World War
World Zionist Organisation 222, 234
foundation and purpose 146
move to Germany 47
breakaway group formed 167
Weizmann removed from presidency 182

Yesh Din 326
Yom Kippur disturbances 142 ff
Yom Kippur War (the October War, 1973) 27, 252 ff

Zeid Hussein 57
Zionist Commission
established in Palestine 40, 80, 122
operation 83, 86
role of David Eder 141-42
British Army's disapproval of 81, 89, 132
Palin Report's criticism of 82 ff, 138
criticism by Curzon 84
criticism by senior civil servant 94
denial of influence in Churchill White Paper 117
Zionist Congress
expresses wish to live in harmony with Arabs 117
only Palestine acceptable as a state 43
opposes partition 162
removes Weizmann as president 222